CW00692561

LETTERS OF DOROTHEA PRINCESS LIEVEN

DURING HER RESIDENCE IN LONDON

1812-1834

EDITED BY

LIONEL G. ROBINSON

Elibron Classics
www.elibron.com

Elibron Classics series.

© 2005 Adamant Media Corporation.

ISBN 1-4212-1683-3 (paperback)
ISBN 1-4212-1682-5 (hardcover)

This Elibron Classics Replica Edition is an unabridged facsimile
of the edition published in 1902 by Longmans, Green, and Co.,
London, New York and Bombay.

PRINCESS LIEVEN'S LETTERS

1812–1834

Princess Lieven,
(aged about 20)
From the picture by Sir Thomas Lawrence. P.R.A.
in the National Gallery.

LETTERS OF DOROTHEA, PRINCESS LIEVEN, during her Residence in London, ⌖ 1812–1834

EDITED BY

LIONEL G. ROBINSON

WITH TWO PHOTOGRAVURE PORTRAITS

LONGMANS, GREEN, AND CO.
39 Paternoster Row, London, New York
and Bombay. 1902.

PREFATORY NOTE

THE following letters—which, with one or two exceptions, were addressed to Princess Lieven's brother General Alexander Benckendorff—were given by his widow a year after his death to her son-in-law Count Rodolph Apponyi, whom many will still remember as Austro-Hungarian Ambassador in London. General Benckendorff, after a brilliant military career, was on the accession of Nicholas I. to the throne appointed to a post of confidence which until his death kept him in close relations with the Emperor, and in his position as Chief of the Third Division he was practically in charge of the political police system of the Russian Empire. The letters now published are all that have been preserved, and they are printed without omitting anything but purely family matters which would have no interest for the general public. In translating them I have endeavoured as far as possible to give a literal rendering of Madame de Lieven's style, and by so doing may have retained certain Gallicisms which might have been expressed by English equivalents, but in this way the original forms would have been lost.

For the historical threads by which the letters are connected I have made free use of Sir Spencer Walpole's 'History of England from 1815,' of Miss Martineau's 'History of the Peace,' and of the Greville Diaries. For the notes, by which it is hoped many events will be elucidated, the various memoirs, diaries, and correspondence relating to the period are cited.

The letters cover the whole period of Count (afterwards Prince) Lieven's embassy in London. On his arrival, of all the allies of Great Britain the Russians were the most popular, socially and politically. Before his departure, on more than one occasion it needed the greatest tact and caution to prevent war breaking out between the two Powers. These letters may not conclusively fix the blame for this revulsion of feeling upon either country, but they may induce students of history to modify their judgment as to the share of responsibility which each incurred in this untoward change in international politics.

My sincere thanks are due in the first place to Count Alexander Apponyi, to whose confidence I am indebted for the use of these letters. He thought, in view of the recent publication of a portion of Princess Lieven's correspondence, and of the announcement that a further instalment was to follow, that the strictly confidential tone of the letters to her brother was no sufficient reason to longer delay their appearance. He was, moreover, convinced that whatever verdict the English public might pronounce upon the way in which Madame de Lieven discharged her duties as Ambassadress, friendly and hostile critics would alike recognise her intense patriotism and her earnest concern for the greatness and influence of Russia.

I am indebted to the Earl of Ilchester for kindly consenting to the reproduction of the portrait of Princess Lieven now at Holland House, painted by Mr. G. F. Watts, R.A.—a noteworthy link between the past and the present—and to the Trustees of the National Gallery for allowing the reproduction of Lawrence's portrait of the Princess, painted while she was resident in London. I have further to express my obligation to Lord Rowton, Lord Edward Fitzmaurice, M.P., to Hon. F. Leveson-Gower, to Mr. N. Harris Nicolas, C.B., and specially to Mr. Guy L'Estrange, for much assistance and useful counsel, which have greatly lessened my labour and have, I hope, mitigated its imperfections.

BIOGRAPHICAL NOTICE OF
PRINCESS LIEVEN

DOROTHEA (DARJA) CHRISTOROVNA BENCKENDORFF was born on December 17, 1785, at Riga, where her father, an infantry General, was Military Commandant. A branch of the family, which was of the Mark of Brandenburg, had settled in Esthonia and entered the Russian service. General Benckendorff, however, found a German wife in Baroness Charlotte Schilling, of Cannstadt, an intimate friend and companion of the Princess Maria of Würtemberg, who afterwards became the wife of the Emperor Paul I. of Russia ; and Madame Benckendorff, on her death in 1797, commended her four children to the care of the Empress, who conscientiously undertook the charge and stood their protectress as long as she lived. By her will the Empress bequeathed the various portraits of her ' good and saintly friend Benckendorff' to her children, and one special miniature to Constantine because he most resembled his mother. The Empress in her will further rehearsed how she had discharged her duties as mother to her good friend's four children, educating all of them, providing dowries and trousseaux for both the daughters, and investing a capital sum in the Foundlings' Bank, of which the interest was to be divided among the sons and daughters during their minority, adding, ' I pray the Emperor to protect the four children of a lady who was my most intimate friend, and the memory of whom will be ever dear to me.'

The elder daughter, Maria (the Masha of the following letters), in course of time became Lady-in-Waiting to the Empress Maria Feodorowna, and married Lieutenant-General I. I. Schewitsch.[1] Her younger sister, Dorothea, although a Lutheran, received her education at the Smolny Convent

[1] Further details respecting the other members of the Benckendorff family will be found in the notes and Appendix.

School, on leaving it was appointed Maid of Honour to the Empress in 1799, and in the following year was married to Lieutenant-General Count Lieven—who, notwithstanding his military rank, was only twelve years her senior. There is no lack of legends regarding the precocious intelligence of Dorothea Benckendorff, nor of the talents as hostess and talker which she displayed at an age when the majority of her contemporaries were still in the schoolroom, but there are no authentic sources whence the story of the first years of her married life can be drawn. It was only on the appointment of her husband as Russian Envoy to the Prussian Court in 1809 that Madame de Lieven came before the public, and from the meagre references to her presence in Berlin it is fair to infer that she did not create any great impression upon German diplomatists and politicians. Her husband's or possibly her services were, however, so far appreciated by their own Government that two years later Count Lieven was appointed Ambassador to London, with the object of restoring those friendly relations between Russia and Great Britain which had been suspended after the Treaty of Tilsit. The task was not a difficult one, as both English Ministers and London society were ready to welcome the return of their former allies, and in proof of its good will Parliament in 1813 had voted 200,000*l.* for the relief of the distress in Russia. Madame de Lieven was well qualified to use her opportunities, and promptly took up the position of a leader of fashion. Her cleverness was generally recognised, but her tact was shown rather in her fastidiousness than by her geniality, and the impression she produced was that she was as fully conscious of her own superiority as she was of the inferiority of those with whom she was brought in daily contact. Not only her contemporaries but her biographers took her at her own valuation, but it is with astonishment that we find one of the latter, the most prominent writer at the present time on Russian policy in Europe, Prof. Kleinschmidt, speaking of her 'discretion, her instinctive dislike to gossip and intrigue '—which, so far as we can judge, formed the staple of her daily life. Her tastes as well as her duties—for it must be assumed that she was the guiding spirit of the Russian Embassy in London—led her to cultivate the friendship of those most capable of advancing the interests she wished to promote. In this way she established intimate relationships with Wellington and Canning, Aberdeen and Palmerston, Peel and Earl Grey ; and not the least interesting characteristic of the following letters is the place occupied in her esteem by each statesman according as he rises or falls in power or position. That her so-called friends did not appreciate these shifting sands of sentiment in the same degree may be gathered from the remarks which some have left on record, especially the Duke of Wellington and Lord Palmerston. But what is more surprising is that a woman so astute should have so far been able to deceive herself as to the opinion which British statesmen entertained with regard to her intrigues. ' I do not doubt,' wrote the Duke of Wellington, ' the inclination of the lady to do this country all the mischief in her power in return for much kindness and good will with which she was treated during a long residence here ' ; [1] and again, a month later, he writes : ' Nobody knows better than I do the lady whom you mention. She can and she will betray everybody in turn, if it should suit her purpose.' [2] Lord Palmerston's estimate of her character was not more flattering, and he freely expressed it in his letters to his brother, Mr. William Temple, who for some time was British *chargé d'affaires* at St. Petersburg. Against this, however, must be placed the late Lord Chelmsford's remark when the early careers of both were under discussion : ' Well, after all, it was Madame de Lieven who made Palmerston.'

The relations between Princess Lieven and Metternich have recently been brought before the public by M. Ernest Daudet, and the nature of the letters which passed between them has been partially revealed. From the correspondence with her brother there is little to be gathered beyond the fact that Madame de Lieven continued to interchange letters with the Austrian Chancellor down to the end of 1825, and that the rupture of their friendship coincided with the change of Russian policy consequent upon the accession of Nicholas I. The actual date at which the acquaintance between Metternich

[1] Letter to T. Raikes, November 23, 1840.   [2] *Ibid.* December 23, 1840.

and Madame de Lieven began cannot be ascertained, but in 1819, at the Congress of Aix-la-Chapelle, they were thrown together socially and politically, the chief aim of Metternich's policy at that time being to bring the views of the Emperor Alexander into more complete accord with those of Austria, and to restrain his more liberal instincts. In this design Metternich found a valuable ally in Madame de Lieven, while he was doubtless at the same time attracted by her social and intellectual qualities. That the feelings thus engendered assumed a warmer tone as each learnt to appreciate the other is beyond doubt, and after the breaking up of the Congress they continued to correspond in terms which bore witness to the depth of their mutual regard. Metternich's letters, however, are not wholly convincing as to the extent of his devotion to the lady to whom he unburdens himself apparently without reserve, and one doubts whether either of them would have sacrificed position or career in order to live altogether in each other's society. So much of this remarkable correspondence has now been published that it is to be hoped that the whole of the letters in an authentic shape may be given to the world, for they cannot but reflect credit to the head if not to the heart of the statesman who for a whole generation was the Dictator of Europe and the Nestor of politicians.

Meanwhile Madame de Lieven had not been inactive in London, and long before her correspondence with Metternich closed she had already obtained considerable influence over Britis' statesmen, and there is good reason to suppose that durir the Regency and the reign of George IV. she was possessed of considerable political and social power. There are, however, but few references to her in the memoirs dealing with the earlier period of her husband's embassy, except as one of the leaders of fashion—as a patroness of Almack's and as the introducer of the waltz into that aristocratic assembly. The statement that the Prince Regent expressed to her his dissent from the views of his Ministers and his accord with those of the Emperor Alexander, on the occasion of the abortive Congress of Châtillon, cannot be substantiated, and it seems hardly probable that it should have any basis of truth, for at the time the negotiations were being conducted M. de Lieven had been only a few months in England and Madame de Lieven was but five-and-twenty years old. At the same time, there is little doubt that the aims of Great Britain and Russia in the settlement of the peace of Europe were identical, and that the relations between the two Powers were extremely cordial, when Count Lieven presented his credentials. It is no less true that on his recall the two countries had drifted apart, and the actions of each had become the constant source of suspicion to the other, and the breach then created has never been closed, but has gone on ever widening. If the following letters throw any light upon this change of opinion, their publication needs no other justification. The charge commonly brought against the Lievens by those who have written of this period, and of the statesmen who were the principal actors, is that they misrepresented to the Russian Foreign Office and Court the real state of public feeling in England, and that they made mischief between the two Powers. This charge was especially brought against Madame de Lieven, who had convinced herself that she was competent to advance the interests of her own country more effectually than the Emperor or his advisers. By disposition and training she was an Ultra-Tory, and on her coming to England she found Lord Castlereagh, Lord Liverpool, and the Duke of Wellington at the head of affairs, and wholly in sympathy with her opinions. To the Duke of Wellington she seems to have made great advances, which were met in a friendly spirit; but some years later, on the question of the independence of Greece, she did not scruple to transfer her devotion to Canning, and the Duke's vanity was probably as much wounded as his sense of political rectitude was offended by so complete a *volte-face*. About the same time he was sent to St. Petersburg to congratulate the Emperor Nicholas on his accession to the throne, and incidentally to arrange a common action in regard to Greece and Turkey. Notwithstanding the Emperor's formal promise to take no independent step, the Russian Government had already despatched orders to its representative to quit Constantinople, and Wellington returned to England without having obtained the revocation of this step. The conviction of having been duped on this occasion warped his judgment on all matters in which the interests of Great Britain and Russia seemed to be at variance, and every proposal by the latter was viewed by him with distrust. This feeling became more strongly marked as the negotiations with regard to the independence of Greece proceeded, and impelled him to draw nearer to Austria.

At no time, probably, have personal feelings and private interests played so important a part in political history as during the period of M. de Lieven's embassy in London. The settlement of the Greek, the Spanish, the Portuguese, and the Belgian questions, although springing from national movements, was alternately promoted and delayed out of consideration for individuals rather than in view of the well-being of the peoples concerned. Madame de Lieven fully realised this condition, and, regardless of party, she endeavoured to turn to her own uses and to the advantage of her own country the instruments she found ready to her hand. She was ready to work with Canning, because he supported the views of Russia with regard to Greece—and had no confidence in Turkey ; and after his death she probably did all in her power to undermine the Duke of Wellington's influence with the King and with his party. That she ever went so far as to take part in the intrigues of the Duke of Cumberland—as has been asserted on the authority of the Duke of Wellington—is open to doubt, and certainly these letters do not lend any colour to such a story. At any rate on such a point the intended victim (real or supposed) of such a plot would not be the most trustworthy witness to its existence. That Madame de Lieven had the ear of George IV. is probably true, and that she took every occasion to exasperate him against his Prime Minister is not less likely ; but she knew also that there were limits to diplomatic discretion which she could not overstep without danger to herself.[1]

[1] The following passages from the *Wellington Correspondence* (vol. iii. pp. 55, &c.) will explain the Duke's state of mind with regard to the efforts of the

The accession of William IV. brought with it the return of the Liberals to office, with Earl Grey as Prime Minister. Madame de Lieven's relations with this statesman are too well known to need recital, although it is difficult to understand the attraction which the Liberal leader's policy could have had in her eyes, his aims and his methods being alike unintelligible and distasteful to her. Possibly, as in the case

Lievens to upset his Government : ' To attain this object all is fish that comes to her net. She wants to attain this, not from any personal dislike to me or any of its members, not because we entertain any notions hostile to the Russian Government, but because we are an English administration. . . . I know she has been concerned with the Duke of Cumberland, as well as with everybody else. . . . The person to whom she looks is Lord Grey ! Why ? Because Lord Grey entertains some old Opposition opinions of Mr. Fox that the Turks ought to be driven out of Europe.' (Letter to Earl of Aberdeen, July 29, 1829.)

' I concur in your letter to Lord Heytesbury about Prince and Princess Lieven. They have played an English party game, instead of doing the business of their Sovereign, since I have been in office. I have the best authority that both have been engaged (as principals) in intrigues to deprive my colleagues and me of power since January 1828 ; that they have misrepresented our conduct and views to their Sovereign, and that they are the sole cause of coolness between the two Governments which exists at the present moment. . . . In another country, in Russia itself or France, or with another Sovereign, or in a different state of society . . . would amply justify our interference to have Prince Lieven recalled. But it is my opinion that this measure would do us more harm than good.' (Letter to Earl of Aberdeen, August 24, 1829.)

' I have known that since the year 1826 Prince and Princess Lieven have taken pains to represent my conduct, whether in or out of Government, in the most unfavourable manner in St. Petersburg. I believe their displeasure commenced in a conversation which I had with Prince Lieven at the end of 1826 upon the turning of the Protocol of April 1826 into the Treaty of July 1827. . . . I was out of office from April 1827 to January 1828, during which time I know the Prince and Princess wrote of me all the evil that they thought and much more than they knew. From the time I returned to office the Prince and Princess have been what is called in regular opposition to the Government. They have misrepresented to their Court all that we have done and particularly all that I have done ; they have been parties to all party intrigues against the administration ; and really, if I had not the very best authority for what I say, I could not have believed it possible that persons who have been so long employed in public office in this country would have committed the extraordinary indiscretions of which they have been guilty. . . . I know all that I have stated in this letter is true, but I can prove nothing, and I will not complain of any man so as to deprive him of his office without being able to prove that which I state against him. Besides, to tell you the truth, I am perhaps vain enough to think that I am too strong for Prince and Princess Lieven, and that I prefer to suffer a little inconvenience to taking a step which might require from me some explanation.' (Letter to Lord Heytesbury, September 8, 1829.)

of Canning, she hoped to shape a Liberal policy to absolutist ends, and it was the consciousness of her failure which may have prompted her to boast, even to her brother, of greater influence than she possessed. Up to the very day when her husband's recall was notified to him she had no misgivings as to the strength of her position or of diminished prestige. The rebuffs to which Russian diplomacy had been exposed in the settlement of various international questions had shown that the methods of the Russian Embassy in London were not satisfactory, and the selection of Sir Stratford Canning as Lord Heytesbury's successor at St. Petersburg, in spite of the remonstrances of Count Nesselrode, rendered necessary the presence of another representative of Russia at St. James's. The actual reason for the Emperor Nicholas's objection to Sir Stratford Canning has never been clearly ascertained, and the latter strenuously denied the truth of the alleged cause. Palmerston's persistence has generally been explained by his vanity, which prompted him to withdraw the promise he had given to Madame de Lieven that Canning's nomination should be cancelled ; but it would seem from these letters that the Cabinet had endorsed Palmerston's promise, and had allowed Lord Durham to give a similar assurance to the Emperor. Under these circumstances it seems difficult to adopt without reserve this misunderstanding as the only reason for the recall of the Lievens. In our ignorance of the rivalries and intrigues of the Russian Court it is impossible to estimate how far there may have been potent agencies at work at St. Petersburg, but that the Lievens did not at once fall out of favour with the Imperial family is shown by the simultaneous appointment of Prince Lieven to take charge of the Tzarevitch in his travels, and by the assumption by Princess Lieven of her dormant duties as Lady-in-Waiting on the Empress. The prospect, however, of living in the society of the Imperial family had little attraction for the Princess, notwithstanding the protestations of ardent devotion so frequently recurring in her letters. Whether she had formed the secret determination to reside in Western Europe, and consequently created the cause of her short stay of less than a year at

6

St. Petersburg, or whether she fled from a situation for which she had no ambition, it is impossible to guess. The utmost that can be said is that some time afterwards, when writing with reference to her abrupt ending of her service at Court, she made use of the expression, 'The master has not forgiven and will never forgive me.' The death of her two elder sons shortly after her return to Russia may have accounted for her disinclination to remain in that country, of which the climate was so fatal to her family. At any rate, she decided to leave it, and settled herself provisionally in Paris. Her original intention had been to return to London, but, as she had expressed it years previously in one of her letters to her brother, 'a centrifugal force drew her to Paris,' and there she remained with slight intermission for the rest of her life. Her attachment to M. Guizot and his devotion to her were honourable to both, a beautiful sunset to a stormy life ; and it was doubtless with absolute truth that she could write her last words to him, 'Je vous remercie pour vingt années d'affection et de bonheur.' With this portion of Madame de Lieven's life, however, we are not on this occasion concerned. We shall know it more completely when M. Guizot's papers—now in the hands of M. Ernest Daudet—are published, and we shall then learn, what is now only surmised, that, although without any official position, she still occupied herself with politics and continued intimate relations with the statesmen of her own and of other countries. In 1848 she followed Guizot to England, and took up her residence at Brighton, where she met Metternich, who was also a fugitive. In 1850 she returned to Paris, where she remained with the exception of a few months after the outbreak of the Crimean war, and died in her house, which had previously been Talleyrand's, in the rue Saint-Florentin, on January 26, 1857. In accordance with her express wish she was placed in her coffin in a velvet dress and with a diadem on her brow, and transported to Courland, to be laid beside her two sons in the family vault at Mesohten.

In this country Madame de Lieven's reputation has not escaped the penalty which all who take an active part in political life must incur, and, unfortunately for her, the relations which she maintained with both parties, instead of protecting her, exposed her to the criticism of the Tories and Whigs alike. The Duke of Wellington and Lord Eldon spoke and wrote of her as bitterly as Lord Palmerston or Charles Greville, and we may be sure that they either led or voiced the opinions of their respective coteries. By some she was called a gossip-monger, by others a spy, and by all a political *intrigante*. In some ways she may seem to have merited these harsh epithets, and she doubtless well knew the dangers to which she exposed her reputation. It was one of her duties to write every week a letter to the Empress-Mother giving her the gossip of the English Court, and it is not unlikely that many of her clever and possibly unflattering reflections on English men and women were passed round the Imperial Court at St. Petersburg, and ultimately found their way back to England embellished or disfigured in accordance with the laws of scandal-mongering. These letters were part of the price which the Ambassadress had to pay for the distinction she had obtained for her husband, and it is not for outsiders to find fault with the ways in which the Imperial family exacted payment for its favours. With regard to the other charge, Madame de Lieven was undoubtedly in constant correspondence with Count Nesselrode after the Congress of Verona, and the Russian Secretary of State looked to her to keep him informed of the trend of English opinion and of the sentiments of English politicians. The methodical and laborious despatches of Prince Lieven would have availed little to shape Russian diplomacy had they not been supplemented by his wife's keener appreciation of passing events, and by the personal judgment which she brought to bear upon the leading men of the Cabinet and the Opposition. Madame de Lieven lived before the days of telegraphy, when personality played a far more important part in politics, and diplomacy required prompt and independent action on the part of Ambassadors. It behoved the head of each mission to know everything about his colleagues as well as about the politicians of the country to which he was accredited ; and Ambassadors' wives played

their part according to their powers. Madame de Lieven's
rôle in this respect differed but slightly from that of others
similarly placed, but she brought to its discharge rare qualities
—a shrewd and ever active mind, an unquenchable curiosity,
and the power of extracting confidences even from those who
distrusted her. Her *salon* was no more and no less a
centre of political activity or intrigue than were Holland
House or the *salons* of Lady Hertford and Lady Jersey.
Politicians met and discussed their hopes and their chances,
and Madame de Lieven's drawing-room differed only from
those of other political leaders in that it welcomed alike
members of the Ministry and of the Opposition. Madame
de Lieven cannot be blamed if during her husband's embassy
so many important problems, national and dynastic, had to
be faced, nor that in their discussion personal feeling and
prejudice were allowed to play so prominent a part. Doubtless she took up each cause with the firm conviction that the
interests of Russia prescribed a certain course, and in order
to support them she was willing to run the risk of being
misjudged by those to whom Russian views were unpalatable.
If she showed herself hostile to the independence of Belgium,
on the other hand it was owing to her skill that Wellington
was brought to assent to the enlarged limits of Greece ; and if
she sympathised with Don Carlos in Spain, she consistently
opposed Dom Miguel in Portugal ; and in each case because
she believed that Russia's interests were better served by a
more supple policy than that which commended itself at first
sight to Nicholas and his advisers. At this distance of time
it is possible to judge how far events have justified Madame
de Lieven's anticipations, and, what is of even more importance,
whether the price paid—the breaking of the bonds which had
united the policy of Russia and Great Britain—has been of
greater profit to the former or to the latter country. Madame
de Lieven would probably have deprecated this estimate of
her official career in London, but it cannot be gainsaid ;
although it is doubtful if she fully realised the actual outcome
of her methods.

Of a character so complex and so thoroughly national it
is impossible for a foreigner to speak with any assurance

Madame de Lieven embodied in an excessive degree the characteristics of the political woman. The intense activity of her mind prevented her from feeling lastingly, and her abrupt changes from ardent affection to intense dislike might convey a want of depth of sentiment to those who measure feeling by reticence or by discretion in words and acts. To us her exaltation and depression may alike seem excessive, and her adulation of her Emperor fulsome or hysterical; but her whole life showed that she was capable of warm and sincere attachment. We are less able to condone the easy indifference with which she put aside those whom she at one moment flattered and cajoled. She applied with too facile cynicism La Rochefoucauld's maxim as to the treatment of both friends and enemies, but she was as able to forgive as to forget when circumstances counselled oblivion of the past. Probably few women of her talents and intelligence were ever less endowed with mental resources. She cared only for 'human documents,' she had no taste for books, and we may infer equally little for literary and abstract discussions. She had a horror of solitude, and an even greater dread of being bored, while her insatiable avidity for news not seldom brought upon her the latter penalty in her efforts to avoid the burden of her own company. Notwithstanding all these defects, if defects they be, as judged by our present standard, Madame de Lieven was endowed with qualities which in her own day made her conspicuous in that brilliant galaxy of *femmes d'esprit* who marked the Restoration period in France and the reactionary movement in Europe. It is because Princess Lieven was essentially typical of her time, and stood in the front rank of the distinguished persons of her day, that it is believed that her familiar letters —written without view of subsequent publication—will be found to possess more than ordinary interest, and will throw some fresh light upon the events and personages of her time.

CONTENTS

ILLUSTRATIONS

LETTERS

OF

DOROTHEA, PRINCESS LIEVEN

TO HER BROTHER

1813–1834

1813–1815

THE CLOSE OF THE WAR—ENGLISH SOCIETY—FRIENDLINESS
TO RUSSIA—PRINCESS CHARLOTTE

[The position of affairs in Northern Europe at the moment at which this correspondence begins may be briefly summarised. Napoleon's invasion of Russia had failed, and on October 19, 1812, the retreat of the French army had commenced, and had been conducted without serious disaster until November 6, when the frost set in and the horrors of the homeward march began. General Kutusoff pushed steadily forward, and Platoff with the Cossacks hovered persistently on the flanks of the French army. Disasters followed in rapid succession. On November 27 the Beresina was crossed, and shortly before reaching Wilna Napoleon quitted the army on December 5, and set off in all haste for Paris, delegating the supreme command to Murat, King of Naples. The defection of the unwilling German allies soon followed, and after some fencing Prussia finally threw in her lot with Russia, Hardenberg signing a treaty with Kutusoff to furnish 80,000 men for the ensuing campaign. The French retreated across the Vistula on February 3, but it was not until March 27 that Prussia formally declared war against her former ally. Almost simultaneously the Austrians came to a secret arrangement with Count Nesselrode that their troops should be withdrawn to the right bank of the Vistula and the Duchy of Warsaw abandoned. Berlin was speedily evacuated (March 5) by the French, who were retreating

on the Elbe, closely followed by the Russians. General Count
Wittgenstein and a corps under Baron von Tettenborn occupied
Hamburg on March 18. The French, however, concentrated a
force round Magdeburg to oppose General Dornberg's advance,
which was temporarily stopped by Marshal Davoust (March 26), and
this is probably the French ' victory' to which Madame de Lieven
makes reference. The Emperor Alexander had joined the army at
Warsaw, Kutusoff being left in supreme command until his death
shortly before the concentration of the Russian and Prussian forces
round Leipzig. Of Madame de Lieven's two brothers it would seem
that Constantine Benckendorff was serving in Prince Wittgenstein's
division, and Alexander was with General Tchitchagoff's in the
country between Thorn and Danzig.]

I

London : April 6, 1813.

My dear Alexander,—I am delighted to have the means
again of writing to you direct, and to tell you how much I
congratulate you on our successes and the happiness your
share in them especially gives me. It is noble to have carried
on this great war—gigantic in its proportions and worthy of
Russians only—to have passed in the space of five short
months from the banks of the Moskowa to those of the Elbe ;
but it is nobler still, after such a succession of victories and
triumphs, to show such moderation.[1]   This it is which raises
our Emperor above all who have occupied, however worthily,
the throne ; and Europe is lucky in having her destinies left
in the hands of Alexander. The Alexander to whom this
letter is addressed is mentioned in every newspaper ; also I
thus learn to-day, by extracts from the ' Moniteur,' that we
have got a drubbing on the Elbe, but inasmuch as no details
are given I am more disposed to believe that I have to congratulate you upon some further advantage over the enemy.[2]
One acquires without difficulty the art of interpreting French
official reports : it consists in simply substituting the word
' defeat' for that of ' victory,' when they claim the latter.

[1] The first triumph of the Allies in Germany was the brilliant rescue of the
citizens of Lüneburg from the French by a small body of troops under the
command of Count Constantine Benckendorff.—*Alison*, xvi. 193.

[2] Referring to an engagement with the French under Prince Eugène, who
managed for a short time to hold the Russians and Prussians at bay on the banks
of the Elbe.

Constantine wrote to me a short while since from Hamburg,[1] and I have had many opportunities of writing to him of late, as we are now such near neighbours. As for you, the elder, you are wandering so far afield that I am never sure if my letters reach you. Even when you have no defeat of the French to announce, I am eager to have a few lines from you. My thoughts are ever on the Continent. This beautiful England is always the same—an endless chain of perfections which appeal to the reason but leave the imagination untouched. For a couple of months you may be enraptured by the country, for everything seems at first so beautiful, and then so extraordinary, that one's sense of admiration is constantly excited ; but when one has seen everything, and grown tired of admiring, one wishes to feel, and England is not the country of emotions. Personally I ought to be supremely happy, for I am here under specially favourable auspices. I am everywhere received as no other foreigner has been, and I flatter myself that I have been a success, but never would I wish to die in this country. I am always astonished at the Anglomania which has seized upon sc many of my fellow countrymen. One feels the reaction when living with the English. I am talking, however, too much about these people and their views ; but for myself I prefer to think of those on the other side of the sea. Write to me, dear Alexander, I entreat you. My husband sends you a thousand good wishes. He is very busy, and, I think, is doing well. He is esteemed and liked. All the members of our little group are well ; send us news of your own, for it is always a pleasure to us to welcome Russians. Good-bye, my dear good brother. I embrace you with all my heart. Do not forget me, and that I wish every success to our brave army and for its heroes who belong to me.

[Before the next letter was despatched important events had occurred. Napoleon had returned and assumed the supreme command. A formidable force had been brought together near Jena, and the first operations were made with the view of effecting a

[1] Hamburg, after a rising of the citizens (February 24), had been abandoned by the French and occupied by the Russians ; the latter, however, a few weeks later had to evacuate the city on the approach of Marshal Davoust.

junction between his main army and the troops under Prince Eugène Beauharnais, a movement which the Russians under Wittgenstein and the Prussians under General Blücher determined at all costs to prevent. A series of sanguinary battles round Lützen, Leipzig, Bautzen, and Hochkirchen followed, with varying success, but notwithstanding the frightful losses sustained by the French, including many guns and prisoners, they succeeded in forcing the passage of the Spree and entered Breslau (June 1). Almost at the same time Hamburg was evacuated by the Allies and occupied by the French and Danes under Marshal Davoust, who continued to hold it until after the conclusion of peace, May 30, 1814. An armistice for six weeks, and finally until August 10, preparatory to a Congress, was then arranged through the mediation of Austria ; but during the time Prussia drew a levy *en masse*, and Austria hastily calling together all her available troops on August 11 formally declared war against France, which was followed by the declaration of a treaty of alliance between Austria, Prussia, Russia, and Great Britain.

The campaign which ensued extended from Brandenburg to Bohemia, from Saxony to Silesia, and, although the French could claim the victory in several important engagements, especially round Dresden, the superior forces of the Allies steadily advanced. On October 15 and four following days the battle (Völkerschlacht) raged round Leipzig, and at its close Napoleon was forced to retreat, having lost upwards of 50,000 men and 300 guns. On the previous day Baron von Tettenborne had entered Bremen.]

II

Richmond : 16/28 September 1813.

It is long since I have had news of you, my dear Alexander. You have never told me how far your health was benefited by the baths of Dobberan.[1]   All I know is that you have resumed active service, and I am sure that you will be all the better for the change. Here we are all delighted with the reassuring bulletins which you are careful in transmitting. Your chief displays a skill which should ensure your constant success. How the world is turned upside down since we

---

[1] Once a fashionable watering-place in Mecklenburg, ten miles from Rostock, on the shores of the Baltic, much frequented by members of the Grand Ducal family. In 1807 H. Crabb Robinson, the *Times* correspondent at Altona, took refuge there to avoid arrest by the French authorities in Hamburg. (*Diary*, i. 240.)

last met—what a glorious year you have passed through, and how well chosen was your motto as the true one to follow in order to reach your present position—and more especially that which lies before you, for everything is now organised for the accomplishment of the great work !

The Emperor is admirable—and much admired, as I can testify ; moderation and loyalty go well when combined with strength. His glory is solidly founded.

I shudder in thinking that poor Moreau was wounded by his master's side.[1] The Emperor should recollect that the safety of the world at this time depends upon his life. If he were conscious of this truth, he would not expose himself to danger.

How I wish we were in possession of Hamburg, for I have not so much pleasure in writing to you when I know that my letter must make long wanderings before reaching you. It communications are re-established by some direct channel, as I trust, let me know, dear Alexander, if you have any commissions I can execute for you here, or if there are any things you wish to be forwarded.

Adieu. I am in good health and charmingly established in the most beautiful spot in beautiful England. I often think of you, dear Alexander, and I am ever forming wishes for you and all about you. My husband joins me in much love. He is overburdened with business.

Again adieu. Do not forget me.

[The conclusion of a Treaty of Concert (June 13) between Great Britain and Russia had led to increased friendliness between the two nations and their rulers. The Prince Regent having decided to confer the Garter upon the Emperor, it was necessary that a new statute should be passed. A chapter of the Order was consequently held at Carlton House on July 27, at which Count Lieven was present, and the Bishop of Salisbury, the Chancellor of the Order, having received the opinions of the knights present on the propriety of the proposed statute, the Emperor of Russia was declared duly elected, and a special envoy despatched to St. Petersburg with the insignia of the Order.]

[1] See Appendix.

III

Stratham (Streatham ?) Park : Tuesday, 6/18 October 1813.

Dear Alexander,—A messenger is being sent off to-day to Vienna, and I am taking advantage of this opportunity to write to you, as there must be frequent messengers thence to Petersburg. Since my last letter we have been spending a few days with Lord Liverpool at his house near Dover. On our return we found Léon Narischkine, who had come to spend a week with us, and is now back again at Brighton. His health is even worse than in your time. The Woronzows are settled in London[1] and often come to see us—the sister is still expecting her confinement. My husband and I are going this week to Brighton, on the invitation of the Prince Regent, ' to meet ' the Queen, who is coming there for a short time. I am delighted at this opportunity of again getting some sea-bathing. Balmaine's matrimonial intentions have received a check ; the lady says ' No '—but nevertheless continues to write to him unceasingly. By the way, the Marchioness (sic) of Southampton[2] has fallen in love with Léon Narischkine,[3] who by [her proceedings ?] would be made to seem her lover. She follows him everywhere and without respite, and he is a little ashamed of his bonne fortune. Beroldingen[4] often comes to us ; he is a thoroughly good sort. Fritz Pahlen[5] arrived the day before yesterday from

---

[1] Prince Semen Woronzow, G.C.B., had been Russian Ambassador in London 1784-1806. He obtained permission to reside in England, which he continued to do until his death in 1832. His daughter Catherine married 1808, as his second wife, George Augustus, eleventh Earl of Pembroke.

[2] Frances Isabella, daughter of Lord Robert Seymour and granddaughter of first Marquess of Hertford, married, as his second wife, George Ferdinand, second Baron Southampton, and was left a widow in 1810.

[3] Léon Narischkine was a member of the princely family to which Peter the Great's mother belonged.

[4] Count Joseph von Beroldingen served in the Austria service during the war with the Wurtemberg Contingent. Appointed envoy from Stuttgart in London 1814, transferred to St. Petersburg 1816, Minister of Foreign Affairs in Wurtemberg, 1823-48, died 1868.

[5] Frederick von der Pahlen, younger son of Peter von Pahlen, Governor of St. Petersburg in 1801 and one of the conspirators against Paul I., was Minister successively at Munich, Washington, and Rio de Janeiro, Councillor of State,

Brazil with the intention of making a short stay in England.

I shall see Brighton again, where I passed such a pleasant time with you, dear Alexander, and I leave you to guess what regrets this recollection will evoke. Come back to us next year with Michael [Woronzow]. You will have the pleasure of seeing this beautiful England again, and give me still more by seeing you. My husband is writing to you to-day. . . . [1] sends you all kind messages. He goes on in much the same way as usual, and Balmaine daily delivers himself of atrocious puns. We are living very quietly, seeing people every day, for the distance from town is so trifling that we are easily reached—and our house is large enough to lodge a number of guests.

Adieu, my dear good brother ; let me have news of you, and love me as I deserve to be for my affection for you. I wrote to papa last week, and I hope he has already received my letter. Good-bye again, dear Alexander; I embrace you tenderly.

[The advance of the Allies had continued without interruption, although the French were still holding several places in Germany, of which Hamburg was the most important. The rising of the Dutch at the end of November was followed by the evacuation of Helvoetsluys (December 5), and the almost simultaneous taking of Breda by a party of 300 Cossacks under Count Benckendorff, who gave themselves out as the advance guard of a large army. For this brilliant exploit, doubtless, he was presented by the Prince Regent with a sabre, of which mention is frequently made in the following letters. The campaign in the Netherlands was carried on without serious check. The Prince of Orange, who had embarked at Deal on November 25, arrived at Schevening, and made his entry into Amsterdam on December 1, and before the close of the year most of the principal towns had surrendered to the Allies, with the exception of Bergen-op-Zoom and the port of Brille, which latter was held for the French by Admiral Verhuel, who, according to Baron Humboldt, was the reputed father of Napoleon III. In these incidents Constantine Benckendorff, who had become General of Brigade, took a con-

Governor of Kherson, and one of the signatories of the Treaty of Adrianople, 1829, died 1863.

[1] Blank in original.

spicuous part. His advance guard entered Amsterdam on November 23 ; the main body, coming ' by post ' by way of Zwoll and Hard-erwyk, arrived a week afterwards. In the following campaign, after having cleared Holland, Count Benckendorff found himself con-fronted at St. Trond, near Liège, by General Maison coming from Antwerp. A serious battle ensued (January 24), in which the French were forced to retire, and the passage of the Meuse assured to the Allies. After the Battle of Craon, near Soissons (March 7), Count Benckendorff, who commanded a cavalry division, effectively pro-tected the retreat of the Russians, and again saved the situation at Bar-le-duc (March 26), where Napoleon had completely out-generaled and defeated Tettenborne and Winzingerode.

Lord Castlereagh, Secretary for Foreign Affairs in Lord Liverpool's Cabinet, left England for the Continent (December 27) to confer with Metternich at Basle, prior to the meeting of the abortive Congress of Frankfort.]

IV

To Alexander and Constantine Benckendorff

London : December 27, 1813.

I received yesterday, my good brothers, your letters of 19th inst. from Breda. I reply to both together, but I am sure that Alexander will be the first to receive my letter ; for Constantine will have had some good reason for going from Bremen to Berlin, and there my letters will not have an absorbing interest for him. Alopeus'[1] letter to Jacoby[2] was passed on to him at once, as he was dining with us—and Natalie's[3] to me is charming. Pozzo will take charge of this letter ; his departure, combined with that of Lord Castle-reagh,[4] will give some respite to my husband, who has latterly been literally overwhelmed with work. We are going into the country to-morrow for a few days. If the weather does not turn to frost the stay will be pleasant enough, but if it becomes cold it will be unbearable. Your

[1] Or Alopæus, Russian Minister at Stockholm. His arrest by the Swedish authorities after the invasion of Finland by Russia in 1808 almost brought about a war between the two Powers. He was related to Madame de Lieven's mother.

[2] Herr Jacoby, after the treaty between France and Russia in 1805, had been sent by the King of Prussia to bring about a reconciliation with Great Britain. He remained Prussian Envoy for several years.

[3] Subsequently married to Constantine Benckendorff.

[4] To attend the Congress at Vienna.

letter from Breda, dear Alexander, was read by us to the whole English Ministry, assembled at our house. Liverpool remarked that it was a pity that you had not 80,000 men instead of the 4,000 under your command. As a matter of fact this campaign in Holland, which might be brought to a close in a few days, looks now as if it will cause some trouble.[1] If it does not, come and see me, my dear Alexander, it will give me so much pleasure. My dear love to Constantine, whom everyone here regrets. Potocki[2] especially sends a thousand greetings, and all the others desire to be remembered. Adieu, my good friends. I love you both dearly, singly and together.

[In the long interval between the last letter and the date of the next the face of Europe had been completely changed. France had been invaded, and after a brilliant campaign, in which Napoleon's genius was never more conspicuously displayed, the Emperor of Russia and King of Prussia entered Paris on March 31. On the following day Napoleon was deposed by the Senate, and a month later embarked on board a British frigate, was landed at Elba on May 4, and the Peace of Paris was signed at the end of the month. The Congress of Vienna assembled on November 1 to settle the affairs of Europe, at which Great Britain was represented by Lord Castlereagh and the Duke of Wellington, and the other Great Powers, except France, by their respective Sovereigns. From various causes, which have often been discussed, the policy adopted at the Congress was imposed by Russia and Austria. France docilely followed the lead of Austria. France above all things needed peace, and Great Britain was indifferent to continental affairs which did not affect her interests. Four important questions, however, were discussed by the diplomatists at Vienna on which no formal decision was taken, but within the next few years all demanded solution. First, was France to be admitted to the European Concert without control over her domestic affairs? Second, in the restoration to each State of its former territory, was each State to be left free to make its own constitution, or were the Allies to intervene and establish absolute monarchy? Third, was the integrity of the Ottoman territory included

---

[1] General Decaen, who had been sent by Napoleon from Antwerp to relieve the pressure on Marshal Macdonald's retreat, was forced to abandon Breda, North Holland, and fall back behind the Waal.

[2] Probably Count Stanislas Potocki, a great traveller, a man of fashion, and an accomplished scholar, son of General Count Stanislas Kortka Potocki, Minister of Public Worship and Justice.

in the general guarantee given by the Allies ? Fourth, what should be done with regard to the American Colonies of Spain ? In the course of the previous summer the Allied Sovereigns of Russia and Prussia had paid a visit of nearly three weeks to the Prince Regent, and were received with great enthusiasm in London, Oxford, and other places which they visited.]

V

Streatham Park (five miles from London) :
5/17 November 1814.

I am at once uneasy and angry because of your silence, dear Alexander, and for your not having informed me of your arrival in Russia. Each mail which comes in raises the hope of a letter from you, but so far this has not been realised. What are you doing ? Where are you ? After a very pleasant stay at Brighton, where we had a gay time as long as the Queen stayed, we returned here [1] with the intention of remaining here until the spring. We see a good many of the diplomatic body and several English people : among others Mrs. Burrell [2] very frequently—and I find plenty to amuse me. Michael Woronzow [3] often comes to see us—his departure is postponed, I believe, until quite the end of the year. Léon Narischkine will be starting somewhat sooner in order to join his mother somewhere on the Continent. He is

---

[1] 'Streatham Park was worth anyone's seeing six months ago. . . . Count Lieven is my tenant, and pays me liberally ; but so he should, for his dependents smoke their tobacco in my nice new beds, and play a thousand tricks that keep my steward, who (sic) I have left there, in perpetual agony.'—Mrs. Piozzi to Dr. Gray, *Autobiography*, ii. 269.

[2] Mrs. Drummond-Burrell, Clementina Sarah, only surviving child of James, Lord Perth (who, but for the attainder of 1715, would have been eleventh Earl of Perth), married, 1807, Peter Robert Burrell, 'the chief of the dandies' ; assumed the name of Drummond on his marriage ; succeeded his father as second Baron Gwydyr, 1820, and his mother as Lord Willoughby d'Eresby, 1828 ; Deputy Grand Chamberlain at the coronation of George IV. and Joint Hereditary Grand Chamberlain at that of Queen Victoria.

[3] Prince Michael Semenovitch Woronzow, born at St. Petersburg, educated in London, where his father was Ambassador, entered the Russian army, served in the Caucasus and in the campaign against France, Plenipotentiary at the Congress of Aix-la-Chapelle, 1818 ; Governor of Bessarabia, 1823 ; commanded the Russian troops at the siege of Varna, 1828, and in the campaign against Schamyl. He took great interest in the development of the Crimea and in the building of Sebastopol. Died at Odessa, 1856.

a good deal with us when not at Brighton, and he has recently been an inmate of our house for quite a week. At this moment he is at Brighton, where he has gone to take leave of the Prince Regent, who is staying on there for some weeks longer. We know nothing of what is going on at Vienna, except that there is dancing and other amusements. Potocki has not yet returned here. Matters are not going on well in France, and two hundred persons—chiefly military—were arrested the other day in Paris. There is general restlessness of public opinion, and one does not foresee how the Government will succeed in quieting the clamour of 30,000 officers dismissed without pay. The Duke of Wellington is very unpopular there : and I think he will be obliged to return home.

I have no news of Constantine—as a rule, the art of letter-writing is seemingly little practised on the Continent, for I have not had a line from anyone for a century. Do not be a sluggard, dear Alexander, I entreat you. Tell me what you and Petersburg are doing.

VI

Streatham Park : December 8 (N.S.), 1814.

At last I have had the pleasure of receiving your letter from Petersburg of October 22, and I thank you much for it, my dear Alexander. I am answering it to-day by Woronzow, who undertakes to have this letter forwarded to you from Warsaw, where he is going to stay for a while. I heard almost simultaneously of Constantine's accident and his promotion. I am delighted that this business has been brought to such a satisfactory close—but I am very sorry that you have not his luck. Why is this ? Is it true that you are already or will soon be quartered at Odessa ? It is a long way off, and gives me small hope of seeing you here. In the course of the next fortnight we are going to join a large shooting party at Lord Cholmondeley's about a hundred miles from here. We shall probably stay there for a week, and then come to town, where we remain until the fine weather returns. I should very much like to make a trip to Paris, and I do not

altogether despair of so doing ; but there must be a new
Russian Ambassador at the post, in order that my visit may be
en règle. I have felt much regret at losing both Woronzow
and Léon Narischkine : the latter is going to Brussels, and
thence—God and his aunt alone know where ; his mother will
be in Paris in a few days. Nothing is so far officially decided
with regard to Balmaine, but there is little doubt that he will
be attached to the Embassy. For the present he is the devoted
attendant of the Marchioness of Lansdowne,[1] at whose house
at Southampton we recently spent a few days. I hear that
Constantine is starting for Petersburg, so that through him
you will have all the latest news of London and your acquaintances. Miss Mercer appears to be much taken with
Nicolas Pahlen, after having been equally so with Léon
Narischkine. She has a warm heart, but a cool head—nevertheless, I believe Pahlen might marry her, if he wished it
seriously. Good-bye, dear Alexander ; write to me, I entreat
you—and tell me what is said at Petersburg about 'la belle.'[2]
Here it is asserted that everything is broken off. My dear
love to you—do not forget me.

VII

I thank you a thousand times, dear Alexander, for your
letters, which reached me by the courier. I received them in
Norfolk, while staying at Lord Cholmondeley's seat,[3] where I
spent a fortnight in amusing and agreeable company. There
was a great shooting party, and my husband distinguished
himself. We have been back a few days, and the day after
to-morrow we return to London, as the frosts in the country

---

[1] I.e. Dowager Marchioness, widow of John, second Marquess, who died in
1809. She was the daughter of Rev. Hinton Maddox and widow of Sir Duke
Gifford ; married Lord Lansdowne in 1805.

[2] Presumably Madame Narischkine, who had for some time been the
Emperor's *confidante.* Her place was taken temporarily by Madame Gerebsoff.

[3] Houghton Hall, built by Sir Robert Walpole, first Earl of Orford, whose
only daughter married third Earl Cholmondeley, grandfather of Madame de
Lieven's host, who was created Marquess Cholmondeley 1816 and K.G. 1822.
He had been British Envoy to Berlin in 1782.

begin to be unpleasant. By the time this letter reaches you Michael will, I expect, already be with you : remember me most kindly to him. I cannot make out why we saw so little of each other here ; for in good truth I like him exceedingly, and I am sure that if he knew me better he would think well of me. Léon Narischkine must by this time be in Paris ; he made a great fuss about getting away to join his aunt, but it strikes me that their meeting will not take place immediately. Potocki is still at Vienna, awaiting from day to day his appointment to London. My husband has had no news of what is being done at Vienna ; so that we are not better informed than any other newspaper readers, for whom the most contradictory reports are provided. What, however, seems most certain is the restoration of Poland, or rather its annexation to Russia. I do not know which form the arrangement will take, but the matter is much discussed here in talking and writing. The Burrells, who were of the party in Norfolk, have given up all idea of travelling, so that we shall keep them in London through the winter, and they will be a great resource for me. I intend also to see as much as possible of the Pembrokes. By the way, their refractory son has just returned home. He managed to escape from the Sicilian prison, where he was confined, and has disposed of his wife, who was very much his inferior, in a convent. I have no very high opinion of this Lovelace, who marries, runs away, loves, and ceases to love three times in a week.[1]

Balmaine has just been making a journey with the Marchioness of Lansdowne in the north of England, where he has been instructing himself in the rearing of cattle and the cultivation of crops, and he tells us that he has seen pigs measured by the yard. He is, if it were possible, more simple and more funny than he ever was. . . .[2] is ever dogmatising and arguing, and his bursts of laughter are even longer and louder than at Brighton. Both send you all kindly greetings. Prakoushkin will be starting shortly for Petersburg. My husband has presented himself with four

---

[1] For other versions and details see Appendix.
[2] Blank in original.

saddle-horses, which interest him a good deal. He is quite delighted at finding himself again in town. We hear that you are having a gay time at Petersburg, with a constant succession of balls and fêtes. Have you fallen in love, and with whom ? The Prince Regent is gone back to Brighton, and I suppose will remain there until March. I I can get no tidings of your sabre,[1] and I am sorry to let slip this opportunity of sending it you by the courier. As soon as I get back to town I will send to Rundell & Bridge to ascertain what has become of it. I am grieved to hear that dear Masha [2] thinks it necessary to go into the country : when I recall our winters and our country-houses, I think she is to be pitied. But why is she going, if, as it appears, her monetary affairs are in a satisfactory state ?

Good-bye, my dear Alexander ; write to me frequently, I entreat you—your letters give me the greatest pleasure. Tell me the Petersburg news. What you say of my sister-in-law does not surprise me, but my idea is that the best thing to do is to laugh at anything of which one does not feel guilty. Probably we have both been lazy and nothing worse—and it is never too late to mend one's ways. Good-bye again, my dear good friend—my best love and wishes to you.

[The quarrellings, the intrigues, and the festivities of the assembled monarchs and diplomatists at Vienna were rudely disturbed by the news that Napoleon had escaped from Elba and had landed (March 1) near Cannes. In less than three weeks, after a triumphal progress, he reached Paris (March 20), where he lost no time in carrying out his promise, made at Lyons, to settle the constitution on a more liberal basis than the Charter of Louis XVIII. This was rendered necessary by the distrust of the Republican or ' patriot ' party, which was actuated more by hostility to the Bourbons than by devotion to Napoleon. It is unnecessary to refer to the events of the ' Hundred Days,' which ended in the final downfall of Napoleon. The deliberations of the Vienna Congress were resumed, and the three Sovereigns of Russia, Austria, and Prussia, who again met in France, concluded on September 26 the solemn compact known as

[1] A present from the Prince Regent to General Alexander Benckendorff in recognition of his brilliant achievements in Holland and Hanover.
[2] Marie Schevitch, sister of Madame de Lieven.

the Holy Alliance, by which they bound themselves to 'live united by the bonds of a true and indissoluble fraternity, and on every occasion and in every place to lend each other aid and succour ; regarding themselves in relation to their subjects as fathers of families . . . and as agents of Providence to govern three branches of the same family.']

VIII

London: April 19, 1815.

Dear Alexander,—I am enclosing herewith a letter from young Montgomerie,[1] whom you knew here and of whom you have often spoken to me. He wishes to serve under you, and has asked me to forward his letter. He is waiting impatiently for your permission, and would start at once to place himself at your disposal. As I am altogether ignorant as to your whereabouts at this moment, I decide to send my letter to Prince Pierre Wolkonsky,[2] who should be acquainted with the quarters of the army, and who, I hope, will have the kindness to forward my letter.

What events have happened during the last few weeks! and how a little foresight might have warded off the calamities which now again threaten Europe. Happily the energy and the force which the Powers are showing promise a speedy ending to this fresh crisis. I hope so sincerely, and also that, as last year, you will take advantage of the peace by coming to England. Let us make a rendezvous at Brighton in August. See if it be not possible to make an end of this business by that time.

Here there are a few grumblers who want peace preserved, but everyone who claims a grain of common-sense understands that it is only by bayonets and cannon-balls that that man [Napoleon] can be faced and Europe preserved from his domination. Meanwhile he is not at his ease in Paris.

[1] Probably Mr. Montgomery, one of the stewards of Almack's and a member of the *coterie* known as 'the Dandies.' In 1815 he, with Lady Harriet Butler, made up the first set of quadrilles danced in London at Almack's. See Gronow's *Reminiscences*.

[2] Prince Pierre Michaelovitch Wolkonsky, aide-de-camp to Alexander, whose life he saved at Austerlitz, re-organised the staff of the Russian army, and was appointed its chief in 1813, went through the campaign 1812–1814, and was Minister of the Household to Nicholas in 1824.

He is in the hands of the Jacobins, who are very powerful throughout France ; and, while awaiting his opportunity to gain the upper hand, the most despotic of men is forced to wear the republican livery, as he is altogether without money. His words just now are all honey, but, like the bees, his emblem, the sting is not far off. The French are the most despised and the most despicable of men. At this moment they are expecting that another revolution, as peaceful as that which they have just gone through, will restore the Bourbons ; and they will welcome them back with the same indifference as they saw them depart—this is the superlative of *canaillerie.* The Duc d'Orléans is here ; [1] I don't know why, except that these princes are always just where they ought not to be.

The Prince Regent has at length sent the sabre. I have not yet seen it, but my husband tells me that it is very beautiful. I will send it to you by Montgomerie —an excellent opportunity. I am waiting impatiently for news of you ; I am firmly convinced that you have rejoined the army. Poor Constantine hardly appreciates this new campaign now that he has taken to himself a wife. Léon Narischkine after a few months spent in Paris, has returned in the general stampede of the Russians from France. He only stayed a fortnight, and is now off again, seeking first for his mother, next for his aunt, and then for the army. We have here Madame Gerebsoff, the Lapouchines, Demidoff,[2] Sergius Wolkonsky, Pahlen, and . . . who has arrived from Spain.

I am going out a good deal this year, and my health suffers. Late hours do not suit me, yet the need of distraction urges me to go everywhere. This will last as long as I can bear it. Good-bye, dear good Alexander. You are the object of my best wishes, write to me as often as possible,

---

[1] Afterwards King Louis-Philippe.

[2] Nicolaï Mikitch Demidoff, aide-de-camp to Prince Potemkin in the Turkish war, raised and equipped a regiment which took part in the defence of Moscow. After the peace he travelled much in Western Europe, and finally fixed his residence in Florence. He devoted his time and ample means to the improvement of industry and agriculture in Russia, and endowed the Moscow University with a natural history collection.

and let me know the surest way of writing to you. Would not Woronzow be a good intermediary for our purpose? My husband sends his kindest remembrances, and I am with you heart and soul; the children often talk of you, and all your friends ask after you. Good-bye. I hope we may meet this autumn.

IX

Harley Street: July 4, 1815.

Dear Alexander,—I hear that the *corps d'armée* to which you are attached is on the march, and that consequently you are coming nearer to me. I am sending this letter to Michael Woronzow, who has kindly undertaken to forward all mine. The work in France seems accomplished, and we have nothing further to do there except by negotiation. I conclude, therefore, that you will stick to your regiment just long enough to justify asking for six months' leave, which you will come and pass in England. In a week's time I shall be going to Brighton, where I shall expect you. Do come, my dear brother, it will make me so happy to see you again. I will not send you your sabre; it awaits you here. I am afraid it may go astray between you and headquarters, and it is far too beautiful to run any risk.

I have spent an agreeable season at London, having had plenty of amusement, and my health has been so good that I have taken part in all sorts of dissipations without feeling any bad results. I see that already there are several of my friends at Brighton. Mrs. Burrell, Miss Mercer, the Duke and Duchess of Devonshire, possibly Lady Harriet [1]—all these are coming and going, so that I expect to enjoy myself thoroughly; but not so much as last year, when you were there. But do not fail to come, dear Alexander; I promise to let you stay out even till one o'clock in the morning. My husband desires to be most affectionately

---

[1] Lady Henrietta Elizabeth Spencer, daughter of fifth Duke of Devonshire, married 1809 Lord Granville Leveson-Gower, son of first Marquess of Stafford, created Lord Granville 1815. She was one of Madame de Lieven's warmest friends, and her Diary (published 1894) contains frequent reference to the Princess.

C

remembered to you. We have been having Boutaignine [1] here for the last fortnight, and he has only just started on his return to headquarters. Balmaine is just now with Pozzo,[2] but may return here at any moment. Constantine writes frequently. I hope he will soon get back to his wife, who cannot bear their separation. Good-bye, dear Alexander ; my scapegrace boys are at Brighton awaiting me. I only wish that among other scapegraces I might find you also. Do come, I pray you. I embrace you, my dear Arras, most affectionately.

X

London : November 8 (N.S.), 1815.

Since your last letter of the month of April I have not heard a word about you, dear Alexander. I was under the idea that you were attached to the *corps d'armée* which was marching through Germany, and I was constantly expecting some intimation from you where to address my letters. A few days ago a letter from papa tells me that you have never quitted Kovno.[3] I pity you too much to scold you ; but I find in the very motives of the pity with which you inspire me reasons why you should have remembered me. In fact, at Kovno you might have thought even of a sister, for you could scarcely have found there anything better to do. Poor dear little brother, I do pity you, and myself too : I was looking forward to seeing you here. I had fixed in my mind that the date of your coming would fall in with that of my visits to different parts of the country, that we should have travelled about together, that we should have amused ourselves together, admired together this beautiful country and these splendid country seats ; and should have laughed together at the *gaucherie* of their owners, but we should have agreed, as I in truth have found out, that one might gladly consent to be *gauche* as the price of the happiness which these people enjoy and spread around them. Moreover, one

---

[1] General Boutaignine had gone through the campaign, and had accompanied the Emperor Alexander to Paris and London.

[2] Pozzo di Borgo ; see Appendix.

[3] On the River Niemen, midway between Tilsit and Wilna.

finds beneath these little attractive exteriors so great a fund of good-nature, cordiality, and good sense that one must sometimes shift the compliment and acknowledge oneself to have been very *gauche* for having passed judgment on them. I first went to stay with my friend Lady Harriet, now Lady Granville, whom you doubtless remember. She is the person with whom I am most intimate. She is very clever, her house is most pleasant ; with her I made several visits to neighbouring country houses, and then went with her to spend several weeks at her brother's, the Duke of Devonshire, whose establishment is worthy of an emperor.[1] The company was numerous and well selected ; the house magnificent, and the surrounding country most romantic. We were obliged, however, to quit all these, and now since a week I am back again in London. I expect, however, to be paying several more visits between this and January ; my health, which was very indifferent during the two months I stayed at Brighton, is now quite restored.

The Orloffs[2] have started for France and Italy ; she is quite well again, and has even grown stout. We have, however, very few Russians here, a Count Lavadovsky, a young scapegrace, who has some cleverness, but lodged in the worst brains. On the other hand we have a superfluity of Austrians commencing with two Archdukes, who are travelling all over the country. Prince Paul Esterhazy[3] has been sent here as Austrian Ambassador in succession to the late Merveldt. He is a pleasant acquisition for our circle ; his wife is coming in the spring. We are promised the two Mesdames Narischkine, Princess Sergius Galitzin and her sister Comtesse Woronzow, quite a fashionable list. By the way, speaking of 'fashionables,' I met a number at the Duke of Devonshire's, all of whom claimed to be your friends : among others a Mr. Nugent. I wonder whether you recollect him ; he is an accomplished musician, and very agreeable company. Montgomerie has been to the little (West) Indies, instead of following the war with you, as he had

[1] Chatsworth Hall, Derbyshire.
[2] See Appendix.   [3] *Ibid.*

requested ; he is come back thin and yellow. Old Woronzow, the Pembrokes, and Madame Balmaine are at Paris. You have heard of Balmaine's strange destiny ; he is appointed commissioner at St. Helena to look after Bonaparte.[1] He is at this moment in Paris, but we expect him shortly, and he will start with the commissioners of the other Powers. . . . is also at Paris ; he is seeking a more distinguished post, but I suspect that the post will have none of him—thus the embassy is now altogether restricted to workers, so that I can claim from it no ' society' men—and in many ways this is much less troublesome.

I have not yet despatched your sabre, because as long as the war lasted I did not like to expose it to risk (a phrase which, if taken literally, sounds ridiculous ; but the truth is that the sabre is far too gorgeous to be exposed to danger of loss), and, as I told you, I imagined you to be on active service. Now, however, I will despatch it by the first courier my husband is despatching to Petersburg, which will be very shortly, and you should receive it soon. I shall address it to my mother-in-law, where it will be perfectly safe until you claim it.

This is a very long letter, but I hope it may make you blush for your forgetfulness. Write to me, therefore, dear Alexander, as I am most impatient to receive a word of tenderness from you. My boys are in excellent health, and send kisses to you, and my husband his best greeting. Good-bye, dear good little brother, try and love me, and tell me that you do so. My fondest love to you. The Princess Charlotte is still a recluse, and leads a very sad life ; there is no question of a husband for her. What is our good Macha doing, she too writes to me so rarely ?

---

[1] He subsequently married the daughter of Colonel Wm. Johnson, whose widow had married in 1815 Sir Hudson Lowe. Madame Balmaine, referred to in the text, was the Count's mother. For details respecting Count Balmaine see Lord Rosebery's *Napoleon*, p. 142, &c.

1816–1817

XI

London : Tuesday, January 9 (N.S.), 1816.

Dear Alexander,—Two letters from you received at the same time have made me quite happy. One of them, it is true, was not very recent, as it bore the date of the month of July—the other that of October—and the day before yesterday one from Valiki Lonki[1] dated November. Thanks for having at last bethought yourself of me. You shall now see how diligent in writing I am going to be, now that at least I am assured that it is in Russia that my letters will have to seek you, for I assure you that for six months I was in ignorance of your whereabouts, firmly believing that you were on the march with some army corps in Germany. Did Prince Pierre Wolkonsky ever forward to you a letter which I sent under cover to him at Warsaw ?

I have been moving about a good deal of late. I have been twice to Brighton ' by command ' of the Prince Regent, the first time to stay there during the Queen's visit, and on the second occasion to amuse the Archdukes, who, by the way, are not very amusable. After that I went to spend a few days with Lady Jersey,[2] Lady Cowper,[3] and others, and to-morrow I am off to the Marchioness of Salisbury's,[4]

[1] A small town of the Government of Kharkow, in Southern Russia.

[2] Sarah Sophia, daughter of tenth Earl of Westmoreland, married at Gretna Green, in 1804, to George, Viscount Villiers, afterwards fifth Earl of Jersey. She succeeded to the head partnership of Child's Bank, was a prominent leader in the fashionable world, and known as ' Queen Sarah.' Died 1867.

[3] Emily Mary, daughter of Peniston Lamb, first Viscount Melbourne, married first, in 1805, Peter Leopold, fifth Earl Cowper, and second, in 1839, Henry John, third Viscount Palmerston. Died 1869.

[4] Lady Emily Mary Hill, daughter of first Marquess of Downshire, married 1773 first Marquess of Salisbury, K.G., and lost her life in the fire which

and elsewhere—and finally I shall settle down in London, where for the last six weeks I have not passed three consecutive days.

My life in England is now very different from what you knew it. For this it only needed to give way to a little dissipation, and now I am literally fought for. It is not fashionable where I am not, and I have even arrived at amusing the English and amusing myself at the same time. This may last as long as it will, but I declare that I have no desire to die here. General Flahaut [1] is in England—you have doubtless heard speak of him, and perhaps met him when in Paris. He is half proscribed, but as Talleyrand, who is his real father, protects him, he has been allowed to escape from France and has taken refuge here. No one talks of anybody except him, and he is declared delightful. Miss Mercer has very distinctly set her cap at him, and if he is well advised he will marry her. Mrs. Burrell has just got a little daughter, and is not beautified thereby. We have a very agreeable man, Prince Paul Esterhazy, as our Austrian colleague. His wife is coming shortly; she is grand-niece of the Queen of England. I don't know how we shall get on together. Balmaine is gone back to Paris, while awaiting the fitting out of the ship which is to convey him to St. Helena. It was Nesselrode's department which caused the post to be offered to him; for my own part, I should never have thought of recommending him for it. Sass is here, and desires to be remembered to you ; he is in love with a young lady who is still more in love with him. Léon Narischkine is in Paris with his aunt ; poor Léon, if only his affairs were now to take a turn for the better ! I promise you very shortly another long letter. I wanted to reply at once to yours, and to assure you of the punctuality which I intend to observe in our correspondence, but there must be no laziness on your side. If you receive this at Petersburg, take upon you to kiss the little brother, his wife, and *la Cadette* for

destroyed the west wing of Hatfield House, 1835. Her diary of the events of her long life is quoted from freely by Sir H. Maxwell in his *Life of the Duke of Wellington* (1900), for whom the Marchioness had a great regard.

[1] See Appendix.

me. I will write to them all without fail in the course of the week. Your sabre is ready packed to go by the first courier, but before he sets off my husband must receive one from Petersburg whom he has been expecting for the last three weeks. I kiss papa's hand if you are still with him. I will write to him also. My husband sends his affectionate remembrances, my boys are delightful, everybody here remembers you. When shall we see one another again, dear Alexander ? Good-bye, dear little (*sic*) big brother.

[The story of the life of the Princess Charlotte, the Prince Regent's only child, is one of the most pathetic chapters in the records in the Royal Family of England. Her birth at Carlton House on January 7, 1796, brought about no reconciliation between her parents, the Prince of Wales and the Princess Caroline of Brunswick, between whom differences had arisen almost immediately after their marriage. At a very early age she was taken from her mother and placed under the care of governesses, and persistently neglected by her father. On the latter being named Regent this estrangement became more marked, and he avoided acknowledging her as heir presumptive to the Crown. In 1813 she was placed under the care of Miss Cornelia Knight, and in the same year became engaged to William, Prince of Orange ; but the restoration of his father to the throne of Holland would have necessitated her living in that country, and the match was broken off, but renewed again in 1816, and again broken off, greatly to the annoyance of her father, who ordered her summarily to dismiss her household. She thereupon left Carlton House and drove to her mother's house in Connaught Place, but eventually, at the instigation of her friends, was induced to return, but shortly afterwards removed to Cranborne Lodge, Windsor, where she lived in great seclusion, her mother soon afterwards leaving England. On May 2 she was married to Prince Leopold of Saxe-Coburg, and died in child-birth, November 1817. The best tribute, perhaps, to Princess Charlotte's merits and virtues was that at a time when party spirit was not specially scrupulous, neither side attempted to make political capital out of her misfortunes.]

XII

London : 1/13 February 1816.

Dear Alexander,—Since Sass will convey this letter to you, what need I add to the thousand and one details which he will give you about me and about London ? I count upon his finding you at Petersburg. At all events, he will bring you the famous sabre; do not scold me if you have not received it sooner. I know by sad experience the carelessness of our chancelleries ; your sword would have fallen into the waters of oblivion, as so many of my letters and my packets have. I thought it, therefore, wiser to wait for someone in whom I have confidence.

Here I am once again settled in London after having made the round of all the country seats of the kingdom. I never enjoyed England so much as during the past twelve months. I see and know a number of people, and really enjoy myself. You would be satisfied now with my habits of life ; to begin with, no more walks, the same hours as the rest of the world, plenty of society, and, finally, I live like the rest of my fellow-creatures—and do not feel the worse for it. Why are you not here, my dear Alexander ?

It seems that the marriage of the Princess Charlotte with Leopold of Coburg is really to take place. He is expected here at any moment. This will give fresh life to the Court circle. Miss Mercer is very much taken with Flahaut, whom we have here with several other French refugees. They are made much of by the Opposition, of whom I see as much as of the Ministerialists. We have found means of being on equally good terms with both parties. Balk is still here, and sends his kind regards. He is just off to Brazil as Minister. He is a strange personage, reminding me somewhat of the Senator Manteuffel. Stiff like him, pedantic like him, and wearisome like him. Moreover, we have no other Russians here just now except Tchitchagoff,[1] but we are

---

[1] Admiral Tchitchagoff played an important part in the Russian campaign. In May 1812 he had been sent to conclude the Treaty of Bucharest with the Turks. He was then given the command of the 'Army of Moldavia,' and ordered

threatened with a swarm in the spring. Léon Narischkine is, as you know, with his aunt in Paris, which, at all events, is better than Bessarabia, where he talked of going. I leave to Sass the task of replying at length to all your questions ; do not spare him unless you are anxious to spare yourself. Good-bye, my dear Alexander, my dearest love to you. My small boys send you their love. Alexander has outstripped Paul by more than an inch. My husband is also writing you a short note to-day ; he is in all the horrors of contracts and patterns of cloth. He has to clothe the whole army, and this gives one more trouble than all the politics in Europe. Tell me everything about Petersburg. Is it true that Madame Gerebsoff is the ruling star ? And my Prince of Orange, does he succeed ?[1] I hope so. Farewell, my good friend ; love me always, and write to me frequently.

XIII

London : 16/28 May 1816.

Dear Alexander,—A courier brought me some weeks ago two letters from you, and I was indeed happy to receive them. I know not how it happens that, each of us being equally desirous of having news of the other, we enjoy this pleasure so rarely. We live at such a wide distance apart that I do not feel any confidence in writing to you except by the aid of a courier, and for these couriers my husband always makes me wait wearily weeks, and even months, before sending one off. At last one is to be despatched—and here too is my letter.

We have been having festivities of all kinds lately. The

---

to attack the French from the south and to cut their communications. He reached the Beresina on July 31, and was able to inflict such heavy loss upon the French on their retreat that after that battle they offered no serious resistance to the Russians.

[1] William, afterwards King of Holland, born in 1792, educated at the Military School, Berlin, and afterwards at Oxford, entered the English army ; passed with rank of lieut.-colonel into the service of Spain, 1811, aide-de-camp to the Duke of Wellington in the Peninsula and in Flanders ; wounded at Waterloo ; married, 1816, Grand Duchess Anna Paulowna, sister of the Emperor Alexander I., towards whom, after having received his *congé* from the Princess Charlotte of Wales, he had turned his attentions.

Princess Charlotte is happy and contented ; they are both of them prodigiously in love—he with his wife, and she with her husband and her freedom. I have my own part in the latter : for I can see her just as often as formerly, and she is always charming. London society is very gay and brilliant this season. I amuse myself like the rest ; I keep late hours, I dance, but I do not walk, and I find the exchange excellent for my pleasure and not even bad for my health.[1] I see a number of people at home on fixed days, and without vanity I may say that my *soirées* and those of Lady Jersey are the most agreeable and the most brilliant.

I do not know what we shall be doing this autumn. I have a great wish to go and enjoy myself in Paris for a fortnight, and I am hoping that my husband will give me this treat as soon as Parliament is dissolved, Ministers off to their shooting, and the clothing of our army safe on board ship.

I am very anxious about Constantine. What is the cause of this strange misanthropy ? I hope he is by this time in Germany, and I am impatiently looking for tidings of him. I am told that you are going to get married ! I have been told it so often that I no longer think or believe it. Will you announce it to me yourself shortly ? And is there beauty, wit, and a fortune ? The union of these three qualities (? conditions) is delightful—find it, or don't marry. My husband holds you in great affection and sends his love. We often talk of you between ourselves, and oftener still wish to have you with us. The boys are going on famously.

Good-bye, dear Alexander, write to me from your horrid garrison town. How is it that you are not in France ?—that would have made me so much happier. I embrace you from the bottom of my heart, my dear good brother. Do not forget me. Good-bye.

---

[1] During the season of 1816 the waltz was first danced at Almack's, the leaders being Lord Palmerston and Madame de Lieven, and Baron de Neumann and the Princess Esterhazy, according to the volume on ' Dancing' in the Badminton Series. But from Lady Burghersh's ' Letters' it would seem that Madame de Lieven had introduced it three years earlier.

XIV

Harley Street : October 30, 1816.

My dear Alexander,—I received yesterday your letter from Gaditch [1] dated August 18, and I take advantage of a courier whom my husband is despatching to Petersburg to reply to it. I do indeed sympathise with you in the weariness of your dull garrison town, but I can assure you that beautiful London offers precisely the same commodity, although perhaps dressed in finer clothes. The arrival of a number of our countrymen has detained us in town, just as we were setting off to pay visits and take a holiday in the country, so we were unable to go anywhere. However, in these disappointments we had the satisfaction of not feeling them so acutely as we might have done had any other Russians fallen upon our hands All this autumn's gathering has been agreeable and accommodating, and has given us far more pleasure than trouble. Marie Antonsona, who stayed with us five weeks, has had much success, not so much by her beauty as for her obliging and charming manners. The Prince Regent was very much taken with her, and expressed himself in the most gallant style. I have found her extremely engaging, with a marked desire to be on good terms with me. As I ask nothing better than to be friendly with all Russians who are ready to show their good-will we were soon on a friendly footing, and, in fact, I find that she gains immensely upon closer acquaintance. She has plenty of tact, a clear judgment, no pretentiousness, and is accommodating and reasonable in all things.

We have, in addition, Prince Alexis Gortschakoff and Count Wittgenstein,[2] both excellent personages, whom the

---

[1] Or Gadjatsch, a town in Government of Pultava.

[2] Louis, son of Count Sayn Wittgenstein, a Pussian General in the service of Russia.   He was born 1769, fought at Austerlitz, took part in the invasion of Finland 1809, commanded the army covering St. Petersburg, which he saved by defeating the French at Kliostizy 1812, Commander-in-Chief of the Russian and Prussian forces 1813 ; Field-Marshal 1825, but fell into disfavour in consequence of his want of energy in the Turkish War; created Prince by the King of Prussia, 1834.   Died in January 1843.

Prince Regent welcomed very cordially, and I think they are going back well satisfied with their stay here. There now remains only Colonel Pancratieff, the Emperor's aide-de-camp, who has brought some horses as a present to the Prince Regent. He is well mannered and sensible, without a touch of that swagger so common to our young officers. We see him daily, as you may understand.

The Grand Duke Nicholas [1] will arrive here in the course of the next fortnight. I believe that the Court here will entertain him, and I expect that his stay will be more satisfactory than that of the Grand Duchess. I see a good deal of the Coburgs, and as a matter of fact I claim to be the most intimate friend of the Princess Charlotte ; at the same time showing enough prudence and reserve to prevent her father taking offence, for the family relations are the same as in your time. Her husband is behaving very well ; she is greatly attached to him, and very submissive. I will not answer for the duration of their conjugal happiness, but it is certainly to be hoped that it may be lasting. Both of them desire to be remembered to you.

You will do me a favour, dear Alexander, to burn this page of my letter. I know by experience how important it is even to exaggerate prudential precautions.

I often see the Duchess of Cumberland,[2] who unfortunately finds herself in such a position as to make a reconciliation with the Queen beyond hope ; and since the Court has quarrelled with her, private persons hold aloof, and subject her to every sort of humiliation. I have taken up such an independent position that I am able to show her attentions despite the general anathema, and a friendliness which I should not have cared to display had she been in a happier position. As things are, I feel myself morally bound not to

----

[1] Afterwards Emperor Nicholas I.

[2] Frederica Sophia, third daughter of Charles Louis Frederick, Grand Duke of Mecklenburg, born 1778 ; married, first, Prince Frederick Louis Charles of Prussia ; secondly, Prince Frederick William of Solms-Braunfels ; and, thirdly, Ernest Augustus, Duke of Cumberland (afterwards King of Hanover) ; died 1841. Queen Charlotte, on learning that the Princess had been divorced by her second husband, refused to receive her at Court or into the family circle.

withhold my sympathy when it may be of some service or even some pleasure to her. As a matter of fact, my most intimate friends, Lady Jersey, Lady Cowper, &c., are just now away from England. They make a very sensible void in London society, in which the first named exercises great influence. The diplomatic circle has been enlarged by the arrival of the Ambassadresses of France [1] and Austria,[2] the former the Marquise d'Osmond, a sort of ghost, very thin, very colourless, and a very delightful person ; the other, the Princess Esterhazy, small, round, black, animated, and somewhat spiteful. I get on equally well with both. The latter is a great-niece of the Queen of England, through her mother, the Princess of Thurn and Taxis. This relationship, however, gives her no sort of precedence here, as she is regarded as belonging to the *corps diplomatique*.

Here is a lot of small details, dear Alexander, but I expect that you will read them to Gaditch, for otherwise they will bore you intensely. My husband is strong in health, in spirits, and influence ; he is really much and generally esteemed.

By the way, Wittgenstein has been talking of you in most flattering terms as an officer. Your friends Yarmouth and Company are, as usual at this season, away shooting. Madame Narischkine has been giving much trouble to her mother. Remember me kindly to General Sacken,[3] merit and ability are seldom found so well united as in his case. His companionship has always seemed to me most highly agreeable.

My children are growing apace, are learning somewhat, and are as thorough little scamps as you could wish. Paul is the leader of all the disturbances at the school where he is (he is at a different school to his brothers) ; he boxes in a ring

[1] La Marquise d'Osmond, whose husband had served in the army and Diplomatic Service under Louis XVI., and after the Restoration was successively Ambassador at Turin and London (1815–19). He had distinguished himself as a cavalry officer and had lost a leg at Leipzig.

[2] Princess Theresa of Thurn and Taxis married Prince Paul Esterhazy.

[3] General Fabian William Osten-Sacken, born 1752, died 1837. A distinguished General, who took a leading part in several campaigns and was appointed Governor of Paris in 1814 by Alexander.

he makes as much noise as a regular John Bull, and, as I should scarcely have anticipated from his earlier years of childhood, is extremely courageous. The other two are also getting on very well. Here I am at the end of my thin page of paper ; you will have had enough of me, so I end in embracing you most heartily. My husband does the same, he is very fond of you. Good-bye. Write to me more often.

[Madame de Lieven's first reference to English politics is in connection with the riotous proceedings of the 'Spencean Philanthropists,' so called after Mr. Spence, a Yorkshire schoolmaster, who was one of the earliest propounders of the doctrine of the nationalisation of the land. He advocated, in 1800, the plan that the State should take over the ownership of all the land in the country and devote all the produce to the support of the people ; but the only result was that the enthusiast was prosecuted for promulgating such an idea. In 1816 the writings of William Cobbett, and the more constitutional reforms demanded by the 'Hampden Clubs,' rendered the free discussion of real or supposed grievances less dangerous. The Society of Spencean Philanthropists was established, but speedily took up other questions besides the unequal distribution of land, and attracted to its meetings more dangerous fanatics and demagogues. 'Orator' Hunt was, for a time at least, connected with the body, and attended a meeting held in Spa Fields on December 2. A large crowd assembled, with banners and arms, and, following the lead of a young man named Watson, who carried a tri-colour flag, marched off to seize the Tower of London. A gunsmith's shop on Snow Hill was attacked and plundered, and a gentleman in the shop shot. The rioters then marched along Cheapside to the Royal Exchange, where they were met by the Lord Mayor and Sir James Shaw with five constables, who without difficulty dispersed the mob, after having secured several of the ringleaders.]

XV

London : 1/13 December 1816.

My dear Alexander,—I have just finished writing half a dozen letters to Petersburg, and before closing my budget I must remind you of my existence by a few lines. You will no longer grumble, for it is scarcely more than a fortnight ago that I sent you a volume.

By the way, and before I forget it, why do you never

mention Cretoff? I dreamt about him last night, and I am possessed by an eager desire to have news of him—what is he doing? We have the Grand Duke Nicholas now in England![1] He is generally liked, and is really charming: the only fault I find in him is a mania for uniforms, but I only allude to this to show the impossibility of perfection in men. His relations with the Prince Regent are excellent— and all the merit is his, for his manners are most captivating. I invited everybody just now in town to meet him. He has the faculty of setting people at their ease, and this is very needful to encourage the *gauche* English. With women he is very timid ; but his taste is good, and he pays his court with deference. He has been generally successful, and I am very proud of the fact. He has gone off now to Scotland, and he will be back in London in a month and will stay as long here. He gave a big official dinner here in honour of the Prince Regent but dinners bore him and he likes evening parties better.

We have had trouble in London ; mobs assembled, became excited, and set about pillaging the town. This was all the more amusing as nothing serious came of it all—one man injured and some gunsmiths' shops sacked. There is, however, a fear lest serious consequences may ensue, and every precaution has been taken. There must be fresh outbreaks from time to time, the misery among the poor is extreme, and the English people are not submissive. Nevertheless they are so accustomed to popular outbreaks in this country that this prospect causes no anxiety. Princess Charlotte and her husband frequently inquire after you, and desire to be remembered to you. Here is my husband urging me to finish my letter, so that he may close his packet. This is a pity, for I was just beginning to be talkative—I say a pity, because I am thinking of Gaditch, and its snow-fenders and other

---

[1] 'You may remember the present Emperor Nicholas fourteen years ago in London, when he lived in the large house at the end of Stratford Place. He was then one of the Grand Dukes of Russia, travelling for his amusement ; a fine-looking youth, making a conspicuous figure at Almack's in the waltz, and whirling our English beauties round the circle to a quicker movement than they had previously learned to practise.'—T. Raikes, *Visit to St. Petersburg*, 1824-30.

pleasures of the same kind. Good-bye, my dear big little brother. I implore you to love me ; this is only as it should be, for I have a great affection for you—husband and wife embrace heart and soul.

XVI

Harley Street : July 1 (N.S.), 1817.

My good Alexander,—Do not scold me for writing seldom to you ; you know how one spends one's hours in London ; my best intentions are ineffective, perfectly idle occupations over-ride the best intentions. What a nuisance that you are not in France, with your army corps ; I have regretted it a thousand times.

We are going to spend some weeks in Paris this autumn, as we were not able to do so in the spring. The project delights me as an enjoyable *bagatelle*. I must, however admit that after London everything seems to be rather frivolous ; I refer, of course, to serious matters, in which by moral comparison with this country other countries must necessarily lose. Apart from this, from the point of view of mere pleasure, I give to them all pre-eminence over England, but I have become so serious minded that this consideration is of little interest.

You know the Duke of Devonshire has gone to Petersburg. If you happen to be there at the same time as he be amiable and attentive to him ; you will find him very clever, and I am afraid of the judgment of fools on him.

Miss Mercer has just married Flahaut, and for that has given up an inheritance of 30,000*l.* a year. There has been a good deal of marrying in London lately ; the Duke of Devonshire's departure has tired out the hopes and patience of several aspirants.

Mademoiselle Georges [1] is here, and also Talma.[2] I have

[1] Marguerite Joséphine Wemmer, daughter of an army tailor, born at Passy, 1787 ; educated by Mademoiselle Raucourt, a famous actress ; admitted to the Comédie Française under the name of Mademoiselle Georges ; made her *début* in 1802 as Clytemnestra in *Iphigénie en Aulide* ; performed at Dresden and Erfurt before the Emperors Napoleon and Alexander (1808) ; finally retired from the stage in 1855 ; died at Passy, 1867.

[2] François Joseph Talma, son of a Brabant dentist, born in Paris, 1763 ;

not yet seen them. They have acted in dualogues; the public was only moderately pleased, as French declamation is scarcely appreciated here. We still have the Duke of Wellington here, who enjoys himself very much and is very agreeable. Princess Charlotte and Prince Leopold wish to be remembered to you. Her accouchement is to be in October; they are the happiest couple, and I often go and see them in the country.

Good-bye, dear Alexander, I embrace you with all my heart. I think of you a great deal, and I want you very much indeed. Will you not come to England one day? I showed old Woronzow a Russian merchant's letter that you sent me, and he wept from compassion. We are soon expecting Lisa and her father. Good-bye again; my husband embraces you.

XVII

London : 14/26 November 1817.

My dear Alexander,—Will my letter reach the married or the bachelor brother? I think that I might congratulate you as much in one case as in the other. You see how accommodating I am ; but I am meanwhile somewhat curious, and you would do well to let me know the real state of the case. I received at Paris your letter from the town with a barbarous name in the depths of Russia. I spent three weeks in a whirl of pleasure and novelty—and I am somewhat dazed thereby. After five years of serious habits the ways of Paris diverted me a good deal, but I cannot say that they pleased me, and I believe that one would tire of this constant frivolity sooner than of anything else. What, however, is quite certain is that I am very glad to recall in London my life in Paris, and to find myself again among the silent English to whom I can repeat French gossip. Do not betray me— or they will have a poor opinion of my taste.

educated in London and afterwards in Paris, where he was admitted to practise as a dentist, 1782-1784. Abandoned his profession for the stage, and after having, with some difficulty, been received at the Comédie Française, made his *début* in Voltaire's *Mahomet*, 1787, and continued to act until a few months before his death in 1826.

The King (of France) received us with marked kindness, as did all the Royal family. We had numerous grand dinners, attentions from all sides, and the choice of our pleasures. That which I appreciated the most was the short visit of Michael Woronzow to Paris while we were there. He showed us the utmost friendliness, and I parted from him with many regrets.

A very sad event has marked our return here. That charming Princess Charlotte, so richly endowed with happiness, beauty, and splendid hopes, cut off from the love of a whole people. It is impossible to find in the history of nations or families an event which has evoked such heartfelt mourning. One met in the streets people of every class in tears, the churches were full at all hours, the shops shut for a fortnight (an eloquent testimony from a shop-keeping community), and everyone, from the highest to the lowest, in a state of despair which it is impossible to describe. I have personally suffered more, perhaps, than most—for we were very intimate, and she had shown me more actual friendship than to any other woman—and it was impossible not to feel the attraction of her charming qualities. Poor Prince Leopold is in a most distressing state, and the Prince Regent also feels the blow acutely.

The Duke of Devonshire is back again from Russia, delighted with his reception by the Imperial family, but not altogether pleased with his welcome by others. I can understand what has happened ; they amused themselves at his expense, and altogether wrongly, for, notwithstanding his dull demeanour, he is full of cleverness and wit, and his reception will give people here a bad idea of Russian courtesy. I wish that, instead of laughing in our country at the *gaucherie* of foreigners, you would not send Russians abroad who do far worse than make other people laugh at them by making themselves actually and rightly despised. I met some such at Paris who really made me indignant, and it was with quite patriotic pleasure that I met a Michael Woronzow.

Good-bye, dear Alexander, you are so far away, I have so little confidence in the way my letters are forwarded to you and whether they reach you at all, that I do not write to you more frequently. But you well know that, writing or silent, I love you with all my heart. I think of you often and with great affection. My husband sends his love. My boys are in rude health ; Paul accompanied us to Paris, and thoroughly enjoyed himself. Good-bye, dear little brother ; always love me.

1819 1820

[The Congress, or rather the Conference, of Aix-la-Chapelle, ostensibly held for arranging the final evacuation of French territory by the Allies, was made the excuse for bringing together once more the principal personages who had assembled four years previously at Vienna. The chief business transacted was the settlement of the actual amount outstanding of the original indemnity of 700 millions of francs and the date of the withdrawal of the troops. The former was settled at 265 millions, and the latter fixed for November 30, the Duke of Wellington taking throughout the lead in urging a liberal and friendly treatment of France, which at the same time was freed from the surveillance and control in domestic affairs imposed by the Treaty of Vienna. A secret agreement, however, provided for an armed intervention in the event of a revolution in France. The chief outcome of the Conference was the triumph of Metternich, who wrote that 'there is to be no change in the existing order of things,' and, at a later date, 'The Congress has encouraged the friends of order and peace in all nations, and everywhere alarmed innovators and factionists.' No other matters were treated officially, except the general principle of governing Europe through the Five Great Powers, who undertook to maintain peace ; but the slave trade question was mooted, and Mr. Clarkson, the prominent abolitionist, was received by the Emperor Alexander, as was also Robert Owen, of New Lanark, both of whom had long conferences with the Tsar.

After the close of the Congress the Duke of Wellington, on his return to England, was appointed Master-General of the Ordnance with a seat in the Cabinet. On the other hand his French colleague, the Duc de Richelieu, who had succeeded Talleyrand some months previously, found that his position was wholly untenable in view of the attitude of the ' Doctrinaires,' whose representative, M. Decazes, was Minister of the Interior and practically Prime Minister. The Duc de Richelieu, who had been Governor of Odessa (in the Russian service) during the Empire, consequently resigned the Ministry of Foreign Affairs and was succeeded by General Dessolles.]

XVIII

London : 3/15 January 1819.

My dear Alexander,—I have just finished spending six weeks at Aix-la-Chapelle, a fortnight at Brussels, a month in Paris, and finally a week almost beside my own coffin. I have been in great danger from an inflammation of the throat and lungs ; and I assure you that the idea of not having given news of myself for so long worried me considerably during my fever. I make amends at once—as you see—and begin by congratulating you on your little daughter,[1] and on your happiness, in which I take a lively interest ; but it is needless to say so, because you know how much I love you.

We have come back very well satisfied with our journey— my husband much pleased by the favour and confidence displayed by the Emperor, and I by the interest of the scene passing under my eyes. The meeting at Aix-la-Chapelle is without doubt an event memorable by the satisfactory results which it should produce, and most noteworthy by the simplicity and concord which presided over the discussion of so many great questions. For my own part I made some interesting acquaintances, of whom I shall always retain a pleasant remembrance. The delight, too, of having had Constantine there was, as you can easily guess, fully appreciated by me. He did not altogether attain the aim of his stay at Aix-la-Chapelle, but he has every chance and many promises that he will do so ere long. The Empress Mother[2] was, as ever, most gracious ; my mother-in-law thoroughly enjoyed her short stay with us, and my boys won her heart completely. I have seen again the whole of this Russian Court, and thought it most accommodating in coming from so far to meet me ; I renewed my tender passages with the Grand Duke Constantine. In a word, I have enjoyed the recognition of so many friends of the past in so brief a period that had it not been for a sharp attack of illness, the result of my fatigue, I

---

[1] Annette von Benckendorff, married 1840 Count Rudolph Apponyi, and died in 1900. These letters were bequeathed to her by her father.

[2] See Appendix.

should have been disposed to have taken all this journeying
for a dream.   After having got rid of the Congress and its
grandeurs, we went to refresh ourselves at Paris, where we
found an epidemic of delirium, so acute was the strife of parties.
The crisis at one moment threatened to become dangerous—
these Ministers in disgrace, those in favour, hopes on one
side, fears on the other, courtiers in dire perplexity, unable
to distinguish the rising from the setting sun, so frequent
and prolonged were the fluctuations.   All this makes up a
curious spectacle, which might have been amusing did it not
threaten to become tragic ; for, to close all, comes the resignation of the Duc de Richelieu, whom all Europe should and
does regret.[1]

We are expecting Michael Woronzow immediately ; he
proposes to spend six months in England.   I left Madame
de Nesselrode [2] at Paris, where she will stay until next summer.
I saw a good deal of her while we were there.   She is a
clever woman, with whom it is a pleasure to me to associate.
There was a swarm of Russians in Paris, but as they did not
go into society I saw only old and inevitable acquaintances,
among these the Princess Souvaroff, who has treated herself
to a superb set of teeth.   Of the others I have no news to
tell you.   I returned yesterday from Brighton, where I
have been spending some days as the guest of the Prince
Regent.   He is more polite and friendly than ever to us.

---

[1] Armand du Plessis, Duc de Richelieu, son of the Duc de Fronsac and last
member of the direct line, was distinguished in early life as a linguist.   In 1789
he took service, first in Austria, and afterwards in Russia, but joined the army of
the *Emigrés* under the Prince de Condé in 1792.   After a short stay in England
he returned to Russia, and was named Governor of Odessa in 1803, then a small
colony, and afterwards Governor-General of New Russia.   He returned to France
in 1814, and after Fouché's dismissal became Minister of Foreign Affairs and
President of the Council ; attended the Congress of Aix-la-Chapelle, 1817, which
freed France from foreign occupation, but retired in the following year.   He was
sent to London to congratulate George IV. on his accession, and took office once
more after the murder of the Duc de Berri, and held it until December 1821.

[2] Marie Dimitrijevna Gourjew married Count Nesselrode 1812, the diplomatist
and statesman, of German-Russian parentage, born in 1780 in Lisbon harbour on
board a British vessel, so that Pope Gregory XVI. said of him that he represented
in his own person a Quadruple Alliance.   In the opinion of his contemporaries
he was rather dexterous than distinguished in diplomacy.

'All Russia' has been talking to me of your wife, dear
Alexander; they find her charming, witty, sensible—in fact,
everything needed to make you thoroughly happy. I enjoy
this praise of her because it assures me of your happiness.
Will you not at last have the luck to exchange your dull
quarters for some more civilised spot, and more within reach
of my letters? This one will be specially favoured if it
reaches you before the end of the year. Good-bye, my dear
Alexander. I embrace you, your wife, and my little niece,
who without doubt is pretty. My husband sends you a
thousand good wishes.

XIX

London : 2/14 May 1819.

My dear Alexander,—I hardly know if I ought to congratulate you on your new sphere of activity. I will
wait for your impressions after a certain interval ; but this I
know without a moment's hesitation, that I am delighted
with a change of residence which will give me more frequent
opportunity of having news from you and giving you the like
of myself. Thanks, too, for having already taken advantage
of the situation, for I have already received your letter of
March 27. I will write at once to Michael Woronzow and
ask him to undertake your commissions, and as he is on the
spot he can both execute them and see to their forwarding.
He is expected here at the end of the month, with his wife,
with whom, it is said, he is much in love. Have I dreamed
it or not that formerly she had the reputation of being a
great coquette ? Ten years may probably have sobered her :
at all events, she is a person of good style, well educated, and
rich, which is never a drawback.

The year has begun badly for me—I have been out of
sorts ever since my return to England. I verily believe
that the little breath of continental air which I inhaled has
re-adapted my life to its requirement, and that I have had
enough of London fogs. Such is the inconsistency of human
nature that I should receive with delight the news of another
appointment, but, as Nesselrode said to me, there is only Paris

or Vienna—and Paris, Heaven preserve me from it and it from me, yet I believe there is a centrifugal force between it and me.

My children are well and are studying diligently. Constantine is undoubtedly the most capable and will not rest satisfied with being a nobody. Paul is the handsomest, and he is also clever.

London is going through its ordinary round of amusement.

[The commercial depression which followed the resumption of specie payments, although in no way resulting therefrom, had made itself felt throughout the country ; wages fell, employment was difficult to procure, and food, especially wheat, maintained a high price. Meetings were held, chiefly in the open air, by operatives in all parts of the country, and political questions were discussed as much as the low rate of wages. The Midlands and Lancashire were the chief centres of agitation, but at Glasgow, Leeds, and elsewhere large meetings were held, but no breach of the peace was committed. On August 16 a meeting was held in St. Peter's Field, Manchester, 'to consider the propriety of adopting the most legal and effectual means of obtaining reform in the Commons House of Parliament.' Large numbers from the adjoining districts flocked in, and it was estimated that upwards of eighty thousand people, including a number of women, were assembled to hear 'Orator' Hunt and his friends address them on the subject of Parliamentary Reform. The authorities, either warned by the Government or acting on their own discretion, had taken elaborate precautions. Special constables had been sworn in, the Cheshire and Manchester Yeomanry, and a large military force— including a regiment of infantry, a troop of horse artillery with two guns, and six troops of Hussars—were held in readiness in the neighbourhood of the meeting ground. The magistrates, on being informed that the meeting was assembled, had given the Chief Constable a warrant to arrest the reform leaders. This officer declared that he could not execute the warrant without military aid. The Manchester Yeomanry, only about forty in number, were the first to advance, but were almost at once broken up into small groups and completely hemmed in by the crowd. The officer in command of the Hussars, taking the order of the principal magistrate, ' Disperse the crowd,' ordered his men to charge, and a frightful scene of confusion ensued on the efforts of the closely packed crowd to escape. The actual loss of life, however, did not exceed six, of whom one was a special constable and another one of the Yeomanry, and some seventy people were taken to the Infirmary. When the news became known in London a Cabinet Council was immediately summoned, at which the law officers of the Crown gave it as their opinion that the conduct of the magistrates was justifiable, but public opinion did not endorse this view.]

XX

Camden Place, Kent: October 5 (N.S.), 1819.

Dear Alexander,—You have heard what has happened, and that I am on the point of again becoming a mother, without having scarcely had the time to realise that I was in that way. You do not know, however, how much I have suffered, and how incapable I have been of any exertion—hence the reason of my idleness in writing. I must, however, send you a line to say how much your appointment to the Emperor's military household has delighted me. My husband is very glad to have you for a comrade. We have had staying here for several weeks the Count Capo d'Istria.[1] I have never known a foreigner in England make himself so thoroughly popular as he has done ; everybody recognises him to be a man of ability, of tact, and of excellent judgment ; everything in him, including his appearance, has charmed everyone —in a word, he has been a complete success. On his part he has done justice to this country, which he knows better after a fortnight's visit than many who have lived here many years. We have been spending three months in the country, where we are well, and above all comfortably, established. The children are especially happy here, and have profited in all ways. I am going to town to-morrow to get through my ' event,' and afterwards, if I live, I shall come back here. Michael Woronzow is returning to you with his wife in a similar condition—they left us a fortnight ago ; he is an excellent husband, and they get on very well together. Your *protégé* Nevachoff only spent a few weeks in England, my husband being obliged to send him to Warsaw, as there was no one here whom he could employ as a special messenger. He

[1] See Appendix.

was here during the visit of Count Capo d'Istria, throughout which we were overwhelmed with invitations, race-meetings, and even journeyings—for my husband accompanied him in his travels over the greater part of England. I did what I could so long as I had strength to do anything.

Things are getting a little noisy in England—that is, there is a good deal of talking and a good deal of writing, and as usual the best intentions are the least wise. The discontented are doubtless numerous, but I see no real danger in the situation ; do not suppose that we are on the eve of a revolution from what you read in the newspapers. The Ministers, at all events, do not seem disturbed, for they are scattered in every direction; some at Spa, others in Italy or Ireland, and the remainder at their country houses. The Duke of Wellington is playing the British farmer, and, as in all things, acquits himself with good grace, but I suspect that it bores him somewhat. Farewell, dear Alexander, I embrace your wife, your little one, and yourself with all my heart. Love me always and write to me sometimes—if in four weeks' time you do not hear that I am dead.

[King George III. died on January 29, 1820, at Windsor, six days after the death of his son, the Duke of Kent. At the same time the Prince Regent, now George IV., was at Brighton in a state of health which, for a time, caused serious anxiety. He, however, speedily recovered, and one of his first acts was to refuse to allow the alteration in the Liturgy involving the Queen's name. The Ministry, which had formally resigned, was re-appointed, the Earl of Liverpool as Prime Minister, Viscount Castlereagh, Secretary for Foreign Affairs, Mr. Canning, President of the India Board, and Viscount Palmerston (not in the Cabinet), Secretary at War, being the most conspicuous members. In less than a fortnight after the new King's accession they again proposed to resign in consequence of the King's attitude on the inclusion of the Queen's name in the Prayer Book, but they eventually gave way, and at a meeting of the Privy Council on February 12 the name of the Princess of Wales was struck out, and in the new form no allusion was made to her as Queen. Little notice was taken of the matter at the time, either in Parliament or by the newspapers of the Opposition. In the House of Commons (February 21) Mr. Hume drew attention to the subject, but refrained from finding fault with the use the King had made of his prerogative in fixing the forms of the Church Service. Mr. Tierney, the leader of the Opposition, refused to prejudge the case, but called upon the Ministry in the name of justice to give Parliament some information and to submit the whole case to its inquiry. Mr. Brougham, the Queen's legal adviser, urged that in considering the question, 'the voice of party ought to be extinct,' and deprecated broaching the question at that moment, when the only effect would be to defeat the ends of justice, and 'to drag the subject through the mire of every hustings.' This wish was fulfilled, for in the general election which followed the Queen's position was seldom discussed, and the general result was a trifling increase in the number of the ministerial supporters. The truce, however, was not long observed on either side. On June 6 Queen Caroline arrived at Dover after six years' absence, and proceeded to London, where she was received with great enthusiasm by the people. On the same day the King sent a message to Parliament commending to the Lords an inquiry into the Queen's conduct, and forthwith the matter became a party question. The Opposition, led by Mr. Brougham and supported by Mr. Tierney, arguing strongly against the appointment of a committee to hear in secret the charges against the Queen, challenged the Government to bring specific charges against her. Mr. Canning, while defending the conduct of the Ministers, urged that when the Crown sought the advice of Parliament it could not be withheld, but added, 'I never will place myself in the situation of an accuser against this individual.' This was doubtless the view of other Ministers. The debate was ultimately adjourned, on the motion of Mr. Wilberforce, in order to see if a compromise could not be effected. On the same night, however, the Lords, by a majority of 79 had agreed to the appointment of the Committee, and fifteen peers, were chosen by ballot to serve on it. Negotiations ensued between the Prime Minister and Mr. Brougham; and Lord Castlereagh and the Duke of Wellington on the part of the King, and Mr. Brougham and Mr. Denman, on behalf of the Queen, were named to discuss and settle the terms of an arrangement. The questions to be examined were : (1) the future residence of the Queen abroad, (2) the title she might think fit to adopt on the Continent, (3) the non-exercise of certain rights of patronage in England, (4) the suitable income to be assigned to the Queen when abroad. The question of the Liturgy was not specifically mentioned, but the Queen's advisers felt themselves entitled to bring it forward in connection with that of her residence abroad, and on this point the negotiations were practically abortive, as neither side would give way. After many postponements Mr. Wilberforce proposed two resolu-

tions, which practically called upon the Queen to listen to the advice
of Parliament, and to forbear to press further the adoption of those
propositions on which any material difference of opinion existed,
but would by no means be understood to indicate any wish to shrink
from inquiry.   Mr. Brougham opposed the resolution, and was supported by the Radicals, but it was ultimately carried by 391 to 134
votes.   A week later, June 26, the adjourned debate on the Royal
Message was resumed, again adjourned, and finally discharged, and
subsequent proceedings were left to the House of Lords.   On July
4 the Committee presented its report, declaring the necessity of
further proceedings upon the charges against the Queen, and Lord
Liverpool forthwith introduced into the Upper House a Bill of
Degradation and Divorce.   Ministers would doubtless have been
glad to shift the responsibility upon the Committee, for the popular
feeling, noisily expressed on the Queen's entry into London, became
daily more marked.   Sympathy with the Queen was a ready way of
expressing dislike and disapproval of the King, and in London
especially this feeling was but thinly veiled.   The King's Ministers
came in for a full share of popular disfavour, and although no effort
was made in either House of Parliament to displace them their
authority in the House of Commons especially was greatly weakened.
The Queen's trial commenced on August 17, and was continued with
several adjournments throughout the autumn.   The case was so far
concluded that on November 6 the Bill was read a second time by a
majority of 28, but four days later, when the question was put that
the Bill should be read a third time, the majority dropped to nine—
contents 108, not contents 99—and Lord Liverpool thereupon moved
its abandonment, which was agreed to without a division.   The
result was received with great enthusiasm and illuminations in the
principal streets were general, including that of Marlborough House,
the residence of Prince Leopold.   The only political incident of
importance arising out of the Queen's trial was the resignation of
Canning.   It was first tendered after the failure of Mr. Wilberforce's
mediation ; but the King requested Canning to remain in office,
abstaining as completely as he thought fit from any share in the
proceedings respecting the Queen.   He therefore attended no
meetings of the Cabinet upon the subject, absented himself from
England during the progress of the Bill, and after its withdrawal
again tendered his resignation, which was then accepted.]

XXI

London : February 8, 1820.

My dear Alexander,—I am much disturbed by what my mother-in-law writes concerning papa, and by not receiving any direct news from him or from you for so long. For pity's sake tell me how he is ; I write to him by every courier, and send my letters under cover to my mother-in-law. Does she pass them on to him ? Find this out for me, I beseech you, for I gather, to my horror, from her letters that she is failing, and consequently might as likely as not be sending on my letters to China, if she had any correspondents there, instead of to Revel. I must recount to you her series of blunders, which have placed me in a very awkward position. Immediately after my confinement my husband wrote to her as well as to the Empress Mother, because the latter has always wished to be godmother to each of my children. He told his mother that he left it to her to ask or not for this favour, according, as in her judgment, the Empress Mother was expecting this request from us or was not desirous of acting. On this simple sentence, would you believe it ! my mother-in-law takes upon herself to say to the Empress Mother that not only are we desirous of having her as godmother, but that we wish the Emperor to be godfather. As you may guess, we had never entertained such a thought, and had I had four-and-twenty children I should never have been guilty of the indiscretion of putting forward such a request. However, she managed to settle the business somehow, and writes to say that the Emperor and Empress accept with much pleasure the right to hold the child at the font— a thing of which we never dreamed for a moment. But this is not the end of the trouble. Before receiving her letter I had written to her to say that as far back as last May (months before its birth) the Prince Regent himself had expressed his wish to be the godfather of the child. Under these circumstances I could not with decency do otherwise than accept the offer—so that at the baptism it must be he who will hold the child and it must be named George. And now, what does my mother-in-law do but go about saying that it is from vanity that I wanted the Prince Regent for godfather! When I say that she tells this story, it is because she wrote to me in these very words, and that ' meine kleine Eitelkeit ' (my bit of vanity) has caused this ' misch-masch,' inasmuch as it is impossible to have a second godfather when the Emperor has consented to act as such. I have told you all this because I should be extremely grateful, should the opportunity offer, if you would explain this matter, in which my mother-in-law makes us play the most foolish part imaginable. I never asked anyone, and it was absolutely spontaneously that the Regent offered to act. In truth, I hoped that he had forgotten all about it, and so fully did I think so that when, a few days after my confinement, Wellington came to see me I told him that he must stand sponsor for my boy. The Prince Regent, however, was not to be disposed of so easily, for he sent for my husband to talk the matter over. Nothing remained, therefore, but to submit with good grace. Now the result of all this business is that, notwithstanding this embarrassing wealth of godfathers, my poor child is not yet a Christian. Either I was ill, or the Regent was away, and now that he is King there is at least three months' full mourning—during which there can be no question of baptism.[1]

We are expecting the Duc de Richelieu here to greet the new King. Will anybody be sent from our Court on a like mission? I suppose so. I wish you could impress upon our people the colossal stupidity of the English—the King's above all—in considering themselves more honoured by Colonel N.N., an envoy, if he should happen to be a prince, than by Marshal N.N. if he be untitled. Our friend Nikita is here—a magnificent ' Highness '; it must be admitted that the English don't think him any the cleverer on that account.

---

[1] A somewhat similar misunderstanding arose with regard to the naming of the late Queen Victoria. Her father, the Duke of Kent, had chosen the name of Alexandrina, after her godfather Alexander I. The Prince Regent wished her to have the name of Georgiana, which, as it could not stand first, was omitted altogether.—Greville, *Memoirs.* i. 22.

This letter has grown old upon my table—but at length I despatch it to-day, February 1-13, by a courier going by way of Paris. My dear Alexander, I implore you to send me news of papa—I am very anxious.

The King is now out of danger, but one could not have been nearer death than he was for a time. The Queen—that is the great question of the moment—what is wanted is to 'un-queen' her, but how is it to be done? There will be a scandal in London, and there will be plenty to laugh about, except for the Ministers, who find it no laughing matter, I warrant you, but meanwhile perspire in the Council Chamber. Wellington is the only one who laughs at everything, and, above all, talks of everything. He is charming, agreeable, and accommodating in the highest degree; he is a most excellent resource for us, and is quite happy if one will pet him. The truth is that London bores him, and that he is never so much at ease as in our house.

Good-bye, my dear Alexander ; I have gossiped finely to-day, but won't you be gossipy also ? Put aside for awhile your производство[1] and everything which ends in руки and in укн, and tell me in good French that you always love me.

XXII

Dear Alexander,—I entreat you to send on at once the enclosed letter to papa ; Krudener will tell you all about myself, for he has seen a good deal of us during the few days he has been staying here. It is he who will convey this letter to you. We are one and all going on well here : at any rate, for the moment nobody is conspiring, and everyone is on amusement bent. This is the epoch of obligatory pleasures in London ; personally they bore me, and I look forward with impatience to the time when, instead of going to a rout, I can go off to sleep, even to the hootings of the owls. We have plenty of them at our place in the country ; but we have also

---

[1] Production &c.

that beautiful English turf and foliage, and the fresh air un-
tainted by coal-smoke.   Do you recollect Mrs. Burrell, and
do you remember how she was turned out of the Prince Regent's
circle ? [1]   Well, now she is one of the King's select and most
intimate group.   He does not give audience to his Ministers,
but he receives Mrs. Burrell.   She belongs to the 'great'
Opposition, but she is a friend of the new Star.[2]   I am giving
you a bit of Court gossip, as if you were not fully satisfied
with such as our own Court could supply.   But a boudoir
revolution is so exciting even in England that I cannot refrain from being highly diverted by this one, but it is not a
laughing matter for everybody.   Good-bye, my dear Alexander,
a thousand tender things to your wife—when is she expecting
her confinement? Does little Anna talk yet?   Is she pretty?
Tell me some of her prattlings.   My husband sends his
love.

XXIII

London : November 6, 1820.

My dear Alexander,—I have to thank you for a letter to
myself and for another to my husband, which we have just
received, with the many details that you give us about our
boy, I am delighted to know that he is at school, and equally
pleased to find that you are prepared to show some stern
ness in dealing with him.   I have been really anxious about
the Court favour he has received ; he has his faults, and what
he needs to overcome them is rigid supervision rather than
indulgence.   He has always been extremely idle, and it was
partly because he thereby hindered his brothers' progress
that we thought it advisable to separate them, and it must be
allowed that since his departure they have been going on
famously.   Probably my mother-in-law has told you of my
husband's intention of spending a couple of months at Peters-

---

[1] It appears by a letter from Drummond-Burrell, dated October 11, 1818,
that he and his wife had left England for Italy and had taken a villa on the Lake
of Como, but no reference is made to any misunderstanding with the Prince
Regent.   She had been friendly with Lady Hertford, and possibly this may have
caused the coolness of the King after Lady Jersey's rise in Court favour.

[2] The Marchioness of Conyngham.

burg next summer. He has need of a holiday to look after
his private affairs, to get into touch with Russia, to mix with
his fellow-countrymen, and to see his own country again.
Eight years of absence almost makes a foreigner of one, and
that is a condition to be avoided. He is therefore going to
ask for a few months' leave of absence during the fine
weather ; he will go to Russia with the two elder boys, the
other is too small to face so long a journey. I shall stay
with him, but not in England (for we are not rich enough for
me to play the Ambassadress while he is spending so much
on his travels) but at some baths near Frankfort. I shall go
and see Constantine, too, and shall await there my husband's
return, and go back with him to England, or trot off elsewhere should he be sent to another post. Not to see you
and our dear father will be a keen disappointment to me,
but it would be impossible for me to leave my small boy
here. He is a sweet, gentle creature, dear Alexander ; I wish
you could see him. Whenever shall we see one another
again ? We are at the opposite ends of Europe, but that
reflection does not facilitate matters.

Heaven knows what is coming to pass in this England.
We are not near settling with the Queen —if she is white-
washed, the Radicals will triumph ; if she is found guilty, they
will bring about a revolution, that is the pleasing alternative.
Prince Leopold[1] has broken completely with the King and
the Government by going to see her (the Queen) since the
trial ; he declares that in his opinion the proceedings have
cleared her, and that consequently he treats her as perfectly
pure and innocent ; he has judged and decided before the
House of Peers has pronounced. His profound sagacity has
anticipated the judgment of the highest tribunal. The
King will never see him again. I divide my time in London
between the Ministerial and Opposition *salons*. Lady Jersey

[1] Prince Leopold offended the King by visiting Queen Caroline, and he consequently was not present at the King's coronation. He further estranged
George IV. at a later date by protesting against the alienation of certain Crown
jewels which had been possessed by his wife, Princess Charlotte, to the
Marchioness of Conyngham.

holds her club in the latter ; it is most amusing for a neutral. I must end, my dear Alexander, by asking you to give the enclosed to my son. Good-bye, my husband embraces you and your big nephew also. Paul is as tall as his father, and a splendid fellow.

1822–1825

CONGRESS OF VERONA—SPANISH AFFAIRS—CANNING'S INFLUENCE —DEATH OF ALEXANDER—WELLINGTON'S MISSION

[In the interval which elapsed between the trial of Queen Caroline and the meeting of the Congress of Verona, several important events had happened which affected the policy of Great Britain towards its continental Allies. The Tory Ministry, although still remaining in power, had been modified by the introduction, in January 1822, of Mr. Peel into the Cabinet as Home Secretary in the place of Lord Sidmouth ; and on the death of Lord Londonderry (Viscount Castlereagh), in August of the same year, Mr. Canning, who had been nominated Governor-General of India, was gazetted Secretary of State for Foreign Affairs on September 16, notwithstanding the reluctance of the King to admit him to his Council. On the day following, the Duke of Wellington, who had been selected to replace Lord Londonderry, set out to represent Great Britain at the Congress of Verona, with instructions to frankly and peremptorily declare that Great Britain would not be party to any interference by force or by menace in the struggle in Spain.

The meeting of the Sovereigns of Austria, Russia, and Prussia on this occasion was the natural outcome of the policy foreshadowed at Paris in 1815, and endorsed subsequently at Aix-la-Chapelle in 1818, at Troppau in 1820, and at Laibach in the following year. The five Great Powers were in effect to police Europe, although the policy of the Pentarchy was more euphemistically described by its supporters as that of maintaining peace. The chief promoter of the Holy Alliance was Prince Metternich, and his chief aim was to uphold Austrian influence in Italy, and as the limits of the smaller continental States and the wishes of their inhabitants were of very slight interest to Lord Castlereagh, he had raised no discordant note at any of the Congresses which had assembled during his tenure of the British Foreign Office. Public opinion in England had never cordially accepted the views or the fair words of the framers of the Holy Alliance. This distrust was deepened by the policy of Metternich in Piedmont and Naples, where popular feeling against the autocratic government of their restored rulers, Victor Emmanuel I.

E 2

and Ferdinand IV., had shown itself in serious disturbances of public order.   At the Congress of Troppau (1820) Metternich proposed to uphold the absolutism of Ferdinand, but Russia and France wished to remove the revolutionary features of the Constitution without suppressing it.   England held that the Powers under the Treaty of Vienna had guaranteed only the territories of the various States of Europe, and refused to interfere in their domestic affairs.   Metternich, however, managed to win over Alexander I. to his views.   In the ensuing year King Ferdinand attended the Congress at Laibach and accepted the arrangements imposed upon him by Austria, whose army had occupied his kingdom on the ground of restoring the King's authority, while in Piedmont Charles Felix was established by Austrian arms on the throne vacated by his brother Victor Emmanuel I.   In Spain an even worse state of affairs was brewing, and, separated from France only by the Pyrenees, it was so far removed from the influence of the Northern Powers that the latter were especially desirous to strengthen the hands of Ferdinand VII., whose restoration they had effected and with whose policy they sympathised. On his return from captivity Ferdinand's chief aim had been to remove all traces of the comparative liberty which Spaniards had enjoyed under the Constitution of 1812.   During the years which followed Ferdinand's return, affairs in Spain grew steadily worse. Her American colonies, from Mexico to Paraguay, had revolted against her since 1810, and her feeble efforts to recover them only served to disorganise more thoroughly the finances and to excite the discontent of the mother country.   Colombia, the States of La Plata, Chili, and Peru were already independent, and on the eve of the meeting of the Congress of Verona Mexico was hesitating between Iturbide and the Republican party.

Ostensibly the Congress of Verona was summoned to deal with the affairs of Greece, which had not escaped the revolutionary fever ; but on passing through Paris the Duke of Wellington found out that the condition of both Spain and Portugal would engage immediate attention, for in the eyes of Metternich the dangers to the European Concert were more to be apprehended in the south-west from French intervention than in the south-east from Russian encroachment.   Ferdinand having found that his efforts to govern by means of a camerilla led to insurrection against his authority which he was powerless to control, and forced to choose between abdication and concession, convened the Cortes and proclaimed the Constitution of 1820.   Revolution and counter-revolution ensued, and Ferdinand was suspected of intriguing with each party by turn, the Decamisados, the 'Armies of the Faith,' the Moderados, and finally with the

Exaltados or Radicals. The presence of a large body of French troops on the Pyrenees was equally a matter of suspicion. On the one hand, it was asserted that Ferdinand had invited French intervention ; on the other, it was alleged that he claimed the protection of the Holy Alliance. In any case, the three northern monarchs considered a further Congress opportune, and they met at Verona, where the predominance of Metternich's policy of intervention was accepted without reserve by the monarchs attending the meeting. The views, however, of France and Great Britain were not in accordance with the absolutism of Austria and Russia, which, with Prussia, would gladly have dispensed with the offer of the co-operation of France in Spain, as they were eager to bear down the opposition of Great Britain, which had categorically refused to take part in intervention, ' come what might.' In France, however, the Legitimists were still the strongest party in the Chamber, but the Duke of Wellington's efforts to induce France to observe complete neutrality in order to prevent the intervention of the northern Powers had been only partially successful. M. de Chateaubriand replaced M. de Montmorency, the leader of the war party, as Minister for Foreign Affairs, but ultimately he was forced by the action of the Spanish Government to side with those who insisted upon intervention. The Russian, Austrian, and Prussian Ministers accredited to Madrid were recalled, and the French Ambassador shortly afterwards was also withdrawn, and the French troops under the Duc d'Angoulême crossed the Spanish frontier.]

XXIV

Harley Street : 10/22 March 1822.

My dear Alexander,—You are quite right to scold me ; but when I reflect that your anger of December only reaches me in March, I am quite discouraged from making amends in March in order that you might gather the fruits some time next autumn. It is not distance alone which is fatal to correspondence, but the want of regularity and certainty in the interchange of letters. It is disastrous, my dear little brother, I pity you most truly for the long distance which now separates you from your wife. A quite recent letter from Constantine, however, tells me that he and you have been brought together, but that cannot be for long. Where are you actually at this moment ? How long do you stay there? and what are you thinking of doing next? That is the big question which at this moment all Europe is asking. I answer it in accordance with my hopes, that is : ' not going to war.' No one can tell where this might lead us, and it seems to me that there are plenty of reasons for maintaining peace.

I have been passing the winter between this and Brighton, where the King has repeatedly invited us. His palace has become a really delightful residence since he has become so exclusive in the selection of his society, which is now from among the best in England. The majority, doubtless, are from the ranks of the Opposition, but it must be admitted that it is that party which is supported by the great families, the great estates, and the fashion. The Duke of Wellington is also regularly invited when we are summoned to Brighton. Bloomfield has retired ;[1] you remember he was formerly the Regent's factotum ; his dismissal caused a good deal of talking. Lady Pembroke has been at the point of death, and is not yet altogether out of danger. The Woronzows—father, son, and daughter-in-law—are still in Paris, but all your other acquaintances are in London. Lord Yarmouth[2] is awaiting with indecent impatience the death of his father, but it should be said in his defence that the poor old man has become quite childish. Colonel Cooke[3] is still the purveyor-in-ordinary of lovely caskets and extravagant fashions. I hesitate to name others, lest you should do England the bad compliment of saying that you have forgotten all about them. Paul is in Paris, where he is studying with a tutor, and attending some lectures at the Collége de France. This is my husband's excellent idea ; we shall see how it will turn out. We are expecting him home to-morrow for

---

[1] See Appendix.

[2] Francis Charles, Earl of Yarmouth, afterwards third Marquess of Hertford.

[3] Major-General Sir Henry Frederick Cooke, C.B., G.C.H., son of John George Cooke, of Harefield Park, Middlesex, born 1783, died 1837 ; entered the Foot Guards 1801, served as A.A.G. in Spain and Portugal, aide-de-camp to H.R.H. the Duke of York 1814-27. He was one of ' the Dandies,' and several of his letters are preserved in the ' Wellington ' and the ' Raikes ' correspondence. Frequently referred to in Raikes's *Diary*.

the Easter holidays. My little George is a most winning child, and without him I should feel myself childless, so totally separated am I from the others. My husband is very busy, and goes out very little into society ; I go partly from duty and partly from pleasure, for I like the bustle and the gossip. The King of England's projected journey for the summer seems to grow vaguer as time goes on. Personally I should be sorry if it were given up, for I had been looking forward to the occasion for making a little jaunt on the Continent. His (the King's) health has visibly declined of late ; he is much thinner and aged, and he is very nervous about himself. You will have heard of the death of poor Minette—it gave me real sorrow. Constantine is happy and delighted with his little post. What about your little girls, my dear Alexander ? Are they pretty ? to whom are they like? Embrace your wife for me, I love her with all my heart because she makes you so happy. Love me always, dear Alexander, and tell me so sometimes. My husband sends his best remembrances.

4/16 April.

Here is a letter, grown old in my writing-table drawer, the opportunity for despatching it never having turned up till to-day. Between these two instalments of my letter the famous outburst of the Divan of March 3 has astonished us.[1] The general opinion is that it must bring about war. The worst side of the matter is that all the Jacobins are in favour of it, and they are but sorry apostles. But, after all, will it now be possible for us not to be launched upon it ? You will be far better informed when you receive this letter than I am when writing it. My husband has received your two letters, and was intending to reply to them to-day, but the despatch of a courier is like the day of Judgment—one has not time to think of one's little sins. He desires me to

---

[1] Russia's protest against the massacre of Christians in Constantinople, in the Archipelago, and throughout Asia had been treated with contempt. The Sultan claimed his right to repress rebellion in his own dominions as he thought fit, and demanded the surrender of such as had taken refuge on Russian or Austrian territory. Russia at once recalled her Ambassador.

say that he will certainly write to you by the next courier, who starts in a week's time.

XXV

London : 4/16 September 1822.

My dear Alexander,—At last you have got stationed somewhere where my letters can reach you. This gives me courage, although I am in the midst of the horrors of a hurried departure. I am only writing on this occasion in order to congratulate you on having rejoined your wife, and on being stationed in a city instead of among dreary villages. We are leaving this in a couple of days for Verona. Our absence probably will not be long, but in all likelihood will be determined by that of the Duke of Wellington. He starts to-morrow to attend the Congress, which will have grown impatient at his delay. A serious attack of illness has detained him up to the present moment :[1] but the new Ministerial arrangements would in any case have prevented him from starting sooner, for it is only to-day that Mr. Canning has been appointed to succeed Lord Londonderry. You will have been shocked by the latter's tragic death, which has upset everybody. I have lost a very faithful and much trusted friend.

The King is better than he has ever been for years : he is very much in love, behaving very well, and most kindly disposed towards us. Your friend, Lord Yarmouth, is at last become Marquess of Hertford ; his father is dead, leaving him a clear annual rent roll of 160,000*l.* His idea is to devote the greater portion of it to buying votes in Parliament in order to make himself a power with which the Crown must count.[2] He has quarrelled with the King.

Paul goes back to Paris to study law, and to pick up

[1] On Castlereagh's death the Duke of Wellington received the King's commands to attend the Congress of Vienna (Verona) in his place, but his departure was delayed by a sharp attack of illness.—Maxwell, *Wellington*, ii. 166.

[2] Writing to Lady G. Sloane-Stanley, Mr. J. Jekyll says : ' Among the *on dits* of the day they have conjured up a party among the Ministerialists against Canning with the Duke of York at its head. To this also they ascribe the new Lord Hertford's rage for buying seats in Parliament.'—Jekyll, *Correspondence*, p. 136.

some knowledge of political economy. We are quite satisfied with his progress. My little George, whom I adore, will remain at Brighton during our absence. There would have been some risk in making him travel so rapidly and so late in the autumn, and he will be perfectly happy where he is. I am going with my husband chiefly because by so doing I shall save the cost of living in England ; this would mean a double expenditure, which our means cannot afford. You have recently seen our dear papa, dear Alexander, and I hope you will have good tidings to give me of him. I am writing to him to-day. Good-bye, my dear little brother ; you shall have news of me from Vienna. I embrace you and love you with all my heart ; repeat both assurances to your wife, whom I love well. Please ask her to accept the dress which I send herewith ; it is of the latest English fashion.

XXVI

Verona : October 23, 1822.

My dear dear Alexander,—I received at Salzburg the letter which you wrote to me from papa's house. I am writing to him to-day, and to you also to thank you for your scrap. It was a long time since I had had any news of you. Our direct line of correspondence is for the time being so well established that we really ought to take advantage of it. You are no longer in any of those provincial garrisons, and I am not on the other side of the sea. I am very glad to find myself here—my curiosity is altogether satisfied ; it is perhaps a more interesting meeting than any of the previous ones. The feminine element is weak ; there is not a single woman (of distinction ?) here—and those who are gathered here are thorough barbarians,[1] so that I am the sole representative of my species. The duration of the Congress is uncertain ; they talk about four weeks, but in my opinion

---

[1] 'Ou celles qui s'y trouvent sont (ou font ?) les Hurons.' It is possible that this may be a hit at Madame Récamier, who came to Verona escorted by M. de Chateaubriand. He had recently returned from his travels in the backwoods of Canada and the United States, and somewhat wearied his listeners with his stories, in which the North American Indians figured prominently.

that is too modest an estimate.   We shall probably not stay to the very end ; our going will follow close upon that of the Duke of Wellington, who will take his departure before the opening of the Italian Congress.   His health is much broken, and I am really afraid lest the Congress should give the finishing stroke.   My husband takes part in the conferences, and his time here is fully occupied ; so I am very much in doubt if we shall be able to see anything of this beautiful Italy— but I regret this the less because the season is now so far advanced.   Moreover, I shall be in a great hurry to get back to England as quickly as possible, on account of my small boy.   That, in fact, is the only thing which occasions me in any way to regret a journey which for my husband and myself has only had agreeable episodes.   Paul has gone back to his studies at Paris ; Constantine is still happy at Stuttgart, he is a little too devoted to the King of Würtemberg.[1]   This does him some harm, and I regret not having the chance of being able to talk to him on this point.   Our route hither did not lie by way of Stuttgart, and we were in a hurry to arrive here.   I am not writing to my mother-in-law to-day : make her my respects when you see her next.   There is no lack of Russians here, diplomats and others—all of whom look upon me as a foreigner, especially your comrades, my dear Alexander.   Good-bye, write to me.   Your letter will in all probability find me still at Verona.

XXVII

Verona : December 1 (N.S.), 1822.

My dear Alexander,—I received yesterday your letter of November 3–15, and I am answering it at once in case of accidents, for the courier's starting-day is not at all regular. I begin by reminding you that on the day of our leaving London (September 20) I wrote to you and at the same time forwarded a dress for your wife, another packet for Masha, and a third for papa.   Not one of you has ever mentioned

---

[1] The King was out of favour with both the Emperors of Russia and Austria.

the arrival of these packets, which were sent by the official
courier. Since coming here I have written to both you and
papa ; but it looks as if nothing had reached you—I cannot
understand it. Here we have been for two months sitting in
Congress. Europe is quite interesting, and the circle in
which I live puts me in a position altogether conformable to
my curiosity and my taste. Every evening the Congress
assembles *chez moi*. Both Count Nesselrode and Prince
Metternich urged me to allow this as a resource for them,
and I find every advantage in such an arrangement, because
it brings me into daily contact with those who are most
noteworthy, either by the part they play in Europe or by
their personal attractions. I already knew Prince Metternich
fairly well by meeting him on several occasions, but here
I have associated with him on the most friendly terms.
The Duke of Wellington, too, who is the best and firmest of
my English acquaintances, comes to see me constantly.
These two stars, looked upon antipathetically in the Emperor's
ante-chamber, have completely deprived me of the society of
my fellow-countrymen, so that at Verona I see all Europe
except Russia. I must, however, except Nesselrode, who is
a perfect gentleman, and Pozzo and Tatischeff[1]—who as
members of the Congress call on me daily. I am sorry to
find that those who should be on the best of terms with me
are precisely those who keep me as much at a distance as
they would an enemy. Because I have spent ten years in
England they look upon me as an Englishwoman, and
because I see Prince Metternich daily they think me an
Austrian. Conclusions such as these, without a shadow of
reason, do not reflect much credit on the intelligence of your
colleagues. It is, moreover, quite opposed to the Emperor's
principles to depreciate the personages who have drawn upon
me these strictures. I have good reason for supposing that
the Emperor is well aware of the ill-will of which I am the
object, and that he disapproves of this antipathy. I know
that an attempt was made to make him share it, but the plot

---

[1] Russian Ambassador at Vienna.

failed : he treats me with much kindness, and I flatter myself that he quite understands me. For myself I may say that I have made all possible advances to the Russians, but they have replied to them in the way I have just told you. Nevertheless I am always polite to them when we meet, although I am altogether indifferent to their tittle-tattle and in no way affected by it. I tell you all this in answer to your letter, because you seem to think that I am worried by my fellow-countrymen.

December 7.

My letter has lagged, and I take it up to finish it. The Congress is dispersing. By the end of next week everybody will have left, ourselves included, each taking his own route ; the Duke of Wellington has already started. I shall regret Verona. I have spent a pleasant time here ; my husband has been well occupied, acting as plenipotentiary at the Congress.[1] This experience has suited him completely ; one forms a better judgment on the spot than at a distance, and his acquaintance with affairs could never have been so complete or so useful for the State if he had stayed in London. We are returning there for I know not how much longer, it is now ten years that we have been fixed there—a long time. I told Count Nesselrode that I found it so, and further that we should feel grateful if he would consider the possibility of giving us another post so soon as the service would allow of such change. The choice, it is true, however, is a limited one, lying between Paris and Vienna. To the latter Tatischeff, a man of great ability, is going to be sent as Ambassador, while Pozzo at Paris is doing his work admirably well.

I expect you will not be seeing the Emperor again at Petersburg before the end of January. Meanwhile speak of us to Nesselrode when you see him. He will be able to tell you much about me. I like him excessively, and I trust him

---

[1] His actual position was not clearly defined, and he does not seem to have assisted at the meetings of the Congress—all the acts being signed by Nesselrode and Pozzo di Borgo.

completely as a most true and loyal friend. I like his wife also very much, and regret that she has not been here with him. She is a clever woman. Farewell, my good Alexander ; here is a very long letter for you, write me equally long ones. Forward the enclosed to papa. I assure you that I write constantly to him, generally addressing my letters to my mother-in-law. I do hope that she does not forget to pass them on. My kindest remembrances to your wife and to Mademoiselle Annette. I hear from Stuttgart that Nathalie is very ill, and I am fearful about her lungs. Constantine is off to Innsbruck with the King of Würtemberg to meet the Emperor there.[1] Farewell, my good brother, I embrace you heartily ; my husband is at Venice, but will be only away a few days.

[At the opening of the Session of 1823 the King's Speech stated that 'he had declined being a party to any of the proceedings at Verona which could be deemed an interference in the internal concerns of Spain on the part of Foreign Powers, and had used his most anxious endeavours and good offices to allay the irritation unhappily subsisting between the French and Spanish Governments, and to avert if possible the calamity of war between France and Spain.' In the debate on the Address in the House of Commons Mr. Brougham made an impassioned speech, which was received with emphatic applause from both sides of the House. He denounced the conduct of the European Powers in their attempt to stifle the freedom of Spain, and bitterly inveighed against the claims of Russia to pose as the champion of civilisation. 'Resistance to this band of congregated despots was a matter of duty, and the duty of England was in consequence plain. It behoved us, however, to take care that we did not rush blindly into war. An appeal to arms ought to be the last alternative we should try ; but still it ought never to be so foreign to our thoughts as to be conceived impossible, or so foreign from our counsels as to take us unprepared.' Sir Francis Burdett, Mr. Hume, and other Radicals spoke in the same strain. Mr.

---

[1] The interview, whatever its ostensible object, was not wholly satisfactory, for on January 2, 1823, the Würtemberg Cabinet addressed a circular to its diplomatic agents abroad severely attacking the acts of the three Powers who had called together the Congress of Verona, and formally protesting against the political attitude of those allied Powers as detrimental to the independence of the lesser States.

Canning not having as yet been re-elected, the task of reply was left to Mr. Peel, who mildly protested against the sweeping invectives against our allies, and urged that the recent conduct of Russia towards Turkey proved that the accusation of aggression was unjustified. No division was taken, but Mr. Brougham's speech was translated into Spanish and widely circulated wherever, either in the old world or the new, that language was spoken.]

XXVIII

London : 2/14 February 1823.

Dear Alexander,—I am taking advantage of an English messenger to write to our good papa, and I should not like the enclosed to go without adding a few lines for yourself. The loss which poor Constantine has suffered gives me deep sorrow, and I am sure that you too share in it. The devotion with which he regarded his wife [1] was so entire that I cannot imagine how he will be able to become reconciled to his loss. He writes to me saying that he will go back to Russia. My first intention was to accompany him, but my husband would not allow me to do so in my present state of health. Since our return from Verona I have not once left my bedroom. I have a recurrence of fever every alternate day, and it seems doubtful if I shall get over it before the fine weather. This journey in the middle of winter, a winter more severe than anyone can remember, was too much for my frail machine. I get along fairly well as long as I take care of myself, but I cannot bear the cold.

You are, I expect, not overburthened with news just now. Here we are suffering from a superabundance in this respect, but of very inferior quality. The opening day of the parliamentary session was marked by the display of violent opinions by all parties—that is to say, that we were attacked from all sides.[2] The first explosion, however, once over, matters began to calm down, and my belief is that very

[1] Madame Constantine von Benckendorff was a Mademoiselle Alopæus.

[2] The attack upon the Ministerial policy in Spain was led by Brougham, who vehemently upbraided the Government for not having resisted more openly the pretensions of Russia to interfere in Spain.

shortly all sensible people will grow calm. England materially has everything to lose by a war, and the moral advantage of being the standard bearer of all the Jacobins of Europe can flatter only the Radicals.

The King is still very far from well, but he wants us to go and stay with him at Brighton. It is possible that the doctor may allow me to go there next week.

[The papers relating to the negotiations between France and Spain were laid before Parliament on April 14, and on the same night Lord Liverpool in the Upper and Mr. Canning in the Lower House explained the course adopted by the King's Government. Lord Fitzroy Somerset had been sent on a confidential mission to Madrid in the hope of inducing the Spanish Government to come to an understanding with France, but the attitude of the French Government, and the speech of the French King at the opening of the Chambers, rendered a peaceful solution impossible. The formal debate, however, was postponed until April 24, when in the House of Lords a vote of confidence in the Government was passed by 142 to 48 votes. In the House of Commons the debate lasted over three nights, taking the form of an address to the King protesting against the right of the Sovereigns assembled at Verona to make war on Spain on account of her political institutions, and 'to represent to his Majesty that, in the judgment of this House, a tone of more dignified remonstrance would have been better calculated to preserve the peace of the Continent, and thereby secure the nation more effectually from the hazard of being involved in the calamities of war.' The question was debated at great length and with much ability on both sides, but, the Opposition seeing that they would be defeated by a large majority, Mr. Brougham concluded his speech by requesting the mover of the Address, Mr. McDonald, 'to sacrifice his own feelings to the general unanimity and to abstain from pressing the House to a division.' Mr. Canning, however, objected to this course, and the Opposition rose as a body to leave the House ; but the doors having been closed in anticipation of a division, the Speaker put Mr. McDonald's motion, which was negatived without a division. Public opinion endorsed the prudence of the Ministers, and although much sympathy was expressed for the Spanish people, the occupation of Madrid by the French and their subsequent march upon Cadiz were accepted as inevitable.]

XXIX

London : 15/27 April 1823.

My dear Alexander,—A thousand thanks for your letter from Berlin. I must tell you that I am rather anxious about Constantine. I mistrust great moral efforts in a sorrow such as his. Strength of mind in such cases often translates itself into failure of body. Give me every particular about him. Poor dear Constantine, I grow sad when I think of him. I hope you found our dear father in good health, mine is very far from what I could wish. I am still troubled by rheumatism in the head, and I can't regain my strength. The weather is atrocious, damp and cold ; and it is warmth that I absolutely need. Paul is better, but is to be sent to Aix-la-Chapelle, where the waters are a specific for such cases as his.

We change to-morrow into our new house : [1] a delicate attention which I owe to our dear Count Nesselrode. At last we have space in which to bestow ourselves, our children, and even the secretaries.

The English public is beginning to display a little common sense, and, what is more to the point, an appreciation of its own interest—the first consideration with the English. They will not spend a shilling on those interesting Spaniards, the objects of their good wishes. Public sympathy certainly points in that direction, but the utmost a Jacobin Minister could offer was a promise of neutrality. Don't tell Bagot [2] my opinion of Mr. Canning, they are intimate friends. This opinion is not that of everybody, but I give it you as my own special conviction. The King is most good, I wish that on our side they would take more kindly to him.

Count Nesselrode will with this give you a letter for

---

[1] The Russian Embassy was transferred from Harley Street to Ashburnham House, (30) Dover Street, at the top of Hay Hill. The house was pulled down in 1899.

[2] Sir Charles Bagot, G.C.B., P.C., second son of Sir William (First Lord) Bagot, born 1781 ; Under-Secretary for Foreign Affairs under Canning, 1807–14 ; Minister at Paris, 1814 ; Envoy Extraordinary to the United States, 1815–20 ; Ambassador to St. Petersburg 1820-24, at the Hague 1824 ; Governor-General of Canada, 1841-3. Died at Kingston, Canada.

papa; take care to pass it on to him, as it contains one for Constantine, whom I expect to be at Revel rather than at Petersburg.

I congratulate you, my dear Alexander, on being once again united to your wife and children. When shall I see the bunch? Next year, I hope, for I have made up my mind to make a trip to Russia in the summer to see our dear old papa. Good-bye, dear brother. I embrace you heartily, ask your wife to think kindly of me.

XXX

London: 1/13 May 1823.

My dear Alexander,—I have heard indirectly of your arrival in Petersburg, and of Constantine also, and I am told the latter is well. In the dearth of direct news from you this information was very welcome. I wish I could report satisfactorily about myself, but to tell the truth I feel seriously and decidedly ill. Possibly there is nothing really alarming the matter with me—nothing that the fine weather will not set right—but this fine weather is still in the future, and every day I feel more and more out of sorts. Rheumatism of the nerves is the name the doctors give to the ills of which I am the victim, and at times my legs are so much affected that walking is quite impossible.

I am expecting my son from Paris; it will be a great pleasure for me to have him with me again, but he will be starting shortly for Aix-la-Chapelle to take the waters.

We have heard of the sudden dispersal of all the Emperor's staff at the War Office. What does this mean? Perhaps nothing at all: but at a distance one attributes everything to intrigue or *finesse*.[1]

Here everything is quiet; people are watching the course of events in Spain, and are anxious about any hitch which may complicate the business or cause it to drag on for any

---

[1] No political importance was attached to this proceeding, which was thought by some to have been due to the Emperor's fear and hatred of Freemasons, of whom there were many in the higher ranks of the army.

F

time, and above all they are afraid lest anything should draw England into war. Personally, I believe that everything will be peaceably arranged, for, in fact, when things seem to be most topsy-turvy they often have the knack of settling down of themselves.

Good-bye, my dear Alexander. I send no messages to Constantine, for he will certainly have started before this letter arrives. Kiss your wife and children for me, love me always and write to me. My husband sends a thousand good wishes.

XXXI

London : August 6 (N.S.), 1823.

My dear Alexander,—I have not written to you for some days, but I feel the need of writing to you often and of drawing near to you as much as the distance allows. It separates us from one another at a time when my heart and spirit are bowed down by sorrow. Your grief cannot be compared with mine, which will sadden all the future joys of my life. Write to me as often as you can, my good brother. What is Constantine doing? Where is he? You keep me quite in the dark respecting him—it cannot be possible that he is not going to look after his little children.

My health, instead of improving, is getting worse, and my duties here prevent my pursuing steadily any course which might re-establish it. I have already had to decline one invitation from the King to stay at the Cottage at Windsor. He has just sent to ask me again to go and spend a few days there ; he thinks that Windsor will do me good. But Windsor life will assuredly do me harm ; late dinners and long evenings do not suit me ; but how can I, in my situation here, do otherwise than bend to its requirements ?—the more so, too, as by not complying I should be preventing my husband from being brought in closer contact with the King. You don't believe me when I say that I have had enough of this life of an Ambassadress in England. It is too grandly delightful here not to be unbearable anywhere else ; but what is the good of getting people to like you, when etiquette forbids your forming intimacies? Do not imagine, I entreat you, that this complaint arises from pride; and don't speak to others about it, for those who do not understand my feelings will think me vain, and God knows that I am not that —but only sick and sad-hearted.

My husband is very busy—fresh points are continually arising—I can only hope that they won't get tangled; but there is need, not only of the greatest care, but of much skill on the part of all concerned to avoid the rocks which beset the course of affairs. We are anxiously waiting for good news from Cadiz[1]; matters must be brought to a climax— and a satisfactory one—without delay. When matters drag on they are dangerous.

Good-bye, my dear brother. I embrace you tenderly. Love me and say a thousand tender things to your wife and children from me. I am not writing to Constantine, as this letter is for him as much as for you. I address it to you because there is greater likelihood of your being in Peters- burg. Good-bye, dear Alexander.[2]

XXXII

London: 8/20 October 1824.

I wrote to you a few days ago by the post, my dear Alexander, and I am sending this to-day by the courier—one of those rare bits of luck. The Emperor's absence has made my husband delay the sending off of the bag; we can go back, therefore, to the old routine, and, as by this time you are also back at Petersburg, our correspondence can resume its former regularity.

The Osarofskys[3] are still here—but now without aim or

---

[1] The French under the Duc d'Angoulême crossed the Bidassoa on April 7, and entered Madrid on May 23. The siege of Cadiz began on August 10: it was bombarded from the sea on September 23, and finally surrendered on October 3, the Cortes having determined to make no further resistance.

[2] There are no letters preserved which relate to Madame de Lieven's stay in Italy during the winter and spring, 1823-4. Meanwhile she had apparently commenced her correspondence with Earl Grey, although the first letter of the series, edited by Mr. Guy L'Estrange, is dated September 3, 1824.

[3] Count Osarofsky had come to England on a special mission from the Emperor of Russia to thank the British Government for its good offices in bringing about a temporary understanding between Russia and Turkey.

object. It is we who will have to leave them, for we are going to spend some time with the King. The autumn is still genial, the foliage fresh and green as in summer—yet what a difference from that beautiful Italy where I was this time last year! There are certain things of which one should never know the existence if one cannot always enjoy them, and I place in the front rank of the blessings of life the enjoyment of a fine climate.

We are going to send Paul away soon; he is now fairly well again, and it will be a wrench to my heart to separate from him. I still keep my dear little George with me; we simply worship him, he is the most fascinating child in the world.

Schilling [1] is here and expects to remain some weeks longer. He is blessed with a rare amount of intelligence and of vivacity. With his taste and capacity for every sort of scientific study this country interests him exceedingly. He tells me that he sees very little of you at Petersburg. How is this?

I am without news of Constantine for some weeks. Persons who have just returned from Baden tell me that he is growing stout; I am doing the like—we both of us apparently have had to wait forty years for this distinction. Kiss your wife and your three little girls for me. I have been writing so much to-day that both hand and head are tired out. You will hear all the news by the Osarofskys—for, after all, they must set off some day. What is Masha doing? Send her my love when you are writing to her. Good-bye.

XXXIII

London : 16/28 December 1824.

My dear Alexander,—You may imagine how proud I have been of your good fortune, and at the same time anxiously concerned in the danger you incurred. All the newspapers are full of your praises, and you can guess how

---

[1] Paul Schilling—attached to the Russian Foreign Office. He had visited Pekin disguised as a mandarin. He was related to Madame de Lieven, whose mother was Fräulein Schilling of Cannstadt.

proudly my heart beats. I have been waiting from day to day the despatch of a courier to write to you, but as he does not seem to be even now on the point of departure I have lost patience, and so make use of the post to tell you, my dear brother, how deeply my husband and I were affected by your brilliant act of courage.[1] The good fortune to have been able to save the lives of a number of fellow-creatures will be a pleasing remembrance throughout your own.

So far we have received no direct news of that fatal November 7–19. The newspapers up to the present have been our only sources of information, and they make one shudder. I hope they exaggerate the catastrophe, for the thought of eight thousand unfortunate creatures being drowned is too awful. How nobly the Emperor has shown his humanity on this sad occasion! and what a trial for his feelings the sight of this catastrophe must have been ! Everybody here is talking of you, my dear brother, and I am not a little proud of the fame you have won in this sad event. How anxious and how happy your dear wife must have been. I will write to you by the courier ; and this is the reason that to-day's letter is limited to these few words. I embrace heartily my dear sister and your children, and you, my dear Alexander, most tenderly.

Here is a scrap for Paul ; be so good as to let him have it, and tell me all about him when you write. You will have seen Lord Yarmouth on his arrival at Petersburg ; for my own part, I am sorry that it should be seen by strangers at this sad time.

Farewell, my good Alexander ; my health holds out fairly, and in five weeks' time I am expecting my confinement.

---

[1] At St. Petersburg, on November 19, a storm of great violence drove back the waters of the Neva, already much swollen by recent rains, and almost the whole city was submerged ; bridges were torn up, horses, carriages, and people swept away. The Emperor Alexander, who had first watched the scene from the palace windows, endeavoured by his personal example to stimulate the efforts of those engaged in the work of rescue. A few resolute men, among them Count Alexander von Benckendorff, rendered good service and saved numerous lives.—Schindler, *History of Russia*, ii. 246.

[The dissension in the English Cabinet was primarily due to Canning's policy with regard to the recognition of the Spanish colonies. The Duke of Wellington, who had never adopted Canning's views, was the chief of a small minority in the Cabinet who supported the King's attitude that such a step involved a secession from the alliance of the Great Powers, and gave support to revolutionary principles. Lord Eldon (the Chancellor), Lord Westmoreland (Lord Privy Seal), and Lord Sidmouth, who held a seat in the Cabinet without office, were the Duke's supporters. He had objected to the publication of the Spanish papers, and had gone so far as to tender his resignation when the recognition of the independence of Colombia and Mexico was decided upon. The discord in the Cabinet was further accentuated by the indiscretion of Lord Westmoreland, who on a visit to Paris in the autumn had an interview with the King, Charles X., who had just succeeded to the throne, and on that occasion expressed his own views, which were totally different from those of Canning. Lord Westmoreland on his return repeated to the King, and afterwards to Canning, his conversation with Charles X. Canning at once decided to pay a visit to Paris, much to the annoyance of Lord Liverpool and the Duke of Wellington, but Canning remained obdurate to their remonstrances, and it was only by the adoption of his own policy that Canning's withdrawal from the Cabinet was averted.]

XXXIV

London : 19/31 December 1824.

Dear Alexander,—It is only to-day that your letter of October 26 has reached us—so you see how we are posted up ! Thanks, all the same, for this ancient document and for the good news which you are able to give of our boy's behaviour—may it long continue.

I wrote to you a week ago by the ordinary post, as I grew impatient at not being able to convey to you my congratulations and my delight after your splendid act of 7–19th November. I don't know if and when that letter will reach you, so I do not scruple to say over again how much touched and elated we were by your achievement, and that it was with no little pride that we read your name mentioned with honour in every foreign newspaper. What an awful winter this seems to be throughout Europe ! Here the storms are incessant and disastrous.

I am expecting my confinement in five weeks' time, and I am already very much of an invalid and little able to get about. At such times I am always more or less prone to melancholy thoughts—but I am not especially anxious about myself on this occasion. Nevertheless I like to prepare for any eventuality—one feels more comfortable. My husband also is anxious to get over the next few weeks. The birth of another child and the opening of Parliament happening together is a serious conjunction.

The English Cabinet is altogether at loggerheads. Mr Canning poses as a Radical to please the populace—the other Ministers smile approvingly to keep their places. The Duke of Wellington alone is prepared to break a lance for the good cause, but he does not produce any effect. England's moral grandeur is on the down-grade.

We are wholly without news from Petersburg—all eyes are keenly turned in that direction, watching for what the Emperor will do. It must be admitted that he exercises an enormous power in Europe and that he raises the influence of Russia very high. All other interests seem of secondary importance beside that will which holds the balance of peace and war.[1] The Emperor is feared, but at the same time he is the only monarch who is really respected. He is regarded without exception as the profoundest politician in Europe, and before him all other reputations are colourless.

Farewell, dear Alexander, I am tired with having written so much—so I leave you after having embraced you, my dear sister-in-law, and my nieces.

Give me what news you can of Paul.

[Mr. Canning having carried his point with regard to the recognition of the Spanish-American republics had also so far overcome the King's scruples and the Duke of Wellington's opposition in the Cabinet as to obtain Ministerial support in the House of Lords for Lord Lansdowne's Bills for abolishing some of the disabilities of

[1] From a letter from Canning to the Duke of Wellington about this date it appears that in answer to the question whether Russia intended to force the mediation between Russia and Turkey by arms, Count Lieven replied that the Emperor would put himself entirely in the hands of the Allies in the Conference. *Wellington Despatches*, iii. 271.

English Roman Catholics. Both Bills, however, had been rejected in the Session of 1824. A slight concession had been made in favour of the Catholic revenue officers, who were to be freed from all oaths except the oath of allegiance. The Earl Marshal and his deputy, by another Act, were not to be required to take the oath of supremacy or to sign the declaration against transubstantiation. These small instalments of religious liberty had, however, been opposed by the Lord Chancellor Eldon. It was anticipated that in the ensuing Session some further steps would be taken to meet the demands of the Irish Catholics, and Mr. Canning was credited with a willingness to approach this question in a liberal spirit, and also to take steps to allay Irish discontent. On both points differences of opinion, it was asserted, existed in the Cabinet. In the King's Speech at the opening of the Session no reference was made to any measure for the relief of the Roman Catholics, but Parliament was invited to consider without delay the means of pacifying Ireland. In the debate on the Address, on the first night of the Session, Mr. Brougham pointedly referred to the existence of two opposing currents in the Cabinet. 'Measures once designated as Jacobinical had at length been carried by the wisdom and manliness of the right honourable gentleman opposite (Mr. Canning), who, backed as he was by public opinion, and backed by those who filled the benches around, would have triumphed even had he been obliged to have left office on such grounds.' Mr. Canning, in reply, positively denied the notion of a Cabinet divided into two parties and 'that a certain member of it, who was opposed to him on the Catholic question, was also opposed to him on that of South America. The line which was frequently drawn between the supposed Liberals and il-Liberals of the Cabinet Council was by no means a straight but a serpentine line. As it regarded the Catholic question it was nearly straight and direct, but wherever habit did not arbitrarily prevail or personal honour was not pledged the members brought their minds to the discussion totally disengaged.' In one way or another, however, the Catholic question was destined to occupy a greater part of the Session. The Government was determined to impose restraints on the Catholic Association as an unlawful secret society. After a good deal of opposition the Bill passed through both Houses, and in the course of the debate Mr. Canning was challenged by the Opposition to fulfil the expectations he had aroused with regard to a more liberal treatment of Roman Catholics. As soon as the Bill had been disposed of Sir F. Burdett moved that the state of the law affecting the Roman Catholics should be considered in a Committee of the whole House. He was supported by Mr. J. Wilson Croker, Mr. Canning,

Mr. Brougham, and others, and opposed by the Solicitor-General (Sir Charles Wetherall), Mr. Peel, &c. ; but the motion was carried by 247 to 234 votes, and six resolutions were then agreed to, upon which a Bill was introduced (March 23) prescribing a new form of oath to be taken by Roman Catholics in lieu of the existing oath of supremacy. The names on the back of the Bill were those of Sir Francis Burdett, Mr. Plunkett (Attorney-General for Ireland), Mr. Tierney, Mr. C. Grant (Vice-President of the Board of Trade), Sir James Mackintosh, Mr. Canning (Foreign Secretary), Lord Palmerston (Secretary at War), Mr. Wynn, and others from both sides of the House. The opposition to the Bill was led by Mr. Peel (Home Secretary), but it was read a second time by 268 to 241 votes. Before the third reading was taken the Duke of York, in the House of Lords, took occasion, on presenting a petition against the Bill from the Dean and Chapter of Windsor, to announce his determination to oppose to the utmost any fresh concessions to the Roman Catholics ; but his speech, although presumed to explain the King's views, had little effect upon the Commons, who passed the Bill by 248 to 227 votes, and it was carried up to the House of Lords. In that House Lord Harrowby (Lord President of the Council) was the only member of the Cabinet who supported the Bill, but he had with him Lords Camden, Lansdowne, Darnley, and Fitzwilliam, and the Bishop of Norwich, while Lord Liverpool (First Lord of the Treasury) and the Lord Chancellor, three Archbishops, and twenty-four Bishops opposed it, and in the second reading (May 11) it was thrown out by 178 to 130 votes, inclusive of proxies, of whom sixty-five were against and forty-six in favour of the Bill, the Bishops of Norwich and Rochester alone voting with the minority.

The additional expenditure on the army and navy, to which reference was made in the King's Speech, did not exceed half a million for all services, army, navy, and ordnance, and was required not so much for raising the strength of the army in the East Indies as for strengthening the garrison in the West Indies in view of the state of Spanish politics. At the same time, the operations in Lower Burma had been pushed forward with great energy, but the majority of the troops employed were Indian and the expenditure fell upon the East India Company.]

XXXV

London : $\frac{\text{January 20}}{\text{February 1}}$, 1825.

I must thank you, my dear Alexander, for your letter of December 14-26, and must congratulate you and my dear

sister most heartily on the distinction conferred upon you : [1]
and the pleasure to me is doubled by the satisfaction given
to you.

I can well guess that you have your hands full of work,
but I fully believe that such work is satisfactory to you, since
it will be owing to your care that so many poor creatures will
be able to maintain life.

The letters I receive from Paul show me the innumerable
difficulties which lie in his way.   His last news is from Riga,
and my impatience for his arrival at Petersburg is increased
by hearing of these stoppages.   Write to me candidly about
him, my dear Alexander.   Meanwhile we are much satisfied
with the favourable report you send us of our other boys ;
I am deeply grateful to my good sister for all her kindness to
them.   Entreat her to be good to Paul also.   I am still
going about, or rather I drag myself about, and I hasten to
write to you, for I may have to betake myself to bed at any
moment.

Parliament assembles the day after to-morrow, but the
King will not attend, as he has a slight attack of gout.   The
Ministers have been having long conferences ; and they are
at loggerheads upon nearly every question.   The British
army is to be increased by 15,000 men, an enormous addition for this country, but the East Indies are greatly in need
of troops and Ireland is scarcely more than superficially
quiet.   The English and French newspapers are squabbling,
and pin-pricks sometimes make nasty wounds.   Everything
looks unsatisfactory, but we have seen darker clouds roll
away.

The season here is inexplicable ; we have not had a single
frost, the weather is as mild as summer, and the trees are
coming into leaf.

What is Masha doing ?   Good-bye, my dear, dear brother ;
my husband sends his kindest remembrances.   I am sorry to
hear that your health has not been satisfactory.   Are you

---

[1] His appointment as General Aide-de-Camp to the Emperor, and to the
command of the Fifth Cuirassiers.

still at Vaili-Ostroff?[1]   Once more good-bye, my good
Alexander.   Love to my sister and nieces.

XXXVI

London : 2/14 March 1825.

I am very glad, dear Alexander, to be able to write
myself, and to boast of my steady return to strength.   I have
been through a good deal of suffering, but my prudence is so
great that I may fairly expect to have got over all my
difficulties.   I have another boy, much to our mutual regret, but
we are already more than resigned and are prepared to receive
him with all tenderness, for he is remarkably pretty ; your
girls and our boys are determined to tease us respectively.
By this time you will have finished the repairs to your house,
and you will appreciate my congratulations.   I am very glad
to hear the news of the approaching Court festivities.   This
will have a good effect abroad, where all sorts of mischievous
rumours have been set afloat ; a ball is sometimes a more
important event than one supposes.

The news that Paul tells me of himself gives me great
pleasure, and I cannot express myself too gratefully to dear
Count Nesselrode for his goodness in allowing my boy to
commence his career in a way most likely to give him a taste
for his profession.   As for Paul, he is delighted with his
start in life, and speaks in high praise of the Foreign
Office.   I gather also from his letters that his doings at
Court and in society are such as I should have wished.   I
am surprised, however, dear Alexander, that you should
think him too young to be independent.   At twenty years
old he should know how to behave himself; I am convinced
that he can do so, and if he cannot I should still be disposed
to say that he ought to be independent, for at that age
experience is the best master, and, moreover, at that age
not one of your contemporaries (yourself included) had not
been for some time independent.

Our reason for wishing him to make his *debut* in Russia

---

[1] A town in the Government of Pskoff, on the main road to St. Petersburg.

was to awake in him a love for his own country ; we have endeavoured to make him understand his duties towards it. In what concerns his tastes and affections he will need freedom of choice—that is the outcome of his stay in this country —but the fruits of his learning will not be limited to this. If your ideas on this subject do not agree with mine, wait until we meet ; do not let us fall to disputing, especially on paper.

My departure is fixed for June 1, and in any case I shall travel by way of Warsaw, as I have a holy horror of that Prussia. I shall make the journey comfortably ; it is a pity that Constantine cannot go with me.

I am not yet allowed to do much writing, so I must bring this letter to an end. Good-bye, dear Alexander ; if you have any influence in the matter, try and get my poor boys made officers. I confess that it will be a shock to me to find them in the garb of corporals, and it seems to me that their apprenticeship has been long enough. In what branch of the service are they serving, cavalry or infantry ? The cavalry of the Guard is too expensive. They must be in the army, but where and under whom ?

I embrace you, dear brother, my sister, and nieces most tenderly. How glad I shall be to see you all !

XXXVII

London : 7/19 October 1825.

I have just received, dear Alexander, your letter of September 14–26, and I hasten to thank you for it most sincerely. You will have heard that I fell ill immediately after my arrival. I was confined to my bed for over a week, and seemed to have escaped by a hair's breadth from an attack of brain fever. All the worries and fatigue of the last three months seem to have concentrated themselves in my poor body, and so long as I could keep going the machine worked also, but it came to a stop when my carriage set me down here. However, I am better again now, and almost altogether restored.

Your letter delighted me. I can assure you that I think only of Russia, and that everything you can tell me about it interests me supremely. Henceforth, therefore, you will be in no want of materials for your letters. Do not spare me any details, write about everything and everybody, and tell everyone who may care to hear it that I am Russian to the core. I cannot tell you to what a degree those six weeks have brought me into sympathy with our country, nor how devotedly I am attached to our dear Empress. I will not, however, pursue this line, otherwise my letter would be made up of proper names.

What a frightful story is this murder of Arakcheief's.[1] I thought it was only the English who enjoyed the privilege of offering the spectacle of such a catastrophe ; at any rate, it is a novelty with us.

I am delighted to hear that my mother-in-law is interesting herself in Constantine's future, and I shall be most anxious to hear what comes of her care. Alexander has been greatly benefited by his sea-voyage. He is looking very well, and I am in hopes, whatever the Grand Duke Nicholas may say, that we shall make a soldier of him in a very short time.

The younger children are delightful ; the youngest is a very fine fellow, and the exact portrait of my husband—it is almost laughable. They are now fixed at Brighton, and we divide our time between that place and London, for at the present moment there is not a single Cabinet Minister in town. Mr. Canning has taken a fancy to Brighton, so my husband concluded that he could not do better than take up his abode there also. We spend about four days out of ten in London ; and I am just back from Windsor, where I spent a few days and found the King quite rejuvenated.

The Rasumowskys [2] are still here, but are returning shortly to France. Léon Narischkine has already left ; I

---

[1] See Appendix.

[2] Count (afterwards Prince) André Rasumowsky, born 1752, was successively Russian Ambassador at Stockholm, Naples, and Vienna, and in conjunction with Count Stachelberg represented Russia at the Congress of Vienna. He died in 1836.

did not see him before going, for I was too ill to receive
anybody. I believe that he is gone back to Russia with his
wife.

Say a thousand pretty things for me to my dear sister
and your charming children. I often think of you and I
love you with my whole heart.

The weather here is still superb, the days are like July
days, and there is not a yellow leaf to be seen.

My husband sends his best love. Good-bye, dear Alexander; I entreat you to write frequently, to talk about me
continually to my good mother-in-law, and tell her how
much I love her. God keep her in safety, and in two years'
time I hope to see her again. Farewell.

[The death of the Emperor Alexander I., which happened at
Taganrog on December 1, 1825, was an important event for Russia
and for Europe. Inclined to religious mysticism, he was open to
generous impulses, and had a certain amount of sympathy with
freedom of thought and opinion. He fully recognised the advan-
tages of western civilisation, and was friendly to foreign influence in
social matters and to a lesser degree in political matters. For a time
he withstood Metternich's absolutist views, but in the latter years of
his life he had acquiesced in the Austrian Chancellor's policy towards
Italy and Spain. By his death without children the crown devolved
upon his next brother, Constantine, the Governor of Poland, who,
however, had previously renounced his rights. How far he intended
to abide by this resolution was apparently unknown even in the
Imperial family, for on the news of Alexander's death reaching St.
Petersburg, the Grand Duke Nicholas caused the troops to swear
obedience to Constantine 'as legitimate heir to the Empire by right
of primogeniture.' The Council of the Empire, however, held
a packet sealed with the Imperial seal, committed to its authority
by Alexander with instructions that it was to be opened at once in
the event of his death. The President of the Council, Prince Peter
Lapouchkin, broke the seal and found it to contain a letter from the
Grand Duke Constantine to the Emperor dated January 14–26, 1822,
in which he formally renounced his rights to the throne, 'conscious
that he did not possess the genius, talents, and strength necessary,'
adding : ' I shall add by this renunciation a new guarantee and a
new force to the engagement which I spontaneously and solemnly
contracted on the occasion of my divorce from my first wife.'
Something like a revolt ensued. The Liberal party among the nobles

called for a constitution, while a portion of the troops led by Prince Troubetskoi declared in favour of a federative republic. The Grand Duke Constantine persisting in his renunciation, Nicholas thereupon assumed the sovereignty and promptly put down the revolt in a summary and ruthless fashion. As soon as order was restored in his own country, he showed that he intended to inaugurate a more active foreign policy than his predecessor.

The Greek War of Independence, originated in 1820 by Prince Ypsilanti, son of a Hospodar of Wallachia, had been going on without interference from the Western Powers with varying success. From Albania, where it was supported by Ali, Pasha of Janina, the movement spread to the Morea, Athens rose against the Turks, Mavrocordato became the chief leader of the national party, and a Constitution for Greece was promulgated on New Year's Day, 1822. The atrocities committed by the Turks on the taking of Janina and the massacres in Scio and other islands of the Greek Archipelago, aroused public indignation throughout Europe. Beyond proposing to the European Powers, in 1823, that Greece should be placed on the same footing as the Danubian Principalities, Alexander took no steps to arouse the hostility of Turkey. In the following year Canning made no objection to the raising of a Greek Loan in London, and some months later recognised the Greek Government.]

XXXVIII

Brighton : 5/17 December 1825.

A thousand thanks, dear Alexander, for your letter of November 7, and for all your news. Everything you tell me, and everything you may tell me, has become far more interesting than I can say since my short stay in Russia. Everything from there interests me, for my affections are more in Russia than in England.

I expect that about the time this letter reaches you the Emperor will have returned to Petersburg. I see by the newspapers that he has been going about very much, thus showing him to be in good health ; may God preserve it to him.

I am distressed to think that the Grand Duke should see in the step taken by my mother-in-law with regard to

Constantine a proof of my want of confidence in his kindness.   I am explaining myself to him on the subject to-day.

12/24 December.

Alas ! my brother, what a terrible misfortune has befallen
us ! Count Nesselrode's courier has just arrived bringing the
fatal news.   To-day, the anniversary of his birth, we receive
the news of his (the Emperor's) death.   The rumour of this
sad event had been in circulation for the past week, but I
could not bring myself to attach any credence to it.   My
heart revolted at the horrible thought that the Emperor
Alexander could be dead.   It needs all the help of religion to
make us resigned to the decree of Providence.

I must stop writing now ; my health and my spirits are too
much broken to give me courage to quit this retreat.   Write
to me, tell me everything.   How I wish that I were in Russia ;
I feel that I want to see everyone around me in tears.   Ah !
our tears are in truth sincere.

I embrace your wife and children ; write to me very, very
often, and always love your sister.

1826

ACCESSION OF NICHOLAS I.—WELLINGTON'S MISSION TO RUSSIA—
CANNING PRIME MINISTER—THE GREEK QUESTION—DIVERGENCE
FROM AUSTRIA

[The selection of the Duke of Wellington as Special Ambassador
to congratulate the Emperor Nicholas on his accession was as much
due to political reasons as to ceremonial usage.   His name was
better known in Russia than that of any of his contemporaries, and
as the most prominent man in his own country he was best fitted to
represent it on such an occasion.   At the same time it was believed
that Nicholas intended to adopt a different line of policy towards
Greece from that of his predecessor.   Alexander shortly before his
death had called a conference at St. Petersburg, which had urged
the Sultan to accept the mediation of the Powers, but without
practical result.   Nicholas at first thought it was his duty to follow
out his brother's policy, and told the Duke of Wellington that he
abjured all idea of aggrandisement of territory if he made war upon
Turkey.   Almost simultaneously an ultimatum was despatched,
without Wellington's knowledge, to the Sultan demanding the
immediate execution of various treaties and promises.   Count
Lieven was summoned to St. Petersburg to support Count Nesselrode,
whose policy was that if war broke out Russia might fairly claim
territorial compensation.   Wellington, in reply, demanded a written
confirmation of the Emperor's oral repudiation of such a view.
Nesselrode and Lieven insisted upon a similar declaration from
England, and that Russia should not be required to send an Ambassador to the Porte.   Neither side would give way, and Wellington
left St. Petersburg on April 6.[1]   Some sort of understanding had,
however, been arrived at in the shape of identical proposals for the
pacification of Greece, preserving the suzerainty of the Porte, and
granting autonomy to the Greeks, and a protocol pledging Russia
and Great Britain to a joint intercession on behalf of the Greeks with
the Porte, and containing certain pledges of *désintéressement*, was

---

[1] *Wellington Despatches*, new series, iii. 224, &c.

G

notified to the Powers. At the same time, Canning's clearer insight into Russian aims enabled him to see that Wellington had been over-reached, and this discovery did not make the relations between the two English statesmen more cordial. This feeling was reflected in the increased distrust of Canning entertained by the Ultra-Tories, and in the confidence of public support upon which Canning relied to strengthen his more liberal policy.]

XXXIX

London : $\frac{January\ 26}{February\ 7}$, 1826.

I am sending you a line, dear Alexander, by the Duke of Wellington. I am delighted that he is going to see our country, and I am sure that his visit will be greeted with much satisfaction by the Emperor and our people. I rejoice in anticipation both in his success, and in the impressions of our country which he will bring back. He is the finest and noblest character of the day, and he is probably even more distinguished by his feelings than even by his high military reputation. The visit he is paying to our country is a genuine pleasure to him,[1] and England could not send an Ambassador more worthy of the great occasion. Like all the world, he is full of admiration for the splendid conduct of our Emperor. What events ! What a character our Emperor displays ! What respect and admiration has he not gained from the world at large ! What a magnificent race of Princes is ours ! I pity the poor Princes of the rest of Europe ! What a contrast with our own ! If you found me Russian to my heart's core during my stay, guess what must be my feelings at this moment. My health has suffered from what I have just gone through, my every thought has been fixed upon Russia. We are anxiously awaiting the conclusion of the business of the Military Commission. Some examples in high places will be necessary. I agree with what the Duke of Wellington says, ' Where Kings can ride on horseback and can inflict punishment, revolution is impossible,' so on this point I am at ease.

---

[1] Greville, on the other hand, declares that the Duke, on taking leave of his family and friends, ' was deeply affected, as if he had some presentiment that the should never return.'—*Greville Diaries*, i. 79.

I saw with much pleasure, dear Alexander, that your name is mentioned in many honourable and flattering ways Who could have foreseen, when we were discussing the Grand Duke Nicholas last summer, that he would so speedily have fulfilled our predictions? He has indeed proved himself to be a Peter I., and we foresaw the great man of the future. He has already shown what he is capable of becoming. You have not once written me a line since the death of our dear Emperor Alexander, yet I am greedier than ever for letters. You may guess how eagerly we look for news from Petersburg at this moment. What is our beautiful and charming Empress doing? Good-bye, dear Alexander. I embrace you with all my heart ; love me always.

I am anxious about the state of Paul's health. I see very clearly that as soon as the season should allow he must come and live in a more genial climate. With this view I had discussed the matter with Count Nesselrode, and on my coming away Madrid had been suggested. I think Brussels would be preferable, especially as it is within reach of Aix-la-Chapelle, where he has been advised to take the waters. Alexander, too, does not regain strength, and we are at our wits' end to know what to do with him, for he is scarcely fitted for diplomacy. Good-bye. a thousand kind things from my husband. The Duke of Wellington is taking with him his nephew, Lord Fitzroy Somerset [1]—a man of great ability and of the highest character. Make your acquaintance with him— you will be rewarded.

[1] Lord Fitzroy James Henry Somerset, youngest son of fifth Duke of Beaufort, was aide-de-camp to the Duke of Wellington in the Peninsula ; lost an arm at Waterloo ; was Military Secretary to the Commander-in-Chief for many years ; created Lord Raglan, 1852, and on the outbreak of the war with Russia in 1854 was appointed Commander-in-Chief of the Allied Army ; married, 1814, Lady Emily Wellesley, daughter of third Earl of Mornington, and died before Sevastopol 1855.

XL

London : ^{February 18}⁄_{March 2}, 1826.

My dear Alexander,—Count Nesselrode wrote to my
husband conveying to him the Emperor's gracious invitation to
come to Petersburg.[1] Two days later all his preparations were
made. The moment could not have been better chosen, for
there is nothing doing here at present, and he is only too delighted at the thought of going to pay his respects to his new
sovereign. I have had to go through many internal struggles
before giving up the wish to accompany him. I have no
thoughts but for Russia, the Imperial family, and the
Emperor, whose greatness I have long foreseen. The thought
that my husband will find himself in the midst of all these
attractions while I am vegetating on the banks of the
Thames is by no means agreeable. A host of considerations,
too long to detail, oblige me to submit. I implore Constantine (since you are too busy) to write me at length about my
husband and all that he does. I cannot count upon his
telling me himself, for he is a wretched correspondent. I
hope he will be back again in three months' time. He must
follow my example, for even more than I he has to re-assert
his position. I have no time for more to-day than to embrace
you affectionately, my dear, dear brother, as well as your
wife and children, and Constantine and Coco. Paul has full
instructions to have rooms reserved for his father at
Demuth's.[2]

XLI

London : 1/13 August 1826.

You do not write to me, dear Alexander, and I can well
see that it will be for me to make the advances, so here I
begin. My husband has told me much about you, he has come
back infatuated with the Emperor and delighted with you.

---

[1] According to another account, Count Lieven was summoned to St. Petersburg
to support Count Nesselrode in his negotiations with the Duke of Wellington and
to sustain the old Russian policy to which Nicholas was supposed to be un-
sympathetic.—*Correspondence of George Canning*, ii. 46.

[2] The well-known hotel at St. Petersburg.

I rather take credit to myself for having discovered in the Grand Duke Nicholas *le grand homme* ; I had the foresight, others will enjoy the experience. I do not, as you see, forget my own cleverness, in which, however, I admit your right to share, as I remember how often our talk turned upon him. He has already a great reputation abroad, which will increase and be strengthened as time goes on. My husband, who is sober minded in most things, is, I can well see, quite enthusiastic. On his return here he was received with marked attention, and, as you may well imagine, was urged to talk by King, Ministers, and everybody. As I am not, I confess, wholly devoid of curiosity, I have given him but little peace. At the present moment he is very busily engaged with Mr. Canning, and this may go on for several weeks, after which ' Foreign Affairs ' will shift to Paris and we shall enjoy a respite here. Mr. Canning is very good to us, but very gruff to *l'original*[1] ; ask Constantine to explain who that is.

My husband is decidedly thinner after his journeyings and I have not got any fatter, so that we both are in need of a rest to set us up. The boys are well ; the elder Alexander, is impatiently awaiting his appointment to the United States Mission, which had been promised to my husband. I know of no news here which is likely to interest you. The Duke of York, who well remembers you, is very ill, and I fear is not likely to last long. The King, however, is in excellent health. We constantly go for short stays at Windsor, and he continues to show himself full of goodwill towards my husband.

Give me all the news of your dear wife and of my little nieces. I heard with much interest and more pleasure of the new duties imposed upon you by the Emperor's confidence.

[1] Probably Lord Dudley. ' One of the most conspicuous of the eccentric oddities (*les originaux*) who flourished forty years ago was Lord Dudley. I need not speak of his powers of conversation, which were most brilliant when he chose to exert them, of his sarcastic wit and cultivated intellect. These great gifts were obscured by a singular absence of mind, which he carried to such a pitch that some persons maintained that much of this peculiarity was assumed.' —*Gronow*, i. 337.

Your position is a difficult one,[1] but I can well understand that one gives one's self entirely to such a master—and when one's heart is in one's work difficulties disappear.

I have just received Constantine's letter, to which I will reply forthwith by a courier whom my husband is sending off shortly. I did not want to put off writing to you, dear brother. If you have the leisure, think of me sometimes practically—I mean by writing me a few lines, for in thought I am sure you do not altogether neglect me. I love you and embrace you with all my heart.

P.S.—We have this instant received the judgment of the Tribunal, the sentences, and the noble proclamation of the Emperor on this affair.[2] It is an admirable manifesto, and now, thank God, the curtain falls upon this tragedy, and will not again be raised. With Nicholas one knows upon what to count.

---

[1] Count Alexander Benckendorff had just been appointed head of the Imperial Gensd'armes and charged with the command of the headquarters of the Emperor. At the same time he was made chief of a superintending Department of Justice (secret police) attached to the Emperor's private household, and was inseparable from the Emperor's person.

[2] The military tribunal appointed to inquire into the revolt of a portion of the troops on the accession of Nicholas sat with closed doors. The sentences pronounced were remarkable rather for their leniency than for their severity. Of 321 persons accused, almost all belonging to the nobility, five only—including Pestel and Rileief—were executed. The inquiry established the existence of three secret organisations : the Northern Society, established at St. Petersburg, which desired constitutional government ; the Central Society, recruited in the garrisons of Lesser Russia, which was in favour of a republic ; and the United Slavs, whose strength was in the south, who inclined towards Federation. One of the principal leaders, Prince Sergius Troubetzkoi, who aspired to be proclaimed Tsar in the event of the success of the revolt, was also condemned to death, but the sentence was commuted to penal servitude for life, and he was amnestied on the accession of Alexander II., 1855.

1827

LORD LIVERPOOL'S RETIREMENT—CANNING PRIME MINISTER—
PORTUGUESE REVOLUTION—BATTLE OF NAVARINO—THE GREEK
QUESTION

[The state of affairs in Spain had become more than ever complicated. Yielding to the pressure of Great Britain and France, Spain had recognised the Regency of Portugal. King John VI. had died in March 1826, and his eldest son Dom Pedro having elected to remain Emperor of Brazil, transferred the Crown to his child, Doña Maria da Gloria, aged seven years, under the regency of her aunt, Doña Isabella. Dom Miguel, King John's second son, who after his abortive revolt had, since 1824, been living in banishment at Vienna, asserted his claim as the legitimate male heir to the crown, the question being, as in Spain at the same time, on the respective claims of direct female heirs and collateral male heirs. The Portuguese Liberals, headed by Count Villaflor, supported Doña Maria, and the Absolutists, or the 'Serviles' as they were called, comprising chiefly the clergy and the peasantry, were for Dom Miguel. Dom Pedro had previously chosen his brother, Dom Miguel, to be his daughter's guardian and Regent, on condition that he should recognise the Constitution, and should promise to marry the young Queen ; but, pending the fulfilment of these conditions, he assigned the regency to his sister Doña Isabella. At this time the Absolutist party was dominant in Spain, and the leaders made little secret of their sympathy with the Portuguese Miguelites, who, emboldened thereby, as well as by material aid, provoked disturbances in various parts of Portugal. The intervention of England by despatch of the British fleet to the Tagus encouraged the Portuguese Liberals, and the subsequent landing of 6,000 troops at Lisbon at the end of the year restored order, and confirmed Doña Maria's position.

The Duke of Wellington's succession to the Duke of York as Commander-in-Chief was not so simple a matter as Madame de Lieven's words would imply. It was agreed that to no better man could the command of the army be entrusted than Wellington, but it was equally agreed that the post must be non-political. Wellington at this time was the mainstay of the Tory section of the Cabinet, and his acceptance would in honour debar him from political action. Lord Liverpool, however, although in feeble health, still remained Prime Minister, and could be trusted to moderate, if not to counteract, Canning's more Liberal policy at home and abroad. After some correspondence, in the course of which even the idea of the King himself assuming the command of the army was mooted, Wellington's 'dislike' (to use Peel's own word) was overcome, and he yielded to necessity, and Canning had reason to suppose that his most dangerous rival was thus removed from the sphere of politics.]

XLII

Brighton : 6/18 January 1827.

I received your letter of December 2–14 only an hour ago, my dear Alexander, and since we seem to have adopted the plan of devoting a page to discussing the duties of moral conduct, I will make mine as brief as possible. We are both of us in the wrong, but it is never too late to mend. I will write to you in future three letters to one of yours in return. Does this arrangement suit you ? A reply I must have, for without it I shall quickly come to think that my letters bore you.

To-day I am going to chatter to you a little about many things. We are staying here because (the Minister for) Foreign Affairs is here.[1] Our colleagues not having the same liking for Brighton, nor the foresight that Mr. Canning would be coming here, could not find so colourable a pretext for shifting their quarters, and this makes the change all the more agreeable to us. The King is also coming here in the course of the next few days. This will carry us on until the meeting of Parliament, which will take us back to the fogs of London and to more than one political imbroglio. Spain is taking one absurd step after another, and the Portuguese insurgents are thereby emboldened, so that very soon the troops of the Queen-Regent of Portugal will be unable to

[1] Canning, who had caught cold at the Duke of York's funeral, had returned to Brighton, where the Lievens had been staying since the previous August, immediately after the Count's return from St. Petersburg. Canning was also there at that time, and they worked together on the Joint Protocol to be addressed to the Porte.—*Canning's Correspondence,* ii. 131.

hold them in check. Thereupon the English will think it opportune to intervene, and will consequently find themselves at war with Spain, which the French now occupy. The two rival nations will thus be brought face to face ; and although the conduct of the French Cabinet may be absolutely correct, who can foresee to what such a collision might lead ? I grant that I have only strung together a number of gloomy hypotheses, but although I am not often accused of taking a black view of things, this colour just now tinges everything in my eyes.

The death of the Duke of York is an important event for England ; [1] the army loses the best Commander-in-Chief it ever had or ever will have ; the King, a faithful subject, a trustworthy friend and counsellor ; the Government, a man whose personal influence with the great families assured to them the support of this important body in the State ; and, above all, the British Empire loses as heir to the Crown an honourable man, and is left to console itself with the Duke of Clarence, whom no one holds in esteem. The Duke of Wellington succeeds as Commander-in-Chief.

We have not as yet seen anything of Michael Woronzow. He went direct from Dover to Wilton, to stay with the Pembrokes. Old Woronzow is still very fresh and vigorous. I am writing to-day, dear Alexander, by the post, because I did not want my letter to run the risk of delay, which always attends the despatch of a courier. My husband will be sending one off shortly, and he will bring you another letter from me, and I promise that none shall ever go hence empty-handed for you. I am very fond of you, dear Alexander, but I do not like the little pen-pricks which you give me. On my side there is only a little idleness and a great fear of giving offence, but I wish for replies to my letters. In my proposal as to our correspondence I gave, as I thought, a great proof of the modesty of my pretensions. A thousand loves to your dear wife and the children, I should much like to see the one who gives you so much amusement. I embrace Coco also—what is our dear Constantine doing ? Good-bye, dear little brother,

---

[1] Died on January 5, 1827, at Oatlands Park, Weybridge. See Appendix.

my husband sends his kindest remembrances. Continue to love me.

P.S.—Although it may seem somewhat flippant to deal with an Emperor in a postscript, I cannot refrain from adding how everything you tell me about him delights me. Abroad he already enjoys a high reputation. Considering the length of time needed to give a solid seat, one would think that he had stepped over twenty years, so fixed is public opinion concerning him. Europe recognises in him wisdom, firmness, and straightforwardness, and this is become a *credo*.

XLIII

Brighton : $\frac{\text{January 27}}{\text{February 8}}$, 1827.

You see, dear Alexander, that I am doing my very best to fulfil my engagement. This is my second letter within a fortnight. I spoke of so many things in my previous letter that little remains to be said in this. Nevertheless, as I think that I took a somewhat too sombre view of what was happening in the Peninsula, it seems that I owe the Peninsula some apology. It is behaving much better, and here it is generally believed that all danger of war has been for the time set aside. Will it be altogether avoided in the future ? That is a question to which it would be bold to make answer : meanwhile it is convenient to be satisfied with the present. Mr. Canning is very ill, and nothing is more likely than that he may die. Many people are finding satisfaction in this thought ; I am not one of them. He is a man of extraordinary talent, and he is honest. He is not a Jacobin, and he is the only member of the English Cabinet who is well-disposed, entirely well-disposed, towards Russia. He is absolutely opposed to the Austrian policy, and as anti-Turk as it is possible to be. On the other hand, one cannot but deplore the imprudence of his speeches. A man whom vanity and success carry away to the extent of giving to his words a meaning at variance with his intentions is not a statesman. I regret it, but we have cause to love Canning, and for that reason the other considerations do not trouble me. The King is wonderfully well, and enjoys his fine bizarre pavilion, his good table his very noisy music, and his fat Marchioness, of whom, however, he is getting a little tired. We dined with him the other day in company with his Ministers, whom he had not seen for two months, not even the Duke of Wellington. Parliament has re-assembled ; I don't know what will be done should important questions arise, for Canning, should he recover, will be an invalid for a long time. I expect that without him neither foreign politics nor the Catholic question will be touched upon. Diplomatic questions are in a state of complete stagnation ; my husband will stay on here until Canning is better, for it is here that he fell ill and remains. The King too will remain at Brighton for some weeks longer. Is it true that the coronation of the Emperor as King of Poland is to take place in May ?

I embrace you, dear Alexander, and your wife and children. My husband is much attached to you ; we often talk of you. Tell me that at least sometimes you think of us.

P.S.—I wish you to tell Count Nesselrode that I love him as much when I am silent as when I am writing to him, but that I feel that he has enough to do without my letters. Tell him that we are respected, that we are feared, and that it is recognised that the world has to deal with a Cabinet which knows how to maintain its dignity and its wishes. This is how Russia should be regarded. Metternich and Canning hate one another as cordially now as in the past ; the former cannot stomach our intimacy with England, and there are many others whom it annoys, but for my own part I can only see in this fuller proofs of its usefulness. As between the two Ministers, who hate one another, Canning is not the greater rogue—that is absolute truth. To sum up, may I be whipped for it, but I assert that we ought to love Canning.

XLIV

Brighton : February 17 / March 1, 1827.

This is my third letter, my dear Alexander—this means that it is now your turn, and that I am awaiting your budget with impatience. We shall have news of importance to send you very shortly. A ministerial crisis is looming here ; Lord

Liverpool's apoplexy necessitates the appointment of a new Premier.[1] Who will it be? That is the great question just now of both the home and the foreign policy of England. Both parties are busily agitating, but it seems that in all probability the Opposition will not come into power. The struggle will be between Gothic ideas and modern tendencies, and Canning sides with the latter. He is in favour of the Emancipation of the Catholics, which the others reject, and on this question will depend the choice of the next administration. Canning went back to London yesterday, weak but convalescent. We are staying on for a couple of days on account of the King, but we shall be in town before the decisive moment, which, by general consent, cannot be postponed beyond next week. The news from Portugal is good in so far that the Queen Regent's troops have up to the present defeated and repelled the insurgents,[2] but bad in that these insurgents, who it was believed had been got rid of by being driven into Spain— where, according to promise, they were to be disarmed—re-appear at any moment, and re-appear partly armed and equipped. It is the story of Antæus regaining fresh strength each time that he came in touch with his Mother Earth. This, however, is a game which cannot go on indefinitely— there is an end to patience, as to everything else. In France, too, parties are marshalling their forces, and that which supports the throne is unfortunately not the most respected. Religious excitement is doing much harm there. The poor Empress of Brazil has just died.[3] The Emperor was as bad a husband as he was a bad constitution maker, so she may

[1] Robert B. Jenkinson, second Earl of Liverpool, was successively Foreign Secretary, 1801 ; Home Secretary, 1803-6 ; Prime Minister, 1812-27. He never recovered from his stroke of apoplexy, but his death did not occur until December 1828.

[2] The Queen Regent, widow of John VI., wished to preserve the crown of Portugal for her son Dom Miguel. The adherents of the infant Queen, Doña Maria della Gloria, rose to assert the rights of the latter, but were defeated and driven across the Spanish frontier.

[3] The Archduchess Leopoldina of Austria was married in 1817 to Dom Pedro de Acantara, Pedro IV. of Portugal and Emperor of Brazil. By him she had a son who renounced the throne of Portugal and became Dom Pedro II. of Brazil, and three daughters : Doña Maria, Queen of Portugal ; Doña Januaria, married to Count d'Aquila ; and Doña Francisca, married to the Prince de Joinville.

well have died of her troubles. Do I write enough to you, my dear Alexander, and do you not think that it is about time for you to reply ? Give me news of Constantine. I embrace you, your wife, and your children with all my heart. Good-bye, dear little brother.

[Parliament met on February 8, and in Canning's absence Mr. Peel conducted the Government business in the House of Commons, but, greatly to Lord Liverpool's annoyance, Canning communicated his real views and wishes to Huskisson, President of the Board of Trade, both on the Corn Bill and Catholic Emancipation. Lord Liverpool's illness (he had been struck down on March 1) was urged as an excuse for postponing the discussion of both measures until after Easter, but without success. On the Corn Bill a compromise on the principle of the sliding scale, proposed by Canning and Huskisson, was grudgingly accepted by the Tory party ; but the Catholic question, raised by Sir Francis Burdett and supported by Canning, was after two nights' debate lost by 276 to 274 votes. These two important votes were destined to bear upon the Ministerial crisis, which was obviously inevitable. On March 19 the King, having been definitely informed that Lord Liverpool could never again resume office, sent for the Duke of Wellington, and requested him to consult with his colleagues as to the best mode of reconstituting the Cabinet. It was not until ten days later that Canning was sent for, and the full extent of the disruption of the Cabinet and of political parties was made evident. The King, while he supported Canning's foreign policy, which Wellington hated, objected to Canning's ' Catholic ' views, to which Wellington was indifferent, but to which Peel and the other ultra-Tories were intensely hostile. After the recent evidence of the revulsion of opinion in the House of Commons, it was clear that the anti-Catholic party was for the moment uppermost, and that even the alarming condition of Ireland failed to make the Tories pause in their zeal for Protestant ascendency. Canning from the first gauged the situation, and finally declared to the King that while not claiming any special post for himself he must have the substantive power of First Minister, and be known to have it, or he must retire from office. Under these circumstances all attempts to reconstitute the Cabinet under a respectable figurehead broke down, and at length (April 10) Canning received the King's command to form a new administration. Peel, the Home Secretary, was the only important member in the House of Commons who quitted the Cabinet, but in the House of Lords the Lord Chancellor Eldon pleaded his advanced age as a reason for retirement, and the

Duke of Wellington, finding that Canning intended to be Prime Minister in fact as well as in name, tendered the resignation of his seat in the Cabinet and of the command of the army. Their example was followed by Lords Westmoreland, Bathurst, Melville, and Bexley, and Canning found himself forced to look elsewhere for assistance. For this he turned to the Whigs, who had previously assured him of their support in the event of the defection of the Tories. Copley became Lord Chancellor as Lord Lyndhurst, and as zealous a Tory as he had previously been a Liberal. Lord Dudley became Foreign Secretary; the post of the Lord High Admiral was revived for the Duke of Clarence, but that of Commander-in-Chief remained vacant, Lord Anglesey taking Wellington's place as Master General of the Ordnance. Palmerston, who had been led to expect the Chancellorship of the Exchequer, was objected to by the King and remained Secretary at War, but obtained a seat in the Cabinet.]

XLV

London : 4/16 March 1827.

My dear Alexander,—My humility oversteps the limits I had imposed upon it—for here is my fourth letter. We have been settled in London for the last fortnight. Great things are going on and greater still are expected. The Catholics are swamped (the expression is somewhat 'Gothic'); Mr. Canning has had to give way on this question. I only hope that his Corn Law will not incur a similar fate, for we are concerned in seeing it pass. Public interest is now aroused as to who will succeed Lord Liverpool as Prime Minister. My idea is that in any case Mr. Canning will continue in office, but nothing can be certain until the last moment. Meanwhile foreign affairs as well as ministerial arrangements are delayed on account of his illness, for he is again confined to his bed. The Marquess of Hertford (your old acquaintance) is selected as Special Ambassador to convey to the Emperor the Garter,[1] of which order he is himself a

---

[1] 'Nicholas I., Emperor and Autocrator of all the Russias, invested at the Palace of Alexandroffsky at Tsarkoe Selo, 9 July 1827, by the Marquess of Hertford, K.G.' (*History of the Order of the Garter*). When the question of conferring the Garter upon Nicholas had been raised in the previous year, Canning wrote to Lord Liverpool saying that personally he was against the idea, but that it would be necessary to follow the lead of France (' Canning to Lord Liverpool,' April 25, 1826).

knight, and, moreover, the richest landowner in England and the most flattered by the Government.   He is anxious to get through his short embassy at Warsaw, on the occasion of the Emperor's coronation there.   He will give a grand *fête* and then hurry home.   My husband has formally put forward this request on behalf of the British Government, and I hope and wish that the Emperor will give his consent.   The Duke of Wellington frequently inquires after you ; his command of the army occupies him as much as it pleases him.

A rumour comes from Vienna to the effect that an interview will take place between our Emperor and the Emperor of Austria.[1]   Whether there is any foundation for this, or whether it be only Austrian boasting, I know not.   In either case the story will have a sort of success by disquieting the minds of many.

Good-bye, my dear brother ; all kind of affectionate greetings from us to your wife.   What news of Constantine ?

XLVI

London : 7/19 April 1827.

A thousand thanks, my dear Alexander, for your letters —they give me immense pleasure.   I am replying to them at once—for there is a ministerial crisis in England which leaves much leisure even to an outsider.   The excitement is contagious, and I begin to understand the English from both the pleasing and unpleasing side.   Party spirit just now reigns supreme, and what contemptible passions it reveals ! However, the facts, without embroidery of comment, are as follows : a Prime Minister is required. Mr. Canning, by far the most capable man, is the one on whom for the last two months the country at large has fixed its choice.   The King, on consulting the other members of the Cabinet, finds that none is anxious to assume the post, knowing well that Canning will serve under none of them—yet without him the ministerial crew cannot avoid shipwreck.   Thereupon the King nominates him Prime Minister.   Canning invites his former colleagues to retain their posts, and in reply they

---

[1] The interview did not take place on this occasion.

send in their resignations. Parliament approves thoroughly of Canning's nomination; but the high Tory aristocracy revolts—all the holders of important Court or departmental posts withdraw. The Duke of Wellington sets the example by resigning the command-in-chief of the army, the King nominates the heir to the throne Lord High Admiral and gives him a seat in the Government. Canning assigns a few seats in the Cabinet to members of the outgoing party, breaking up the distinct line of the former administration but retaining much of its colour. Many places are still unallotted, and the Cabinet itself cannot be finally settled for some days. But no matter from what quarter Mr. Canning obtains recruits, he has already given his Ministry a moderate tone, which has met with popular approval, not extended to those who have resigned. A spirit of rivalry and faction too clearly influenced their action, which they will have considerable difficulty in publicly justifying. The King is extremely annoyed, and his firm conduct on this occasion has won for him the good opinion of the country. How greatly I regret the extreme attitude adopted by the Field Marshal, and how undignified it is for him to add to the difficulties of the King and his Government!

Parliament re-assembles on May 1, and we shall then see on the Opposition benches the men who have for the last thirty years been governing the country. It will be a curious sight.

Tell my mother-in-law that I really have no time to write to her to-day, and that there is reason to hope that under Mr. Canning's administration we may be able to sell our corn, albeit on this question he will have many formidable opponents to overcome. Diplomacy has of necessity been in abeyance for a time. It was a question for Mr. Canning ' to be or not to be ' (do you know enough English and enough Shakespeare to understand that ?), and until the Cabinet was completed it was useless to attempt anything—but I rely with confidence upon Canning.

Good-bye, my dear brother, I embrace you with all my heart. I should be glad if you would send my letters, after having read them, to Constantine. They might interest him and more often than otherwise I find that I have no time to give him a second edition.

XLVII

London : 15/27 April 1827.

I have this instant received, my dear Alexander, your letter of March 23 (O.S.), for which I thank you with all my heart. I wrote to you a week ago in the midst of the first flush of a sort of ministerial revolution. Everything, however, has since gone on quietly and circumspectly. The negotiations with the Whigs are not yet concluded, which proves at least that they are not going to have their own way in everything. My opinion is that the result will be a polite understanding, which will assure to the Government the support of the moderates of the party, but not their entry into the Ministry. As to the extreme Whigs like Lord Grey, &c., &c., they have warmly taken up the cudgels on behalf of the outgoing Ministers. Strange and monstrous as such an alliance is, one is almost tempted to say that the Duke of Wellington has lent himself to it, but this is almost too strong for belief. The King is perfectly firm, calm, and resolved. The Duke of Devonshire will probably be made Lord Chamberlain, and as he is the chief of the moderate Whigs this will be a sort of guarantee for the votes of the party. Parliament re-assembles on Tuesday, and it will be the most interesting of all the Parliaments I have seen here.

I embrace you, my dear Alexander, and all that belongs to you.

XLVIII

London : 8/20 May 1827.

I am sending herewith, my dear Alexander, a letter for Constantine, and although I have put into it my budget of news I must take advantage of this lucky chance to add a word for you. I beg of you to speak on every occasion to

H

Count Nesselrode of my devotion and at the same time of
my discretion. What things have happened since I wrote to
him ! However, as one of my letters of last winter may
have indicated that a change in the Ministry would be by no
means displeasing to me, that I attached more importance
to Canning's good will towards us than to that of the former
Ministers, and, lastly, if we are not as completely satisfied
with him as we might desire, yet Count Nesselrode may
believe me that with Canning there is something to be done,
with the old ones there would have been nothing ; worse
than all, they would have been hostile to us on the question
which now promises an understanding between us and
England. Nevertheless Canning's position is still a very
difficult one. The party opposed to him is powerful in numbers, names, and wealth, but happily weak in talent—and, in
a word, they are fools. On his side are to be found all the
cleverest men, who for the time being are tractable, moderate,
and loyal. There never was a more thorough comedy than that
which has just been enacted. It is ridiculous to say that there
are political parties in England—it isn't true. There are only
men who wish to keep their places, and others who wish to
occupy them. These two parties only have a real existence.
They adapt their principles to circumstances, and there is no
more reason to be frightened at the term ' radical ' than to be
proud of the term ' ultra.' The place, not the thing, makes
the man ; just now we are slightly Whiggish, in a little while
we shall be completely so. The Duke of Devonshire has had
an important share in these negotiations, and it is he who
has brought the two parties together.[1] Lord Morpeth,[2] who
caused so much amusement at Moscow by his dancing, is
destined to play an important part. He has no seat in
Parliament.

Lord Hertford sets out for Petersburg in June. His
ambition is to outshine the Duke of Devonshire, but I do not
see how he will find the opportunity. Michael Woronzow is

---

[1] This is confirmed by Greville (*Memoirs*, i. 96.)

[2] Eldest son of sixth Earl of Carlisle, distinguished as a statesman and a
writer. Chief Secretary for Ireland, 1835-41 ; Viceroy, 1855-8 and 1859-64.

still here, and so is Stanislas Potocki.[1]   The latter eats and dances ; the former runs about paying calls, discussing English politics, and enjoys himself.

Good-bye, my dear Alexander.   I embrace all your family most cordially, and Nesselrode also, if he likes.

[On the re-assembling of Parliament the Ministry was at once assailed by the Tories in both Houses.   In the Commons, Canning, supported by Brougham, had no difficulty in holding his own ; but in the Lords Earl Grey separated himself from his Whig friends and joined in the attack upon Canning and the Coalition Ministry. Charles William, third Marquess of Londonderry, K.G., succeeded his half-brother, who had been Secretary for Foreign Affairs in 1822. He had previously served with great distinction in the Peninsular War and had been Ambassador at Vienna.   The actual struggle, however, took place over the Corn Bill, which had already passed the Com- mons.   The Bill proposed a duty of 20s. when the price of corn stood at 60s. a quarter.   The great landowners, taking part with the farmers, urged that at this price corn could not be grown profitably. The Duke of Wellington, although a member of the Cabinet when the Bill passed the Commons, had never thoroughly approved of its provisions.   He now proposed an amendment to the effect that foreign corn should not be taken out of bond until the average price of home-grown corn had reached 66s.   This amendment was carried by 78 to 74 votes, although in reality the Corn Bill was a money Bill, which the Upper House had no right to amend.   An attempt to reverse the decision on report was even more disastrous, the amend- ment being re-affirmed by 133 to 122 votes.   Publicly general dis approval was expressed at the course adopted by the Duke and his friends.   With reference to the King's good will, each party claimed it, but the ultra-Protestantism which the Lord Chancellor for Ireland (Lord Manners) was permitted to display by his disregard of Canning's appointments seemed to suggest that the latter was not very cordially supported.   Lord Grey's attitude was equally ambiguous.   He had separated himself from his colleagues upon a question of absolutely no importance, and therefore presumably because he thought the necessity urgent of protesting against the coalition of the Whigs and Canningites.   His opposition was attributed to pique, because

[1] Not to be confounded with Count Stanislas Korska Potocki, Russian Minister of Public Worship, 1815, and President of the Senate 1818 ; surnamed Princeps Eloquentiæ.   The Count Potocki here referred to was the husband of Countess Anna Tyskiewicz, author of a volume of memoirs published in 1901.

the negotiations had been with Lord Lansdowne instead of with
himself; but this course had been adopted in consequence of Lord
Grey's partial withdrawal from active political life, and of his persistent reference to Lord Lansdowne as the leader of the party.
Madame de Lieven evidently took Lord Grey to task for his attack
upon Lord Lyndhurst and Canning, but he only replied in stilted
language, ' My conduct must be regulated by what I think my own
honour and the public interest require.']

XLIX

Richmond : $\frac{\text{May 24}}{\text{June 5}}$, 1827.

Lord Marcus Hill,[1] attached to Lord Hertford's embassy,
will hand you this letter, my dear Alexander.   He comes
from far, having been to Brazil with Sir Charles Stuart.   He
now wishes to visit its Antipodes, and therefore accompanies
the present embassy.   I am hoping that you will receive this
within ten days of now.   I am here for twenty-four hours,
to get refreshed after that horrid London, which overpowers
me.   My health is no longer suited to this dissipated life, and
my tastes still less so.   I do all that is really indispensable
and neglect nothing which is of any real importance, but I
throw over everything which is unnecessary.

The Duke of Wellington continues his policy of hostility
towards us, even in the matter of the corn duties.   A Bill,
introduced during his Ministry, has been thrown out by himself, because he is no longer in the Cabinet.   However, this
explosion of temper will hurt only himself, for I hope his
amendment will be defeated.   In any case he has seriously
compromised his reputation.   His conduct is bad, perfidious,
and injurious to the country.   Its openly avowed object is to
embarrass and ultimately to upset his rival.   Canning will
hold his own, however, in spite of all this and will show
his strength.   The King, too, is resolved to support him,
and on such occasions a King counts for a good deal in
England.

Parliament will, I hope, be prorogued in about a fortnight's
time, unless the Opposition resorts to unforeseen tactics.

[1] Lord Arthur Marcus Hill, P.C., third son of second Marquess of Downshire, succeeded his brother in 1860 as second Baron Sandys.

Once the doors of the House closed, the Ministry will be able to consolidate itself leisurely, for up till now it has been in a state of intermittent convulsion, during which the strongest heads alone could keep steady.

We are very anxious for news from Georgia. Woronzow is much pained and surprised at the discontent aroused by Yermoloff,[1] and he wishes as much as we do that Paskievitch may well and quickly recover the time unfortunately wasted. The fat Stanislas Potocki is still here, dancing, eating, sweating. We will see if we can arrange for him to be presented to the King at Windsor. There has been no Court here, and there will be none for regular presentations. Good-bye, my dear Alexander. I embrace you and all your surroundings most cordially.

[The Greek revolt against Turkish rule had now been going on for nearly seven years. A National Assembly which met in the woods near Epidaurus had proclaimed the independence of their country ; but dissension soon broke out, and two parties with distinct and often conflicting views claimed to represent national feeling. The 'primates' of the Morea and the people of the adjacent islands, under the leadership of Mavrocordato, favoured and were favoured by the English ; the Klephts and Morean fighting men under Kolokotroni were friendly to Russia. At length an arrangement was arrived at. Capo d'Istria, a pro-Russian, was elected head of the Government for seven years, Lord Cochrane was appointed Admiral-in-Chief and General Church General-in-Chief. An attempt to succour the besieged garrison of the Acropolis (May 6) resulted in a severe defeat, and left the Greeks practically helpless. The Turks felt themselves strong enough to set the sympathies of Russia and Western Europe at defiance. The reduction of the Protocol into a treaty therefore became of pressing importance. Lord Liverpool's retirement and the subsequent intrigues, added to Canning's illness, had greatly impeded the free discussion of a policy of intervention, against which the British Cabinet had protested in the cases of Italy and Spain. A draft treaty binding Russia, France, and

---

[1] General Yermoloff had been in command of the frontier force during the previous year, and had met with serious reverses. He was now replaced by Paskievitch. General Yermoloff had distinguished himself in the campaign of 1812, when he commanded the advance guard of Kutusoff's *corps d'armée* during the French retreat from Moscow.

Great Britain had been settled at Paris at the end of January, but it was not until Parliament had been prorogued that the matter was seriously taken in hand. The Greek Treaty, not less than the Portuguese expedition, offended the Duke of Wellington and the Ultra-Tories as leading to possible embroilment with one or other of the Great Powers, for the treaty not only specifically recognised for the Greeks that 'they shall be governed by authorities whom they shall themselves choose and nominate,' but intimated that the signatories were prepared to support this claim. The treaty, however, which thus inferentially founded the kingdom of Greece, was at length signed at London on July 6, and was formally laid before the Porte on August 16, just a week after its chief author's death. The treaty was at first strongly opposed by Metternich, but ultimately he assented to it on behalf of Austria, and persuaded Charles X. to adhere to its provisions on the understanding that the King of Greece should be selected by the Greeks from one of the European ruling families. It is only due, however, to M. de Metternich to state that he foresaw the difficulties which would arise in the event of the Great Powers supporting Greece in her revolt. Early in the year (1827), when on a visit to Paris, he warned the French Ministry that the Porte could only be induced by force to consent to the independence of Greece. 'Il faut bien savoir ce qu'on veut. Si c'est la destruction de l'empire ottoman, allons tout de suite au but. Partageons la Turquie et remanions l'Europe ; autrement laissez la Grèce à elle-même, ou ne vous en parlez pas.' Neither France nor England, however, would listen to such language, and popular enthusiasm for Greek independence supported the Governments of both countries.]

L

London : 1/13 July 1827.

I am sending you a line, my dear Alexander, as covering to the enclosed letter for Constantine. The last courier brought me nothing from you ; do take advantage of such occasions to send me a few words. You will hear through Count Nesselrode that our affairs are progressing satisfactorily. Once Mr. Canning embarks, the ship must speed on her course ; the difficulty has been to start, to induce him to go on board. A man may be bold enough so long as he is in the second rank, and yet lose his courage in the first ; and such has been Mr. Canning's case. At last, however, he is moving, and with us, and to hold back is impossible. On the contrary, his interest and his honour alike force him to go forwards ; and it might seem that he has taken pains to impose this obligation on himself in every possible way : since he has been guilty of the most inconceivable impropriety in announcing the Treaty.[1]   One must swallow many disagreeable things, but so long as one attains one's object (and I believe it to be attained) it is useless to worry about trifles. We are awaiting the arrival of our fleet, for now that the word has been said everyone is impatient to act.   The Austrian intrigues have carried M. de Metternich further than he intended, and he is now in a nice predicament ; so much the better.

Michael Woronzow is suffering from his eyes : his wife dances, and they are leaving in six weeks' time.   I am always ailing, and very ailing, from palpitation of the heart, which gives me little respite ; and this has been the case for the last six months.   My husband takes no notice of it.

Good-bye, my dear Alexander, I love and embrace you tenderly, and your wife and children also.   Tell me how my mother-in-law is going on.   I am disturbed by her accident, notwithstanding the reassuring news the Emperor sends concerning her.   What news of Masha ?   Send her my best love.

[Madame de Lieven's claim for Canning as the sincere friend and ally of Russia can only have been with regard to his anti-Metternich policy.   He had, at least since the downfall of Napoleon, expressed his distrust of the 'Apostolical' party of which the Austrian Chancellor was the head, and on more than one occasion had measured swords with Metternich and had been by no means worsted.   ' The insane and revolutionary policy ' of Great Britain which Metternich and the Duke of Wellington denounced had found support among the Liberals of the Continent as well as among those of our own country, and the extent of his loss to this party can be measured by

---

[1] The Treaty (with an additional secret article conveying a threat in case the Porte should decline mediation in the affairs of Greece) was signed at London July 6, 1827.   It pledged Russia and Great Britain to joint action.   The *Times* some time previously had published, greatly to Canning's annoyance, the substance of the Protocol upon which the Treaty was based.--*Wellington Despatches*, iv. 323.

the widespread grief his death evoked.   He was anxious to frame a
policy in which Russia and France could unite with Great Britain,
holding that the two latter Powers could liberalise the absolutist
tendency of the other partner.   For Russian diplomacy he had
always shown distrust, and on more than one occasion had
upbraided its mouthpieces with insincerity.   His objection, too,
to the Garter being sent to Nicholas on his accession to the throne
is evidence that he was by no means a devoted admirer of that
ruler.[1]]

LI

Richmond : $\frac{\text{July 29}}{\text{August 10}}$, 1827.

My husband has started for Portsmouth to see our fleet,[2]
and I, very ill, am left behind.   I was dying to see Russia
again, but the wish could only be gratified at the risk of killing
myself.   I am writing to you, dear Alexander, in the hope of
consoling myself for this disappointment.

A thousand thanks for your letter of June 22 and the
enclosure from Constantine.   Your letters and his are always
a joy to me.

We have just lost Canning [3]—I say ' we,' because his loss
really touches us personally among the many great interests
affected by this catastrophe.   I say ' we ' also as Russians, for
he was the sincere friend and ally of Russia.   After him—
well! we shall see.   The grief for his death is general, even
his enemies praise him now that he is no longer here.
England does not contain another man of equal genius.
The mercantile class is in dismay, the people in tears;
everybody who is not Metternichish is in despair.   No one
knows what may happen, and the vaguest conjectures are
afloat.   It is more than probable, however, that we shall drift
back to the old *régime*, although that can bring about only
confusion.   Ireland would probably rise without much delay ;

---

[1] See letter to Lord Liverpool, April 25, 1826, published in *Canning's
Despatches*, ii. 33.

[2] On its way from the Baltic to the Mediterranean and Greece, the Russian
fleet, under the command of Admiral Siniavin, called at Portsmouth.

[3] Died August 8 from the effects of a chill, consequent on his attendance at
the Duke of York's funeral.

in a word, we shall witness many strange things, and that speedily.

Michael Woronzow is bathing at Brighton, but returns to us, I believe, in company with Admiral Siniavin. I am so ill (in bed) that I cannot write more to-day, but you shall have a long letter by the courier. My best regards to Count Nesselrode and tell him 'Nun wird die Wirthschaft wieder anfangen.' [1] I embrace you cordially.

What a misfortune for Capo d'Istria to arrive at such a moment, and what a difference !

[Russia and Persia could scarcely at any time have been described as friendly neighbours, but in 1800 began a struggle which with slight intervals lasted for over a quarter of a century. In that year the Czar of Georgia, the last of his line, renounced his crown in favour of the Russian Emperor. This act was repudiated by a large section of the Georgians, who regarded the Shah as their Suzerain, and war ensued, ending in 1802 by the Russian occupation of the chief places in the country. After a restless interval, war, fomented by France, between Russia and Persia broke out in 1811, lasting for two years, when in 1813 the Treaty of Gulistan, negotiated by Sir Gore Ouseley, formally ceded Georgia to Russia and gave to her all the Persian territory north of Armenia, together with the right of navigation on the Caspian Sea. In 1825 disputes arose as to the frontier line, and Prince Menschikoff was sent to Teheran as Special Envoy to settle matters amicably ; but his efforts failed, and in 1826 war was declared, and at first the Persians were wholly successful, only one advanced post (Shishah) being held by the Russians. But the arrival of an army under General Paskievitch, in which General Constantine Benckendorff (Madame de Lieven's brother) held an important command, changed the aspect of affairs. The Persians, who had all along been encouraged by Turkey, were defeated on the banks of the Zezam and again more decisively at Ganja. The Russians then offered terms, which the Persians refused, and a prolonged campaign with varying gains and losses ensued. Ultimately Russia asserted her power, and Persia was forced to cede the remaining Armenian provinces and to pay an indemnity of eighteen million roubles. This was known as the Treaty of Túrkmanchái, which laid down the boundary existing up to 1884.

Metternich, who since the Congress of Verona had not ceased to protest against ' the insane and revolutionary policy' of Canning, was

[1] ' Now the business is about to begin again.'

generally credited with having encouraged the Porte to disregard the demands of the Greeks for autonomy, and finally to resist the coercive action of Russia and the Western Powers.

On the death of Canning it seemed as if the intrigues which had surrounded his accession to the Premiership would be renewed, but without delay the King sent for Lord Goderich, Secretary for the Colonies and at War, and confided to him the task of making up the Cabinet. The principal changes were the introduction of Mr. Herries as Chancellor of the Exchequer at the King's desire, notwithstanding Huskisson's strong opposition ; and the Duke of Wellington's resumption of the Command-in-Chief.]

LII

Richmond : 8/20 October 1827.

The last courier from Petersburg has brought your letter of the beginning of August, my dear Alexander. A wretched date to bear in mid-October. As for the letter itself, I am indeed grateful for it, and it is by no fault of yours that it is not fresh ; who is responsible ? I am writing to Constantine. This war with Persia is deplorable. Our troops display the most conspicuous courage, but to expend it against such enemies, and at the end of a twelvemonth to have to repel their attacks, is most annoying. However, there is nothing to be done but to force them to a peace, of which we shall have the honour and the profit. This is quite clear, and we must bring it about speedily. Here we are treading gingerly on ground obstructed by timidity or excessive prudence. One cannot blame the Ministry, for their position allows them no alternative, and so far they have not tried their strength ; they have, therefore, every reason to be cautious. My hope is in the force of events, which will upset all their cautiousness. They will be bound to do something if the Turks continue to act as fools, and their patron Metternich *idem*. For my part I have come to the belief that Metternich, the man of cleverness, is dead, for there is not a trace of it in his present conduct. It is some usurper of his name who has quarrelled with everybody ; who clings obstinately to all the political blunders which his vanity provoked ; who just now has personally offended the King of England (hitherto his admirer) in the matter of the Duke of Brunswick ; [1] and who, to crown his blunders, at the age of sixty acts like a simpleton. I am truly not sorry for this galaxy of stupidities, for there is less risk of his being able to recover his former influence. I could have been more certain on this point with Canning, but I think that even with the present Ministers there is quite as little danger.

Mr. Huskisson is the strong and important feature of the Cabinet.[2] He is a man of as bold ideas as Canning, but with more character and determination. He has not the same talent as a speaker. Lord Dudley [3] combines much real ability with so exaggerated a diffidence that he is capable of asking his colleagues if he dare say ' perhaps ' ; an honourable man, of much talent, immensely wealthy, but he is an amateur Minister. Lord Lansdowne [4] is the most distinguished of the great aristocrats of this country, without a spot on his great reputation, a remarkable orator, and a man of merit rather than of superiority. As for the other Ministers, they are only padding, including the Premier.

Show this page of my letter to Count Nesselrode ; it may interest him, and he may rely upon the truthfulness of the portraits. As to the Cabinet as a body, all its members profess the political principles we should most desire, for they have grown old in their distrust of Austria. There is

---

[1] Metternich's offence was that, in his anxiety to prevent the quarrel between the Duke and his subjects coming before the Confederation, he made friendly advances in the hopes of bringing about a settlement. The *trait de berger* to which Madame de Lieven refers is Metternich's second marriage at this time to Maria Antonia von Leykham, Countess of Beilstein.

[2] William Huskisson, born 1770 ; secretary to Lord Gower when Ambassador to France, 1790 ; Under-Secretary for the Colonies, 1795 ; Secretary to the Treasury, 1804 ; Chief Commissioner of Woods and Forests, 1814–22 ; President of the Board of Trade, 1823–7, representing Liverpool in Parliament after Canning's defeat ; Secretary for the Colonies, 1827–8 ; accidentally killed at the opening of the Liverpool and Manchester Railway, 1830.

[3] John William Ward, ninth Baron Ward and fourth Viscount Dudley, created Earl of Dudley, 1827. Died 1833.

[4] Henry, third Marquess of Lansdowne and fourth Earl of Kerry. Chancellor of the Exchequer (as Lord Henry Petty) 1806–7. Held many offices in subsequent Whig administrations and had a seat in the Cabinet up to 1858.

some talk of finding a place in the Ministry for Lord Holland,[1] but for the present the proposal is quite vague. Even should it be carried out, there is no reason that we should feel annoyed, quite the reverse. Lord Holland has to make reparation for the ill he has done us, and you will see that he will do more to favour us than if he had nothing to reproach himself with. On the Eastern Question he could do more than the Government itself, especially in what concerns Russia.

Portugal haunts the Ministers even in their dreams, and for the moment they have thoughts for nothing else. In this business they are afraid of some of Metternich's shuffling tricks, and this by no means inclines them to forbearance.

The Duke of Wellington still looks very coldly on me ; I can wait, for it really is of no consequence. He cannot forgive me for having preferred the Minister friendly to the Greeks to the Minister friendly to the Turks. The King has certainly restored him to office, but not to favour, for he has only seen him once for half an hour since he was restored to the chief command of the army. His friendly relations with the Ultras are displeasing to the King. Just now the Duke is on a most intimate footing with the Austrian Ambassador.

This is how the gossip runs, my dear Alexander, but it is the principal food of diplomacy. I am rejoiced to hear that the Empress has had such a satisfactory time, and I hope her health will be speedily restored. I think the choice of the name of Constantine in the very best taste. The Emperor must be very delighted.

Good-bye, dear little brother, write more frequently. I have need of the pleasure which your letters give. I am

---

[1] Henry R. Vassall-Fox, third Lord Holland, nephew of Charles James Fox, Lord Privy Seal 1806-7. During his lifetime Holland House, Kensington, became the chief resort of Whig politicians and of the most distinguished literary celebrities of the day. In 1824 by Metternich's order he was refused admission to Austrian territory as ' a person notoriously of very bad sentiments, and known as an enthusiastic adherent of Radicalism.' George IV.'s objection to his holding office nearly rendered Lord Goderich's attempts to make a Ministry abortive. He was, however, Chancellor of the Duchy of Lancaster between 1830-40 when the Whigs were in office ; married, 1797, Elizabeth, divorced wife of Sir Godfrey Webster and daughter of Richard Vassall of Jamaica. He died in 1840.

worried about my wretched health.   You will laugh at me, as you did at Constantine, but I become dreadfully thin—do you understand that?   However, so far as concerns my size and weight, I get accustomed, and that is in itself a consolation, but to feel oneself gradually dying is very different sort of trouble.   All my best wishes, dear Alexander, to your wife and children and yourself.

[The battle of Navarino was fought under conditions which gave rise to violent controversy and marred the lustre of a brilliant feat of arms.   Sir William Codrington, commanding the Mediterranean Fleet, while cruising off the coast of Greece received instructions to forward to the Provisional Government of Greece the demand for an armistice, a similar demand being addressed to the Porte by the three Powers.   Meanwhile the admirals of the allied fleets were to prevent any supplies of arms and men being sent to the Turkish forces, and they were told that 'any hostile proceeding would be at variance with the pacific ground' which the Powers had assumed. In other words, a blockade was to be effected, but any attempt to enforce it by arms was to be avoided.   In explaining this ambiguity, Mr. Stratford Canning, the British Envoy at the Porte, had added that when all other means were exhausted the will of the Powers could be enforced 'by cannon shot.'   The Greeks assented to the armistice, the Turks refused it, and an Egyptian squadron entered Navarino harbour on the south-west of the Morea on September 9, two days before Codrington's arrival.   He at once communicated with the Turkish admiral requesting the latter not to provoke hostilities, but without result.   On September 21 the Turkish fleet put to sea, and Codrington at once prepared for action; the opportune arrival of the French fleet under Admiral de Rigny induced the Turks to put back into port, and on September 25 Ibrahim Pasha consented to an armistice of twenty days.   The news that Lord Cochrane had made a descent on Patras reached him immediately afterwards, and he was with difficulty persuaded to allow the armistice to stand.   In the absence of the French fleet, and with his own force weakened, Codrington received news on October 1 that the Turkish fleet was putting to sea, but on the display of force the Turks again put back, and a similar attempt was defeated without bloodshed on October 7.   On the 13th the French fleet under de Rigny and the Russian under Admiral Heyden arrived at Navarino, and Ibrahim, unable to reach Patras, revenged himself upon the inhabitants of the Morea.   The three admirals, on learning of the atrocities committed

by the Turks, conferred together, and agreed that the mere presence
of the allied fleets was insufficient to protect the Greek population.
On October 20 they therefore stood into the harbour, and after four
hours out of the Ottoman fleet of sixty men-of-war there remained
only one frigate and fifteen smaller vessels.

The news of this victory reached London at the time when the
intrigues which had hampered Canning in the formation of his
Ministry were revived. The rivalry of Huskisson and Herries, the
annoyance of the Whigs at the exclusion of Lord Holland and Lord
Wellesley from the Cabinet, and the obvious inability of Lord Goderich
to deal firmly with his own Cabinet, brought it speedily into general
contempt. On the matter of the battle of Navarino it was also
divided, one section wishing to censure Codrington for allowing the
peace with Turkey to be broken, another anxious to allow Russia
alone to give the Greeks their independence, while others were
disposed to let the allied admirals pursue actively the policy which
they had inaugurated. Outside the Cabinet there were not wanting
those who openly declared that the coincidence of the arrival of the
Russian admiral with the outbreak of hostilities was not wholly
fortuitous, and that the policy of Russia was to embroil Great
Britain irretrievably with Turkey, and to profit by the situation thus
created. Such a theory logically involved the suggestion that the
massacre of the Moreans, which finally led to the intervention of
the allied fleet, was brought about by Russian intrigue, but for this
disgraceful thought no evidence was forthcoming. On the other
hand, it was asserted, probably with as little foundation, that the
aggressive attitude of Turkey had been secretly provoked by Austria.]

LIII

London : 4/16 November 1827.

Dear Alexander,—Why don't you write to me? The
couriers arrive, and the fire-ships arrive, but your letters do
not arrive. Well, well, *vive* Navarino ! There is a treaty
which has not been stillborn, as M. de Metternich predicted—
quite the contrary, the child is remarkably lively. We
are delighted, the English Government a little frightened,
and the French the reverse of satisfied, except for the
fact that it distracts public attention. As for the Austrians,
it goes without saying that they are furious and greatly
disturbed. The English public is full of proud boasting,
there has been burning and sinking of ships and much

massacring—all this is to their taste. The masses do not stop to ask the cause : the Opposition is squabbling, and asks by what right these things have been done. 'We are playing the game of Russia, she alone will profit by this business ; our Ministers are incapables, who allow themselves to be duped by Russia.' Others say : 'Let us at least know what will fall to our share. England is mad to want to fight for mere sentiment, what are the Greeks to us ? The Turks have always been our faithful allies.' The Ministers—who, by the way, do not belong to a very intrepid race—are sorely embarrassed by these remarks, and they need to be taken by the shoulders daily to shake up their courage. Their followers at the same time are proud and boastful ; they say, and with perfect truth : 'Here is a noble act, a fine policy unalloyed by self-interest, with a really big battle into the bargain, such as our bluejackets need from time to time to enliven them and to keep up their traditions.' Such talk, however, disturbs me very little ; the Ministry have gone too far to retreat now. If the Porte gives way all is well, for we shall have got what we wanted. If there should be a war, England would enter upon it with goodwill, for wars have always turned to her advantage. This one will profit us also, so that all is well. Meanwhile Greece lives again. What glory for this century, and for Christian kings !

I fancy Count Nesselrode will find that my portraits of the English Ministers have some resemblance. They are about to send us an Ambassador, Sir William A'Court.[1] Everything is satisfactory with regard to him except his unlucky star, which up to the present has brought about a revolution wherever he has been sent—Naples, Madrid, and Lisbon. For my own part, I care only for doctors who are lucky, and I do not know why it might not be made the rule to accept only lucky Ambassadors. This is childishness,

[1] Sir William A'Court, G.C.B., second Baronet, Secretary of Legation at Naples, 1801 ; of special mission to Vienna, 1807 ; Envoy to the Barbary States 1803, Naples 1814, Spain 1822 ; Ambassador to Portugal, 1824-8, when he was raised to the peerage as Lord Heytesbury ; and was Ambassador at St. Petersburg, 1828-32 ; nominated Governor-General of India 1835, but did not take office ; Viceroy of Ireland, 1844-6.

perhaps, but I do not pique myself on being strong-minded. I had hoped that it might have been Lamb who would be sent. It was proposed to him, but he was afraid of the climate and of the cost of living, so he is to go to Lisbon.

Dom Miguel[1] is expected here shortly. He is afraid that he will be assassinated, or at the least that the populace will throw mud at him. It is true that he is not popular here, but he will only need to be looked after carefully, and he is quite willing that this should be done.

The King of England is everything we can wish ; the affair of the Duke of Brunswick has quite disenchanted him with Metternich. He agrees with me that it is Metternich who brought about the battle of Navarino. He trusts the Emperor and his loyalty. I am curious to see what will be thought (in Russia) of the King's request for the *cordon bleu*[2] for the Duke of Devonshire. The demand is somewhat unusual, but there are several good reasons for it. He passes for the Emperor's friend (that is the English expression) ; he is also a friend of the King, the head of a powerful party, which has great influence and will be more powerful by and by, well disposed towards Russia, devoted to the Emperor—in a word, the person who is the most favourably inclined to us in this country ; above all, *grand seigneur* in the highest degree and a Knight of the Garter ! The King looks upon this favour as if it were for himself and as if we were still in the year '13.

Good-bye, my dear Alexander ; I am ending this letter in a headache which almost makes me blind. I am impatient for news of Constantine, and I am impatient about many things. In the course of the next fortnight important events will happen. The news from Constantinople, subsequent to the Navarino battle, is awaited here with the greatest anxiety. A thousand caresses to your wife, your children, and Coco. Good-bye, my dear brother. I embrace you tenderly.

To be quite correct, I ought to efface the whole fourth

---

[1] See Appendix.

[2] The riband of St. Andrew of Russia. The Duke also received the red riband of St. Anne and the Cross of St. Alexander Newsky, March 18, 1828.

page of this letter. My husband is afraid to undertake the King's commission without making some previous inquiries—so there is something put off until the next time. I am very sorry for it, for the King's insistence is most marked. He said to me, 'It is the greatest proof of friendship the Emperor can give me,' and the King deserves that some evidence of it should be given him. Well, well! dear Alexander, I believe that a woman is often bolder than a man, for I should have said the thing quite naturally, and very likely the Emperor would have taken it kindly, and the result would have been a King delighted and a fine fellow made supremely happy. Here is my migraine again, which makes me shriek with pain. Kindest regards to Count Nesselrode.

[The most immediate outcome of the battle of Navarino was the downfall of Lord Goderich's Ministry, which was hastened by the King's assumption of the right of dispensing honours for an action of which the Cabinet did not wholly approve. The Prime Minister recognised the weakness of that body, and hoped to strengthen it by the introduction of Lord Wellesley and Lord Holland; and on the King's refusal, Goderich, on December 13, sent a letter of resignation, to which Lord Lansdowne and Huskisson were ready to adhere. Lord Goderich, however, had added, without the knowledge of his colleagues, a postscript which put his resignation upon domestic reasons—the state of Lady Goderich's health. The King, ignoring the letter, took advantage of the postscript, expressed his regrets, and sent for Lord Harrowby, one of Canning's most trusted supporters. Lord Harrowby, however, declined the task, and on December 19 Lord Goderich had withdrawn his resignation. Two days later the squabble between Herries and Huskisson was renewed over the chairmanship of the Committee on Finance Neither would give way, and Goderich, acknowledging his helplessness to preserve peace in his Cabinet, was told by the King to 'Go home and take care of himself,' and after an interview with the Chancellor (Lord Lyndhurst) the Duke of Wellington was empowered to form a Government with the assistance of anyone except Lord Grey. With reference to the trend of foreign politics it may be stated that while Great Britain hesitated to take any definite line, and wished to postpone any decision until Codrington's views and explanations were obtained, France had expressed her willingness that Russia should be allowed to occupy the Danubian Principalities and to exercise severe pressure

I

on the Porte. Austria, however, wholly unprepared for war herself, was most anxious to prevent any advance of Russia upon her eastern frontiers or the permanent weakening of Turkey.]

LIV

London : 5/17 December 1827.

How much I thank you, dear Alexander, for your letter of November 9—21, and for the pretty little message of charming taste and friendly interest which you give me from the Emperor. I am touched and delighted that he should bestow a moment's thought on me. It seems to me that he is quite right, and this conviction both my heart and my vanity endorse. Our affairs at Paris are going prosperously and superbly ; they startle both friends and enemies, and one can easily see that both have a fine fear of us. The Emperor seems to be well aware of the truth of this, for no better means could be taken than to appease by his good faith the fear which his power arouses.

I repeated to you in my last letter the gossip inspired by speculating on the consequences of Navarino. Since then these speculations have gone on *crescendo*. There is little said about Greece, it is of Russia and Russia alone that people talk, and we shall have to submit to a fine shower of invective when Parliament meets ; that is, Ministers will be told plainly and flatly that they are fools to believe in our protestations or even in our assurances. All this is part of the Opposition tactics, while Ministers conjugate the verb ' to tremble '— or at least such of them as still hold to the ancient *régime*. Huskisson and Lansdowne are not among these, yet you would scarcely believe the trouble Lord Holland takes to give them courage and to inspire them with confidence in Russia. It is indeed strange to find in him so valuable an auxiliary. Lord Grey, too, the most redoubtable of the opponents of the Ministry, will spare our feelings, at least upon this point. I am doing all in my power to rally him to our side : and all my arguments turn upon this very obvious little truth—'You cannot hinder us from being powerful, attach yourselves to us by complete confidence in the Emperor's straightforwardness ;

that is a chord you can always touch with effect, and therefore there is no ground for apprehension.'

Metternich is fallen lower in public esteem than at one time seemed possible. His intrigues at Constantinople have been exposed to the world, and there is in them so much malice, blundering, and excessive bad faith that no one is at pains to defend him. Esterhazy has been guilty of buying a newspaper to defend his master,[1] which affords a fine opportunity of attacking him still more bitterly. In a word, he is altogether brought low.

8/20 December.

P.S.—While this letter was waiting for the courier to get into his carriage, lo! and behold, another ministerial crisis bursts upon us. Lord Goderich, this Prime Minister who is as cowardly as the most timid woman, declares that his nerves will no longer stand the strain. He has given in his resignation and rushed off to the country. Two days later he cries for mercy, and it is accorded him—because in the interval it was found impossible to replace him without swaying altogether to the right or altogether to the left. Meanwhile you may guess what ridicule and contempt this casts upon the administration : and this at the moment Parliament is about to meet, and when there are so many thorny questions of policy needing defence. The King is wrong in making so much fuss; he should accept Lord Holland willingly, for he will have to do so in some way. Here we are awaiting impatiently to know whether it is to be peace or war—but my idea is that it suits M. de Metternich to make us wait. There! good-bye, my dear Alexander. I embrace the whole family with all my heart, you especially. Write to me constantly. By the way, do me (or rather do the man at the Embassy) the service to remind Count Nesselrode that he has not yet sent the full-length portrait of the Emperor for which my husband has asked him, and which Pozzo di Borgo has already received. Why is the London Embassy treated so scurvily ? I have still ringing in my ears the words of

---

[1] Presumably the *Courier*, which defended the Austrian policy.

Count Nesselrode at Petersburg, 'that it is highly improper that the portrait of the Emperor is not hanging at the Embassy.' Another request. Countess Woronzow has left at the Foreign Office a little parcel addressed to me containing a boa. As it is of very discreet proportions, ask that it may be sent to me by the first courier. Many apologies, dear Alexander ; my husband's kindest remembrances.

1828

[The readiness of Huskisson and several of his friends to give
their co-operation removed Wellington's immediate difficulties, but
it did not ensure permanence to his Ministry. The Roman Catholic
question was not to be made a Cabinet question, and the Protestant
ascendency in Ireland was to be clearly expressed in the selection
of the Viceroy and the Irish Lord Chancellor ; but William Lamb
was allowed to remain Chief Secretary. Lord Lyndhurst as Lord
Chancellor, and Dudley, Palmerston, and Grant continued in their
respective offices. Peel returned to the Home Office and became
leader of the House of Commons, Goulburn Chancellor of the
Exchequer, while Herries, who had been the cause of the crisis, was
rewarded with the Mastership of the Mint, and Lord Anglesey was
sent to replace Lord Wellesley as Viceroy of Ireland. This coalition
naturally offended the extreme Tories as well as the extreme Whigs,
but Huskisson, in defending his position on the occasion of his re-
election for Liverpool, expressed himself in terms which showed how
hollow the alliance really was. He was reported to have said that the
' Duke of Wellington had assented to a continuance of the system of
free trade and of Canning's foreign policy.' On the earliest opportunity the Duke in the House of Lords denied the existence ' of any
such corrupt bargain.' The Canningites, however, for a time consented to work with the Duke, who showed no disposition to go back
upon the foreign policy of their late leader, but to carry out the
Treaty of London. Moreover, the fact that Lord Dudley, who had
signed that Treaty, was still Minister of Foreign Affairs was a
guarantee that the friends of the Turks would not have their way.
The utmost concession made to them was a reference in the King's
Speech to the fight at Navarino as 'a collision, wholly unexpected by
his Majesty,' who further 'deeply lamented that this conflict should

have occurred with the naval force of an ancient ally.' Meanwhile the Ambassadors of the three Powers, who had remained at Constantinople for some weeks after the battle of Navarino, had withdrawn (December 8) previous to the collapse of Lord Goderich's administration in consequence of the issue of a *Hatti Sheriff* by the Sultan calling upon 'the faithful' to take up arms, and of the refusal of the Porte to abide by the terms of the Treaty of Ackermann. Russia thereupon called upon the allies to carry out the Treaty of London, intimating at the same time that in the event of their refusal she would act alone. The French Government at once announced its intention of acting energetically by blockading Constantinople and assenting to the occupation of the Danubian Principalities by Russia. The British Cabinet was hopelessly divided. Wellington suggested that Greece should remain under the suzerainty of the Sultan, that even its quasi-independence should be limited to Morea and the adjacent islands, and that it should pay a heavy annual tribute in addition to a large indemnity to Turkey. These proposals were rejected by the Cabinet, even Peel and Aberdeen protesting against them. Wellington, however, stubbornly refused to be drawn into hostilities against 'the ancient ally.' Codrington, who had fallen under his displeasure, was recalled on the ground that during his absence at Malta another Egyptian fleet had entered Navarino harbour and had carried off to Alexandria upwards of 5,000 Greeks, chiefly women and children, who had been sold into slavery. Before the arrival of his successor Codrington had succeeded in re-establishing, in conjunction with the Russian and French fleets, the blockade of the Morea, which reduced the Turks to great straits, and he ultimately concluded an agreement with Mehemet Ali at Alexandria to withdraw Ibrahim Pasha's army from the Morea.

Already divided upon its foreign policy, Wellington's Cabinet was not better agreed upon domestic legislation, while its hold upon the House of Commons seemed very precarious. The Ministry was badly beaten upon Lord John Russell's motion to repeal the Test and Corporation Acts, which, although they had virtually lapsed, had to be met by an Indemnity Act which was passed each Session 'to forgive good men doing good service to their country.' Peel proposed a compromise in order to avoid the alternative of resignation or a conflict with the Upper House, and this was accepted by both Houses. Roman Catholic Emancipation was then brought forward by Sir Francis Burdett on May 8, and on the resolution three members of the Cabinet (Peel, Goulburn, and Herries) voted for it and three (Huskisson, Palmerston, and Grant) against it, and it was carried by 272 to 266. Peel seemed to be most personally affected by this vote, and hinted retirement, but was induced to remain on the understanding that the Duke should not commit himself to any irrevocable course of action.   When the resolution was brought forward in the Lords by Lord Lansdowne, on June 9 it was noticed that the Chancellor's (Lord Lyndhurst) tone was very different from that he had used in his attack upon Canning's Bill a year previously, but the resolution was nevertheless rejected by a majority of 44 votes.   On the Corn Bill there was even more open dissension among Ministers.   The Duke of Wellington wished to deal with the subject himself, but his proposals met with very little support even in his own Cabinet—and finally led to Huskisson's resignation.   This was, however, for the moment averted, and a new Corn Law on the basis of a compromise passed both Houses.   The disfranchisement of two corrupt boroughs, however, was to be the ultimate cause of the break up of the Coalition Cabinet.   Penryn and East Retford had been proved to be notoriously corrupt, and it was proposed to substitute Manchester and Birmingham respectively for representation in Parliament.   This was the view of the Canningite section of the Cabinet, but the Tories wished to have the seats thrown into the counties concerned.   Peel was, as before, ready with a compromise which was to give one seat to a manufacturing town and the other to the county division in which it was situated. After much wrangling it was arranged that the seat for East Retford should be given to the 'hundred of Bassetlaw,' instead of to Birmingham and the Penryn seat to Manchester.   In the House of Lords, however, Lord Carnarvon, who had charge of the Penryn Disfranchisement Bill, gave up the point and consented to the seat being thrown into its county.   Thereupon the Liberals in the Commons proposed that the Retford seat should be transferred to Birmingham.   Fresh disputes broke out in the Cabinet, which came to no decision, and Peel supported the proposal for giving the East Retford seat to Nottinghamshire.   Huskisson, followed by Palmerston and Lamb, voted on the other side, but was defeated by a majority of eighteen votes.   On the following day Huskisson wrote to the Duke a letter which the latter interpreted as a formal resignation of his office.   All attempts to explain its meaning in a different way having failed, the Canningites felt that the only course for them was to take the hint thus roughly given to them and to retire from a Cabinet in which their views were always at variance with those of its chief.   The withdrawal of Palmerston, Grant, and Lamb was unhesitating, but Lord Dudley separated himself from the Foreign Office with more reluctance.   Sir Henry Hardinge became Secretary at War.   Sir George Murray, who had been Quartermaster-General to the Duke in Spain, took the Colonial Office, and Lord Aberdeen was promoted from the Duchy of Lancaster to the Foreign Office. In these intrigues Madame de Lieven played an important part. Prince Esterhazy, the Austrian Ambassador, however, thought that the part she had taken had been so far successful that through her means the objects of the Russian Court had been attained.]

LV

London : 5/17 January 1828.

My dear Alexander,—Your letter of December 10/22 has caused me the greatest delight. You tell me that the Duke of Devonshire is to have the Blue Riband.[1] This is a good, a kind, and a useful act of our Emperor. He has an easy, quiet way of doing things admirably suited to his power. I blushed a little to think that my little scrap of paper was the cause of this great favour. I will not brag about it, but I feel deeply that it implies confidence in me. My husband waits for instructions before announcing it to the King.

You will hear to-day of a ministerial revolution. There has been a traitor in the Cabinet, an occult power behind the throne—gout in the King's leg and inflammation of the chest. The intriguing doctor takes from him forty ounces of blood, and on the same day tells him that his Ministers are quarrelling among themselves. We are only ten days off the meeting of Parliament, the Ministry must be re-arranged, and the Speech from the Throne settled. The King protests that it will be his death, and that he must shift from his own shoulders a burden which his physical sufferings will not permit him to undertake. So he hands over to the Duke of Wellington the trouble and danger of making a Cabinet. You can well imagine that Wellington's name alone causes a sensation in the public mind. Everything will now once more be topsy-turvy here. England, however, is no longer suited to an apostolic *régime*, and Wellington knows this, so he is negotiating with Canning's friends. If they stand by him the Treaty will be ratified, if they retire everything may be upset. I am asked on all sides, ' What will the Emperor say?' I reply that the Emperor will much regret if England

[1] Of St. Andrew of Russia.

detaches herself from his policy, but that he will not, on this ground, be disturbed in the very least. ' He will do without England precisely what he would have done with her : never will it be said of him that having intimated his intention he fails to carry it into execution.'

As a matter of fact the post of a representative of the Emperor Nicholas is an easy one—to be firm and haughty, yet moderate, and to let come what may.

I had already read in the English newspapers the text of Constantine's letter some days before receiving it ! You have no idea of the interest with which the English public has followed the details of the visit of Abbas Mirza to our camp.[1] This is just the sort of food which the English really need. I am delighted, too, that Constantine should have such a memorable event to look back upon.

Dom Miguel has soft manners and a ferocious expression. He is altogether in the hands of Austria. I pity his subjects. We have managed to get rid of him by means of *fêtes*. He is madly devoted to dancing, but one would say that he was being whipped, so much bad humour does he manage to get out of his amusements.[2]

Admiral Codrington has written to the Duke of Clarence a letter overflowing with enthusiasm for our brave sailors and with friendliness for Admiral Heyden.[3] The Duke tells me that a brother and a fellow-countryman could not express themselves more warmly. Between ourselves, the Duke of Clarence, although full of pride for the battle of Navarino, which he thinks was won by himself, is nevertheless at heart wildly philo-Turk. You can hardly believe how many English are of the same way of thinking. The truth is that

[1] The Russians, after the taking of Erwán in the previous October, had pushed on, meeting with little resistance, and reached Tabreez, where the Shah, Abbas Mirza, had made his quarters. He sent a flag of truce, and afterwards paid a visit to the Russian camp.

[2] 'Dom Miguel has been with the King at the Cottage these two days. He has been received with great magnificence ; they say he behaves well enough, but is very shy.'—*Greville Diaries*, i. 117.

[3] The Russian Admiral in command. After the battle the Emperor Nicholas sent to Admiral Codrington a letter of congratulation together with the Grand Cross of St. George (of Russia).

the Eastern Question has never been clearly explained to the English public. The Ministry which has just collapsed might have done so in Parliament—I will not answer for the intentions of their successors. Austria is on the best footing of friendliness with all those who by general opinion are to be the new actors. These insolent Austrians talk about making Russia tremble, at which I simply shrug my shoulders. Good-bye, my dear Alexander ; perhaps before closing this letter I may be in a position to tell you the names of the new Ministers. I almost hope that they may be Tories without alloy. In that case the House will bundle them out in a fortnight. If the Canningites remain, the Cabinet might be really strong.

LVI

London : 8/20 February 1828.

My mind is occupied with a single matter, and I doubt if I shall be able to speak to you of any other to-day, my dear Alexander. The Duke of Wellington is Prime Minister— the Duke of Wellington is Austrian. He prefers the trickiness of M. de Metternich to the straightforwardness of the Emperor Nicholas. Very well, so be it, we are in such a position that this need not disturb us. He is formally bound to the execution of the Treaty, and he must comply with it ; but he will try to do so in a slack and dilatory fashion, while we do so vigorously and at once. Austria is of the same humour, let us therefore adopt our own line. England can do nothing hostile to us, what pretext could she have ? We shall not give her one. And where are her means ? She has none. It is doubtful if the English public would make sacrifices even for a point of honour ; how thoroughly indisposed would she then be to make them with a disloyal object ? Our cause has gained a good deal in public opinion since the opening of Parliament, because all the speakers have been favourable to us. If the former Ministry had held together we should have been attacked by the whole Tory phalanx which is hampered by the Turks and Austrian *good faith*. This phalanx is now pressed into the service of the new Government, and is forced to espouse its recognised doctrines—or common decency, at least, requires that it should remain silent. The Whigs alone talk on this question, and all the men of ability are on their side—all are warmly in our favour, all admire the forbearance and moderation of the Emperor, all trust to his honour ; and, moreover, the English Government cannot have forgotten that in 1792 Mr. Pitt's Ministry was overthrown by the Whigs for wishing to support the Turks against Russia.[1] We have recently made the discovery of several worthy friends, and among the most useful is Prince Leopold. You would scarcely believe the warmth with which he has espoused our interests. He loudly defends Russia, and we owe not a little useful advice to his zeal and goodwill. We can count, too, upon other friends in the Cabinet, but they are overawed by that despot, Wellington. He makes it understood that he is the master, how long he will continue to be so I cannot say. My dear Alexander, I am in a furious rage—I have forgotten all about my health— but at the same time I am more proud than ever of being Russian. Well, come what may, Russia is there, strong in the good faith and in the will of her Sovereign—supported by all her might. Now we shall have good cause to thank heaven for the monarch it has given us. I should like to go to sleep and only wake to hear that our armies were in motion—and that they are pushing forward rapidly. I don't know if I deceive myself, but it seems to me that our influence and our reputation are engaged in this business, and we should act promptly in order that Europe may not have time to interfere by intrigues and combinations. I am full of hope in God and our Emperor. Good-bye, dear brother, I love you with all my heart and entreat you to write to me. In a few days you will probably have another letter from me : but I much doubt if I shall have to withdraw a single word of what I have written to-day.

[1] Pitt's Ministry was not upset in 1792 ; but in March 1791, Russia and Turkey being at war, Pitt proposed to Prussia and Holland to intervene with Great Britain and to force Russia to make peace. Parliament supported him, but the proposal produced a scare in the country. Fox attacked it, Pitt's colleagues wavered, and two or three days later he withdrew the threat of inter- vention, suffering thereby loss of reputation at home and prestige abroad.

LVII

London : 16/28 February 1828.

I am writing to you, my dear Alexander, because there happens to be a courier, but I have not a scrap of news to send you. A week's squabblings, the Sultan's *hatti-sheriff*,[1] provocation, direct and indirect—none of these make the slightest difference to the Field-Marshal. He will not have a war, therefore war will not be made. His obstinacy and his stupidity may be the cause of serious ills, so much the worse for England ; I don't see how it can be any the worse for us, and consequently I don't allow myself to be worried about it. The Duke's position, however, is not yet quite solidly assured ; Ministers are at loggerheads in the Cabinet, and even quarrel openly in Parliament. The country scarcely knows what is the tone of the Government ; some find it too liberal, others too apostolic, everybody is dissatisfied, everybody is suspicious and distrustful, but everyone submits because they cannot see whom else to take. The Ministry is there for want of a better, but I do not think it will last long ; yet a good deal of harm may be done as long as it remains. I am disturbed because the peace between us and Persia has not been already concluded, the delay is most inopportune. Austria is triumphing here ; it is her turn to take the lead ; our position is painful, but bravado has never intimidated me. I await events with calmness, the dignity of Russia in the hands of the Emperor is in good hands. Good-bye, dear Alexander, we all have our thorns, and I expect things are not going on very peaceably at Petersburg, and that you are already thinking about the spring.

Where is Constantine ? I have not heard a word of him since his interview with Abbas Mirza. Tell him, or write

[1] This declared that the impending war was to prevent the Christian Powers interfering with Islamism. It ended : ' Let the faithful then have no thought of their arrears or of pay of any kind. Let us sacrifice willingly our properties and our persons, and struggle, body and soul, for the support of our religion. The worshippers of the Prophet have no other means of working out their salvation in this world and the next.' The Turkish Government complained of the publication of this document, which was only a letter of private instructions addressed to its own officials.

to him, all my loving remembrances. I embrace you and your wife with all my heart.

LVIII

London: 16/28 March 1828.

Dear Alexander,—What tears and what regrets do I not give to that good, excellent mother whom we have just lost.[1] Your letter to my husband and that of the Empress-Mother have brought us this sad news. I am quite upset by it, I assure you. What touching conduct our adorable Imperial family has shown towards that dear good lady ! I am as much moved by this behaviour as by the death of our own good mother. What a beautiful life, and what a beautiful end ! This sad news arrived just as my husband was despatching a courier, and I am very glad that he should in a measure be forced to distract his thoughts from the memory of his mother. He has not a minute to himself; he is working himself off his head ; the moment is a serious one. However, it is no surprise for us. England is a coward, and nothing less. She is afraid to go with us, afraid to go against us, and she thinks herself safe by halting mid-way between her two fears. The attitude is not very dignified for her, but it is not harmful to us, and that is the essential matter.

This Government is contemptible and cannot last, Ministers blackguard one another like draymen. At the moment I am writing it is not certain that Huskisson will not give in his resignation this evening. The immediate cause of the quarrel between him and the Duke is the Corn Bill, but the quarrels are of daily recurrence and upon every question. The Lower House does not support the Government, the King does not like Wellington, the nation, which expected mountains and marvels from his firmness, in the absence of talent, is beginning to see that he temporises on every question. Hesitation and half-measures are the order of the day, and opinions concerning him are somewhat sobered. The state of France, moreover, disturbs him ; the stream runs strong, public opinion urges the Government forward, men's

<hr>

[1] See Appendix.

minds are moved. It is feared here that it may be thought necessary to give them some occupation abroad, lest they may find it at home. Portugal can be taken up or left alone.[1] If taken up, it would plunge England more deeply than ever into the complications of the Peninsula, and would force her (horrible prospect) to spend money. If left alone, from that moment England would be felt to fall to the depths of political insignificance. Austria is pushing Wellington forward, but I doubt if he is disposed to advance much—by choice, yes, but from cowardice, no. Everything has gone against him since he has been Minister; he is really routed, and does not know how to recover himself. The important decision taken by our great Emperor was a thunderbolt to him ; the effect upon the public, magical. There were only two feelings evoked, fear on the one side, pleasure on the other. I repeat, then, that all persons of intelligence are on our side, and among these Lord Holland deserves special mention. He is making ample amends for his former errors ; he will not listen to argument on the subject of Turkey, but wishes her outside of Europe. He would be glad to see the Emperor arrive at Constantinople, that he might do as he liked with it, that we might have a port in the Mediterranean— in a word the only difficulty is to restrain him. He admires the Emperor beyond everything, and his wisdom above all his other qualities. He is ashamed of the miserable policy of England, of this great country which returns to a narrow plan—I prattle too much about a mere detail ; for on the whole, dear Alexander, our Emperor has given us the grandest possible moral position. May God bless his noble projects.

I am overjoyed to find that our last episode in Persia has been brought to a close ;[2] you have no conception of the terrors which that business aroused. They saw us already in the Great Indies. As for me, I am glad that there is

---

[1] Dom Miguel, who had been appointed Regent of Portugal, landed at Lisbon on February 22, and took the oath to the Constitution. The English troops were recalled, but the fleet and marines remained. Dom Miguel after a very brief interval usurped the Crown and annulled the Constitution. The English Minister then ordered the marines to be landed and to occupy Fort St. Julian.

[2] Peace between Russia and Persia was signed February 28.

the money the more and a war the less, and an army corps at liberty to go and frighten the Turks on this side of Asia.

We still have some good friends in the English Cabinet (one, Lord Palmerston, brother of Mr. Temple, who is just now *chargé d'affaires* at Petersburg) and many more outside the Cabinet ; the King, too, is well disposed towards us. He has personally much friendly feeling for the Emperor, and very great confidence in his character. The blue riband for the Duke of Devonshire has pleased him (the King) beyond measure ; as for that requested for Lord Hertford, the King boasts that he has nothing to do with it. He hates Hertford, it is all Wellington's affair.[1]

I have had many inquiries here as to the possibility of volunteers being allowed to serve in our war. Lord Grey, for instance, would much like to send his son to join our army. Lord Yarmouth,[2] too, is eager to serve. What answer shall I give them ? Instruct me on this point. My dear Alexander, I am indeed proud of being Russian, and I can assure you that my pleasure is renewed day by day, for no one talks to me about anything except our great undertaking, and our part in it is so fine and so clear. There is, however, one reflection which occurs to me. Hitherto we have been fighting against the Turks with small armies and dreaming of great conquests ; now we have a grand and magnificent army, and no ambition. This is real greatness.

I am a little annoyed, I must admit, that my husband should have asked for leave for private business. I have done my utmost to hinder it, my reasons being the importance of the present state of public affairs ; his, the future welfare of his children and his duty to look after it. There is reason in this, and I say no more. Possibly, however, these affairs will

[1] Frances, third Marquis of Hertford, K.G., the bearer of the Garter to the Emperor Nicholas on his accession, had been decorated with the Order of St. Andrew of Russia.

[2] Richard, afterwards fourth Marquess of Hertford, born 1800, was at this time a captain in the army, lived chiefly in Paris, died unmarried, 1870, leaving his property to Sir Richard Wallace, ' the son of my dearest friend,' whose widow on her death in 1898 bequeathed his collection of pictures and works of art to the British nation.

become clear and easy of solution because they are just now so perplexing. I hope so, indeed. If only I could wring the neck of this Government, how pleased I should be. At the same time the Duke of Wellington and I are on good terms. He comes to talk with me of a morning, but the word 'Turkey' has never escaped his lips or mine. If I were to break out some day, I am sure that we should come to blows. Good-bye, my dear brother. I loved my dear old mother-in-law, so that I am, in sober truth, quite upset by the sorrow her death causes me. What touching honour the Emperor paid to her remains! How greatly he does honour to himself by such acts. I adore our Emperor from afar, I wonder what I should do if in his presence. Do they know how to love him in Russia? Good-bye again, dear Alexander ; if Constantine is with you, give him my dearest love, as well as to your wife and children.

[The withdrawal of the Russian Ambassador from the Porte was not, however, followed immediately by a declaration of war, and Wellington's resistance to the suggestions of Russia and France to give effective assistance to the Greeks held those Powers in check for a while. But Nicholas, having at length made an advantageous peace with Persia, was determined to take more active measures. At the same time the three Ambassadors—Stratford Canning, Guilleminot, and Ribeaupierre—were ordered to take up their quarters at Poros, an island in the Archipelago, to draw up fresh terms for the settlement of the Greek question. On April 26 Nicholas formally declared war against Turkey, and the Russians a few days later crossed the Pruth, the Czar himself accompanying them. A month later the Danube had been crossed and the Dobrudscha overrun as far as Varna, of which the surrender was obtained through the treachery of the Turkish Commander. But after some serious reverses and being unable to seize Schumla and the Balkan passes the Russians were finally forced to recross the Danube. Meanwhile, in Asia Minor, Paskievitch had taken Anapa and stormed Kars. The French also, after some hesitation, despatched a force under General Maison to the Morea, which before many months drove out the remaining Turkish troops, M. de Martignac, who had replaced M. de Villèle, proving more desposed to follow public opinion. Palmerston was only giving expression to the views of the Liberal section of the Cabinet, who wished that Russia should take her own course, and, if she thought right, to carry out the Treaty of London. He wished, moreover, to limit the rights of Russia as a belligerent, especially in the matter of the blockade of the Dardanelles ; and in the negotiations which ensued much ill-will against Russia was aroused. In the end, however, Lord Aberdeen, who was acting in concert with Metternich, was obliged to give way, and Russia voluntarily assented to waiving so much of her belligerent rights as interfered with the commercial interests of neutrals. Canning's death, in fact, had brought about a change in the attitude of the English Ministry, of which the policy now was to avoid all foreign complications, and this object was more likely to be obtained by allowing each of the three nations to put its own interpretation on the Treaty, with the result that while Great Britain made a feeble naval demonstration and France sent her troops to the Morea, Russia alone entered upon war, and from the terms of her ' declaration' it was anticipated by some of the shrewder English statesmen that Russia by her individual action had freed herself from the obligations of the ' protocole du désintéressement' by which she had bound herself in the event of joint action by the allies which she had provoked at Navarino. Lord Aberdeen opposed Lord Palmerston's view that Russia should be allowed to act alone holding that the Treaty was no longer binding upon the other Powers.

It is interesting to contrast with Madame de Lieven's self-satisfaction the opinions which were held of her by those whom she thought she had fathomed. Lord Palmerston, writing to his brother Hon. William Temple, April 4, 1828, who was then *chargé d'affaires* at St. Petersburg, says : ' The Duke is evidently very anxious to break with Russia. He has a strong personal dislike to Russia. He has had violent quarrels with the Lievens, and thought himself not civilly used at St. Petersburg. A great many little things have contributed to set him against the Lievens. Mrs. Arbuthnot and Lady Jersey, who have both influence over him, both hate Madame de Lieven. . . . Madame de Lieven was foolish last year when Canning came in, and too openly expressed her joy at the Duke's retirement, and was, too, to a certain degree uncivil to him.'

A month later, May 8, he writes again : ' The Duke has the strongest dislike to Russia, more, I think, from personal feeling than from political.'[1]]

[1] Ev. Ashley's *Life of Lord Palmerston.*

K

LIX

Brighton : $\frac{\text{March 22}}{\text{April 3}}$, 1828.

How can I express to you, dear Alexander, the feelings which have filled my heart in reading your letter of March 1/24. The touching respect with which the Emperor has honoured the memory of my excellent mother-in-law on the occasion of her funeral, the tributary tears he shed on her remains, that touch of delicacy by which even the Princess's maid was remembered—all these trifling details, which so strangely mark the nobility of his character, are so many titles to the blessings of Heaven and the devotion of his subjects. The man whose heart is filled with such feelings deserves every prosperity, and he will enjoy it.

As for myself, I received with tears the news which concerns me—tears of gratitude, tears of remembrance for that dear incomparable lady, whose honours the Emperor allows me to inherit.[1] The favour is indeed great, and the way in which it is conferred renders its value still greater. Never has a like honour been received with greater emotion, and this I have not been able to refrain from telling the Emperor. Here is my letter to him. I hope you do not think that I am wrong in having written it.

I had a long talk with the Duke of Wellington a few days ago. I am not mistaken in anything which I have said to you concerning him. Everybody whose judgment was at all enlightened awaited impatiently, but with entire confidence in the Emperor, the entry of our troops into Turkey[2] ; others there are, certainly, who anticipate this event with dismay. For my part I am not sorry that those who look at things askew should get a fright, and am delighted with the annoyance of those who look them in the face.

I share heartily, dear Alexander, in your and my dear sister's grief for the sad loss that she has just sustained ;

[1] Madame de Lieven was appointed a Lady of the Bedchamber in succession to her late mother-in-law.

[2] General Wittgenstein with 150,000 Russian troops began to cross the Pruth early in May.

our troubles have so much resemblance that I can readily sympathise with yours. My husband and I came here to Brighton yesterday for a few days' rest to set us up again. Parliament has adjourned for a fortnight, Ministers are away in the country, and London is taking a holiday. Good-bye, my dear Alexander, I embrace you with all my heart, and am truly grateful for the interest you take in the favour which the Emperor has conferred upon me. My husband joins me in affectionate remembrances.

LX

London : 7/19 May 1828.

My dear Alexander,—A thousand thanks for your delightful letter of April 5–17. You will receive this by Paul, as my husband, not having been able to get leave (as I had anticipated) to go to Petersburg, has decided on being represented by his son. This is doubtless an official irregularity, for which, however, Paul is not to blame. He is rather a victim, for I was on the point of asking you to obtain for him permission to join the army. He has not ceased worrying us about this ; he is burning to fight. My intention was to ask you to get him passed as an officer, and then to have him regularly attached to Pahlen, Woronzow, or someone. It seems, however, that he must quench his military ardour, and devote himself to a tedious partition of the family property and to matters about which he really understands nothing ; but in your absence from Petersburg my husband had no one to whom he could entrust his interests.

The reports made by French diplomats and others at St. Petersburg have scattered dismay in our party, and have caused M. de Wellington & Co. to crow lustily.[1] We no longer wished for war ! we wanted no indemnity ! If we began our march, we were to be prepared to stop, as soon as any grey-beard, figuring as a plenipotentiary, should appear and hold up his hand. I, however, held my ground, and asserted that if this were true my Emperor Nicholas has

---

[1] Under pressure from the English Government, the French had temporarily suspended the despatch of troops to the Morea.

been juggled, and this is so unlike him I would not believe it unless he himself told me. Upon this arrives that happily conceived declaration [1]—and you should have seen the long faces of some and the delight of others! We are a great people, dear Alexander, and my heart—wholly Russian and wholly Nicholas's—swells with pride.

Wellington is in a very bad humour, and no wonder; he must give way, that is his only chance. Lord Palmerston (Cabinet Minister and *our* Minister) said to me : ' After all, whether for those who, like me, trust, eyes open or eyes shut, in your Emperor, or for those who distrust him, or pretend to do so, there is one and the same course—and that is to show confidence in him and to act upon this principle.' What a foolish position both England and Austria find themselves placed in! These intriguers have been very clever—they emerge from their well-spun web covered with glory! A single word of the Emperor has scattered them to the winds! How imposing to Europe must be the sight of this Emperor at the head of his army assembled for a great and noble purpose. All our official documents are first-rate, the order of the day is admirable.

I really believe that I have not written to you since our peace with Persia was settled—and it deserved a passing word. It was grand, good, magnificent, such as Russia should always conclude, and it is in every way solidly arranged. In truth, the Emperor knows his business well.

The Duke of Wellington has been obliged to make himself a Liberal very much after the fashion in which Sgana-relle (in Molière's comedy) made himself a doctor.[2] The Lower House will no longer be satisfied with obscurantist theories, and in everything which concerns home politics the measures of the Government must be based upon enlightened principles, otherwise it will be unable to keep itself in power—and Wellington desires above everything to remain Prime Minister. The Catholic Emancipation Bill has passed the

---

[1] This was the declaration that Russia, if abandoned by her allies, would still proceed to carry out the Treaty alone, ' but she would consult her own interests and convenience as to the manner in which she would do so.'

[2] *Le Médecin malgré lui.*

Commons, but the Lords are going to throw it out. This struggle between the two Houses must have its usual ending, and in two or three years' time the Peers will no longer dare to say No!

On our business the most complete silence has so far been maintained by both parties, but at last it will be broken. Wilson [1] brings it forward this evening, and the debates will be curious.

The King is altogether well disposed towards us—if he could, he would ; [2] but Wellington is as obstinate as a mule. At the same time he will give way rather than give up his place. By the way, I think I told you last time that, for fear of tearing each other's hair, I never talk with him about our affairs. Scarcely had I finished my letter when we were already quarrelling so seriously that I at once put the scene on paper—and if I can find it I will enclose it with this letter. [3] It will show you the extent of his good will for Russia and the whole point of his logic. It is in this, as in everything else, ' This is, because I say so.' He gets no further than that. How delighted I should be to see him forced to flatter us.

This is a long letter for an invalid—for I am writing from my bed. Dear Alexander, I know the Emperor's great and good qualities, and I am afraid to find one bad one—but why will he forget that he owes it to us to be careful of his life ? This thought worries me—the duty of all of you is to remind him of this at all times, even though he should get angry. I pray for him daily, God knows with what fervour.

[1] Sir Robert Wilson, M.P. for Southwark, who was deprived of his military rank and decoration.

[2] ' They say that Madame de Lieven did really say something to the King about the change of his Ministry, and that his Majesty answered her that if his Ambassador at St. Petersburg should presume to criticise the conduct of the Emperor in the internal affairs of his Empire his Majesty would instantly recall him.'—*Croker Papers*, i. 423.

[3] Missing. Palmerston, writing to his brother, May 8, speaking of the members of the Cabinet and their attitude, writes : ' Ellenborough is even more adverse than the Duke ; Aberdeen is Austrian, and Bathurst anti-Russian and Austrian. All these would give anything to get out of the Greek Treaty, which they hate. The Duke, I believe, is in correspondence with Metternich and this to play his game of delay and procrastination.'— Evelyn Ashley's *Life*, vol. 3.

I embrace you, my dear brother. Write to me—or rather, make Constantine write to me, and remember how I prize every line from him. There was a sentence in your last letter which I have taken care to make known : ' If the Sultan had loyally been made to tremble, the Emperor would have stayed in his new house at Peterhoff! You—the Georges Dandins—have willed it ! '

At the moment of closing my letter I have had a visit from one of the Ministers after leaving the Cabinet Council. He tells me that the squabbling among them during the last two days has been greater than ever. Wellington violent against Russia, Huskisson as violent for her—and no decision of any kind arrived at. W. swears that the fleets shall not act again together, but he gives in on the question of Conference [1]—a fine Conference it will be, in face of such a resolution.

LXI

London : 6/18 June 1828.

The opportunity of a courier—for which I have been waiting impatiently for some time—has only been fulfilled to-day. I especially wanted to write to you, my dear Alexander, about Lord Heytesbury, and that my letter should precede his arrival at headquarters. He, however, has already started, and the messenger will not be despatched for some days : so that it is by Lord Heytesbury himself that I must tell you all the good I think of him. He is the most European Englishman of my acquaintance, the most straightforward diplomatist, and of all the Duke of Wellington's Ambassadors the one who holds the most enlightened opinions and the most conciliatory views, and he is, I might add, the most independent in politics. I think the Emperor will be well pleased with him. From all that I have heard from his own mouth and from others I should be disposed to think that he might be a most useful person-

---

[1] The Conference assembled in London in the course of the year, Prince Lieven representing Russia, Prince de Polignac France, and Lord Aberdeen Great Britain.

age at this juncture, and I therefore recommend him to you for a kindly welcome.

We are awaiting news of the Emperor—I mean, of his doings and goings—with eager anxiety. I have no thoughts but of him and of the war. Write to me, make Constantine write, or at least get someone to write for both of you. Just think of the fever you would be in if you were in London while the Emperor and his soldiers were campaigning on the Danube.

Good-bye, my dear Alexander, I embrace you most heartily.

LXII

London : 18/30 June 1828.

The opportunities of writing to you are so rare, dear Alexander, and my desire to do so is so great, that I am hungrily awaiting the courier. Possibly you will be less anxious to read than I am to write ; diplomacy must seem a stupid business when one is fighting. In a single march you may decide what it would take years to discuss—and what discussions ! with four different Ministries. For this is the situation—fall after fall, we are now landed in the arms of our declared enemies, and the proof that nothing is so satisfactory as an assured position is to be found in what is now going on. Wellington absolute master, Wellington the enemy of Russia, has suddenly become tractable. With Huskisson by his side he would do nothing, because Huskisson would have had the honour and glory of anything which might have been to our advantage. No sooner is Huskisson got rid of than the Duke ranges himself on our side. Why ? A variety of motives must be taken into account. He has knocked at every door, to the right as well as to the left—no one is disposed to attack us. His good friend Metternich even deserts him, because to do anything it is necessary to have the means, and England will not give him a shilling. The English Opposition is wholly on our side. Wellington is well aware of its relations with us ; he knows, too, that it is so well informed of the action of Russia that there are no means of hoodwinking it. Huskisson has in his hands the threads of all Wellington's dealings with our Court, and Huskisson is now an adversary not to be despised.

Portugal, moreover, is preparing complications far more dangerous for England than Eastern affairs are likely to become. All this comes upon the Duke at once, and so, like a very harlequin, he makes a pirouette, and what was black yesterday is white to-day. This is pitiable—almost contemptible—but it is delightful. One after another our enemies have had to humiliate themselves—a formidable coalition was being formed against us, and to-day all Europe is on its knees.

The conduct of the English Cabinet is really enough to make one laugh. We have had every sort of proof of its inconsequence and of its stupidity. Wellington thundered loudly against the idea even of sending a Plenipotentiary to us. 'Never,' as he grandly asserted, 'never will we support Russia's wicked aggression by the presence of our Ambassador.' Metternich sends M. de Homburg, and then, crack !—Heytesbury is hurried off. The '*Jamais*' of Wellington is familiar to us—his dictionary of the French language must be unique.

Lord Aberdeen is a wretched Minister : he is an honourable man, and nothing more.[1] At the best he is Chief Clerk in his office—but not more Minister of Foreign Affairs than I am. He has always been looked upon as Metternich's Seyid ; and consequently when, after his nomination, he asked me to give him an interview, I told him quite frankly that I was extremely sorry to see him Foreign Minister. He seemed a good deal annoyed by my attack, and by the motive which prompted it. He replied that he desired nothing better than that my words should be repeated in the House of Lords, for then he would find the opportunity of

---

[1] 'Among his colleagues, the Earl of Aberdeen stands distinguished (bold as the assertion may to some appear) for that union of feebleness with presumption, of incapacity in every other man's eyes with all-sufficiency in his own, which constitutes the ridiculous in character.'

publicly declaring that the charge made against him was altogether unfounded—that he was neither knave nor fool, and that one must be one or the other to have any regard for M. de Metternich.[1]   This is not bad for a beginning.

Wellington has managed to dominate the English nation, but whence he derives his prestige I know not.   For a week after the ministerial changes there was a kind of insurrection against those at headquarters who pretend to govern the State.   According to these malcontents, the Ministry would not last a couple of days.   Wellington made light of this outburst, took up an attitude of defiance, and his critics took fright.   Wellington, although thoroughly mediocre, is not without guile.   He fools the Ultras—he fools the Liberals still more, on the Catholic question—the latter are as completely satisfied that he will bring about their emancipation as the others are convinced of his unalterable intolerance.   It is quite clear that both parties are being duped ; meanwhile each defends with eagerness the honesty of the common patron of two hostile extremes of opinion. But as a matter of fact the people is easily deceived, and one comes naturally to such a conclusion when one sees this nation, reputed so staid and wise, becoming a puppet in the hands of so mediocre a Minister.   These mystifications of Wellington, however, must have their limit.   This Grand Vizierate is anti-constitutional.   It is also contrary to the real feelings of the nation,[2] which some fine day a man will arouse from its lethargy.

[1] Aberdeen called on Madame de Lieven to explain that he was not all in the interests of Metternich and Austria (*Palmerston's Journal*, June 8, 1828).   On June 12 Lord Palmerston writes : ' Lieven told me that the conferences had been resumed and were attended by the Duke as well as by Aberdeen ; but that the Duke's feelings of dislike to Russia have in no degree abated and that he is just as impracticable as ever.'

[2] Greville, writing on June 18, says that ' so far from the Duke's Government having any difficulty in standing, there does not appear to be a disposition in any quarter to oppose it.   Not only in Parliament there is no opposition, but the Press is veering round and treating him with great civility.   The Government seem well disposed to follow up the Liberal policy, to which they have been suspected of being adverse, and have already declared that they do not intend to deviate in their foreign or domestic policy from the principles on which the Government was understood to act previous to the separation.'—i. 134.

I have not yet told you the actual causes which led to the changes in the Cabinet, but my previous letters must have prepared you for them.

Wellington was at variance on nearly every question with his colleagues, each of whom was trying to upset the other, the stronger always proving that he had right on his side against his weaker rival.   There was nothing surprising in this, and the King took no part in the squabble.   He stood altogether aside, and therein, I think, he displayed his wisdom. He is careful to show himself equally polite to all parties, because he sees that before long he will have to turn to one other than that now in power.   He discussed all this with me the other day, and talked at length about his policy.   He does not like the Field Marshal, but he is obliged to put up with him.   He will not push him over, but he will not stoop to pick him up if he falls.   The King is always most amiable to us, expressing himself most friendly disposed towards our Emperor, whom he continues to trust, and thoroughly opposed to Metternich.   It is most praiseworthy of him to maintain this attitude, for besides his Grand-Vizier, his brother the Duke of Cumberland[1] stops his ears to any other influences.[2]   For us the latter is simply horrid, and acting throughout with the utmost duplicity.   The Duke of Clarence is ill-disposed also, but then he is half-imbecile.   On the other hand, the Dukes of Gloucester[3] and Sussex and Prince Leopold are all that can be desired.   In the Cabinet the only partisan we have is the Chancellor,[4] and he takes small part in politics.   He is the only man of real ability in the administration.   In point of fact, Wellington is simply the whole Government; if he breaks his nose (this literally

---

[1] See Appendix.

[2] 'In the middle of all this Madame de Lieven is supposed to have acted with great impertinence if not imprudence, and to have made use of the access she has to the King to say all sorts of things against the Duke and the present Government. Her dislike to the Duke has been increasing ever since that cessation of intimacy which was caused by Canning's accession to power, when she treated him very uncivilly in order to pay court to Canning.'—*Greville Memoirs*, i. 132–3 ; see also *Croker Papers*, i. 423.

[3] See Appendix.   [4] Lord Lyndhurst.

happened to him the other day, in falling from his horse) you may count upon the Ministry collapsing.

The Whigs are still for us, and are enjoying our successes. The mien of the Ultras was highly amusing when the news of these arrived.   They are always so *anxious* lest the Emperor should meet with serious difficulties—they are so fearful lest the plague should break out among our troops, &c., &c.   This is enough to make me laugh, and I am not sufficient diplomatist to conceal the fact that I am laughing at them.   This may be a mistake, but it is a little womanly enjoyment to which I must treat myself.

The passage of the Danube with the Emperor at the head of his army, confiding himself to the Zaporogians,[1] so recently his enemies, was a grand act, and I can understand the enthusiasm it evoked among the troops.   I hope to see all Europe share that enthusiasm, and it will shortly.   One cannot watch this drama, its origin, and its probable outcome without having one's nerves electrified ; but for God's sake watch carefully over the Emperor—that is my constant anxiety.

Dear Constantine, it is now to you that I address myself, for I really have not strength enough to write a second letter.   I have just received your letter of May 31–June 12, and wish to tell you how much pleasure it gave me ; for your letters are both interesting and precious to me—please go on sending them, as they are also very useful.   I show so much of them as is advisable to those whom it is judicious to inform. I pray for you, and for our great Emperor.   I take pleasure in the delight of our friends, and in the dismay of the fools — among whom, by the way, I reckon some knaves, 'the Original'[2] at their head.

I embrace you tenderly, my two brothers.   I do not wish to withdraw a single word of what I said about Lord Heytesbury in the letter which he brought you from me.   I am

---

[1] Or 'Dwellers beyond the Cataracts,' a tribe known as the Cossacks of the Dnieper.   In 1708 their Hetman, Ivan Stepanowitch Mazeppa, having joined Charles XII. against Peter the Great, they were deprived of privileges and military organisation.   A number of the tribe settled in the Balkan provinces.

[2] Lord Dudley.

satisfied that he will make himself popular with you all, if only
at Petersburg he is anything like what he showed himself to
us here.   He is strong, open, and above-board—he sees and
thinks with us on what is going on here, while on the
Eastern Question he is irreproachable.

Capo d'Istria's line of conduct in Greece is admirable, and
this is admitted even here.   Lord Aberdeen in conversation
expressed to me his appreciation.

[Dom Miguel's usurpation of the Portuguese throne had been
anticipated by our Minister, Sir F. Lamb, by whose orders the
British troops, which were under orders to return home, were
detained.   The Ministry, while approving this act, nevertheless
decided to recall the troops on the ground that it was not possible
for them to interfere in the internal affairs of another country.
This decision left Dom Miguel free, but the 'Constitutionalists'
determined on resistance.   The inhabitants of Oporto, supported
by the garrison and other regiments, declared for Dom Pedro
and marched on Lisbon ; but, instead of pushing on boldly and
seizing the capital, they halted on the banks of the Mondego to
await the arrival of help and a competent leader.   Dom Miguel thereupon collected his forces, attacked and defeated the Constitutionalists,
who fell back upon Oporto and afterwards retreated over the Spanish
frontier.   Oporto was declared to be blockaded, and the English
Government, while refusing to recognise Dom Miguel, acknowledged
the blockade.   The troops which had crossed the Spanish frontier
were not given up, but allowed to embark at Coruña for England.
All the European Powers withdrew their representatives from Lisbon,
and Dom Miguel was left unrestrained to deal with his subjects with
the utmost cruelty.

There was, moreover, a personal element in this Portuguese
question which cannot be altogether left out of account.   On the
final downfall of Napoleon John VI. had been continued on the
throne of Portugal, holding with it that of Brazil, where he continued
to reside.   Portuguese affairs were managed by a Regency of which
Lord Beresford, Wellington's nominee, was the most influential
member as well as Commander-in-Chief of the army.   During
Beresford's temporary absence in 1820 the revolutionary fever spread
from Spain to Portugal, and a Constitution was adopted by both
soldiers and people in which no place was left for Lord Beresford
and his English officers, who thereupon returned home.   Wellington,
who was but human, considered that he had been treated by the
Portuguese with the grossest ingratitude in return for what he had

done for them, and when Dom Miguel appeared on the scene and subsequently forced himself on to the throne, the Duke may not have been able to resist the temptation of allowing the ungrateful Portuguese to 'stew in their own juice.'

Meanwhile Wellington's attitude was provoking not only hostile criticism abroad, but much uneasiness at home. Although a member of the Cabinet which had signed the Treaty of London, and pretending to carry out Canning's policy, he withdrew as much as possible from the operations in favour of Greece, and devoted his efforts to protecting the interests of Turkey. He had consented to the dispatch of troops to Portugal, but on assuming the direction of the Government he recalled them and recognised Dom Miguel's blockade of Oporto, and had prevented Doña Maria's adherents, who had been brought to Plymouth, being despatched to the Azores for the protection of those islands. His policy had isolated Great Britain and weakened her voice in the European Concert. At the same time it must be recognised that the policy of the English Government was logical. Dom Miguel's seizure of the throne had been sanctioned by the Cortes (June 26), and by whatever means its vote may have been obtained it presumably represented public opinion. In the case of Greece, Sardinia, and Spain, Great Britain under Canning had refused to interfere in the internal affairs of the countries concerned, and the Whigs who had then supported that policy could not now effectively attack its application in the case of Portugal.

The question of Catholic Emancipation, having been temporarily shelved by the Lords' vote, was now directly brought before the Irish people by the changes in the Cabinet. Mr. Vesey Fitzgerald, on his appointment as President of the Board of Trade, had to seek re-election for the county of Clare. He was known to be in favour of the Catholic claims, and his seat was considered safe. The English Catholics, however, decided to put forward O'Connell, and to test the point whether a Catholic could sit and vote in Parliament without taking the oath. In the interval between the nomination and the election, the debate on Lord Lansdowne's resolution had taken place, and in its course the Duke of Wellington made a speech which conveyed the impression that, great as were the difficulties in the way of making changes, there was even greater danger in resisting them altogether. He recalled the fact that on a previous occasion when a Bill concerning the Roman Catholics in England was brought forward, it was allowed to pass almost without comment by the Irish Roman Catholics. 'If the public mind,' he concluded, 'was now suffered to be thus tranquil, if the agitators of Ireland would only leave the public mind at rest, the people would become more satisfied, and I certainly think it would be then possible to do something.' This speech led to a general impression that the Duke intended shortly to emancipate the Catholics as he had already relieved the Dissenters. So ambiguous a declaration, however, had no effect upon the result of the Clare election. Under the leadership of their priests the freeholders came to the polls in large numbers, and after a few days Mr. Fitzgerald withdrew. A protest was lodged at the time against O'Connell's return, but the sheriff certified that the election had been legally conducted, and the question of the member's admission to the House could not arise until it was seen whether or not he would take the oaths. The Session, however, had only three weeks to run, so O'Connell did not offer himself for admission before the recess.

The Clare election had, nevertheless, made the prompt settlement of the Catholic question imperative : for the power exercised by the Clare electors was in the hands of other electorates, as had been shown in the case of Waterford two years previously. The time for coercion had passed, and in the event of disorder the Government seriously distrusted even those upon whom it relied for support. Lord Anglesey, the Viceroy, saw that the moment for making concession had arrived, and his arguments convinced Peel, but Wellington still hesitated. Peel wished to resign,[1] but Wellington, recognising the difficulty of finding another leader of the Tories in the Lower House, was most anxious to retain him in office.]

LXIII

London : 2/14 July 1828.

I am beginning this letter to day, dear Alexander, although the courier is not starting at once, in order that I may be more certain to have the time to send you some lines when the occasion arrives. Where, I wonder, will the courier find you ? Will the Turks, the mountains, and the heat have allowed you to advance? Shall you bring matters to a close in this campaign? These are the questions that I am constantly putting to myself, and to which I find no satisfactory answer—except by repeating to myself the worth of our Emperor and his firmness of will. I have in him that blind faith which one places in Providence, and that enlightened faith which his imposing character inspires. In this way I calm myself—and wait, but not without raging of

---

[1] *Peel Memoirs*, i. 181.

spirit and stamping of feet. Here everything is marked by the most astonishing inertness ; to do nothing is the ruling principle of the Duke of Wellington's policy. This may do for a time, but that time, alas ! may extend to six months ; still it cannot last for long—difficulties accumulate daily, and must end in bringing him face to face with them.

In Portugal it is impossible to have compromised one's country more than England has done. She insults Dom Miguel by breaking off all diplomatic relations with him and recalling her Ambassador. She insults Dom Pedro by recognising the blockade of Oporto, and showing favour thereby to the Miguelist party. Nevertheless it is evident that the one or the other must be the legitimate ruler ; and so she disobliges both. But she will not get easily out of the mess. Spain, which to-day is trembling before the double danger of having a constitutional neighbour and of having to recognise a brother's usurpation (beware of Don Carlos !), will to-morrow be forced or disposed to intervene in the matter ; and for some motive or principle, whatever it may be, England will not dare to let Portugal become the prey of Spain without taking part in the scramble. Hence enormous expenditure, endless complications, and long anxiety for England.

In Ireland the state of affairs is delightful. Wellington seems to have supposed that he would satisfy the Catholics by his speech ; but they paid no attention to it, regarding it merely as a bit of unskilful knavery. And now Mr. O'Connell, professing the Catholic religion and chief of the Association, is going to oppose the re-election of Mr. Fitzgerald, who has just been appointed Cabinet Minister. At first sight this would seem an act of folly, inasmuch as, being a Catholic, he would be unable to take his seat ; but there is no law hindering his being elected. He therefore harangues the Catholics, stirs up the priests, and urges the Irish not to get drunk. This last injunction has set all England laughing. Who for a moment would think that the electors would obey it ? What happens ? An enormous meeting is held, no one drinks, no one fights ; the Minister is sent to the right-about, and the Catholic is returned by a majority of 1,300 votes. The

' London Gazette ' is obliged to announce that O'Connell has been elected member of Parliament, and the Minister returns as he went.   The example once set, the Catholics perceive that if they hold together they are the stronger side—a pleasing threat for an intolerant Government.   It may be all a farce, but it may end in a tragedy.   For the present O'Connell will not, it is said, present himself to Parliament. He will wait for next session to come and create a scandal at a more favourable moment.   The session is now drawing to a close ; everyone is going away, and no one wants to fight. If next session, when Wellington is bound to fulfil his pro- mise to do something for the Catholics, he should cite the case of O'Connell as proof of the danger of emancipating such a powerful body war will flare up in Ireland ; if, on the other hand, he gives way his Government will thereby be weakened, because it will be a concession extorted by force, so that in one way or the other the state of affairs is critical for the Ministry and perilous for England.   What conclusion do I draw, my dear Alexander ?   Well, this—all the better for us and all the better for the whole world.   This England is too insolent—she needs to have troubles, and she will have plenty.   This is for your ear alone, and so I am going to put this sheet under lock and key until I hand it to the courier.

LXIV

3/15 July.

While I was writing to you the despatch from Karassou of June 12/24 announcing the surrender of Hirsova and Kustendji arrived.[1]   Bravo ! bravo too for having managed to make mention of Wellington's regiment in the account. There was never a cleverer bit of irony than this ; all Europe will be laughing at his expense.   He will be the only person to take the matter seriously ; that is to say, he will be quite flattered at seeing his name associated with glory as far away as the Black Sea.

    I was unable to finish yesterday.   There will be arriving with you shortly an English officer, Lord Bingham, who will

---

[1] Two towns in the Dobrudscha which had been occupied by the Russians.

pass for being an officer in Lord Heytesbury's *suite*.[1]   He is a weak little man, a trifle stupid, to whom this favour has been accorded because he is pro-Turk—it was refused to Cradock because he is pro-Greek.   The truth is that Lord Bingham will be anything you wish, and will probably become enthusiastic about the Russian army.   He will be a peer some day.   His departure was quite kept secret by Wellington's orders, who had the idea that mothers here had designs upon his happiness or his fortune.

Dörnberg[2] is as good as gold.   I read the letters which he sends to the King : they are even better than if we ourselves had dictated them.   He is devoted to the Emperor, and understands him : he shrugs his shoulders at Wellington's policy. The latter has been made acquainted with the contents of these letters : he is annoyed, but has profited by them.   The Duke of Cambridge was the tell-tale.   This Duke of Cambridge is a trifle mad, but an honest man and wildly enthusiastic for the Emperor.   Münster is just as good as Dörnberg.

Lord Holland, impatient with the lethargy of Parliament, is going to make Ministers speak out about our affairs ; I am anticipating rare fun.   How awkward they will feel ; for the truth is that they court us because they cannot afford to quarrel with us.

Portugal is settled—Dom Miguel has made himself the master.   We shall remain wholly indifferent, and leave all the worry to the others.

How I am chattering ! and at a time when you are at Schumla, busy with more important matters.   I cannot help shuddering at the thought that fighting is going on, and the Emperor !   Do not let him forget that he is Emperor.

[1] Lord Bingham, afterwards third Earl of Lucan, an officer in the First Life Guards, was attached to General Woronzow's Staff; he commanded in 1854-5 a cavalry division in the Crimean War.   Lord Heytesbury accompanied the Emperor during the campaign in Bulgaria, not altogether to the satisfaction of the Russian Government, which held that the embassies should remain at the capital instead of following the Sovereign.

[2] Baron von Dörnberg, a Hanoverian diplomat, who acted as the Regent Münster's agent in London.

My health drags on from one day's bulletin to the next, for I can think of nothing else. The children are in the country ; I often go there too. My little George has become arch-Russian, with his tutor of a most redundant name.

Parliament will rise at the end of the month. The Duke of Wellington's health is a cause of some anxiety to his colleagues. He will do everything himself, he overwhelms himself : he is in everything, business, balls, and visits—in a word, he wishes to be the universal man.

The English Admiral who succeeds Codrington is the officer who early in his career was with Bonaparte at St. Helena,[1] and the only one of the English authorities of whom Bonaparte had a good word to say. He is a worthy man according to all reports. I do not know him, but I regret Codrington. I have heard countless pretty things said of our Admiral ; the whole English fleet is devoted to him on account of his straightforwardness and his conciliatory ways.

I stop, dear Alexander, because I cannot go on longer. Write to me, send me good news, for I am panting for some. My husband embraces you most affectionately.

LXV

London : 13/25 July 1828.

Dear Alexander,—Fighting the Turks is not everything : you ought to write and tell me about it, but since you left Petersburg you have not sent me a single line! The bulletins are admirable both in matter and style. Pray kiss the writer of them for me ; he is a man of intelligence. They tell everything without boasting, simply and with dignity. The last from Kurassow[2] (July 2 N.S.) is delightful, and the little summary appended to it may well give M. de Metternich and Co. the jaundice.

---

[1] Admiral Sir Pulteney Malcolm. He pleased Napoleon, who would talk with him for three or four hours at a time. He soon ceased to be on speaking terms with Sir Hudson Lowe.—Rosebery, *Napoleon*, pp. 32, 33.

[2] Probably identical with ' Karassou ' of the previous letter, and the headquarters of the Russian army in the Dobrudscha.

Read the debates in the Upper House which I mentioned in my last letter. How plain is the ill-will of the Ministry; but it matters not. In the Treaty they go beyond their intentions, and quite against their wishes. In fact, it is always Sganarelle; Sganarelle, by the way, is very much out of breath. He cannot sleep at night, he worries himself to death by day. At sixty that sort of thing cannot go on for long.

Ireland is giving the Government a good deal of trouble; there is a sense of remorse, and every day the sore grows worse.

Nothing can be more contemptible than the way in which Ministers have acted towards Portugal. Their pet, Dom Miguel, reigns, it is true, and in an absolute fashion, and my belief is that they are in a hurry to treat with him; but common decency prevents them from putting politeness aside. Palmella [1] will not let slip any opportunity of raising difficulties for England. He has come back persuaded that the real cause of the defeat of his side was the recognition of the blockade of Oporto by England, France, on the other hand, having declined to recognise it. It is curious to notice how in everything which deals with enlightened opinion France is always in the van and England in the rear.

Parliament rises the day after to-morrow, but probably not for long; Irish affairs may oblige it to meet again in the course of the autumn.

Write to me, my dear Alexander, if you do not wish to be wearied by this ever-recurring refrain. I embrace our dear Constantine, the refrain applies to him also.

Madame Bagration [2] has announced her visit to London;

[1] Palmella, the head of the Constitutional party, had applied in 1823 for British troops to give strength to his policy, and, although Lord Liverpool had then refused the request, the British fleet was sent to the Tagus. In 1826, in view of a threatened invasion of Portugal by Spain, Canning despatched a body of troops. Meanwhile, Palmella had come to England as the accredited Minister of Dom Pedro and the young Queen of Portugal. Later on Count Barbacena arrived as Chamberlain to Queen Doña Maria, claiming also to be Minister-Plenipotentiary for Dom Pedro.

[2] Princess Bagration, daughter of Count Paul Skravousky (Schavrousky), a great-niece of Prince Potemkin and widow of a Russian General, the last member

I will take care that she has no occasion to complain of or to praise me ; I am only sorry that such a bad sort should be Russian. Old Woronzow has aged very much, and I doubt if he can last much longer. I have aged also, but it is possible I may still go on, and in truth I should be sorry to bring things to an end.

There has been a serious quarrel recently between the Duke of Clarence and the Duke of Wellington.[1] Mr. Peel has also had a quarrel with the Prime Minister.[2] The little good which this Government does is due to Peel, who is an enlightened politician on every subject except the Catholic question. He holds his own against Wellington, who is afraid of breaking with him.

You must not infer that Peel is Russian ; but he insists upon a loyal and liberal policy.

LXVI

London : 10/22 August 1828.

My dear Alexander,—We are burning with impatience for news from Schumla ; but while awaiting its arrival and the courier's departure I will begin a letter to you, so that I may not be taken unawares at the last moment.

The Duke of Wellington perseveres in the more conciliatory and more urbane tone which he has recently adopted. Possibly he may hold to this course as long as he did to the contrary one. I do not trouble myself to decide whether his present tactics are the result of constraint or of conviction. Notwithstanding his mediocrity, he is not without a certain

of a family which had occupied the throne of Georgia for over a thousand years. She privately married, in 1834, Colonel Cradock (Caradoc), an attaché to the British Embassy at Paris, afterwards second Lord Howden and Ambassador at Madrid. She was possessed of an immense fortune, and at an early age had, by the Emperor's orders, been married to Prince Bagration as a reward for his military services. She lived in France and Italy, and was distinguished by her debts.

[1] This arose out of the Duke of Clarence's eccentric conduct at the Admiralty, but more especially in consequence of his behaviour towards Sir George Cockburn, one of the Lords of the Admiralty, which ended in the resignation of the Duke of Clarence as Lord High Admiral.

[2] Peel had supported Lord Anglesey's recommendation that the time was come to concede political equality to the Roman Catholics.

amount of cunning in his character ; but he has been so ill-disposed towards us that it will be a long time before his pleasant ways will have any influence on me.

He reverted to some of his former coquetries with me during our recent stay with the King at Windsor, where he came to spend the day. He was most attentive, and we talked on every subject except Turkey. He complained that I had treated him badly, that I did not invite him to come to see me as I did formerly—in a word, he endeavoured to entice me ; but I preserved my dignity, and most certainly I shall not again become the dupe of his sagacious demeanour, which is all he possesses.

The King is better disposed towards us than ever. He made me a long harangue the other day of which the whole burden was praise of the Emperor, and he added : ' I am determined to trust myself to him in all things, and I tell those who attempt to stuff my ears with contrary advice, " I promise you to distrust the Emperor Nicholas when he shall have deceived me, until then allow me to hold to my belief in him." ' He was very much delighted with the way in which the Emperor had expressed himself with regard to the Bruns-wick matter.[1] This affair greatly occupies his mind, and he has drawn a parallel between the Emperor's line of conduct and Metternich's, and, turning to some persons standing by, he said aloud in English, ' Nothing (is) so beautiful and loyal as the Emperor Nicholas's behaviour, and nothing so rascally as Metternich's.' Ask your friends what is the meaning of ' rascally ' in English, and you will see that the expression is pretty strong. Wellington was standing by and must have heard this remark. I told the King everything which was likely to maintain him in this excellent disposition and to arouse his vanity. At the same time he deserves from us the highest praise, for, as I think I have told you, everybody about him,

[1] Metternich had been active in attempting to bring about an amicable arrangement between the Duke of Brunswick and his subjects, the idea of any member of the Bund being called to account by his subjects being altogether repugnant to his mind, while the hope of gaining an anti-Prussian vote was not wholly absent from it.

except his lady,[1] is detestable.   Cumberland is truly infamous, and moreover has considerable influence with the King, but he has not succeeded in shaking the latter's opinions with regard to us.   He has now gone away, but has announced his intention of returning in November, with the object of showing himself in Parliament as the patron of the anti-Catholics.   In this connection he will do the greatest possible mischief.   The great aristocratic families will range themselves under his banner, the favour with which the King is supposed to look upon him will increase their numbers, and he will hamper the wise designs attributed to the Government on the Emancipation question.   He talks of putting down by force the spirit of rebellion in Ireland (rebellion indeed! when six millions of people are groaning under the proscription of their religion).   In other words, he wants civil war, for what he says comes to this : ' If we cannot subjugate them it is better to separate altogether from Ireland than to admit a single Catholic into Parliament.'   Such a view may lead to many difficulties, but all this is to our advantage.

Portugal, too, is good business for us, for she will give England interminable worries ; so much the better, but we need not hurry to extricate her from them.   Everything which hampers this country weakens her, and it is high time for her pride to be humbled.

I notice a great inclination to make much of Charles John,[2] and it does not require much wit to discover the reason.   I don't know if you have heard of the quarrel he has picked with Prince Gustavus about the title assumed by the Prince of Sweden.   Wellington spoke to me about the matter, saying that he wanted to settle to it (by the way, he is always eager to settle everything), that in point of fact the King of Sweden was in the right, and that all this fuss about the marriage with a Princess of the Netherlands was rubbish.   He said that he might have understood it had it been a question of keeping his daughter at home, but now ambition comes upon the

---

[1] Marchioness of Conyngham, who at this time, according to Greville, had been paying great attention to Madame de Lieven.

[2] Charles John XIV. (Bernadotte), King of Sweden.   See Appendix.

scene, and the Prince is detained at Vienna.   I replied that all
this was quite in M. de Metternich's own style ; to have at
hand a nursery of pretenders to draw from as opportunity
suggested—to use either as a bait or a menace.   'Bah, Bah,
Bah ! that would be bad policy ! '   'Do you find, then, that
he pursues a good one ? ' and he went off with a really hearty
laugh.

The Duke of Clarence cannot put up with the rough ways
of the Prime Minister, who wishes to control the naval
patronage.   The royal Prince desired to give promotion only
to those who had earned it, without reference to their
parliamentary influence.[1]   This, however, by no means meets
the view of the Government, and hence have sprung cavillings
and pin-prickings, which have ended in seriously annoying the
heir to the throne, so he has sent in his resignation, and hence
a scandal.[2]   It remains to be seen whether in this business
Ministers will gain as much in patronage as it causes them to
lose in popularity : for the nation was especially glad to see
the navy kept outside political influence.   I am sufficiently
cross-grained (that is, I have enough cause for righteous ill-
will against the Government) to be highly diverted by all
this squabbling, for I really do not like this Clarence.   He is
very ill-disposed towards Russia ; possibly he will be just the
reverse in a short time, for this is the way in which the
English are consequent to themselves.   How well I know
them since the last eighteen months.

You cannot believe how annoyed they are here with the
boastings of the French papers about the Expedition to the
Morea, yet in truth England deserves the contempt which
they throw upon her.[3]   What has she done for Greece ?   Or,

[1] This is endorsed by Greville, who says that the Duke's system of promotion
was more liberal and impartial than that of his predecessor (i. 140).

[2] The King's letter dismissing the Duke of Clarence from the office of Lord
High Admiral was dated August 11. Wellington told him that he must go, but
that he might resign if he preferred to do so, which he did. The reason alleged
was that he had exceeded his powers.— *Wellington Correspondence* (N.S.), iv. 595.

[3] 'During the month of March the Duke of Wellington said to several of the
foreign diplomatists in London : "If the French send a single soldier to the Morea,
I shall declare war with France." And yet in July he agrees to 20,000 men being
sent there !' ('Princess Lieven to Earl Grey,' August 6, 1828 ; *Corr.*, i. 122.)

rather, what has she not done against Greece ? And, after all, this powerful and wealthy England will not give a shilling or a man,[1] and is obliged to leave all the honour to others. Bad faith and impotency, these are the most distinctive attributes of the English Government ; straightforwardness and strength are ours. We may be well satisfied with our share, my dear Alexander, and I am quite pleased to be older than the Emperor. I shall think of that only for my country's sake.

LXVII

14/26 August.

At last the courier is about to start. I don't know what to add to my letter unless it be that my anxiety about Schumla increases every hour—it is in my heart and in my head—what is going on there ?

The Duke of Wellington has gone to Cheltenham to recruit. He is looking very ill. Prime Ministers don't live long ; his relations with the King are very uncomfortable, and a little embittered. He wishes to be the master, and the Master is obliged to hold his tongue for the nonce ; for Wellington is strong from the fact that there is no one to take his place—but his autocratic ways irritate the King. Pray tell Count Nesselrode the remark attributed to the King concerning this Prime Minister : 'King Arthur must go to the devil, or King George must go to Hanover.' Neither the one nor the other has yet started on his journey.

Lord Strangford,[2] a very hero of intrigue and confusion is being sent to unravel the most complicated question now before the world. You have no idea of the harm done to the Government by such a selection ! A man damaged in reputation in every way, whom Wellington, more than anybody else, has caused to be made known in the worst possible light. However, so much the better if the Portuguese business gets into a greater mess—and meanwhile there is

---

[1] A loan for 800,000l. had been contracted in London in 1824, and Lord Byron, Trelawney, and Colonel Stanhope were among many others who took up the Greek cause, and fought for it.

[2] See Appendix.

one more Turkish envoy the less in Europe.   The King does not get on at all with Lord Aberdeen.   He has even taken a very strong course on the occasion of his birthday by inviting Lord Dudley and leaving out the actual Minister of Foreign Affairs.   Esterhazy, too, was not invited, and has fallen ill of the annoyance of seeing such decided preference for Russia while Austria is ignored !   The King has very accurately gauged both the pleasure and the pain.

Good-bye, at last, dear Alexander—good-bye, dear Constantine.   May heaven preserve you both—may it watch over our Emperor and his glory.   It seems difficult to believe that it will not, yet my poor woman's heart is troubled and anxious.   I embrace you a thousand times with all my heart.   Do you know that you have not written me a single line since you left Petersburg ?

LXVIII

Richmond : 2/14 September 1828.

My dear Alexander, henceforth my only brother,—Last evening I learnt by a letter from Count Nesselrode to my husband the overwhelming tidings that our angelic Constantine had been snatched away.[1]   One after another I lose all whom I love—my cup of sorrow is indeed bitter.   That dear, dear Constantine, what a misfortune for us !   How I loved him, how good and tender he was to me !   Good Alexander, love me now more than you have ever done ; I have need of tenderness, of consolation ; no one but you can supply that natural tie of which my heart feels the need so keenly.   Poor dear Constantine, what will become of his poor children ? Did he think of them, did he know how much we should grieve for him ?   Dear Alexander, tell me all particulars, or get someone to send them to me.   I am as certain of your sorrow and of your regrets as I am of my own ; what a good

[1] General Constantine Benckendorff died of fever contracted during the campaign at Pravadi, at the taking of which place he had been in command. In the army, numbering about 120,000, which had invaded the Dobrudscha the hospital entries exceeded 210,000 in the nine months May 1828 to February 1829.

brave loyal creature was Constantine : what a treasure was his noble heart.

4/16 September.

I take up my letter to say always the same thing : write to me, dear brother. Tell me everything—all that bears upon the cause of our sorrow—tell me the day which we should the most bewail. Did anyone think of sending you some of his hair ? If so, share it with me, dear Alexander ; but do not send it except by a courier, I entreat you. Good Constantine dead in the midst of strangers ! he who loved so dearly everyone belonging to him ! Good Alexander, this is a loss for which we shall never console ourselves. The order of nature wills that we should lose our parents—but a brother, why need we be deprived of him so early ? How little we know what we wish, or why we wish it—I, who was so eager for this war, had I but known what it would cost me ! That is a regret which time will never efface.

My dear, dear Alexander, write to me, tell me about him, about his children. Love me, I beseech you.

Tell me where he is to be buried—oh ! sad, sad thought.

LXIX

Richmond : September 27/October 9 , 1828.

My dear Alexander,—What do you expect me to think of your silence at such a time ? From whom should I expect the sad but precious details, and some marks of affection, if not from you ? And you say never a word. I wrote to you four weeks ago as soon as I had received the sad, sad news. My grief to-day is as keen as on the first day—it is more bitter perhaps, because of the total ignorance in which I have been left of the last moments of our dear incomparable Constantine. I know nothing, and I want to know everything. I am miserable and neglected. How can you so forget me, dear Alexander ?

Everything is black around me, our affairs are going

badly. It was only natural to infer, as fear alone had made the English Government give way, that it would stiffen itself again as soon as the chances of war no longer smiled upon us. This it seems unhappily is the case just now. I seem to be in a dream when I hear of our great Emperor and our great army being brought to a standstill by a handful of barbarians, and that Europe is beginning to have doubts as to the power of Russia. I cannot understand what it means.

Wellington has gone back to all his former ill-will, or rather that ill-will which he had concealed only of necessity shows itself again without restraint. However, we may rest satisfied that the state of home affairs will prevent him from thinking of a foreign war. Nevertheless I firmly believe that without Ireland he would have drawn the sword against us the very day he learnt that the Emperor had resolved to blockade the Dardanelles. In this matter, moreover, public opinion is not on our side. The Government this summer laid such stress upon our renunciation of belligerent rights in the Mediterranean that it is now very difficult to know what to say to the public at this juncture. If only this complication might be turned to our interest—that is, if we could starve out Constantinople and force the Sultan to sue for peace—all might be well ; but, if it cannot be so adapted, we must be on our guard at every moment against the vengeance which England will think only proper to take upon us on account of the idea—a general idea at home and abroad—that she has been duped in this business.

The arrival of the little Queen of Portugal [1] in England adds another element of confusion to this strange business. However, her arrival is on the one hand an affront to Austria, and on the other a real political embarrassment for England. In this respect, therefore, it is good. That Austria continues to behave infamously towards us ; her delight makes me

<hr />

[1] The young Queen Doña Maria, aged nine years, had left Brazil before the news of Dom Miguel's usurpation was known. It met the Queen at Gibraltar, and in consequence her Chamberlain decided to bring her to England, instead of continuing her journey to Vienna, as originally intended. She arrived at Falmouth September 24, and was welcomed by a royal salute, and received by both the Portuguese and Brazilian Ministers resident in England.

all the more furious because we have never furnished her with the least cause of annoyance.

The King is still in bed. He is always deeply interested in whatever happens in our country, and will only believe news which is favourable to us.

Home affairs are in a veritable state of chaos. With prudence the Government might yet extricate itself, but the step is a difficult one. Ireland is arming—that is, the people. If nothing is done for the Catholics, an explosion is inevitable and stern repression will follow. If, on the other hand, their rights are recognised, the Tory aristocrats, the natural supporters of the Government will leave it in the lurch, and it must topple over. It looks like an inextricable dilemma. For my own part I look forward to a change of Ministry ; and it would not be wholly impossible for the Whigs to come in with Wellington as their leader, for as for principles he has none. If he can once persuade himself that emancipation is a necessary political measure, he will unite himself to the Whigs without a thought of his previous espousals.

Good-bye, my dear Alexander. What will become of those poor children ? Was there a will, and were there any arrangements made for their education ? Poor little Marie, who will take care of her ? If only it were I ! I am quite overwhelmed. I cannot reconcile myself to this cruel blow ; I weep every day as I wept on the first news.

Good-bye, my dear brother, I embrace you tenderly.

LXX

Richmond : 13/25 October 1828.

In losing that dear, dear Constantine I have lost both my brothers. You have been able to forget me, dear Alexander, at this sad moment. Does not your heart reproach you at all ? I am reduced to seeking from strangers details of my loss because my own brother refuses to send them. Your silence has increased my sorrow. May God pardon you !

I am writing to you because my husband is just sending

off a courier, and my heart will not allow me to treat you as you have treated me. Two lines even would have been an immense consolation for me!

Since my last letter I have had a long *tête-à-tête* with the Duke of Wellington. I found in him a remarkable change—much gentleness, and great friendliness. Speaking of the blockade of the Dardanelles,[1] he said that the Emperor was fully justified in declaring it, that he paid no heed to either newspapers or outcries, that he would be severely attacked in Parliament, but that he would know how to defend strongly what he told me. He expressed great regret that our operations were not progressing favourably, adding that 'there was no such thing as a little war; when once entered upon, it should always be regarded as a great and serious matter—that was the only way in which to conduct it satisfactorily. You have clearly begun the campaign with too few troops.' He went on to make a long speech about military affairs of which I understood nothing. He then went on to talk about his own position, which he asserted to be stronger than that which any Prime Minister had ever held in England. I amused myself a little at the expense of his ministerial colleagues, and laughingly he admitted that he had taken none but the imbeciles (what strange vanity!).

He discoursed at great length on the affairs of Portugal. He is furious about the coming of the Queen, furious against Barbacena, still more furious against Palmella, whom he accuses of being the author of all this intrigue.[2] He wishes the Queen to go to Vienna, and that Dom Miguel should marry her; in fact, he said enough to convince me that Barbacena will need strong nerves to resist the double attack

[1] Lord Aberdeen addressed to *Lloyd's* a letter dated October 1, 1828, announcing the blockade of the Dardanelles by Russia and its recognition by Great Britain.

[2] 'The arrival of this young Queen in England is the work of an intrigue, and is intended to give and will give us a good deal of trouble' (Memo. for Earl of Aberdeen by Duke of Wellington, September 19). Palmella had received credentials from Dom Pedro, Emperor of Brazil, to act as Ambassador for Doña Maria as Queen of Portugal. The Regent, Dom Miguel, had at the time no accredited agent in England. Subsequently M. d'Asseca was appointed as his representative.

made upon him by Lebzeltern [1] and the Duke of Wellington. I have not as yet seen this Lebzeltern. I am staying in the country, and am in no hurry about meeting him. The remarks of the Austrians about us are most insulting—but one may expect anything from that Cabinet and from the ' Seyids ' of M. de Metternich. To come back to Wellington, the impression left by his visit was that he was trying to deceive me by the calm and conciliatory tone in which he discussed our affairs—I am convinced of his ill-will towards us. His change of language can only be deceit. However, I took everything in good part and in complete innocence.

I have been to pay my respects to the little Queen of Portugal : [2] she is a charming child—like the Austrian family, but much prettier. Barbacena is absolute master, actually and formally. Palmella remains in the background—and is clever enough for both. As he is wanting in character, it is to be hoped that Barbacena has sufficient for two—a perfect equilibrium would thus be maintained.

I am making, as you see, a sort of gazette for you, for you say—when you say anything—that you like my letters to take this shape.

The English public and their newspapers are very ill-disposed towards us. If our campaign had been successful we should have had everyone on our side and the ill-wishers would have been reduced to silence ; as it is, there is a general loosening of tongues. This is somewhat hard to bear : but it will change. However, among the few ad-herents who still stick to us I should name at the head of them—Lord Holland ! Such is the world !

Good-bye, my dear Alexander. I cannot cease to love you, but I cannot, either, cease to complain.

P.S.—Defeat the Turks, for the love of God ! Europe is growing insubordinate since it thinks that we cannot do so.

---

[1] Lebzeltern had been despatched by Metternich to demand officially that Doña Maria should be sent to Vienna. To this Barbacena offered the strongest opposition. The English Government favoured the Austrian view.

[2] Her Majesty the Duchess of Oporto—as she was officially styled—was received at Plymouth by Lord Clinton and Sir William Fremantle, representing the King.

[The campaign undertaken by Russia against Turkey under the provisions of the Treaty of London was far more momentous politically than from a military point of view. The latter, however, had for its historian Major Moltke (afterwards Field-Marshal von Moltke), who had attempted the reorganisation of the Turkish army. In the first year of the war Russia took the field with a force variously estimated at from 100,000 to 150,000, under the command of Prince Wittgenstein, and crossed the Pruth in May 1828. After a few unimportant engagements, including the capture of Braila, the whole of Dobrudscha was practically in the hands of the Russians. An attempt, however, to capture Schumla, the key of the Balkan passes, was beyond the power of the Russian army, which, terribly decimated by disease, at length found some compensation in the occupation of Varna (October 10), which had surrendered after a protracted siege, but under circumstances which most unfairly gave rise to charges of corruption against the Turkish commander. In the West, how-ever, Wittgenstein had been unable to make any advance, and was obliged to recross the Danube and abandon the siege of Silistria and the greater part of Roumania. In the following spring Diebitch was appointed to the chief command (May 1829). He at once assumed the offensive and attacked the Turkish fortress of Silistria, and, having defeated the relieving force, forced it to surrender (July 6). With a portion of his forces he then pushed through the Balkans, turning the entrenched Turkish camp at Schumla and masking his advance. After a long and laborious march he found himself in the plains of Rumelia and within touch of the Russian transports in the Bay of Bourgas. Without delay, although his army had been reduced by disease to scarcely more than 20,000 men, he advanced on Adrianople. The Ottoman army, disorganised since the abolition of the Janissaries (1826), was unable to make a stand, and Mahmoud, imposed upon by Diebitch's determined attitude, sued for peace at the instance of Great Britain, Austria, and Prussia, who were equally misled as to the Russian General's position and the weakness of his forces. This situation, however, had not been reached without war with Russia having on more than one occasion been scarcely avoided. The blockade of the Dardanelles—which Russia, having at first waived, afterwards enforced as part of her belligerent rights under the Treaty of London—was not admitted by England until after much keen discussion, at one time nearly ending in a rupture. At the same time Metternich was anxious after the campaign of 1828 to force Russia to make peace with Turkey. He made overtures to the English Cabinet, and undertook to obtain the co-operation of Prussia, while England should make overtures to France in the same sense.

Prussia, however, refused to act against Russia, and France was equally indisposed to prescribe a rule of action for Russia or to take advantage of her difficulties. The campaign of 1829 completely changed the aspect of affairs, establishing the full rights of the victorious Power. The Treaty of Adrianople, signed September 14, imposed upon Turkey conditions which altered the face of European politics ; while the negotiations by which it was preceded and followed displaced the preponderance of Austria in Eastern Europe and of Great Britain in the councils of the Great Powers. Wellington's vacillations and Aberdeen's incompetence had obliged the British Ministry to abandon in turn every position it had taken up, and it had to submit to seeing the kingdom of Greece constituted upon lines which would bind her by feelings of gratitude and dependence to Russia. Wellington—who in this matter had abandoned the policy of Canning and followed his own instincts— found that he was wholly without influence, and he summed up the position of England when he wrote : ' The Greek affair was the most unfortunate in which Europe was ever engaged.' Wellington, in fact, having delivered Europe from thraldom to France, had unwittingly handed over not only Europe but Asia to the thraldom of Russia. He was unable to realise that Metternich's policy in Eastern Europe was doomed by the Treaty of Adrianople as clearly as that of Russia was established, that the attempt to constitute Turkey as a factor in European politics was antiquated, and that the best hope for England to make her voice heard was in unison with France and Russia.]

LXXI

Richmond : 12/24 November 1828.

Dear Alexander,—What a fresh misfortune for Russia, for the Emperor, and for us ! I am overwhelmed with grief, and my heart yearns for you as one who can best understand my trouble. At last your two letters from Varna have reached me. Pardon me my complainings and my doubts, dear brother, and do not throw reproaches at me. I have more need than ever of all your affection ; let no cloud ever come between us.

I am writing by the post, although my husband is busy getting ready a courier ; but I am impatient to let you know that I have received your letters, that they have done me good, and have given me as much pleasure as I am capable of enjoying.

I am anxious, too, to tell you what I have in my mind about that poor little Marie. My first feeling was the desire to have whole charge of her myself, and further reflection has strengthened the wish. Between us you and I will know how to extend to these dear children undivided care and attention. Let me, then, have Marie; I am sure that I can bring her up well, and I am still more sure that I shall love her.

Dear Alexander, your letters are a real comfort to me. You have no idea how necessary they are to me. I will write to you at length by the courier. I am very glad to think that you are in the bosom of your family; what a pleasure it must be to you. Paul writes to me that you have been to see him since his illness. I thank you most heartily, for I know the value of the visit of a man overwhelmed as you are with business.

I jumped for joy at the news of the taking of Varna. I am delighted to think that the Emperor is back again in his capital, and that he is taking a little rest.

Lord Bingham has come back enchanted with the Emperor and the Russians, quite as highly as he formerly was with the Turks; he is a poor little creature, but a babbler a talker, and this does not come amiss at the present time.

I embrace you, dear Alexander, you, and your wife and children and our dear Coco.

LXXII

Richmond: 16/28 November 1828.

Dear Alexander,—I wrote to you last Tuesday by the post, and to-day I am preparing this letter to go by the courier.

My first thought when writing to you is always our troubles; the terrible losses we have suffered, first our dear Constantine, then our adorable Empress Mother. [1] The latter

---

[1] The Empress-Dowager, widow of the Emperor Paul I., was Princess Sophia Dorothea of Würtemberg, 'She was a Sister of Charity enthroned as an Empress.' Madame de Lieven had been in the habit of sending her weekly a

sorrow arouses many sad thoughts, for with her Russia sees a whole century disappear.

The present is a rare opportunity, and I wish to take advantage of it. England is not a whit better disposed towards us than she has ever been ; she is worked upon incessantly by Austria, but this influence has made her burn her fingers in an unexpected fashion. At the moment of what is here called our disasters, this Austria was stirring up a crusade to destroy us, so this *magnanimous* and *generous* England thought the moment most propitious. She, however, met with a strong rebuff at Paris, where they thought differently ; and at the same time she sees that we are rising from our ashes, and she is not a little ashamed of having been so completely deceived. In future she will not believe quite so easily that we have no longer an army to fight with, nor will she be so ready to endorse blindfold de Metternich's hatred of Russia. Nevertheless she is still dangerous, because she is stupid ; but we shall surmount the danger because we are clever. Our Emperor displays his wisdom in the course he indicates to his Cabinet. There is much cleverness in this course, and it is worth something more than all the finessing of the Austrian Chancellor.

Talking of him, I should tell you that his Lebzeltern has never dared to face me. I have only seen him once when he was dining with us.[1] He only came up to me to make his bow. Do you recollect his former eager attentions? Now I am the great bugbear of everything connected with this Austria, that is because they are aware that I know them too well.

Lord Aberdeen is a poor diplomatist—there is no sort of plain-speaking which he will not listen to from me. He is easy enough to convince, but that profits nothing. He is

letter on English politics and society. These letters have been preserved but have not been published.

[1] 'I saw him yesterday ; his language is greatly altered. . . . He said to me : "I have fulfilled the object of my mission. I came here to learn the reason why the destination of the Queen's voyage had been changed, and now that I know the reason I am returning to Vienna." ' ('Princess Lieven to Earl Grey,' October 29, 1828 ; *Correspondence*, i. 175.)

merely Wellington's chief secretary ; in order to make any
real use of him, one must begin by getting him to revolt
against his leader.   Now his leader is the most obstinate
mule I have ever known.   I no longer argue with him—I let
him talk, and listen, and in this way I have been able to un-
mask his hostility to us and his devotion to Metternich.
Sometimes, however, he endeavours to draw me out, as, for
instance, when he regrets that we do not continue the war
through the winter.   ' It's a pity—you would be able to
crush the Turks ; you ought to march along the coast to
Adrianople,' and other similar remarks.   Then he assures
me that Wittgenstein's army before Schumla has been
destroyed.   I do my best not to lose patience.   Last August
he was ready to bet his head that we should never take
Varna.   Lord Bingham frequently makes statements which
do us good ; these, joined to what Count Nesselrode writes
from Odessa, have somewhat soothed the alarms of the
British.   My dear Alexander, let us be moderate, but at the
same time let us be firm ; let Russia never swallow one of her
promises ; and let her beat the Turks next spring.   Then we
shall see that this little moral insurrection which was raising
its head in Europe will be completely crushed.   The nations
have dared to doubt our power—this thought must not be
allowed to exist.

The English Government thinks itself strong because
nobody attacks it.   The Duke of Wellington, with his usual
boastfulness, said to me the other day : ' I am the most
popular Minister that England has ever seen ; take my word for
it, I am very strong.'   If he takes as his measure the passivity
of Parliament last session, he is greatly deceived.   It is the
rule always to give a trial to a new Ministry ; it is watched
for a while, until parties class themselves ; and next session
things will go very differently.   But just see how singular
the situation is.   Lord Aberdeen, among his other innocent
indiscretions, gave me clearly to understand that the Catholics
would get their Emancipation ; consequently the Ministry will
have all the Ultras against them, and will have to fraternise with
the Whigs.   This is absolutely certain upon this question,

but on all matters of foreign policy the case is just the opposite, and hence will arise the strangest confusion. Meanwhile, who knows what the Protestant leaven may not do, if Emancipation is only proposed! Instead of a civil war in Ireland, it might break out here—I am speaking of possibilities, and even of probabilities, but circumstances may upset my warnings. Whatever happens, the Ministry will have a serious business on its hands at home, and that is enough to reassure us as to any warlike leanings.

Dom Miguel's broken leg is a most happy accident.[1] The English Ministry fear that it may prove fatal; for my part I hope it may; first because it is permissible to wish evil to a man who has shown such capacity for doing it, and secondly because his death would create an imbroglio in Portugal greater than what already exists there. It seems altogether beyond doubt that the apostolic faction at Lisbon would begin by placing Dom Sebastian[2] on the throne, making the old Queen Regent. Spain will step in to help them, and this is the *hic* of both England and France. Nothing could suit us better than circumstances which would bring them into collision ; I confess that I do not like their present intimacy—it is closer than you imagine. This French Ministry[3] with all its good disposition towards us, seems to me the very counterpart of Lord Goderich's of last year—anxious seriously to do good, and walking straight into everything that is bad. Let us hope that at least the one will not end like the other, with M. de Villèle acting the part of the Duke of Wellington.

The English Cabinet is extremely proud of the evacuation of the Morea, for it felt itself humiliated by the presence of French troops on Greek soil. Taken all in all this Treaty and its consequences have hung on the Ministry like the ears

---

[1] Dom Miguel was thrown from his carriage (November 9) and his leg was broken above the knee.

[2] A nephew of Dom Miguel, his elder sister, the Princess of Beira, having married the Infante Pedro Charles.

[3] On the resignation of the Villèle Ministry early in the year, a step towards conciliation was grudgingly made by Charles X., who entrusted the formation of a Cabinet to M. de Martignac, of the Liberal Right Centre, which carried several Liberal reforms.

on a donkey. It hopes now to have got rid of the matter,
and that nothing will throw further obstacles in the way of its
eager ardour for the Sultan. Ah ! if only we could have
brought our war to an end in one campaign ! But let us put
away regrets and let us now put forth our full strength, and
keep ourselves within the limits of a diplomacy of prudence ;
then winter and M. de Metternich's intrigues will in the
course of time disappear before us. . . .

As you are now back again in Petersburg I will write to
you regularly by the post, and by the couriers also into the
bargain. My letters shall be despatched regularly every
week ; I will make it a strict rule with you, as I did with our
good Constantine. If on your part it were possible to write
me two words at least every fortnight, it would be an immense
boon to me. You write so easily that it could not give you
much trouble, nor cause the loss of much time. Tell me of
anything likely to interest me, tell me about our dear Emperor,
about our angelic Empress. How keenly can I realise
their sorrow and their regrets—what a loss for them as for all
the world. For, not looking beyond her daily duty, what a
useful helpmate was our Empress continuing by her own
choice the burden of a daily reception—a reception which was
wearisome perhaps for the *ennuyés*, but most necessary for a
great Court giving pleasure to the older people and attaching
them to the Court. Then, again, she was a Sister of Charity
upon the throne ! an inexhaustible source of good and useful
works. In truth one cannot too much deplore such a loss.
Think, too, of us, dear Alexander, for whom she has ever
been so maternal and so thoughtful.

I shall await with impatience your decision with reference
to Marie. Let us, you and I, be really father and mother to
those poor children. It is a duty of which we both feel the
obligation in our inmost hearts. May God bless you and keep
you, dear Alexander. I embrace your wife, and desire that
you should both love me. . . .

I must not forget to repeat to you Lord Bingham's
admiration and gratitude, of which a large share is devoted to

the Emperor [1]—but there remains plenty for you also.   He
wished to make out that so far as you were concerned his
reception was due to my recommendation.   I told him
that he was altogether mistaken, for all that I had said of
him (in writing to you) was that he was Turk.   To this he
replied that if I had told the truth of him then, I owed it to
him to say now that he is altogether Russian, and this is
really the truth.

What a long letter, dear Alexander—but patience, I do
not intend to close it until the moment of the courier's
starting.

November 19
December 1

What an anniversary is to-day![2]   I recall what Prince
Metternich wrote to me the day on which the news of the
Emperor Alexander's death reached him: 'The romance is
ended—we are entering upon history.'   The saying was clever
and true.   The courier does not leave until to-morrow—but
I am feeling so ill that I fear I may not be able to add
anything if I do not do so now, and yet it seems to me
that I have said everything.

The King's health is not good, he is changed for the
worse since the summer.   The Duke of Clarence is in danger
every fortnight with an intestinal 'revolution,' and the public
grows anxious.   No member of the royal family has yet
seen the Queen of Portugal—this is an affront in addition to
the harm they wish to do her.

The Duke of Wellington insists that the three thousand
Portuguese refugees assembled at Plymouth should be dispersed, but if I mistake not Palmella and Barbacena between
them will find means of creating worry out of this demand.[3]
They have offered to transport them to Brazil rather than

---

[1] The Emperor conferred upon him the Order of St. Anne of Russia.

[2] Alexander I. died at Taganrog December 1 (N.S.), 1825.

[3] Dom Miguel remonstrated against their presence in England, and Palmella,
advised by Brougham, urged that as they could not be legally allowed to encamp in
British territory they should be sent to the Açores, Portuguese islands which
had declared for Doña Maria.   To this Wellington objected, but subsequently
offered to convey the refugees, as private individuals, to Brazil under the convoy
of a British man-of-war, which Palmella refused.—Walpole, *History of England*,
ii. 577-8.

that they should be treated as prisoners of war. Thereupon Wellington proposes that they should be sent in English ships. Palmella declines the honour ; each abuses the other; correspondence begins, disputes follow, the public is promptly informed of the whole business, and on this question at all events is totally at variance with the Government : for there is but one voice not raised against Dom Miguel. Wellington is as fond of him as of the Sultan, and for similar reasons.

By the way, Lord Strangford just before starting for Brazil began an action for libel against the editor of a newspaper who had called him a liar. The cause has just been heard.[1] The judge decided that it was impossible to prove that he was not a liar, and declined to admit his affidavit. Brougham was on the opposite side, and the case has amused everybody. Lord Aberdeen laughs with the others, and says that at all events he did not make him (Lord Strangford) an Ambassador. The protection shown by Wellington to Lord Strangford is one of the things which causes the greatest outcry against the former. Lord Holland is bestirring himself to organise a strong opposition to the Government—we shall see what will come of it.

Good-bye, then, dear Alexander, for I shudder at finding myself at the end of my third sheet. Write to me, love me—I shall never cease imploring you to do both.

Here is an English almanack for your wife ; I am sending a small collection to the Empress by the same occasion. Alas ! I have no longer a letter to write to our good Empress Mother, and I have to break with a custom of eighteen years' standing. You have no conception how much I feel this sorrow. I repeat, my good brother, I have only you in the world.

As I am in the way of almanacks I am sending one to Count Nesselrode. So please tell him so, with my love.

---

[1] The *Sun* newspaper charged Lord Strangford with no regard for truth, he having quoted from a despatch as dated from the Tagus, which in fact had been written by him after his arrival in London. Lord Strangford took proceedings against the paper, but, being unable to deny the fact on which the charge was founded, was non-suited. See Appendix.

LXXIII

Richmond : 3/15 December 1828.

My son assured me three weeks ago that you were writing to me by the post. I have been impatiently awaiting your letter, dear Alexander, in hopes that it might bring me your opinion as to what should be done with Marie, or, in other words, your decision to entrust her to me. Meanwhile, your letter not having reached me, my fear is that you should have put it into the post without marking on it ' By way of Holland,' and if so it has undoubtedly been sent by way of Sweden, in which case it will probably not reach me for another two months. Do be careful in writing to me to put always '*viâ* Holland' on the outside of your letters, it is the only way of their reaching me in reasonable time.

I am greatly distressed about our retreat from before Silistria.[1] It will have the very worst effect for us in every European capital, and particularly here, where the insolence of the newspapers is without limit. I should dearly love to be able to jump over the winter in a single bound, so that we might make all the world alter its tone.

The approach of the session is stirring all parties to activity. The Catholic question is the foremost in importance and interest for this country. The Duke of Wellington allows the greatest uncertainty to prevail as to his intentions on the subject, and this leaves both parties balanced between hope and fear. The King has returned to Windsor Castle, and his health just now is excellent.

Dom Miguel is not dead : this is a disappointment. The Portuguese who had taken refuge in England are on the point of starting for Brazil.

I am, and my husband is, very impatient with all these delays in the settlement of my late mother-in-law's estate. We believed that Paul would be arriving here almost immediately, but a letter received from him to-day puts off everything to the Greek Kalends. I am so much obliged to

---

[1] The Russians were forced to abandon the siege of Silistria and to recross the Danube, leaving a great portion of their baggage in the hands of the Turks.

you, dear Alexander, for the kindness you showed to Paul during his illness. I beseech you to decide to let me have that dear little Marie ; it will be a new life for me and an interest and an occupation for every moment, which will be an advantage for her and a happiness for me. If our dear Constantine left any written wishes, let me know of them and send me a copy.

How eagerly anxious I am to have news of you after this great misfortune which overwhelms us all ! I cannot get over the idea that that good Empress is not still with us.

There will be several shiftings in the Ministry here, but these are details which have little importance. As for the policy of the Government, it expresses itself solely in the person of the Duke of Wellington. It is said that among others Lord Dudley will re-enter the Cabinet.[1]

Farewell, my dear Alexander. I embrace you heartily, and repeat my constant prayer to write to me and to love me.

LXXIV

Richmond : December 24, 1828.
            January 5, 1829

Dear Alexander,—We came back here yesterday from Windsor—I have never passed so pleasant a time there. The King had got together a delightful party, just the very people with whom I am on the most intimate footing. He was altogether gracious, attentive, and amiable to everybody, especially to us, and full of good wishes for the interests of Russia. He talked to me a great deal about our Emperor ; and he seemed excessively pleased by the Emperor's attention in sending him the model of a salon in Scagliola. He has given it a place of honour in the Long Gallery. The malachite vase which our good Empress sent him some months ago is now the chief ornament of the best drawing-room. He has obviously taken great trouble to place these objects in evidence, in fact it would not have been possible to be more amiable than he was. I am rather troubled, however, by the apparent state of weakness in which his last attack

---

[1] The return of the Canningites to office did not take place on this occasion.

has left him ; nevertheless I hope and believe that he will soon regain strength.

In London they are much disturbed by the sudden recall of the Irish Viceroy.[1] Certainly it is an important event ; the Catholics were looking to him as their protector, and his departure will cause a good deal of noise, if nothing worse. You know that it was the Marquess of Anglesey who occupied this post, the noblest and most honourable of men in England. The little Queen of Portugal is now being petted by all the members of the royal family. The King spoke of her to me with the liveliest interest, saying he was altogether delighted with her. It seems that these Portuguese refugees wish to be sent to Terceira, but that the English Government will not permit them. This is the more strange since at Terceira everybody is devoted to Donna Maria.

My dear Alexander, do write to me about our little Marie's affairs. Let me have her with me, you may be sure that she will be the object of all my care and love. Tell me, I pray, about the Empress's health ; how all these sad ceremonies must have tried her ! I can scarcely bring myself yet to believe that we have lost the incomparable Empress Mother. What lifelong regrets are ours ! How deeply our dear Emperor must feel his loss !

The Duke of Devonshire was with us at Windsor—the King treats him with the same friendliness as formerly. The Granvilles were also there, some other friends of Canning, and a few Whigs. Windsor Castle is a magnificent place. Pardon this wretched scrawl. I am writing in a desperate hurry, why don't you imitate me sometimes ? Farewell, my dear brother. I embrace you with all my heart.

[The removal of the Marquess of Anglesey from the Viceroyalty of Ireland arose from the differences of opinion which had arisen between him and the Duke upon various points more or less remotely connected with Catholic Emancipation. On the forma-

---

[1] Lord Anglesey was recalled in consequence of a difference of opinion with the Duke of Wellington as to the policy to be adopted towards the Irish Catholics. The quarrel was complicated by personal disagreement.— *Wellington Letters*, v. 244, &c.

tion of Wellington's Government he had been named Lord Lieutenant of Ireland in succession to Lord Wellesley. The Clare election had promptly convinced him that order and possibly security could not be preserved in Ireland if some concession were not speedily made to the demands of the Catholic Association. Possibly without O'Connell's display of his influence a collision between the rival partisans of Protestantism and Catholicism would have occurred, for the English Ministry, divided on the question of Emancipation, gave no instructions to the Viceroy. At any rate, Lord Anglesey resented the suggestion that certain justices should be removed from the Commission of the Peace on account of their conduct during the Clare election. Other events supervened, including the un-authorised publication of a letter from the Duke of Wellington to Dr. Curtis, the Roman Catholic Primate of Ireland, and it became evident that the Viceroy had anticipated the intentions of the Cabinet and the wishes of the King in his attitude towards O'Connell and the leaders of the Catholic Association. The Duke of Wellington had not yet made up his mind that the moment for concession had arrived, and he resented the fact that the Marquess of Anglesey should have done anything to pledge the Cabinet. It was easy to prejudice the King's mind on the Catholic question, and it required but little strategy on the part of the Duke and his henchmen in the Cabinet to make it understood that the Viceroy was being recalled or dismissed by the King instead of because he had quarrelled with the Duke.]

1829

VISIT OF THE QUEEN OF PORTUGAL—DUKE OF CUMBERLAND'S UN-
POPULARITY—CATHOLIC EMANCIPATION BILL—RUSSIAN CAMPAIGN
IN THE BALKANS—THE TREATY OF ADRIANOPLE—PROTOCOL ON
GREEK AFFAIRS—LORD ABERDEEN'S POLICY

[The following letters deal with one of the most important phases
of Madame de Lieven's stay in England, and her conduct during the
period has been the subject of controversy.   Sir Spencer Walpole,
on the authority of the ' Wellington Correspondence,' asserts that
Madame de Lieven engaged in a plot with the Duke of Cumberland
for Wellington's dismissal, and adds that her conduct produced a
coolness between the British and Russian Governments.   Greville,
who was in no way favourably disposed towards Wellington, makes a
somewhat similar statement.   He says that Madame de Lieven, out
of hatred to Wellington, who was thoroughly anti-Russian, had allied
herself with the Duke of Cumberland with the view of overthrowing
Wellington.   He adds that she was the medium between the Duke
of Cumberland and the Huskisson party, who were apparently as
much opposed to the Duke on the Catholic question as were the Ultra-
Tories.   Moreover, Lord Aberdeen, writing to the Duke of Wellington (July 21, 1829), says : ' Polignac dwelt very strongly upon the
proceedings of the Duke of Cumberland and their effect.   He thinks
Madame de Lieven is intimately concerned in the whole of his plans,
and that his stay in this country and the arrival of the Duchess are
concerted with her.   He thinks Madame de Lieven's influence
with the King himself is very great, and repeated a speech of his
respecting her which he (Polignac) had heard and within these very few
days (I take it for granted from Madame d'Escars), " qu'elle était la
bête la plus forte en politique en ce pays-ci."   I succeeded in
undeceiving her respecting Madame de Lieven and her influence.' [1]
Two days later Lord Aberdeen again writes : ' From all I can hear
there can be no doubt of her having counselled the proceedings of
the Duke of Cumberland and the visit of the Duchess.   Leopold
told me yesterday that the Duke of Cumberland's remaining was the

[1] *Wellington Correspondence*, vi. 35.

King's doing . . . that his intention was to leave England immediately, but that he stayed at the King's request and that the Duchess
was sent for by his desire.'[1]   This, therefore, it may be assumed, was
the Court gossip of the day, and was current before Wellington's
firm conviction as to its truth.[2]   On the other hand, throughout this
correspondence with her brother (of which Count Nesselrode alone
would have cognisance), the terms in which she speaks of the Duke of
Cumberland scarcely suggest the idea of an intimate alliance between
them, although it is not improbable that so astute a lady may have easily
obtained the confidence of a headstrong obstinate man like the Duke.
Lord Aberdeen, too, thought it necessary to modify his views within
a week of having expressed them so decidedly.   He writes again
to the Duke of Wellington (July 28) : 'With respect to domestic
matters, I am inclined to think that we give the Princess credit for
more activity than she deserves.   That she would do us all the mischief
in her power is most certain, but the knowledge of this makes us apt
to think her at the bottom of every intrigue.   Madame de Lieven
denied so strenuously all share in the Duke of Cumberland's plans,
and so strongly professed her entire ignorance of what he proposed to
do, she so naturally and earnestly described the annoyance of listening
to his repeated grievances and his unmeaning declarations of hostility,
that I am inclined to believe that she does not act in concert with him,
although she might not be sorry to take advantage of their success.
She truly observed, however, that if his success were possible it
would be fatal to anything like a favourable feeling towards Russia
in this country.'[3]   The Russian Government was probably desirous
for the downfall of Wellington, who had stopped the march of its
army on Constantinople, believing that in the event of the Whigs
coming into power a less antagonistic policy would prevail, notwithstanding their repudiation of Canning's Russian policy ; but it is
difficult to suppose that the Duke of Cumberland was so blinded by
prejudice as to imagine that Madame de Lieven could sympathise
with his Protestant bigotry, or that she had any illusions as to his
preference for the foreign policy of the Whigs or of the Canningites.[4]

---

[1] *Wellington Correspondence*, vi. 40.
[2] Walpole, *History of England*, ii. 570.
[3] *Wellington Correspondence*, vi. 58.
[4] In a letter dated August 21, 1829, addressed to Lord Grey, Madame de
Lieven writes with reference to the correspondence which had been going on
between the Duke of Cumberland and the Lord Chancellor (Lyndhurst), a copy of
which Madame de Lieven was sending to Lord Grey : 'I am not sufficiently
in favour with your Ministers for me to wish this further sin to be added
to my charge.   On the other hand, I think I owe it to the many years of
friendship which the Duke of Cumberland has shown me to do him justice

It is, of course, possible that Madame de Lieven in her eager desire to damage the Duke of Wellington may have been willing *faire flèche de tout bois* ; but it is more likely that she was dissatisfied with the position she found herself in, and was aware that her own Government were informed that all was not going on smoothly between the Russian Embassy and English society, as distinguished from the British Government.   The reference to Buckhausen being summoned to St. Petersburg is followed very closely by the notice of Matuscevitz' arrival in London, who was being sent nominally as Ambassador Extraordinary to assist M. de Lieven, but in the opinion of the Duke of Wellington was ' to overhaul' him, in accordance with a recognised custom of the Russian diplomatic service.

The Emperor of Russia at the same time had been seriously annoyed by the tone of the English newspapers, and M. de Lieven had been instructed to call the attention of the British Government to the terms in which its ally was spoken of.   As the campaign in Eastern Europe progressed more favourably for Russia the tone of the newspapers became less hostile, although our own Government was forced to recede from nearly every position it had originally taken up with regard to Greece and the Danubian Principalities, and to submit to the dictation of Russia, whose troops were within striking distance of Constantinople.]

LXXV

London : 3/15 January 1829.

You leave me, dear Alexander, without a word of reply to the innumerable letters I write to you.   Since Varna I have not received a single line ; Heaven knows that I should love you even more if you could only love me and tell me so ; but my reproaches fall upon deaf ears, I get nothing by

when the opportunity presents itself; and I think in the present instance he has a clear case in his favour' (*Correspondence*, i. 277–8).   The fact that this correspondence was shown to Madame de Lieven, who made a copy of it, would, however, suggest that she was on terms of intimacy with one of the writers, and Lord Grey more than once, in writing to Madame de Lieven, refers to the Duke of Cumberland as ' your friend.'   On the actual question of the Duke of Cumberland's constant visits to Windsor and their import, Madame de Lieven writes to Lord Grey : ' Your speculations about party intrigues, and of their being likely to come to anything, appear to me the reverse of probable . . . you may be perfectly sure that I shall keep out of it all. . . . In short, to *know* everything and to meddle in nothing are my chief duties. After which exordium I will tell you, on my conscience, that I know nothing, and that I think nothing is being plotted.   I will say more, I am far from wishing it ' (i. 367).

them, and I will indulge in them no more.   For the love of
God, however, do make somebody reply to me about little
Marie.   Are you going to let me have her with me ?   I have
grown to that hope, and I shall be unhappy if I have to give
it up.

I sent you through the post a few general details about
our stay at Windsor ; but I kept back the more intimate
ones for a safer opportunity.   The King, when talking to me,
began by complaining bitterly of the abominable lies in the
newspapers about our supposed disasters, and he went on
to say that he no longer read these articles, so much did they
irritate and disgust him.   I said to him that, considering
their source, they did not surprise me.   Thereupon he began
to discuss their source (Metternich), and spoke of him as he
deserves—as a man without belief or respect for law, or for
his own word, in fact there was no iniquity of which
he did not believe him to be capable.   I replied that it was
much to be regretted that such was precisely the man who
was giving a lead to the English Cabinet.   Whereupon he
exclaimed : ' Blindness and inclination I admit, but I do not
allow that he can make us carry out his wishes.   If we were
to follow him we should be setting Europe on fire at the four
corners ; I give you my word that this shall not be—that we
take no part in his schemes, and will take none.   Be quite
assured of this.   Wellington is far too prudent for that, in
fact you may take as absolutely sure and true what I am
telling you.'   The emphasis with which he said this to me
gives me an absolute conviction of his sincerity.   He is
everything we could desire, both for the Emperor and for
Russia, and possibly he may show it all the more because his
Ministers are so ill-disposed.   This is one of the best sides of
the King's character ; it disturbs him very little to find himself in contradiction with the wishes of the members of his
Cabinet, when they seem to him not to be acting in a generous and honourable way.   It is on this account that he has
displayed the greatest respect for and the greatest interest in
the Queen of Portugal, to the intense annoyance of his
Ministers.   In fact, this little Queen has quite gained his

heart, and he told me that he always added to his prayers his wishes for her cause. From this you may imagine that the King and his Cabinet make a strange *ménage*. Even this visit of ours to the King is a curious affair ; we alone representing the diplomatic corps, and not a single Minister, but all Canning's friends and some Whigs with whom we are intimate. No wonder, then, that it was said that our set only was invited and nobody outside it ; and this was on the occasion of the New Year's festivities and of the inauguration of the Castle,[1] none preceding and none following us—that is, no one had been there previously, no one has been there since. It was not possible to have contrived anything more significant to his Ministers. In fact, the malice of the affair was cleverly conceived. The King made me clearly understand his repugnance to the present administration ; his regret for the Whigs, his wish for their return. At the same time, however, I found him quite a fanatic on the Catholic question—that is to say, violent against them (*sic*). This is unfortunate, but it explains why he approved of the recall of Lord Anglesey, who was favourable to the Catholics. Nevertheless this recall of the Viceroy is a bad business for Wellington, for he will have in Anglesey an opponent *sans peur et sans reproche*, who will not be afraid to treat him *de haut en bas* in the Upper House. A strong opposition to the Government is being got up there, and in proportion as the last Session was made pleasant and quiet the coming one promises to be lively. If the Ministry is not bludgeoned out of existence, it will be killed by pin-pricks ; for it is no joke to have to face a body of men determined to attack you every day and upon every question. At any rate, a Minister must be there, and he must reply— and that is a delicate way of worrying him to death. Their oratorical talents will also be subjected to a severe trial, and the struggle will undoubtedly be to make a fine show. Wellington's merit, and it is a real one, is his great love of

---

[1] Restored at the cost of upwards of a million sterling by Wyattville. George IV. up to this time had lived at the Lodge in the Great Park, or at the Cottage, Virginia Water.

Walker & Boutall, ph. sc.

Princess Lieven.
(1856.)
From the picture by G.F.Watts, R.A.
at Holland House,
by permission of Rt. Honble the Earl of Ilchester.

order and economy, and it is said that he will be able to show a surplus of a million.[1]   This will sensibly appeal to John Bull's heart ; however, this will not wholly outweigh all his blunders elsewhere.   The public is still ill-disposed in the matter of our affairs ; we must win, and promptly too, some striking victories to restore our reputation and our position. The Emperor's presence with the army had given such importance to our campaign that it was but natural that the public should have thought the result insignificant in comparison with what was expected ; what might have been called a success for a General has been regarded as a reverse for an Emperor.   Moreover, and for the very same reason, we are somewhat effaced in European affairs this year ; Europe thinks that we may be put on one side. This is a wrong idea, which she must not be allowed to assume.   However, all this will soon be set right, I am convinced.   I am sorry that the ill-natured stories which reach me should irritate me, and I await impatiently the moment when our enemies will begin to grow uneasy.   May Heaven crown with success our dear Emperor's undertaking !   That is my most fervent prayer.

Tell me if it be true that the Empress is *enceinte.*   When is her confinement expected ?   Is she in good health ?

I have always wanted to ask you, and have always forgotten to do so, the news, or rather the opinions, about Diebitch.[2]   My own notion of him is founded on the confidence which the Emperor seems to have in him ; my husband thinks most highly of him, and the Duke of Wellington on his return from Petersburg spoke to me of him as a man of considerable talent and shrewdness.   At the same time the general opinion about him abroad is not favourable, and he

---

[1] The surplus of the year 1828-9 proved to be 5,850,000*l.* instead of 3,797,000*l.*, as had been anticipated on the Chancellor of the Exchequer's estimate. The chief increase was on the excise duties on malt and spirits.

[2] He had been appointed to the chief command of the Russian army operating against Turkey.   He was the younger son of a Prussian officer on the Staff of Frederick the Great, entered the Russian service and obtained a commission in the Imperial Guards, saw much service in Europe and Asia, and rose rapidly. He was a little fat man, scarcely five feet high, irritable and vain, known to his soldiers as ' Samovar,' ' the tea-kettle.'

is nicknamed the 'Mack'[1] of Russia.   I hope that Europe
may be wrong and we right in our judgment.

The Portugal business is as bad as bad can be for the
Ministry ; their partiality for Dom Miguel is shown in a
hundred ways.   But what an absurdity it all is !   They declare
him a usurper and support him ; they call Donna Maria
legitimate, and harass those of her subjects who have remained
faithful to her.   All this is beginning to be noised abroad,
and will be discussed with the utmost publicity in Parliament.
You will have some lively revelations on this subject when it
comes to be debated.

I have given you a long letter, my dear brother, but the
knowledge of a safe occasion to write always makes me
loquacious.   Alas ! formerly I took advantage of such to
write to our good Empress and to my mother-in-law.   I have
lost with them my only two correspondents in Russia.   Now
I get no letters and know nothing, so I have to slake my
thirst for them in the 'Gazette de Pétersbourg,' which is my
only resource.   Does not that cause you some little remorse ?

Herewith I am sending an excellent engraving of a
capital portrait of the King, which he sent me a few days
ago.   If you think that it would give pleasure to the Emperor,
lay it at his feet ; if not, keep it yourself.   It is an extremely
good likeness.

I conclude, dear Alexander, by entreating you to embrace
for me all whom you love and I love, and, in a less degree,
those who love me—for example, Count Nesselrode.   I have
included therein wife, sister (for I hear that Masha is at
Petersburg with her children), and that delightful Coco.

If you still know how to write, remember me—it is the one
bit of almsgiving which I shall never cease urging upon you.

Good-bye, my dear brother.   If Buckhausen, our Consul-
general and the bearer of this letter, comes across your path
be kind to him.   He is a man who thoroughly understands
his business—in general, shows shrewdness and intelligence,
and has very correct views on most topics.

[1] The Austrian General who had lost Rome and Naples to the French, and at
a later date had capitulated to Napoleon at Ulm with 80,000 men.

LXXVI

London : $\frac{\text{January 22}}{\text{February 3}}$, 1829.

I have to thank you, dear Alexander, for the letter which Matuscevitz [1] brought me from you ; he had no need of your further recommendation to be welcomed by me—but it, of course, did no harm. We are delighted with him ; he is a man of wit, sound judgment, and tact—in fact, everything to make us regret that he is not to be permanently fixed in London. We have done our best to launch him, and in a few days his own wings will suffice.

Parliament meets the day after to-morrow, and brings everybody to town. The session will be interesting. The public is getting feverish, and begins to believe that after all the Duke of Wellington will emancipate the Catholics. It is a very important event for this country, and if it takes place will find as many supporters as opponents. For my own part, I believe it will be useful in keeping the country quiet —but we shall see. The King is not coming to town ; his health will not allow him. He received Lord Anglesey at Windsor with great cordiality and good will. It is rumoured that Lord Anglesey intends to lay before the House of Lords all the details of his dealings with the Duke of Wellington. As for foreign politics, everything slumbers—and this lethargy will become general until the Catholic question is settled, for this is just now of such vital interest that it absorbs everything else. Moreover, the party which is most desirous of attacking the Government is in favour of emancipation, consequently no questions and no debates will be raised.

Matuscevitz was the bearer of the most charming letter from the Empress to me, which quite overwhelms me. You can imagine how many questions I have to put to him and how interested I am in all he tells me.

[1] Count Matuscevitz was Nesselrode's First Secretary in the Russian Foreign Office, and was sent ostensibly to assist Prince Lieven in conducting the negotiations arising out of the Russo-Turkish War. He made himself very popular in English society, but ultimately became a thorn in the side of the English Government.

Good-bye, my dear, dear Alexander.   I embrace you and love you with all my soul.

LXXVII

London : January 25/February 6, 1829.

The fortunate Matuscevitz will be witness of the most important event in English history for the last 150 years. Catholic Emancipation has been proposed by the Duke of Wellington.   You really should be able to see the rout of the Whigs, obliged on this point at least to vote in support of the Government, while the Ultras are foaming at the mouth and threatening it with all sorts of woes.   Such is the state of affairs in Parliament ; as for the country, we shall see.   Do you recollect a letter which I wrote to you at the end of November (I think), in which I told you this was going to happen ?   And do you remember my remarks thereon ?   Well, I have nothing either to alter or to add.   It is impossible to describe the excitement and agitation in London.   There is no longer any thought of Europe, she is at the bottom of the sea, and for a long spell.   Possibly Portugal may shortly show herself above water, but that is about all.   Elsewhere all is void.

We are delighted with Matuscevitz, and he is overjoyed with everything he sees and hears, and certainly it is a strange spectacle.   I am writing this scrap of a letter, my dear brother, solely because a desire to scribble has seized me in the midst of the gossiping around me.

I embrace you, your wife and children and Coco with all my heart.

The Portuguese refugees were attacked near Terceira by English cruisers, which fired on them, and an officer was killed.   This would have raised a loud outcry had it not been for the Catholic business, and even as it is it will make some disturbance.[1]

---

[1] Out of the 3,000 Portuguese brought to England from Coruña about 650 managed to embark on four vessels for the Açores, under the command of Count Saldanha, Doña Maria having been proclaimed Queen there.   The British Government at once despatched H.M.S. *Ranger* to intercept any ships arriving

LXXVIII

London : 1/13 March 1829.

Dear Alexander,—A *feldjäger* has just arrived from Petersburg bringing to my husband, among others, your letter of February 14/26. I hasten to tell you that I have used all my influence to retard his return to Russia, and I hope to have been successful : and you may count upon his not leaving this country without all that was essential having been settled. With regard to the whereabouts, it will probably be at Warsaw that we shall meet ; for I am reckoning upon travelling with him, especially if the Empress is going to Warsaw. In that case I should probably not extend my journey further, for I should find there assembled all the persons whom it is at all important for me to meet—the Emperor, the Empress, you, and Nesselrode. Besides my husband will only have some tedious business about his estates, which do not concern me, and I could come back to rejoin the children, whom I shall probably leave behind me here. Send me word, therefore, at once, dear Alexander, as to the arrangements for the stay at Warsaw, its date and its length. You will be doing me a great personal favour.

Here everything goes *crescendo* in liveliness, interest, and intrigue ; there is every likelihood now that the Bill[1] will pass, but there will still be much fighting and serious difficulties. The Duke of Cumberland has openly placed himself at the head of the Opposition, so the Ministry will not spare him. I was present last night at the sitting of the Upper House, when the Duke of Wellington openly charged him with taking this part.

Matuscevitz is still delighted with England, and we continue to be charmed with him. I am very glad to hear the news, received by my husband, of the apportionment of the estates, as he was getting anxious at the delay.

at those islands, and to ' use force to drive them away.' On the approach of the four vessels under Saldanha a shot was fired by which one man was killed and another wounded. Saldanha then surrendered and subsequently withdrew to Havre, and the English Ministry abandoned the blockade of the Açores, but not before its proceedings had been generally condemned throughout the country.

[1] The Catholic Relief Bill.

I must ask you, dear Alexander, to deposit with my
bankers, Meyer & Bruxner, of Petersburg, the draft for the
capital in the Foundlings' Bank,[1] bequeathed to me by our
late adorable Empress. I will write and give them notice
of it, asking them to keep it, and to send me an authentic
receipt only. I am writing all this in a great hurry, and without
having time to read my letter over. I may as well repeat, for it
may interest you, that my husband will not be starting for at
least two months ; but he calculates that by that time all
matters of importance here will be on the way to settlement.
I am much more satisfied on my own account than I have
been for some time, and—would you believe it ?—Matuscevitz's coming has been of use to me. Such are the little
ironies of life. He has no idea of his part in it. I am
grateful to you, very dear brother, for the affection of which
your letters are the assurance, the only wish you leave me is
to read them more often. Give me your love—that seems
to me only natural, and I can assure you it is well placed.

One of the singularities of the present state of affairs at
this time in England is that both parties are equally confident
of having the King's support. The Duke of Wellington
openly declared in Parliament that the King supported the
Government measures. The Duke of Cumberland, on the
other hand, gives out that he has the King's confidence. The
two statements are difficult to reconcile,[2] and meanwhile
doubt inspires hope to the extremists of both parties. The
Bill is so extremely favourable to the Catholics that the
Whigs themselves admit that they would never have had the
audacity to propose such a measure even in their own interests.

Your Captain A'Court would not vote in the final division
in the Commons.[3] The recalcitrant office-holders,[4] of whom

---

[1] The Foundling Hospital at St. Petersburg was founded and mainly supported
by the Empress Mother. The money referred to was Madame de Lieven's share
of the Empress's bequest to the Benckendorff family.

[2] Both were in a measure equally correct, and are explicable by the King's
vacillation. See Peel's *Memoirs*, i. 349, &c., and *Greville*, i. 180.

[3] Brother of the Ambassador at St. Petersburg, sat for Tamworth, afterwards Admiral Edward H. A'Court and assumed the name of Repington.

[4] Sir Charles Wetherall, Attorney-General, Lord Lowther, son of Earl of

I think I spoke in my previous letter, have tendered their resignations—but the Duke of Wellington will not accept them. Some interpret this refusal as a proof of strength, others as one of weakness. Just now everyone is so extreme that it is impossible to know how to form an opinion. One thing, however, is quite clear, and that is the Duke of Wellington's attitude of triumph. I should wish you to show my letters to Count Nesselrode—if you think they are worth his acquaintance, or, if not, to limit yourself to offering him my affectionate remembrances.

(Unfinished.)

LXXIX

London: 5/17 March 1829.

There surely can never have been a correspondence in which there was so much prattling on one side and such silence on the other : I see that the only way to make you speak is to impose silence on myself. It is very horrid of you, dear Alexander ; and having said this, I must make the best of it.

Nothing fresh here—unless it be the revival of a scandal, warmed up and renewed, and almost brought into the Law Courts with the object of throwing dirt upon the royal family, but more especially of forcing the Duke of Cumberland out of the country—a satisfaction he will not give to those who seem most to desire it. A certain Captain Garth passes —or allows himself to pass—as the son of Princess Sophia, the King's sister. The promise through someone connected with the Court of a sum of money, and the eager desire to obtain possession of certain letters, show pretty clearly that the royal family is interested in the matter. This latter point is to be settled in a Court of Law—so far there is something undeniable—but the other point is conjectural. This Captain Garth pretends that these letters prove that the

Lonsdale, Commissioner of Land Revenue, and Sir John Beckett, Judge Advocate General. The first was dismissed, but the others were allowed to hold their posts on the understanding that they would support the Bill in Committee. The second reading of the Bill was carried in the Commons by 353 to 173 votes.

Duke of Cumberland is his father, and at the same time that the Princess Sophia was his mother. Whatever opinion one may have as to the truth of this infamous calumny, the royal family is bespattered, for the newspapers daily discuss the affair before the public, some supporting and others denying it. The much desired outcome, however, will not happen. The Duke of Cumberland remains, and all the more will remain, for his honour obliges him now not to have the air of being intimidated by this terrible charge.

With this the Catholic question is being pushed forward simultaneously. Just now it seems as if it would be carried —and in triumph—but it is better to await the final stage before believing it to be passed. The King is well in health, but sees nobody at Windsor, with the exception of his brother, the Duke of Cumberland, and his Ministers when they may have business to transact with him.

The London populace flares up now and again at the doors of Parliament, and generally in an Anti-Catholic mood, but there is nothing really serious in its acts. Throughout the country meetings are held followed by the signing of petitions against the Bill, but not even in London are there any suggestions of threats.

Good-bye, my dear Alexander, I embrace you most warmly. Matuscevitz is not sorry at the prospect of remaining here.

LXXX

London : 14/26 March 1829.

Notwithstanding that my husband is preparing to send off a courier in a few days, I find it more sure to write to you in advance by post, my dear Alexander. I am impatient to get your answer to my questions about this visit to Warsaw, more especially as after all it may turn out that my husband's absence from his post will be limited to the journey to Warsaw to pay his court to the Emperor. It seems to me, moreover, that now that the partition of the estates has been made and that my husband's share in the Russian property (Obrock) is placed in charge of the regular administration and his estates in Courland are managed by a trustworthy agent, his presence there is after all not so very urgent this year ; and since it is greatly needed here it would be most advantageous if he could change into weeks the months of his intended stay in Russia. Probably he will himself say this in writing by the courier, and I shall urge him to do so, because I think he can, and consequently ought to, do it ; but you will hear more decidedly by the courier.

Our countrymen will doubtless have been much surprised to hear of the Duke of Wellington's duel. It is the first he has ever fought in his life, and blame and approval are about equally divided. He might have declined it, but since it has ended satisfactorily he doubtless does not regret having accepted it.[1]

Both parties are busy marshalling their forces, and next week will make a trial of strength in the Upper House. The Duke of Cumberland proclaims himself the uncompromising opponent of the Duke of Wellington, and has aroused (for he has the means) all sorts of difficulties and obstacles. There is no mention of the King in all this business, nevertheless he gives audiences to the Ultras among the peers who ask for them. The final result, however, is still a secret. Eight bishops have declared themselves in favour of the Bill, but the ministerial majority in the Upper House cannot be guessed. We shall learn more as the debate, which begins on Tuesday next, proceeds.

Good-bye, dear Alexander, I am eagerly looking for your next news. People here are beginning to discuss our next campaign, and each prophesies in accordance with his wishes. A very small contingent affect to see us at the gates of Constantinople ; others limit our operations to the taking of a number of fortresses, which would be a pitiable campaign. I have reason to think that the latter forecast comes from

---

[1] With the Earl of Winchilsea, on account of a letter published in the *Standard* newspaper of March 16, for which the Duke of Wellington demanded an apology, which was refused. They met at Wimbledon on March 21 ; the Duke fired first, and missed. Lord Winchilsea then fired in the air, and produced from his pocket a paper expressing his regret for his letter, which, though offensive and violent, would never have attracted public attention.

Vienna, where good will (*à la* Metternich) for Russia continues to be the order of the day.

Good-bye, my dear brother ; I will write to you by the courier. I embrace you heartily ; likewise your wife, and children, and Coco.

LXXXI

London : 17/29 March 1829.

At last a courier, my dear Alexander ! I am so accustomed to seize upon the opportunity of writing to you in safety that I forget that as a matter of fact I have nothing either important or private to tell you which my letters by the post have not already anticipated. My husband has informed both you and Count Nesselrode as to the conclusion he has arrived at with regard to his journey, and I think he has decided rightly. He will not go a step beyond either Warsaw or Berlin, in whichever city he may find the Emperor, should the latter wish him to get back to London as quickly as possible. In this case his absence from his post will be for only a few weeks, its object being solely to pay his respects to the Emperor and to have some talk with his chief, a very useful thing in political business. The reason why he would give up the thought of going to look after his own business in Russia is twofold. On the one hand, his presence there is of less importance, since he has come into his share of the inheritance ; and, on the other hand, he feels that a prolonged absence from his post at this time might be prejudicial to the service.

Let us, however, turn to what is going on here. We are sitting upon thorns. The Duke of Wellington may be thrown over in the next twenty-four hours. The King is furious against the Bill, the Duke of Cumberland is egging him on, and has got all his friends to back him up, old Lord Eldon at the head of them.[1] If the King could show but a spark of courage the

---

[1] ' All yesterday (March 3) it was thought quite uncertain whether the Duke's resignation would not take place and the Chancellor himself said that nothing was more likely than they should all go out. . . .' ' Lord Eldon prevails on all these peers to exercise their rights and demand audiences.'— *Greville*, i. 181 and 197. This was the moment at which the intrigues against the Duke of Wellington

Duke might be upset ; if not, he becomes the dictator, and the saying of the King is fulfilled : ' Arthur is King of England, O'Connell King of Ireland, and myself Canon of Windsor.'

Throughout the present intrigues against the Government there is a solid basis of religious fanaticism and a clinging to the exclusive Protestant Constitution, but over and above this there is a hatred of Wellington. None are so unforgiving as dupes, and the Duke has treated the Tories as imbeciles, as in truth they are in some ways. As for ourselves, it is difficult to think that we should profit much from a Tory Government,[1] but there is no doubt that it would be a great advantage for us to get rid of Wellington, who is, Heaven knows why, the implacable enemy of Russia. Moreover, a Tory Government will be too contemptible to last for any time ; the Whigs will promptly upset them, and they at least are better disposed towards us. But whatever may be the result, changes and confusion are inevitable, and anything which embarrasses England is favourable for us : while with Wellington remaining master, he may become a real danger to us. Thus his dismissal is our chief interest ; after that— the deluge.

The Portuguese question daily becomes more embarrassing for the English Ministry. In the speeches from the throne at the closing of the last and at the opening of the present session it was announced that they would await the decision of the august Chief of the House of Braganza as to the succession to the throne.[2] This august chief has now spoken, and to the effect that he is prepared to maintain by force the rights of his daughter, the Queen Donna Maria, and that never will he come to terms with the usurper, Dom Miguel. Now Wellington is devoted to the usurper, and detests the legitimate heiress, Metternich likewise.[3] What, then, is to be done ?

---

were being hotly pressed ; the reader must draw his own inference as to Madame de Lieven's complicity in them.

[1] Earl Grey's letters to Madame de Lieven abundantly prove that the Whigs were in no way disposed to adopt Canning's foreign policy.

[2] Dom Pedro IV., Emperor of Brazil, who had renounced his rights to the throne of Portugal.

[3] ' In respect to Portugal, you may tell Prince Polignac (French Ambassador

And what is to be the solution ?   As far as I can ascertain, they themselves do not yet know.   Ministers here are very proud of having managed to send an Ambassador to Constantinople.   I hope our war will spoil the pleasure and the success they anticipate.   Mr. Gordon,[1] who has been named, is a disciple of Metternich and a rabid Turk—a good choice to flatter the Turks, but a very bad one if intended to bamboozle them.

19/31 March.

The courier does not start until to-day, but I have nothing fresh or important to add.   There is an attempt to stir up public feeling, and a little display of it would be found useful to coerce the Ministry.   For my part I think the method a bad one, and I do not suspect the Tories of being privy to it ; but here, as elsewhere at critical moments, there are not wanting hot-headed personages ready for a row for the mere pleasure of creating one.   Since this letter was begun my husband's plans have been somewhat modified, and, unless specially summoned, he has decided not to stir from here.   If you should hear anything of the matter, dear Alexander, do us the kindness to let Paul know it at once.   We had arranged to meet him at Warsaw, but if we are not going there he must return to London as soon as possible after having settled in his father's name the arrangements about the landed property.

In accordance with your wishes we are showing every attention to Captain A'Court, whom we find a charming man ; as for Lord Heytesbury, I am delighted to see that he sustains in our country the reputation he made in his own. At the same time I think that I ought to tell you in confidence that among his most intimate acquaintances he has the reputation of being untrustworthy—let us turn this to our advantage.   We have been unable to obtain the least hint

in London) that we are determined that there shall be no revolutionary movement from England in any part of the world.' (' Wellington to Lord Aberdeen,' January 1829, *Despatches*, v. 409.)

    [1] Afterwards Sir Robert Gordon, a cousin of the Foreign Secretary, and, according to Greville, 'a dull, heavy man,' who was substituted for Stratford Canning.

as to the nature of his reports to his Government. Lord Aberdeen only repeats to me that he cannot speak too gratefully of the kindnesses of the Emperor.

Here, on the threshold of April, my anxiety about our campaign revives. May Heaven inspire Diebitch to advance promptly and strike hard—God knows how important this is for us, and how propitious is the moment. We should never be allowed to make a third campaign, but no one can say a word against our undertaking the present one. Write to us frequently, dear Alexander, and give us good news. Shall we receive a bulletin from Adrianople? Good-bye, my dear brother; your letters are always a pleasure to me, and, besides, are of real use. Do not, therefore, discontinue them.

My health is somewhat improved. Tell me your decision about Marie, have my entreaties had any weight with you? How is Coco? A thousand kind things to your wife and children and to my sister.

LXXXII

London : April 7 (N.S.), 1829.

The fate of the Catholic Bill, my dear Alexander, is settled. The Duke of Wellington obtained for it in the House of Lords a majority of 105 votes, which, added to the majority 45 voting against the Bill only nine months ago, when he himself was opposing it, shows that he can dispose of 150 votes according to his own will and pleasure.[1] If, therefore, he has been powerful up till now, we may reckon that he will be henceforth all-powerful; and Parliament will give him an absolutely free hand in those questions of foreign policy which he now proposes to take up and push forward vigorously. The country submits to the Catholic Bill without protest. The King, therefore, naturally submits also. Amen.

[1] The second reading was carried in the House of Lords after three nights' debate on April 5 by 217 to 112 votes, and a week later passed through its final stage by 213 to 109 votes, and the King gave his assent without further show of resistance.

The capture of Sizoboli[1] is a brilliant affair, which has greatly delighted us. God grant that our campaign be sharp, quick, and decisive—Heaven knows how necessary this is.

Dom Miguel maintains his pleasing ways. He recently wished to shoot his sister, the ex-Regent. The pistol, however, did not shoot straight, or was badly aimed, but the princess is confined to her room.[2]

Matuscevitz is away hunting, and for a week is wholly indifferent to what may happen. He is right, for when one lives in England it is absolutely necessary to get away from time to time to the fresh air out of the reach of the smoke and political intrigues of London—otherwise body and mind would succumb.

How much I wish, dear Alexander, that you would reply about Marie ; if you consider my request without prejudice, you must admit that it is reasonable, and will grant me the happiness of having the charge of her. You know that up to the present I have been kept in ignorance of everything relating to the disposal of those dear children. Did our dear Constantine appoint a guardian to them ? I embrace you with all my heart. We are still, and shall so remain until the last moment, quite vague as to our journey to Warsaw. The state of affairs here, and the orders which the Emperor may send, will decide our movements.

[Having passed the Catholic Relief Bill by the help of the Opposition, and thrown a sop to the Ultra-Tories by disfranchising the forty-shilling freeholders, the Ministry rested from their labours. The ex-Chancellor Lord Eldon and the Duke of Cumberland had failed in their efforts to provoke the King to use his prerogative and refuse his sanction to the first-named measure, and none of the terrible results of his refusal, including the Duke of Cumberland's threatened withdrawal to the Continent, had happened.

In foreign affairs the Duke of Wellington had been less success-

---

[1] Or Sozopolis, on the south side of the Bay of Bourgas and commanding the road to Constantinople.

[2] He suspected his sister of having sent her jewels and money to England by a servant. Having forced his way into her room armed with a pistol on which a bayonet was fixed, after a serious struggle Dom Miguel fired at the princess, killing a servant, and stabbed her Chamberlain.

ful His one aim had been to get out of the 'Greek concern,' as he termed it, without being joint guarantee with France and Russia, and he had an equal objection to leaving France and Russia bound together by a common interest. He had allowed his conservatism to be moulded after the fashion of Metternich's, and was unable to realise the strength of Russia. He recalled Stratford Canning from Constantinople, and assented to the appointment of Lord Aberdeen's incompetent cousin to the important post. He endeavoured, but without success, to persuade the French Government of M. de Martignac to assent to the new conditions which the Porte proposed to add to the Treaty of London. These, if adopted, would have made Greece a mere tributary province of the Turkish Empire. This would have been in accordance with the views of the British Ministry, which desired above all things the maintainance of Turkey as a European Power. The unsuccessful campaign of Russia in 1828 had raised the hopes of the Ministry that its policy would be successful. Diebitch's masterful strategy destroyed this cobweb of intrigue, which the substitution of Prince Polignac, Wellington's *protégé*, for M. de Martignac could not sustain. He opened the campaign early in May, and rapidly invested Silistria, of which the siege had been abandoned in the previous autumn. The Turkish army sent to its relief was completely defeated at Koulevtsk, Silistria surrendered, and Diebitch, leaving a force to mask Schumla, brought his troops successfully through the Balkan passes, and after a laborious march reached the heart of Rumelia with 'the shadow of an army, but with the reputation of irresistible success.' England and Austria were wholly unprepared for the situation thus created, which gave to Russia absolute predominance in Eastern Europe. From the outset of the campaign down to the moment when Adrianople voluntarily opened its gates, the Russian Government had maintained that its only object was to enforce the terms of the Treaty of London, that it desired no Turkish territory, and that the independence of Greece should be effectually guaranteed. As late as the month of March, before the second campaign was opened, Lord Aberdeen had assented to the proposal that the Greek kingdom should include certain territory north of the Gulf of Corinth. To Metternich and the Duke of Wellington this pointed to the eventual dismemberment of Turkey in Europe, to which neither was prepared to assent. Whether any secret overtures were made with this view there is no evidence ; on the contrary, it may be fairly inferred from Madame de Lieven's letters to Earl Grey and to her brother that no such scheme at that time was entertained by the Emperor Nicholas. The Governments of Austria and Great Britain thought otherwise,

while the idea of establishing the kingdom of Greece, the outcome
of a revolutionary movement, and recognising its complete independence, was most distasteful to such upholders of absolutism as were
Metternich and Wellington.   To Austria the dangers of a premature
break-up of the Ottoman Empire were more immediate than to
England, and doubtless every effort was made and every argument
pressed by Metternich to insure the co-operation of Wellington.
That the latter used his influence to obtain the appointment of
Prince Polignac as Foreign Minister to Charles X. is beyond doubt,
and it was another instance of Wellington's policy of being content
to meet the difficulties of the day without troubling about the
embarrassments of the morrow.   Polignac, who had expected to
bring over his master to the side of Austria and England, found French
opinion in favour of Greek independence so strong that he
supported the Prussian proposals and the Russian view.   Distrust
of Russia, reasonable or unreasonable, was the mainspring of
Wellington's policy, and no assurances that she was desirous of no
territory for herself, but only the independence of Greece, availed
to establish a franker and more cordial understanding between the two
Powers.   The terms of peace between Russia and Turkey had been
formulated by General Diebitch without reference to St. Petersburg,
where they were confirmed in principle, although it was intimated
to the Western Powers that certain concessions on the amount
of the indemnity and the consequent occupation of Turkish
territory would be considered in a less exacting spirit.   The opposition to the Treaty of Adrianople was due not so much to its terms
as to the fact that it was concluded by Russia alone without any
reference to the co-signatories of the Treaty of London of 1827.
Russia, having made war against the wishes of her allies, had now
made peace without consulting their opinion, thereby showing her
intention of acting alone, especially in her dealings with Turkey
and Eastern Europe.   After all, Austria and the Western Powers
had to assent to the terms of the Treaty of Adrianople, which
virtually placed Moldavia and Wallachia, although retaining the
Sultan's suzerainty, under the tutelage of Russia, and imposed
an indemnity upon Turkey so heavy that the evacuation of its
territory was in danger of being indefinitely prolonged.   No cession
of European territory was contemplated, but certain places in Asia
already in the hands of the Russians were incorporated in the
Empire.   The complete independence of Greece with its enlarged
frontiers was to be recognised, as well as the free navigation of
the Dardanelles for merchant ships of all nations.]

LXXXIII

London : 2/14 April 1829.

In writing to you, my dear Alexander, I feel somewhat like a newspaper correspondent, with this difference, that in that case an anonymous writer will sometimes provoke a reply, whereas you remain inexorably mute.

The news of the frightful catastrophe at Teheran reached us yesterday ;[1] it makes one shudder to read it. I can well understand the Shah's dismay, but at all events it is an atrocity for which he cannot be held responsible. By what a number of tragedies are the annals of our relations with Persia already marked !

The King has signed the Catholic Bill, so that matter has ended in a complete triumph for the Duke of Wellington. He seems to be very well satisfied and not a little proud of his achievement, as he has every reason to be. I made him laugh a little with me at his own skill, and the way in which the others had been duped. He measured and weighed his own strength and the mediocrity of his antagonists. With this to guide him he marched forwards and carried the position. He made his friends keep silence, availed himself of his opponents' help, and disregarded everything else. After the Bill had passed he expressed his thanks to the Whigs, and at the same time made them to clearly understand that he had no further need of them. By this stroke he brought back all the Tories with very few exceptions to his side, and parties have once more resumed the positions they occupied before the Bill. He is now going to adjourn Parliament for a fort-night, and then the session will be over in a few weeks, all the important business having been got through. The House has voted all the money asked for the public service without a single inquiry or hitch, the estimates being quietly passed in the intervals of the heated debates on the Catholic question. So, contrary to all expectation, everything is settled and the country is perfectly quiet. It is the most

---

[1] The murder of the Russian Envoy and his suite by the mob on February 11.

astonishing change imaginable. The general opinion is that now the public will turn its attention, and very rapidly too, to foreign affairs, and that it will display in the discussion of them as much eagerness and determination as it showed on the Catholic question, and possibly its appetite for surprises may have been stimulated.

We are all waiting with much impatience for news of our army. Rapid movements are most to my taste, and from what I am told of the character of Diebitch they are to be expected from him. The Duke of Wellington, with whom I was talking for a long time yesterday, was strong in his praises of our General, but his real Russian hero is, as it always has been, Michael Woronzow.

The Duke of Cumberland declared the other night in the House of Lords that henceforward he would oppose the Duke of Wellington in every way ; he no longer returns his bow when they meet, but it does not seem as if he were thinking of leaving England at present. My belief is that he will go to Windsor and stay with the King.

Farewell, dear Alexander ; I embrace you heartily, which, considering the slight return you make, is most tender. I am anxiously expecting to hear from you concerning the Emperor's movements, although it is more than probable that my husband will be unable to avail himself of such guidance. Circumstances must decide.

LXXXIV

London : 15/27 August 1829.

You have offended me and wounded my feelings, my brother ; the hurt you have done me will never be effaced. Never would our dear Constantine have been capable of treating me in such a way, but then he loved me.

I do not feel that I have the courage to write to you—but to-day I cannot resist the impulse to turn towards you at this great and propitious moment. Our successes have surprised Europe and startled our enemies. Among these enemies the English Ministry is the most bitterly hostile. It is also the most powerful from the means at its disposal, but the most feeble from the meagreness of its abilities.   To-day the Emperor is dictator of Europe, his will is law.   No Power can thwart him—his decision is awaited[1] ;   that he will be moderate, I have no doubt ; he will be generous also, for, being able to do everything, all that he does not do will be placed to his credit.   But for God's sake let him understand his position. The opportunity is great and unique.   To-day he can determine the strength and influence of Russia for centuries. He will associate his name with this epoch in history—let it be glorious and advantageous for our country.

In the interval which has elapsed since my last letter so many things have happened that I scarcely know where to take up the thread.   We left Austria and England barking, intriguing, and failing against us.   All their combinations of a coalition have been upset by the good faith of Prussia and the good sense of the French Cabinet.   The Duke of Wellington's efforts were relaxed of late, because he never once dreamed of our successes.   The battle of Koulevtcha disturbed his temper, but did not arouse his fears.   He fixed his attention upon Schumla, and saw nothing beyond it. Not more than three weeks ago he said openly that Russia could never penetrate into Rumelia until the capture of that position, that only lightly equipped troops could penetrate the Balkans from the side of the sea, and that by no possibility could artillery be brought through.   Everybody bowed before so great an authority, and one fine morning everybody awoke to learn that the Balkans had been crossed and that we were masters of Bourgas and Aidos.   Before this great event, however, and after the battle of Koulevtcha,

[1] This statement is in accordance with Count Pozzo di Borgo's communication to General Tatischeff, Russian Ambassador at Vienna, and repeated by him to Lord Cowley. ' M. de Lieven thought that he carried his point with regard to the blockade of the Dardanelles and the concessions to Greece.   He said that Russia well understood the meaning of war with England, but that she would not shrink from it. Wellington, he asserted, thereupon moderated his tone, and said that he had expressed his personal opinions, not the views of the Cabinet.' Wellington, in transmitting this account to Lord Aberdeen, qualifies it as apocryphal. (Lord Cowley's despatch, July 31, 1829.)

[2] Fought on June 11.   Diebitch at once sent proposals of peace to the Grand

he thought it imperative to have a *préfet* of his own choice in France. He wanted to have M. de Polignac at any cost. He has got him, and with him a body of such followers that France has risen in protest against this lieutenant of the great captain ; and his position, thus attained, leaves him without influence in the country. Anything in the shape of a coalition against us is no longer possible ; so much is fully admitted, so to-day everybody is talking of the Emperor's generosity, because that is all that remains to rely on. England is in a most humiliating position, and this is by no means the least of my joys in the midst of my satisfaction at our successes.

I have established quite lately most friendly relations with Lord Aberdeen. He lays bare to me, with the greatest simplicity, his innermost thoughts ; they are mean and cowardly, but nevertheless, at the same time, they are as thoroughly in conformity with our interests as it is possible to desire. He does not, it is true, direct the policy of the Cabinet ; but as he has so few ideas of his own it is pretty clear that he never speaks but in accordance with the order of the day. This just now is wholly favourable to the Emperor's wishes—you may take my word for this ; let us, therefore, take advantage of an opportunity which will never recur. The Whigs might be in office to-day, and we should not find them more accommodating than this Wellington Ministry, which intended to be so hostile—God grant Russia may always have such enemies, who avail us more than friends. Moreover, do not fail, my brother, to repeat to Count Nesselrode that he has within his reach the principal *rôle*—and doubtless he is aware of it. Matuscevitz talks and acts better than the most ardent patriot.[1] Like the rest of

Vizier, who replied on July 30 with a request for an armistice, which was not concluded until a month later, when the advance of the Russian army on Constantinople seemed imminent. The Polignac Ministry, in which Wellington expressed great confidence, was formed early in August.

[1] Lord Aberdeen reports to the Duke of Wellington that on this day (August 27) a conference had been held on the affairs of Greece, at which Matuscevitz was full of professions of the Emperor's desire to do everything with ' a full concert understanding with us.' He suggests that the Duke should see

us, he is inspired by the Emperor's glory, and it must be allowed that the Emperor is really well served. His Generals make Wellington's military fame grow pale, his diplomatists know how to sustain the honour of his empire. Whatever he may wish will be done—only make him understand how great he is, and how far-reaching is his moral power. Do not, I entreat you, think that in my letters to you I am giving expression to an exaggerated enthusiasm—I only say what is the precise truth ; your zeal for the Emperor and his renown will enable you to use it profitably. Should you dare to mention my name to him at such a moment, tell him, my dear brother, the happiness and the pride with which I am filled by his successes, and the splendid destiny which they assure him. Never was Russia so great as at this moment. The Emperor will know how to retain for her in peace the position he has obtained for her by war.

Farewell. I have never ceased to be towards you what I have always wished you to be towards me—kind and brotherly.

LXXXV

Richmond : 12/24 September 1829.

This morning, my dear Alexander, I received by the courier your letter of August 11, and as my husband is despatching a *feldjäger* to the Court I am taking advantage of it to send you a few lines. Here we are without news of anything beyond the armistice concluded August 17/29, and we are eagerly waiting to see whether peace will follow and upon what terms. Our successes in the field have been so splendid that it will be difficult to make any comparison between the fruits of peace and war, for to maintain a just proportion it would be necessary to swallow Turkey entire. But as we have no appetite for such a meal, and with good reason, we shall, I hope, content ourselves with shaving the Sultan by razing his fortresses—that, however, is no affair of mine. What is certain in all this is the glory of the

Matuscevitz and discuss the proposal for an extension of Greek frontiers. *Wellington Despatches*, vol. viii.

Emperor, and what is speculative is the future of Turkey. In all probability, since we have not wished to do away with her altogether, she will die of exhaustion. Here everyone was jubilant at the news of the armistice, and this was my sole motive for not being grateful for it ; but I am burning to know what will come of it. We shall be able to do whatever we like. Public opinion has followed in the wake of the Cabinet, whose conduct has been nerveless and cowardly, and now leaves its dear Turks in the lurch. We are hated, but feared. The Duke of Wellington must be mad with rage, for he hates us and will not cease to do so. I have nothing fresh to tell you of his position in England. It is unaltered, and its dangers will not be apparent until the meeting of Parliament. Then a plentiful crop will be forthcoming ; but it is their complexity which will be the source of his safety. The Tories wish to upset the Cabinet, the Whigs also ; but as each party is afraid that its fall will turn to the profit of the other it is therefore more than likely that one or the other stretches out a hand to save the Ministry on the very edge of the precipice, for fear of what might follow—for anything is better in the eyes of a Tory than a Whig, and *vice versâ*. I am much afraid that in this way the Duke of Cumberland's dislike of Wellington is profitable to the latter. The King is still on bad, or at least on distant, terms with his Ministry, but that does not in reality mean much. The poor King is in danger of becoming blind ; he has already lost the sight of one eye, and the other is affected. The operation for cataract will be postponed until blindness is complete ; this makes him sad and troubled, but he is always most friendly towards Russia. On the occasion of our last visit to Windsor about a fortnight ago he made a point of inviting Matuscevitz to dine, and took occasion to drink the Emperor's health, after having invited Aberdeen to propose it.[1] The latter did so with good grace ; as a rule

---

[1] ' The King is convinced that Matuscevitz will come back as Ambassador, and says that in order to say something civil to him he expressed the hope that he might return in such a capacity as would enable him to remain. Matuscevitz replied : " Sire, j'accepte l'augure." ' (' Aberdeen to Wellington,' September 30, 1829.) It does not appear from this letter that Lord Aberdeen was present on the occasion.

he is tractable enough, and amuses me vastly by his simplicity, his bluntness, his complete submissiveness, and his
imprudence. (Please excuse the blots on the bottom of the
page.) Matuscevitz cannot tear himself away from England.
It is a dominating passion with him, such as a man might
feel for his mistress. I have met with people who found red
hair attractive, but he is enchanted even with the fogs, those
horrors which I would fly to the other side of the world to
escape.

Ministers here expect a change of Government in France
very shortly. Since Polignac has not proved to be of any
use to them, they will regard his dismissal with indifference.
Aberdeen, however, is distrustful of the opposite extreme,
and so are we all ; but whose fault is that ?

Good-bye, my dear Alexander. Since you have taken
again to writing to me, try to keep up the custom. You
see that I have had no difficulty in resuming it. My husband
desires his kindest remembrances.

LXXXVI

Richmond : 10/22 October 1829.

Glory to the Emperor and to Russia—what a splendid
triumphal war, what a splendid triumphant peace ! We
should all of us indeed be happy, dear Alexander. I wonder
whether at Petersburg you are able to enjoy this twofold
success as I do here. It is impossible to imagine anything
more delightful than the way in which it is taken. Lord
Aberdeen, in a most woebegone tone, began : ' Well, your
glory is now achieved. Russia dominates the world to-day ;
notwithstanding the modesty of your language, you are
omnipotent everywhere, while as for us we seem to have
been your dupes, and are humbled and disgraced.' ' So
much the worse for you, my Lord ; but we did not dupe
you—you duped yourselves. Your own illusions, or those
inspired by your patron Prince Metternich, were your real
enemies.' At last, after bringing his complainings to a close,
he delivered himself of the conviction that an intimate union

with Russia is a matter of urgent necessity. He found in
such an arrangement only a guarantee of peace and tranquillity throughout the world. 'Thank God, my Lord, you
are at last coming to admit as a truth what we have all along
felt, and have endeavoured to impress upon you. But in
order that this truth may bear fruit you must deal frankly in
the matter, and loyally with my Emperor, and that is the
hic.' It is not to the Duke of Wellington that we now look
for straightforward and loyal conduct, and so we may congratulate ourselves upon having nothing more to fear from
our open enemies or from our false friends. At no time like
the present has Russia been so great, or so much feared and
respected. It is felt that she will always carry out her
purpose, and as she only desires what is just and to maintain
what is right she takes no heed of the impotent rage of a
Ministry devoid alike of honour and ability. You have no
idea of the hatred it has for the wretched Greeks, and
especially for Capo d'Istria.[1]   Members of the Cabinet openly
avow it, and declare that henceforward their policy is to thwart
that nation and drive away the President. Wellington, at
the same time, is furious against France (he well deserves to
be called a dupe), for Polignac, who was to have been his
prefect, has almost become his opponent.

Public opinion here is much divided with regard to us—
the peace has its admirers as well as its detractors. Some
think that we have been far too generous, and regret that the
Ottoman Porte should be so long in dying, for no one believes
that it can ever recover vitality. Our war has revealed to
the world at large and to the Turks themselves that there is
no longer any sentiment of nationality or fanaticism existing

---

[1] Wellington's opinion of Count Capo d'Istria was clearly expressed in a
letter to Lord Aberdeen dated November 26, 1829 : 'The good man (!) came to
England emancipated from the service of Russia. I saw him in September 1827.
He laboured to convince me, and he desired me to assure others on his word of
honour, that he had nothing to say to the Emperor of Russia, that he was going
to Greece as a citizen of Greece &c. Yet there was at that time a Russian credit
in his favour amounting to upwards of 40,000*l*. The Emperor likewise had
nothing to say to Capo d'Istria about assisting him till the demand of pecuniary
assistance was simultaneously made upon each of the Allied Powers ! '
Wellington Despatches, vol. viii.

among them. This fact alone shows that its part is played out. The Emperor has deigned to allow it to live on awhile. His glory is increased by his clemency, and this thought enables me to await with patience the moment when at his will Europe will be finally freed from the presence of barbarism.

I have just received a letter from Lord Grey, and I cannot think of anything better than to send you the translation (quite literal) of a passage in it. I had recounted to him the strange visit I had received from Lord Aberdeen. Here is his reply. Show it to Count Nesselrode. It is not without importance to know Lord Grey's way of looking at things. At this moment public opinion runs strongly against the Duke of Wellington ; some are still blind to his faults, but the majority of the public has taken his measure. If only a definitely organised opposition could be found in Parliament he would not hold office for a fortnight after the opening of the session : but, although he is hated *à outrance* by Whigs and Tories alike, they hate one another still more—and herein lies his safety. Nevertheless it is impossible that a clear-sighted people, like the English, will consent long to be governed by a bundle of mediocrities who cannot even claim to act in good faith. It is generally believed that before the opening of the session the Duke of Wellington will be obliged to take into the Ministry, either from the right or the left of the Speaker's chair, someone of marked importance and ability. I have my doubts about this, for to select a man of mark would be to give himself a master, and this the Duke will never do, and if only a mediocrity is selected he will take his place with the master's other slaves and the Cabinet will not be strengthened. I am therefore strong in the conviction that it will meet Parliament in its primitive incapacity.

I am obliged to finish in a hurry, dear Alexander—for I am not feeling well to-day, so must ask you to forgive the negligence of this letter. My husband sends his best remembrances, and I my best love.

(Enclosure)

Extract from Lord Grey's letter, October 20, 1829.[1]

He (Lord Aberdeen) must be, to be sure, the most extra-ordinary man that ever lived, and so different from what I had conceived of him that I cannot recover my astonishment. I am afraid it is not an uncommon thing in politics to find a man professing an intention with a secret determination never to execute it. But it is new in the history of diplomacy, and still more in that of Scotchmen,[2] to meet with such an avowal as you describe Aberdeen to have made, and for what purpose but to expose himself? You could only understand the views of our Government as they were described in the Protocol. You could not read in their hearts the secret intention of acting contrary to them. If you had expressed a suspicion of such an intention (for which perhaps there was some ground), what would they have said ? As to the complaint of your having stipulated for the fulfilment of the terms agreed upon by the allies with respect to Greece, I cannot conceive anything more unfounded. It surely was natural that you should do so ; nay, more, it might perhaps have been a much more just cause of reproach if you had not. And, after all, how is it possible for any man in his senses to feel injured by your stipulating that the terms which you had agreed upon with him to propose should be taken as the basis of an arrangement the details of which were left to be settled with his concurrence ?

LXXXVII

London : $\frac{\text{October 30}}{\text{November 11}}$, 1829.

Matuscevitz is taking this letter, my dear Alexander, and this fact will almost dispense with the need of writing it. If he still bears me in mind when he gets to Petersburg he will be able to tell you more about me than I can convey in a

---

[1] See *Correspondence of Princess Lieven and Earl Grey*, i. 335.

[2] ' The Scotch are noted for their dissimulation.' (Note by Princess Lieven.)

letter. He has been spending the last ten months here, and throughout his stay, from his arrival to his departure, we have treated him with the fullest confidence and friendliness. He owed his reception to the recommendations he brought with him, but it is to himself alone that he owes the maintenance of such good will. His attitude has been irreproachable towards my husband, who cannot speak too highly in his praise, although the temptations of *amour-propre* cannot have been wanting. The public here have attached to his mission an importance flattering to him, and the reverse of flattering to my husband. If the latter has had the good sense to hold himself above the gossip and chatter of the world, the former has the merit of not allowing his head to be turned by suggestions which flattered his vanity. For my own part I should have liked him, for his own advantage, to have resisted the excessive devotion to England by which he is carried away. It is quite a passion with him, and, like all passions, blinds those possessed. He leaves us at a moment when the Ministry seem inclined to show, in their relations with Russia, a more polished *surface* and a more becoming attitude. As for their real disposition, it is, I can aver, as thoroughly hostile to us as it has ever been ; and however much display they may make of the velvet paw, we must not lose sight of the cat and its claws.

Good-bye, my dear Alexander, for truly beside a courier so well informed as Matuscevitz it would be difficult for me to find a word of interest to add. My dearest love to your wife and children, and many affectionate regards from my husband.

LXXXVIII

Richmond : November 4/16, 1829.

I received at the same time your two letters of September 23 and October 6 O.S., and as you know, my dear Alexander, a letter from you is a rare stroke of luck—but two together demand a prompt and hearty expression of my gratitude. Consequently I am sending this to Matuscevitz in Paris, in order that he may be able to get it in all its freshness. I endorse everything that you say, and I admit that the terms of our peace are noble, good, wise, prudent, and magnificent —and I believe that I have told you all this before, and what I thought of them. I am equally satisfied with what you say about the great White Spectre [1] (this name for him will serve between us); let us keep up a shadow of distrust in him— that is about as much as he deserves, but the ground for this feeling or impression should not be entirely put out of sight.

I am most anxious to hear of Matuscevitz' arrival, for there are a thousand things which cannot be explained in letters which he will be able to tell you. He will be a living cyclopædia—article, ' England.' This reflection comes upon me in thinking of what I said to you in my previous letter concerning Lord Grey. You know what is his political position, and his social position is not less eminent and distinguished. He is one of my most intimate acquaintances in England.[2] A man of the highest honour, in whom I have that confidence which an honourable man inspires. If he were not sixty-eight years old [3] he would govern England one day, but his day will not come, although all parties endeavour to have his support. The Government would be glad to give him office, and it is said that at this very moment they are trying to tempt him. It will, however, be difficult to come to terms with Lord Grey alone, and if he enters the Cabinet it will be as the head of his party and with such a following as will give him weight in its counsels. It remains to be seen if the Duke of Wellington will ever consent to give himself a rival. Lord Grey at the present time is everything we could wish with regard to our policy. We have also another adherent in Lord Palmerston, who is sure to play a leading part next session. But I am encroaching upon Matuscevitz' rights. Ask him about all these matters. You will find he has much that is interesting to say.

I congratulate you heartily, dear Alexander, on the

[1] Prince Metternich.

[2] ' C'est une de mes meilleures habitudes en Angleterre.'

[3] Earl Grey was born in 1764, so that at the date of this letter he was sixty-five years of age.

munificence of the Emperor and on the happiness which comes from having deserved it. This feeling will cause you to enjoy it with fuller satisfaction than anything else. I often hear you talked about by foreigners, and I am not flattering you when I tell you that your way of discharging your difficult and delicate duties is a general theme of approval. I am still here enjoying the most lovely country in the most perfect weather.

You are very good in asking me to come and stay at your country house next summer. You know how much I desire to be near you and our beloved Emperor. Last summer he forbade my coming, but who can foresee what may happen in the near future ? Circumstances may, I hope, allow my husband leave of absence from his post, and the Emperor may be induced to permit it—in fact, many things must be arranged, for the times in which we live are fertile in great events.[1]

When will this Greek business be settled ? If you could answer that question, I might begin making calculations as to my future movements ; but to undertake the journey alone, without my husband, is rather a serious undertaking. If only this Europe were slightly compressed. I have traversed it once, and it is just the recollection of that journey which makes me recoil in dismay from another. Good-bye my dear brother, I embrace you and all your family most cordially.

P.S.—I learn at the last moment that this letter will go to Paris by the Russian courier. If only I had known this sooner I should have been less reserved. Of course you understand by the 'White Spectre,' Austria. Let us stick to this name, which suits her well. Good-bye. Nothing new here.

---

[1] It was anticipated in diplomatic circles that Prince Lieven would not return to London as Ambassador, but the Duke of Wellington would not allow any representation to that effect to be made to the Emperor. In compliance with this view Lord Heytesbury writes from St. Petersburg : 'With respect to the Lievens, I shall take no steps for obtaining their recall, but at the same time shall do nothing to prevent the adoption of such a resolution.'

XC

Richmond : 1/13 December 1829.

My dear Alexander,—I am as little able to spare you my joy to-day as I was to worry you with my anxieties the other day. We are indeed delighted with the good news of the Emperor's health.[1] It seems as if I loved him the more since I had been troubled in mind concerning him. May God preserve him to us ! How I have invoked Him in my anxiety, and how I have thanked Him at my relief He alone knows.

You have no idea of how exclusively public attention has been centred upon the news of the Emperor's health. It seemed as if the world had come to a stop during that weary week, so general was the feeling that the fate of Europe hung upon that one life. If I were to say that all felt as we did it would not be the truth ; there were some disappointed—for instance, those of whom ' the Spectre ' is the friend, and in that quarter speculations as to what might happen were not wanting. But I will not allow myself the expression of one harsh feeling in the midst of my happiness, and I give myself up to it entirely with you, who can fully appreciate it. Dear, dear brother, the Emperor must be more careful of himself, and must husband his health, he owes it to us in return for the love that we bear him. Great joys and great fears alike absorb me entirely, I can talk of nothing else. I embrace you while congratulating him from the bottom of my heart.

To my knowledge the King showed a very great anxiety and our good Devonshire was much disturbed. Consequently he was one of the earliest to whom my husband sent the good news. The Cumberlands, too, displayed much sympathy, and as I believe genuine, for it was shown not only in our presence.

[1] The Emperor had been seriously ill from the effects of a chill, and for several days his condition caused much anxiety.

1830

[The Protocol relating to Greece in the Treaty of Adrianople had
been left for ratification by the Great Powers, the negotiations being
carried on in London.   Lord Aberdeen made no secret of his wish to
restrict the newly founded kingdom of Greece to the Morea and a
few adjacent islands, but the Ambassadors of Great Britain, Russia,
and France, who had withdrawn from Constantinople to the island of
Poros in the Greek Archipelago, had agreed to recommend a very
liberal interpretation of the terms upon which the new kingdom was
to be constituted. Great Britain had been at that time (February 1829)
represented by Mr. Stratford Canning, who so little represented the
wishes of the Duke of Wellington that although it was decided at a
conference in London (March 22) to adopt the conclusions of the
Poros settlement, Mr. Stratford Canning's resignation was accepted
with alacrity, and Lord Aberdeen's cousin, Mr. Robert Gordon, was
appointed Ambassador at Constantinople and ordered to take up
his duties forthwith, the French Government also instructing its
Ambassador to resume diplomatic relations with the Porte.   After
much delay and intrigue, which was ultimately cut short by Diebitch's
rapid advance, the Porte assented to the Treaty of London subject
to five conditions (August 15), and a month later (September 19) the
Plenipotentiaries met in London, when a strong divergence of opinion
was manifested.   Lord Aberdeen admitted that although he had
signed the Protocol of March 22, it was with the idea that it would not
be acted upon, but, finding no support from his French colleague,
he was ultimately forced to give way.   The Porte, emboldened by
the dissensions existing between the allies, attempted in several
ways to avoid complying with the terms of the Treaty, and the
Sultan's bad faith made the Russian Government less disposed to
moderate its demands.

One point, however, had been left wholly unsettled—the ruler of
Greece, which was to be erected into a kingdom under an hereditary

Christian Sovereign.   A fitting ruler was long in finding.   As far back
as 1825 the Greek deputation had suggested the Duke of Sussex, or,
failing him, Prince Leopold, but Canning had put aside the proposal
on the ground of the jealousy it would arouse among continental
nations.   The candidate first put forward was Prince Frederick of
Orange, but only to be withdrawn at his own request.   Prince
John of Saxony was next approached, but he also declined, whereupon the name of Prince Leopold of Coburg was again suggested and
found support from the British Government, and, although an objection was raised by the French Plenipotentiary, the candidature was
viewed with no disfavour by the Russian Ambassador, and was
urged by Leopold himself, whose position at the English Court was
in no way enviable.   His most active enemy was the Duke of
Cumberland, who at this time had the ear of the King his brother.
When, therefore, the Cabinet proposed that Prince Leopold should
be put forward George IV. peremptorily refused to listen to the
suggestion, and ordered Lord Aberdeen to propose the name of the
Duke of Mecklenburg-Strelitz (brother to the Duchess of Cumberland).   Prince Esterhazy at the same time put forward an Austrian
officer, Prince Philip of Hesse-Homburg.   There were other candidates who were also named, but promptly withdrawn—Maximilian
d'Este, brother of the Grand Duke of Modena, Prince Charles of
Bavaria, and a French prince (unnamed) who was to marry the
daughter of the Duke of Cambridge.   Lord Aberdeen, in order to
strengthen his own candidate, Prince Leopold, hinted to the King
that Prince Lieven was supporting the Austrian nominee.   This so
annoyed the King that (according to Madame de Lieven) he said
to Aberdeen that it was 'very desirable that they (the Lievens) should
be recalled.'   As a matter of fact Russia supported Prince Leopold,
and George IV., after a further outburst of temper, was forced to withdraw his objections and to submit to his Ministry.   On hearing the
decision of the Plenipotentiaries Prince Leopold, who for some time
previously had made little secret of his wish for the throne of Greece,
began to raise difficulties.   He desired that the island of Candia
(Crete) should be included in the Greek sovereignty, that the allies
should undertake to put down brigandage in the country, and that
the boundaries of the kingdom should be extended to Arta and Volo
on the north.   Much time was spent in overcoming these objections,
but he gave a verbal consent on February 21 ; but even then a
further delay arose, and finally the Plenipotentiaries Lord Aberdeen
and M. Laval were obliged to despatch their colleague Prince
Lieven to Claremont, February 25, to obtain Leopold's signature to a
document signifying his acceptance of the crown.]

XCI

London : $\frac{\text{January 22}}{\text{February 3}}$, 1830.

Many thanks, my dear Alexander, for the letter from you brought by the last courier. The one which my husband is sending off to-morrow has been starting any day for the last three weeks. The interminable delays of the English Government, its bad faith, and its bad manners, all these have made drag on from day to day, I might say from hour to hour, the conclusion of a business which ought to have been finished two months ago. We have to-day come to the actual point of signing,[1] but such is the reputation enjoyed at our Foreign Office by Lord Aberdeen—or rather by his leader, the Duke of Wellington—that my husband is actually in the dark as to whether they intend to sign or to break away. It is delightful to have to deal with such personages. Matuscevitz understands them thoroughly, and can realise the very unpleasant experiences my husband has had to bear.[2] It matters, however, little now, as he has quite made up his mind as to the attitude he will adopt and maintain. There is no longer any idea of conciliating the good will (of the English); Russia will never be able to gain this from them, but must adopt a firm attitude and enforce it by cold but polite language. Inspire them with fear, and all will go well ; and for my own part I may say that a greater coward at bottom than this great Captain could not be found. Of this my husband has already good proofs in many ways. When Wellington threatens one may be sure that he is afraid, and if only one sticks to the point he gives way. He is far too clever, however, not to see that we have taken his measure, and it is for that reason that he so cordially detests us. He would far rather have here some innocent creature whom he could lead by the nose, as he does the rest of the diplomatic

---

[1] The Protocol on Greece was signed on the date of this letter, and reference was made to the Treaty of Peace in the King's Speech on the following day.

[2] The efforts made by Wellington at this time to obtain the recall of Prince Lieven are stated at length in a letter from the Princess to Earl Grey dated January 25, 1830, but they do not agree with the Duke's version. (*Correspondence*, i. 418–9.)

P

body. He has just come through a sharp tussle with his master ; but a crisis now would not be to our taste, for it might have interfered with the Greek business, and our first interest is to settle this question and then come what will. Russia holds a strong and grand position, and her representatives may carry their heads high. The English Ministry, on the other hand, is faring ill. All classes throughout the country are suffering more or less, doubtless through no fault of the Ministry, but it is only natural for the ruled to throw the blame on their rulers, and since it is impossible for this Government to find remedies for so many grievances, and as the confidence which the nation once had in the Duke of Wellington has given place to much misgiving and not a little contempt, it follows that there is a fine opening for the ambitious to arouse a serious opposition, and most certainly he will be roughly handled by the three parties arrayed against him—the Tories, the Whigs, and the friends of Canning. The last named, although very inferior in point of numbers to the other two, are far superior in intelligence, experience, and even in ability. Moreover, they represent the happy medium between the extreme principles and opinions of the others. In a word, it is from this group, I am convinced, that the chief danger to the present Ministry will spring. I doubt much if Parliament will interest itself much in foreign affairs : the state of things at home will absorb its whole attention.

February 6.

I have delayed finishing this letter, dear Alexander, until to-day, and much has happened since I began it. Leopold will have nothing more to do with Greece. The Ministry want him to go away, the Opposition wish him to remain, that they may turn him to account. So the famous Protocol, the excellent Protocol, is hung up until a prince can be found who is prepared to accept the throne of Greece and is at the same time acceptable. For it required a *tour de force* to bring the three Cabinets to an agreement, which now seems likely to collapse. It is enough to drive one mad ; my husband moves me to pity, for he works like a galley-slave. We are, however, once more on the best of terms with the Ministers.

The session has opened ; the King's Speech is regarded as very feeble, the Ministry admit a partial distress in the country, the House of Commons pronounces it to be general and threatens to move an amendment on the Address.[1] The Government expected to find itself in a minority on the very first day, but was saved from defeat in the Commons by a handful of democrats. Such support cannot be counted on, and in the present state of affairs the Government cannot act. Some change must be made, and probably Wellington will find the way by allying himself with one or other party, or by detaching individual members from each. Meanwhile the prospect is by no means favourable to him.

However, I leave England to speak of our dear Russia and our beloved Emperor. Happy, indeed, are we for all the news which comes to us thence. His health before all things, our tranquillity, our prosperity, our glory ! What a contrast with what I am witnessing here ! This calms my feelings. Good-bye, dear Alexander ; love me a little, there are so few now left who love me.

XCII

London : 10/22 February 1830.

I will get this letter ready for the courier, my dear Alexander, and I will tell you about everything except the reason of his despatch, for as soon as one talks about Greece one is plunged into a maze of uncertainty and bad faith. The step made to-day is recalled to-morrow, and one is pretty certain of not speaking the truth if one tells on Friday the decision arrived at on Thursday. Consequently only in the form of a postscript, when closing my letter, shall I allude to the subject.

Parliament is doing better, or rather less badly, for Ministers than was augured from the opening night. Parties have

---

[1] The King's Speech made reference to the distress among the industrial and agricultural classes prevailing in some parts of the country. Sir E. Knatchbull moved as an amendment that the distress was not partial but general. It was defeated by 158 to 150 votes, in consequence of Hume and his friends supporting Lord Howick in refusing to upset the Ministry.

not yet grouped themselves, and there is already some doubt as to the unanimity of their intentions. So long as this exists no certain forecast of the future can be made. On the other hand, there is no doubt that the present situation is one of constant danger to the Government, which at any moment may find its opponents agreed upon some purely incidental question, and as the former has no actual majority in the Lower House it rests upon very uncertain ground.

We have just had a most terrible catastrophe here, and as the name of a member of the royal family is unfortunately mixed up with it I think you ought to know some of the details. The Duke of Cumberland for some time has been paying attention to Lady Graves [1] (sister of the Marquess of Anglesey), whose husband was Chamberlain to the King. The ways of the Court are well understood here, and there was nothing in the present case of the least importance. Lady Graves is fifty years old, the mother of thirteen children, and no longer with any pretensions to beauty. At the worst it was an old affair of mere flirtation, or even nothing more than long-standing habit. It was enough, however, for the Duke of Cumberland's name to get mixed up in it—he is the most widely hated man in England—for the public to take far more interest in the matter than there was occasion for. Lord Graves was informed by caricatures exposed in the shop windows of the gossip which busied itself with this *liaison*. He had a frank discussion with his wife, the result of which was to convince him that there was absolutely nothing but calumny in the matter, having for its political object to damage still further the Duke's reputation. A complete understanding was arrived at between husband and wife, and it was resolved that they should appear a good deal together in society in order to put a stop to these rumours. This decision is substantiated by several letters

[1] Lady Mary Paget, daughter of first Earl of Uxbridge, married Thomas North, second Lord Graves, in 1803. It was said of Lady Graves that she was the first lady of rank who had waltzed at a public ball. This happened at the county ball at Exeter in 1817. Lord Graves was a Lord of the Bedchamber nd Comptroller of the Household of the Duke of Sussex. He and his wife had long lived apart.

written to his wife by Lord Graves, who was detained in
London by his duties at the Custom House,[1] while his wife
was living in the country.   A fortnight ago he received an
anonymous letter enclosing cuttings from numerous newspapers, which agreed in putting upon his reconciliation with his
wife a dishonourable interpretation, insinuating that he had
been paid to bring it about.   He was alone in his dressing-
room, and, seizing a razor, cut his throat.   At the inquest
which followed a servant stated that all he had remarked was
that for some days previously his master had been in low
spirits, and on this the jury returned a verdict of 'temporary
insanity.'   All this was done in the course of a few hours,
and the public at once jumped to the conclusion that such
precipitation was suspicious.   Four and twenty hours later the
newspapers asserted that Lord Graves had been murdered by
the Duke of Cumberland.   It is impossible to describe the
sensation produced by this catastrophe ; but not a man in
his senses saw ought but absurdity in such an allegation.
Putting the case in its worst possible light—that Lord Graves
really believed his wife to be unfaithful—it was a stroke of
ill-luck for the Duke to be brought into connection with a
husband whose only remedy was suicide.   In any case, however, the catastrophe which would have aroused a feeling of
profound pity for the innocent cause has in this case drawn
down upon the head of the Duke of Cumberland a storm of
hatred and abuse the like of which one has never heard.   It
is, however, something of a small triumph for Ministers, who
have so much reason to be delighted that they are suspected,
not altogether without cause, of having stimulated the horrible
things said against the Duke.   For him the consequences
must be most serious, and his friends have advised him not
to attempt to face the storm, as they believe that he would be
stoned by the populace if he were to show himself.   Luckily
he is just now laid up at Kew, but that cannot last long.   The
Duchess, I believe, is altogether ignorant of what has happened,
even of Lord Graves' death.   I have not seen her since, but
her letters, which I receive almost daily, do not suggest that

[1] Lord Graves was a Commissioner of Excise not of Customs.

anything has disturbed her. In any case she is very much to be pitied, and inspires general sympathy. I have dealt at length on this subject because very possibly it will be much commented upon in our country.

The explanations given by the Duke of Wellington to the House of Lords concerning our war have greatly amused everybody.[1] I send you herewith—word for word and in the original—what Lord Grey writes to me on the matter. Get Matuscevitz to translate it for you, as I do not wish to run the risk of altering his views by my version :

'I well remember what you told me of the Duke of Wellington having protested (in talking to you) against the justice of your war. I well remember also the loud reprobation of all his adherents. They must, I think, have been more surprised than either you or me when they found that the cause against which they had been taught to declaim as a violent aggression had turned out at best to be sanctioned by a plea of justice which we could neither deny or resist. The conversation of all partisans of the Ministers was the same with respect to the eventual results of the war,' &c.

In fact, nothing is more adroit than to compare his present assertions with his previous declarations. I regret very much not having kept a copy of a certain conversation of which I sent you a note some time back. This, if read side by side with his speech in the Upper House, would give you some amusement. As I am on the subject of Lord Grey, I must give myself the pleasure of copying that portion of his letter which deals with Lord Aberdeen's speech on Dom Miguel.[2]

[1] A motion was made by Lord Holland on February 12 to the effect that no pacification of Greece would be permanently advantageous to the interests of Europe which did not give Greece sufficient territory for natural defence. After referring to the repeated assurances of the Ministry of the necessity of preserving Turkish influence in European affairs, he accused them of having surrendered everything—' our conduct with regard to Russia was the acme of imbecility.' The Duke of Wellington made the best retreat possible. He had not, he said, advised to blockade the Dardanelles, but he had done all in his power to prevail on the Porte to give satisfaction to Russia, and, having failed, it was impossible to prevent the war taking place. In answer to the question why England did not shield Turkey, the Duke gave no reply.

[2] Letter dated Howick, February 21, 1830.

' As to Terceira I do not think the defence of the Duke of Wellington and Aberdeen at all satisfactory, and I was a good deal amused by the complaint of the latter that the charges against Miguel had been much exaggerated, at the same time that he acknowledges him to be faithless, treacherous, perfidious, cowardly, and cruel.   I do not see how any person the most disposed to exaggerate could say anything worse.'

These quotations will prove to you that Lord Grey's opinion of the present Ministry has undergone a notable change, and my belief is that he is only waiting for the Opposition to ripen to come forward and upset the Duke— with the hope, of course, of taking his place, for after all that is the aim and object of English patriotism.

14/26 February.

I must close this letter to-day, as the courier is on the point of starting.   Well, my dear Alexander, the Greek business is ended, and well ended.   We have a King (Leopold) who just suits us because he does not suit the English Ministers.   They will have the honour, but we shall get the profit.   Leopold is altogether anti-English in all that concerns Greece ; he will be altogether Russian in that he recognises that it is to us that Greece owes its existence at all, that to us she will owe her future preservation and prosperity, and that the protection of the Emperor of Russia will for all time be his most constant and most powerful support.   I hope that people at home will be satisfied with all that we have done, and know that we have fagged hard to obtain this result.

The last courier brought me nothing from you, dear Alexander ; but I hear from Matuscevitz that the Emperor is well, that he is appreciated and loved, and that in every-thing and to everybody he is perfection.   This fills me with joy.

[The French Ministry under the presidency of M. Martignac, constituted in the autumn of the previous year, had been steadily losing such little confidence of the French people as the foolish Press laws of M. de Villèle might have stimulated for any alternative

Government.   The new Ministry, in which Prince Polignac was nominally Foreign Secretary, but virtually, and at the date of this letter actually, the chief, was known in France as 'Wellington's Ministry,' and thereby associated with the name best known in connection with the restoration of the Bourbons.   During his embassy in London and the negotiations connected with the Treaties of London and Adrianople Prince Jules de Polignac had personally commended himself to George IV. and the Duke of Wellington as a man of sincerity and conviction.   His advent to office in France was therefore cordially desired by the English Government, and while this event was almost universally condemned by the French Press it was almost as generally applauded by that of England, with the obvious result that the people of the two countries became more than ever estranged.]

XCIII

London : 7/19 March 1830.

My dear Alexander,—It is ages since I have any news from you—you have everything to tell and I nothing, and yet it is you who are silent and I who gossip.

Just now more attention is being paid to what is passing in France than in England.   Everybody with a grain of sense had hoped that the King would have sacrificed his infatuation for Polignac, who possesses no merits of any sort to justify such favours.[1]   He is a man without sense or ability, of a crooked and obstinate character, and with the narrowest views.   Let the King, if he wishes it, keep him as his friend, but it is dangerous to impose him as Prime Minister on an enlightened people who look for other qualifications than favouritism in their rulers.   It would really look to-day as if the King was prepared to stake the monarchy for Polignac, and it is this line which Wellington advises him to take. The latter finds himself somewhat stronger in Parliament, since by adopting the principles of economy suggested by the House of Commons he has proved himself ready to conform in every way to the wishes of the majority.   Strange indeed it is that the same man should bow to public opinion here

[1] It was a common belief among the lower classes in France that Prince Polignac was the son of Charles X. (Comte d'Artois) and that this accounted for the King's infatuation.   He married in 1824 Hon. Maria Charlotte Parkyns, daughter of first Lord Rancliffe and widow of the Marquis de Choiseul.

and at the same time should advise the French Ministry to resist it. ' Brave for others and timorous for oneself ' is a strange method. However, his ways are well understood here ; his idea of ruling is to obey—that is to say, the Opposition dictates the course which in home affairs the Government must take. In foreign policy it is very much the same, for after all can it be supposed that it is the Minister most hostile to the Greeks who makes Greece an independent and respectable State, or that it is the devoted friend of the Turks who leaves Turkey humiliated, impoverished, and only just able to exist because it suits our purpose that she should live ? The protector of Dom Miguel now heaps insult upon him ! In fact, this great man is a thorough impostor whose tricks have at last been laid bare. To sum up, there never was a Minister who was at the same time so disagreeable and so accommodating.

We are working together harmoniously : externally, at least, things are going excellently ; what lies at the bottom of their minds matters not to us, their hatred is more profitable to us than their love. I am sure Metternich himself will admit the truth of this : for, after all, what has he gained so far by possessing their goodwill, and what have we lost by not possessing it ?

The King is in good health—much in love with his big lady, and much in dudgeon with his big Minister. I don't know how this has come about again.

The Duke of Cumberland appeared in public yesterday for the first time since the sad business of Lord Graves. I have not heard that he was annoyed by the populace. The general opinion about him is less harsh—in other words, people begin to discuss the matter more impartially.

We have been giving a series of dinners and balls, although it is not yet the high season for London gaieties. Before Easter I shall have given nine balls, and this will spare me the necessity of going to other people's dances later on, for I cannot stand London ballrooms in summer.

I read with much interest the accounts of your Carnival ; it seems as if Petersburg had never been so gay as this year. I am delighted on account of both the Emperor and the

public.   These opportunities of mingling are always advan-
tages to the Chief of the State—an Emperor who is much seen
is an Emperor much loved.   It looks as if he had thoroughly
aroused this feeling in the country.

Good-bye, my dearest brother, is there any hope of seeing
you this year?   So many things are possible, so many are
difficult.   What do the newspapers mean by talking of the
Emperor's visit to Warsaw, and afterwards to Ems ?   If he
comes so far I verily believe that I should run on foot to see him,
and to see you also, for I am really hungering for the sight of
one and the other.   My husband's journey to Russia seems
very doubtful.   Will he be able to obtain leave of absence ?
and, between ourselves, would it be prudent to grant it ?
For he has now taken the measure of the English Ministers
and knows them thoroughly.

Good-bye again, my dear Alexander ; I embrace you
and your wife, and your children, and our children, most
affectionately.

[The sovereignty of Greece was definitely declined by Prince
Leopold on May 21.   At this time the state of George IV.'s health
was such as to presage his approaching death, so that Leopold's
relationship to the Duchess of Kent and Princess Victoria may have
reasonably influenced his decision.   But a more cogent reason
was probably the reply which Prince Leopold had received from
Capo d'Istria, the Greek President, to the letter in which he had
intimated his acceptance of the crown.   The Senate refused to
accept the boundaries of the new State as settled by the three
Powers, while the internal dissensions by which the country was
rent seemed to make the task of government hopeless.   Moreover, a
crown manufactured by politicians could have but few attractions to
a man of ability and honour except where there was for its wearer
the prospect of usefulness to his subjects.]

XCIV

London : 16/28 May 1830.

I am writing one more line, my dear Alexander, with one
foot almost in my travelling carriage, but still not knowing
when and if this carriage will bring me to your house.   For
the moment all our future is wrapped in Matuscevitz, who is

to be here in two days.[1]   Then comes in the question of the
King's health—or rather of his death, which is imminent, and
when this occurs the simplest rules of conventionality oblige
my husband to present his respects to the new Sovereign.
So you see here is at least a fortnight gone, and meanwhile
the summer is coming on.   We are eagerly impatient to
start, but we cannot foresee our movements a day in advance.
To-day we are saying that we shall start on Tuesday next,
but he would be a bold man who would venture to foretell
what we shall say to-morrow.   Meanwhile Leopold has
played us a pretty trick.   It is a bad business.   Now everything has to be begun again, just as one believed that everything was finally settled.   Who is going to take what Leopold
has refused ?   Who will take Greece without asking for more ?
Now there is a fresh set of difficulties to overcome—it is a
wearisome affair from whatever side one looks at it.   Here
the effect on the Ministry has been far more serious than they
at all imagined.   Leopold, in order to give a plausible excuse
for his withdrawal from a cause which had lost its charm,
puts forward reasons which suggest distinct ill-will towards
Greece on the part of the English Cabinet and the narrow-
ness of its political views.   This is naturally seized upon with
avidity by all the cleverer members of the Opposition, composed of the Canningites, the Whigs, and the Tories.   Hitherto they have wanted a leader to bring them together, but one
has at length been found in Lord Grey.   No sooner had he
made in the Upper House a speech attacking the Ministry
than all the factions composing the Opposition rallied to his
banner, and now they are all seated on the same benches.
The Ministry is alarmed, but Wellington still shows a bold
front.   We shall see how long he will continue to do so.   The
Duke of Clarence does not like him, and shows it by making
much of Lord Grey, to whom also public opinion has veered

[1] His coming to replace Prince Lieven during the latter's absence caused
Madame de Lieven some misgivings.   Writing to Lord Grey (June 7) she says :
' He (Matuscevitz) is not my friend : that is very evident.   He is enchanted at my
departure, because he wishes to be everything with the Ministers.   This is a
disagreeable discovery, for I had believed him to be really attached to me.'
(*Correspondence*, ii. 4.)

round in a marked manner. The Duke of Wellington has fallen from the high position he used to hold. All this shows that the position of the Government is precarious ; and I think that with the King's death we shall see a notable change. If this should happen all our friends will be in power.

The most delicate questions will be raised by the death of the King. It will be necessary to make provision for a regency in the case of the Princess Victoria's minority. The Duke of Cumberland is caballing for it, and Prince Leopold desires it. Most probably it will be assigned to the Duchess of Kent, the Princess's mother, in which case it will be Leopold who will rule. He has given us every reason for dissatisfaction and complaint on account of his conduct in the matter of Greece, and the English Government would be glad to follow our lead and to oppose the Prince's pretensions. This is a line, however, which prudence warns us not to take. He will be powerful some day, and indeed he is so already by the number of his supporters. He is attached to Russia on principle as well as by esteem—this consideration must not be disregarded. The time to profit by it will be sure to arrive.

I am eagerly looking forward, dear Alexander, to our being able to talk together ; to see our dear Emperor. Will it be at Warsaw ? My husband wants to go at once to his estates. If, however, Count Nesselrode wishes otherwise let an order be sent to that effect to await him at Berlin ; but all this hangs upon the question whether the King (George IV.) dies or does not die. His sister, the Duchess of Gloucester, who had seen him the day previous, told me yesterday that the wounds in the legs had been closed by the doctors for fear of gangrene supervening. Since, however, this relief had been stopped the water is dispersed all over the body. He has become enormous, like a feather bed, while his legs, also swollen, are as hard as stone ; his face is drawn and the features pinched, and he has attacks of choking, and in speaking of Leopold, against whom he is furious, he had a seizure which threatened to be fatal. The internal remedies he has taken to arrest the progress of dropsy have

upset the functions of the stomach, and for three days he
has eaten nothing. Such is the state of the case ; yet only
yesterday Wellington said to me, ' Oh ! the King is well—and
looks well.' Nevertheless Parliament has named a Commission to act in the King's name, and public prayers will be
offered for him in all churches next Sunday. The daily
bulletins are unsatisfactory, and the public is angry at not
being more distinctly informed of the real state of things.

Good-bye, my dear brother, I embrace you tenderly.

XCV

Berlin : $\frac{\text{June 23}}{\text{July 5}}$, 1830.

Dear, dear Alexander,—I was so sad at having to quit
you all that I made haste to get away as quickly as
possible from all the memories of Warsaw. I came here
post-haste, and arrived after a journey of fifty-five hours—
not very bad for a woman methinks.

I have heard here the news of the death of poor King
George IV., which has given me real sorrow. My letters
from London were written on the eve of his death, and I am
sending them to my husband ; for you I have made an
extract from Lord Grey's letter, as it deals with what is most
interesting.

My good brother, I am indeed grieved at our separation.
I love you so dearly, and I have so much need of your love.
Write to me often. You will have seen during our short
union how deeply I feel everything which concerns our dear
Emperor and our beloved Russia. Give me every detail
you can ; do not forget me, and do not let me be forgotten by
that Emperor whom I idolise. I will write to you very, very
often, and I will keep you informed of everything that is going
on, and things are going to be very interesting in England.
According to the letters I receive, it appears that the new
King made advances to Wellington some few days before
his accession, but that means nothing. I repeat it, he may
remain Minister, but he will never be the all-powerful man
he has been ; that is impossible in view of the King's
character, and equally so in view of his own fall in public

esteem.   Here, for instance, is what a member of the Lower House, a man of talent, writes to me :

'*June* 24.—Day after day the Ministers are beaten, routed in a way which would move one's pity if it were not wholly their own fault, or rather the fault of the obstinacy of their leader.   On Monday there was a keen debate on the sugar duties.   Brougham and Huskisson jeered at them, and turned them into ridicule in every conceivable way, and those miserable creatures had not a word to say in reply.   They will only carry their Bill by a majority of seventeen.   This evening they will have to submit to being tortured over the Chancery Bill ; to-morrow there is to be another night given up to the Sugar Duties, and in the Upper House the Galway franchise comes on.   Lord Grey has taken the lead on this question, and is greatly incensed at the Government making it a party question and sending out " a whip " against him.'

My letters from London suggest the idea that the unfortunate Matuscevitz has to bear the burden of a suspicion which has arisen there, God knows how, that he wishes to occupy the post which he has been holding temporarily. The consequence is that he is looked upon with an unfriendly eye by London society.   My first business will be to put a stop to this rumour, and I hope to do him the good turn of getting him kindly received ; for it is bad for business to be looked at askance by 'society' in England, and by clever men who are influential in Parliament.[1]

Good-bye, dear Alexander.   I am half dead with fatigue, visits, and letter-writing ; ach ! how I wish I were back in my quiet corner at Richmond.   I embrace you, dear, dear brother, and love you with all my heart.   I am indeed happy in the thought of those ten days at Warsaw, although I know you say just the reverse for other reasons ; but I enjoyed all sorts of happiness.   *Liebe mich, mein lieber Bruder.*

[1] Madame de Lieven's suspicions, as expressed to Lord Grey, had been dissipated by her journey to Warsaw.   Matuscevitz was to remain in London only so long as Prince Lieven was replacing Count Nesselrode at St. Petersburg as Minister of Foreign Affairs *ad interim.*

Keep an eye on my poor Constantine; be stern, you must, but mingle a little kindness.

Entreat my husband to send me a line by each post: you are as much, and even more occupied than he is likely to be, and I am sure that you never miss writing to your wife. I am horribly sad at being separated from you all.

XCVI

Richmond: 8/20 July 1830.

I begin, dear Alexander, a letter which cannot be sent off for some days, but as my poor head is still weak I am obliged to parcel out my occupations in order to get through them. I must ask you, too, in advance to pardon the incoherences of this letter. I will ramble on according as things come into my mind.

In the first place, there's the King! a quaint King, indeed! a *bon enfant*—with a weak head! At times I think he is likely to lose it, so great is his pleasure at being King! He changes everything except what he ought to change—his Minister. He changes the uniform of the army and of the navy, he dismisses his cooks and his French servants. He will have none but English. The cook-business was the first act of his reign— on the very day of the late King's death. He makes everybody cut off their moustaches; he strolls about the streets, and gossips with the passers-by. He goes to the Guard-room and shows the officer in command his ink-stained fingers, tells him how many letters he has signed, of the audiences he is going to give: talks about the Queen, his wife, and promises to bring her to the Guard-room to make his acquaintance. Every day he attends parade, and puts the battalion through its exercises—and in this way intends to review the regiment. The day after the King's funeral he took possession of Windsor Castle, where the Ministers and great officers of the Household awaited him. He arrived perched outside a small carriage, in which were the Queen and his two bastard daughters. The day before yesterday he paid a visit to Lord and Lady Holland, and invited himself to dinner for next week, to the dismay of

his Ministers.   He also asked Prince Leopold to invite him
to dinner, expressing the wish that Lord Grey should be
one of the guests.   This will be another cause for alarm.
Outwardly his attitude towards the Duke of Wellington is
most friendly and confidential, but to the Duchess of
Cumberland, who asked if he had given him an audience
that morning, replied : 'Thank God, no, Madam.   I am only
too happy not to see him—I wish I might never see him.'
These were his actual words.   He displays a prodigious
activity ; he is delighted with court ceremonies and recep-
tions, is constantly showing himself in public, occupied all
day long in trifles, eager to reform everything at once—in
a word, he is in a state of feverish excitement.   The mob
adores him, he goes about openly and treats everyone
familiarly—that is enough for John Bull.   The contrast
between his ways and those of the late King is altogether
favourable to the present.   In fact England is quite a new
world, and Wellington said to me quite truly : ' This is not
a new reign, it is a new dynasty.'   I suspect that he is not
sorry that the King should waste his time on trifles.   He has
no leisure left for business, which remains under the exclusive
control of the Prime Minister.

I am sending you herewith the translation of a letter
written to me by Lord Grey which I only received on
arriving here.   Although of old date, it explains so clearly
the motives which may have induced the King to retain
Wellington, and gives such a well-defined sketch of the
situation and of the Duke's position, that I am sure you will
find it interesting—perhaps the Emperor may deign to cast
his eye over it.   For the moment Wellington is apparently
as much the master as under the previous reign, but no one
thinks that he can remain so unless he is prepared to alter
the composition of his Cabinet—the proof is that a fortnight
ago he made indirect overtures to Lord Grey, and, a week
later, to Lord Melbourne (a Canningite).[1]   The former

[1] There is no reference to the advances to Lord Grey in the latter's letters, who,
writing on July 2, says that ' there has been no disposition shown on the part of
the Minister to gain any accession of strength from any quarter.'

replied that he could accept nothing but what came as a direct proposal, and recognised as a starting-point a complete reconstruction of the Cabinet. Lord Melbourne, to whom the Duke had offered seats in the Cabinet for himself, Lord Palmerston, and a third at his choice, excluding Mr. Huskisson, replied that he could take no part in any arrangement in which Huskisson and Lord Grey did not figure.[1] Neither reply was to the Marshal's taste, and the negotiations came to an end—I saw him just afterwards, and found him grumpy and pre-occupied. We are on very good terms just now. He went to see my children in the country during my absence. This called for a little politeness on my part, so I wrote to him. He came to see me yesterday and we ended by saying quite tender things to each other : and you may rest assured that we are once more on an excellent footing. He talked much about the King and his favours, remarking that there was no longer need of citing Henry V. of England or Louis XII. of France as forgetting past offences, for William IV. had surpassed them both in overlooking harsh treatment, for ' to tell the truth,' he added, ' I dismissed him (the King) as I would have dismissed any other officer.' [2] He laughed very much at the King's droll doings.

As for the late King he is completely forgotten, and, if remembered, it is only to criticise his morals. It is in the middle and lower classes especially that this side of his character has left a very unfavourable impression—an impression which overshadows much that was striking and brilliant in his reign. His glory is forgotten, and his vices exaggerated ; so true is it that what a nation most appreciates in its sovereign is domestic virtue. Dear Alexander, how happy we should be in having *everything* united in our Emperor. How can we be sufficiently grateful to Providence for this blessing ?

But, to return to England, the present King takes especial

[1] These negotiations were communicated to Lord Grey through Lord Holland.

[2] From the office of Lord High Admiral.

Q

pains to give proof of a line of conduct totally opposed to his brother's. He shows himself everywhere with the Queen, he puts her forward on every occasion ; he is always surrounded by the other members of the royal family ; all this has a good effect. He goes to church in public, he affects simple manners and popular ways, and dispenses charity—in a word, he is, as I have already said, a *bon enfant* with a weak head. He has just invited the King of Würtemberg to pay him a visit, and has done the same by the King of Prussia. He is eager for attentions, after the fashion of a *parvenu.* France is sending the Duc de Mouchy.[1] I shall be curious to know whom the Emperor will send as 'complimenting' Ambassador. Michael Woronzow would be an unexceptionable choice, and would be heartily received by the King. If it should not be he, you know very well for whom my heart yearns—that dear Tolstoy, it would be a delightful pleasure to me. I often think of our pleasant hours at Warsaw. I like straightforward minds, and plain speaking without phrases. How thoroughly I felt at home among you all ! I like some of my English friends well enough, but after all my heart is not laid open to them as it was at Warsaw.

I am still very ill, dear Alexander. I have been bled twice since coming here, and I am forbidden to go about ;[2] but I see some of my acquaintance who call. I have not yet been able to present myself at Court ; but the King, having heard of my accident, sends to inquire for me. I am keeping quite quiet, both body and mind. I really cannot throw hindrances in the way of friends who come to give me their confidences, so I keep myself informed of what is going on ; but that is all, absolutely all, and there I shall take my stand.

I must end this long letter. I am not bringing it to a close until to-day, July 13 (N.S.), and it is disjointed enough,

[1] Charles de Noailles, a member of the old French nobility, who had rallied to the Orleanist Dynasty, while his son subsequently supported the Second Empire. Both the Duc de Mouchy's parents perished on the scaffold in 1793.

[2] The Princess met with a carriage accident on her journey to England and was badly injured.

as you will easily see by the style ; but really my poor head can do no better. Just another word. The King is anxious to assimilate the regiments of Guards to the rest of the army, and to make the Captain of the Guard (Gold Stick) a Court officer, the Duke of Cumberland being one. The consequence is that the Duke wants to get rid of his office for the twofold reason that as a Prince of the Blood it is not fitting for him to hold an office about the Court,[1] and as a Field Marshal he cannot receive orders from a general officer of lower grade, as is Lord Hill, the present Commander-in-Chief.[2] This difficulty makes the King pause ; he is on good terms with his brother, but on infinitely better with the Duchess of Cumberland, who is also much liked by the Queen. Little Prince George of Cumberland is regarded almost as if he were heir to the Crown, while the real heir, little Victoria, is treated rather shabbily. From this you may gather that the Court, even as seen from Richmond, affords much amusement—and I believe that it will do so more and more, so that my letters may possibly become interesting.

So far as regards foreign politics everything that the King does or says shows his desire to be on friendly terms with everybody. I don't suppose, however, that he has so far taken up important affairs, he has been so much occupied with trifles—but their turn will come. Münster[3] is much in favour, and this is as well, as he is quite with us.

Write to me frequently, my good brother, tell me every-

[1] The Duke of Cumberland as ' Gold Stick ' had taken upon himself all the Court functions of the other Colonels of the Guards. The King, who personally disliked his brother, put an end to this arrangement by making the office of ' Gold Stick ' a military one.

[2] General Sir Rowland Hill, G.C.B., son of Sir John Hill, M.P., third Baronet, distinguished himself in the Peninsula. Created Baron Hill 1814, was Commander-in-Chief 1828-42.

[3] Ernest Frederick Count Münster, G.C.B., the Hanoverian Minister, born 1766. He filled many high diplomatic posts, and in 1806 formally opposed the occupation of the Electorate by Prussian troops. He was afterwards Hanoverian Ambassador at St. Petersburg and London, and ultimately held the post of Regent of Hanover until 1831, when he was succeeded by the Duke of Cambridge. He refused both a title and a pension offered him by the King.

thing about our Emperor, I cannot tell you how completely
he has captivated my head and my heart. I try to put myself
on my guard against such enthusiasm, but even when I come
to reflect coolly I find the result the same. I almost wish
that I had some little grievance against him so that I might
not love him so much. Ah, I have found one. He cut me
short when I was talking to him of himself—that is to say,
I did not dare to be as frank with him as I am with others.
That rankles in my memory.

What is that charming Empress doing? Tell me everything. Have you finished 'Oscar'? If Tolstoy [1] is still with
you, embrace him on my behalf. A thousand loves to your
wife, your children, and to Masha. How happy I was to
find myself with my dear little ones; they are so sweet, so
good, and very Russian.

How does my husband get on with his new work? I
could make a letter of nothing but questions, but I am tired
out. I embrace you, my dear good brother. I entreat you
to love me very much, my heart has much need of tenderness,
for it gives you so much of its affection.

Sir Robert Wilson [2] has been reinstated in his rank as
Lieutenant-General. This is generally approved except by a

[1] Count Peter Tolstoy, a man distinguished for his integrity and everywhere
respected. In early life he had served in the Polish campaign (1794-9), was the
intermediary between Suwarrow and Archduke Charles during the Italian
campaign (1799). After the Peace of Tilsit he was for a year Ambassador in Paris,
and in the Russian campaign after Moscow took a conspicuous part. He retired
subsequently to Warsaw, and in 1831 was appointed to command the Russian
Reserve in the Polish War.

[2] General Sir Robert Wilson, born in 1777, served with 15th Light
Dragoons in the Low Countries, 1794; in Ireland, 1798; in Egypt with Sir R.
Abercrombie, and the capture of the Cape of Good Hope, 1806. He was British
Commissioner with the Prussian army, and according to report obtained know-
ledge of the terms of the Treaty of Tilsit by taking the place of one of the Russian
Guards on the raft on the river Niemen on which Napoleon and the Emperor
Alexander I. met in 1807. He afterwards commanded a Spanish brigade under
Wellington in the Peninsula, and then was appointed Commissioner to the Russian
army during the Moscow campaign and the subsequent advance to Paris, having
commanded the Prussian Reserve at Lützen. In 1818 he was returned to the
House of Commons as a Radical for Southwark, and sat until 1831, and for taking
an active part on behalf of Queen Caroline in 1820 he was dismissed from the
army, but was reinstated on the accession of William IV. and appointed Governor
of Gibraltar.

few friends of the late King, who think it an insult to his memory.

[The French Chambers had met on March 2, and the King in his speech had declared that if obstacles to his Government should arise which he could not and did not desire to foresee he should find strength to overcome them in the loyalty of his people.   These words were interpreted as a direct challenge to the Liberal party, which, being in a majority in both Chambers, replied coldly in their respective addresses, the deputies adding an appeal to the King to choose between his Parliament and the parties which misunderstood the mind of the French people.   On March 18 the King received the addresses, and in his reply said : ' I am grieved to find that the deputies declare that their concurrence in bringing about the good I contemplate, no longer subsisted.   I announced my intentions at the opening of the Session.   These intentions are immutable.   The interest of my people forbids my receding from them.   My Ministers will make my further purposes known to you.'   The next day the Chambers were prorogued, and shortly afterwards dissolved.   The new elections, which took place on June 14, were everywhere hostile to the Government, but the new Parliament was summoned to meet on August 3.   In the meanwhile Charles X., on the advice of Prince Polignac, signed on July 25 the five *ordonnances* abrogating the chief features of the Charter granted by Louis XVIII. in his restoration. These suspended the liberty of the press, decreed the dissolution of the newly elected Chamber of Deputies, altered the system of election, convoked a new Parliament for September 28, and added several Ultra-Royalists to the Council of State.   On July 27 rioting took place in the streets of Paris, barricades were thrown up, the city was declared in a state of siege, but the troops either fraternised with the populace or were worsted in several encounters, and the Tuileries on the 29th was stormed by the mob.   After much hesitation the King, who was at Saint-Cloud, consented to revoke the *ordonnances* and to dismiss his Ministry.   His courtiers, however, more clearly appreciating the situation, abandoned their master, and on July 31 Charles X. left Saint-Cloud for Rambouillet, and the Duc d'Orléans was appointed Lieutenant-General of the kingdom.   On the following day Charles offered to abdicate in favour of his grandson, the Duc de Bordeaux, the posthumous son of the Duc de Berri, afterwards called Henri V. and Comte de Chambord.   The answer from the Provisional Government in Paris was that the royal family should start at once for Cherbourg and leave the kingdom.   On August 4 the King set out, lingering on the way, in the hope of a revulsion of feeling, but on August 7 Louis Philippe, Duc d'Orléans, was elected King of the French, and on August 16 Charles X. embarked at Cherbourg for Spithead on board the steamship *Great Britain*. Weymouth was the first landing place of the exiled royal family ; Lulworth Castle, the seat of the Welds, where the Duke of Gloucester had lived for some years, being selected as their temporary residence. Three months later the King offered them the use of Holyrood Palace, of which they availed themselves until they finally settled in Austria.]

XCVII

Richmond : 16/28 July 1830.

Dear Alexander,—I overwhelm you, I know it, but since our meeting I feel so great an impulse to resume our chat that on the eve of every post-day I have an uncontrollable impulse to write to you.   So here I am again, as loquacious as I was at Warsaw.

I am better in health, I have been able to present myself at Court, and the day before yesterday dined at the Palace. The King and Queen received and treated me with marked favour.   What a totally new spectacle the Court presented, and what a completely different nation are the English of to-day !   From grave and depressed they have become possessed of a gaiety, a vivacity, and a movement which makes them scarcely recognisable.   The King, for whom the proverb ' Happy as a king' seems certainly to have been invented by anticipation, imparts to all about him this extraordinary animation.   He shows by his manners, his good-nature, and cordiality, a sense of gratified pleasure which is quite contagious.   I met at dinner all shades of opinion ; he is polite to everyone, and perpetually moving about.   You will see from what Matuscevitz is writing that his regard for his Prime Minister is such as no monarch had the like for a subject.   I must say that I cannot discover that the Duke's confidence in the King's favour has been increased by the latter's speech at the Duke's dinner table.[1]   I congratulated him upon it as one would a man whose power to all eternity

[1] The King, in proposing the Duke's health, said that it was a mistake to suppose that he had any ill-feeling—any feeling but of entire confidence in his good friend the Duke of Wellington.

had been ratified under seal; he answered very frankly that for his own part he would far rather that the King had not made the speech. This is precisely the impression which some of the other Ministers brought away. I cannot, however, help thinking that, expressed thus openly on the eve of a general election, it cannot fail to produce favourable effects for the Marshal.

The King has spared no pains to do honour to the King of Würtemberg,[1] who is very much as he always has been, and I had a long talk with him. He discoursed at length on his own modesty, and on his thoroughly pacific attitude, on the unjustifiable mistrust of which he has so long been the victim, of the ill-natured conduct of the late Emperor and of the coldness of our Court—of the great qualities of the present Emperor, and his wish to be received by us upon a more friendly footing.

18/30 July.

I was interrupted, and can only now take up my pen to finish this letter. I will write you a longer one by the courier whom Matuscevitz is sending off the day after to-morrow.

The events in France are most deplorable, and stir everybody of all classes here. There is a general outcry. I have told my husband, in my letter to him, what the Duke of Wellington said to me about the business. Read my letter.

I have been terribly upset by the accident from which my husband so narrowly escaped.[2] How awkward or misfortunate we have both been. Thank God, he is now all right again, and I have only a strained back.

I embrace you most heartily, dear Alexander, and entreat you to write to me and to love me.

---

[1] William I. His father, Frederick II., Duke of Würtemberg, who had by attaching himself to Napoleon been successively advanced to be Elector and then King, had especially offended Russia by sending a contingent of 16,000 to serve in the invasion of that Empire, and his hostility to Austria had been similarly shown in 1805. His son inherited the ill-will of the Emperors of both countries.

[2] Prince Lieven was seized with serious illness on his way from Warsaw to St. Petersburg, and for three days lay in a critical state in a wretched Polish village.

XCVIII

Richmond : 1/13 August 1830.

Thanks, my dear good brother, for your letter of July 14/26 from Krasnoe-Selò. Thanks for all you say in it—I feel only too keenly the truth of all you say. Yes ! most assuredly I ought to have gone to Petersburg ; so much for poor human counsels. Care for my health urged me towards England, and here I am laid up, without strength, or any immediate hope of getting well. At the same time my stay at Revel had to be given up. But for this I should have passed the summer with you, near the Emperor and that Empress whom I dare to love with all the strength of my heart. I could shed tears of bitter regret, but I forget that regrets are foolish, for one cannot recall the past. Let us then turn to the present, which, alas ! looks badly. The democratic turn taken by things in France disturbs me greatly. Will this new King [1] (to whom I am ready to attribute the best intentions) be strong enough to do what he knows to be right? What a shred of power is left to him ! What a misfortune that it should be left in the hands of an idiot like Polignac to prepare for Europe this labyrinth of confusion and danger. However, it is very good of me to worry myself about other nations ; whatever blunders their rulers may make, we shall never commit them, I am sure. I have such complete trust in the Emperor that being Russian I feel myself altogether at ease and at rest ; and, after all, his wisdom will be a good example for others, and may prevent the less far-sighted from burning their fingers.

Public opinion here remains the same among all classes, who show the keenest interest in the new order of things in France. I doubt if there is any man, however powerful, who would care to run counter to the general feeling. The more moderate express regret that necessity has compelled a change in the destinies of France ; but they congratulate themselves honestly that nothing worse has happened. By 'worse' they mean a Republic, and at all events the

[1] Louis Philippe.

monarchical principle has been saved, and that is what they think important to maintain.

The elections in England are not favourable to the Government ; in all the counties and in the free boroughs the ministerial candidates have been ousted in favour of Whigs, or of Tories hostile to the Ministry. Parliament is to meet on October 20, and meanwhile all the Ministers are away from London. This prevents their coming to any resolution with reference to French affairs, and this policy suits them for the time being.

Count Haugwitz,[1] the Austrian ' complimental ' Ambassador, dined the day before yesterday at Windsor with the King, who drank the health of the Emperor of Austria, accompanying it with a speech full of veneration and attachment for the Emperor Francis, and of the need, especially at this moment, of a close union with Austria. Prince Augustus of Prussia and the Prussian Minister were also at table. In another speech full of personal compliments and praise he drank to the King of Prussia.

May God preserve you, dear Alexander. Good-bye ; a thousand tender messages to all your belongings. I shall look impatiently for news from you, and Europe will also be awaiting it with equal impatience. This is a momentous occasion, it will affect centuries. May Heaven inspire the Emperor, the peace of the world hangs on his decision.

I see by my husband's letter that he is as much in love with his master as I am.

XCIX

Richmond : 14/26 August 1830.

A courier is starting, dear Alexander, and that means a bundle of gossip from me. To begin with, and to ward off any questions about my health, I will begin by telling you that I am a little better, but still quite incapable of walking from the Lazienski Palace to the amphitheatre.[2] What a

---

[1] Count Eugen von Haugwitz, an Austrian General and Commander of the Teutonic Order.

[2] At Warsaw ; a short distance.

delightful walk it was! Heigho! I feel my heart grow heavy, dear brother, when I think how short were the hours that I spent with you. Now that we have got rid of my health, let us turn to that of Europe.

Is France really quiet? and will her neighbours remain so? The new King is very weak and easily led; the National Guard is very republican. Spain is wretchedly governed, Italy terribly oppressed, and the example of France is all the more dangerous as its revolution, it must be admitted, was carried through with moderation and was altogether provoked by the bad faith of the Government. If, on the one hand, the warning is useful to kings, on the other the example is bad for peoples. In any case it is a bad business, for which there is now no remedy, and the only thing to be done is to make it as little dangerous as possible. My belief is that the only wise policy to adopt is to support the new Government. Here, at first, there were plenty of wry faces, but it was found advisable to bend before the inevitable. The Duke of Wellington, who is never wanting in tact and perception when his own security is at stake, very promptly realised that he must recognise ' la Nouvelle France,' or resign. He chose the former course, at an opportune moment. With one hand he offered an asylum to the passing dynasty, and with the other he recognised the coming dynasty. In England he will be warmly applauded on all sides, except by a few Ultras (with 'the Duke of Cumberland at their head), who would have liked to go to war to support the claim of the Duc de Bordeaux.[1] This strain of romanticism and chivalry is all very well in the mouth of M. de Chateaubriand, but it is sorely out of place in the present state of Europe.[2] Everything has become far too positive in the world to allow leanings in that direction.

I had a long *tête-à-tête* with the Duke of Wellington the day before yesterday. He talked of absolutely nothing else

[1] Posthumous son of the Dauphin, the Duc de Berri, afterwards known as Comte de Chambord and called by the Legitimists Henri V.

[2] Chateaubriand had eloquently maintained the rights of the Duc de Bordeaux, but he was supported by only nineteen of his fellow peers, although seventy-six had been created by Charles X. in the previous year.

but French affairs—regretting the past, disquieted with
regard to the future, but determined to give no cause of
offence ; in a word, not to give France the slightest pretext
for suspicion or uneasiness.   He expressed himself strongly
on M. de Metternich's proposal to hold a conference at Berlin.
He said : ' It would be renewing Pillnitz, [1] whence proceeded
all the evils which for so long have weighed down Europe.
We want the reality (of an understanding), and should beware
of the mere form.   The representatives of the Great Powers
have only to discuss frankly and fully among themselves any
point which can throw light upon the situation.   There is
need for anxiety (these are his very words), and there is need
for watchfulness, but there is no need to exasperate France
by making her think that there exists a tribunal sitting in
judgment on her.'

He spoke of Polignac with an indifference which quite
shocked me, saying, with a significant gesture, ' He will lose his
head.'   Such is the man ; I thought him looking very ill, thin
and drawn.   The truth is that things are going badly for him
in this country—the late elections were most disastrous for the
Government, which has lost far more seats than it has gained.
Lord Grey puts the loss at fifty votes on a division, but I
have my doubts, although there is no doubt that throughout
the elections the hostility to the Ministry was very strongly
marked.[2]   Twelve counties have passed into the hands of the
Whigs in England alone, and the county members are the
dominant party in the Lower House.   The Chancellor [3] (who
is a Cabinet Minister) declared to me that it would be impossible to begin the session without getting some reinforce-
ments : that all his colleagues are agreed upon this except
the Duke of Wellington, that they have greatly lost credit

[1] By the Declaration of Pillnitz in 1791 Austria and Prussia agreed to take
common action on behalf of the royal family of France.

[2] Of the eighty-two county members, forty-seven were members of the
Opposition, twelve supporters of the Ministry, and the remainder doubtful in their
allegiance.   Of the representatives of the large cities, twenty-four were Liberals
and only three Ministerialists.   Nominally the Tories still had a majority, but as
a body they no longer even pretended to support the Duke's Ministry.

[3] Lord Lyndhurst.

by the elections, that the ministerial party is weak-kneed, and that Peel by himself is not capable of weathering the storm in the Commons. Nevertheless I persist in thinking that he will try to go on with the materials he has in his hands, and that his tactics will be, as in the last session, to take his cue from the Opposition, and by this device he will always find himself sure of a majority. This is not ruling, but obeying, but it means remaining Prime Minister, and that, I assure you, is all that he cares for. The King does not interfere with him in any way ; he is a poor sort of creature. He thinks he has done everything if he reads very quickly and very carefully every morning the papers which it pleases the Duke of Wellington to send him. He allows nothing to hang about, as did the late King, but he has no opinions other than those which Wellington suggests for him on the margin of the papers. Sometimes he gets his lesson a little late, and then he talks foolishly, and his Ministers have to come to set him right. This was how it happened that he spoke aloud of the Duc d'Orléans as ' an infamous scoundrel.' Wellington told him that he must curb his speech ; and since then when France is spoken of he pinches his lips and holds his tongue. The Duke of Wellington said to me the other day : ' Really my master is too stupid, so that when at table he wishes to make a speech I always turn to him my deaf ear, so as not to be tempted to get up and contradict him.' He admitted to me that the King allows him to do everything, and occupies himself only with getting amusement out of his kingship.

I read the other day a letter from the Marquess of Anglesey in which he gives an account of his visit to Charles X.[1] He found the ex-King tranquil and resigned, throwing on Prince Polignac the fault of all the troubles which had come upon him ; but it was above all the Princesses who did not spare the ex-Minister, and Anglesey describes them as ferocious on this point. The Dauphine [2] absolutely insists upon remaining in England—and after all, that is, I think, how the matter will end.

---

[1] At Lulworth Castle in Dorsetshire, the seat of the Weld family.
[2] The Duchesse d'Angoulême.

Our people will, I believe, be pleased with d'Athalin,[1] the French Envoy. He has the most engaging manners. You know also that he is the husband, or at least the lover, of Mademoiselle d'Orléans,[2] and that she rules her brother. The Emperor, when he was in England, saw the whole of this *ménage* at Twickenham. This reminds me, and in fact the Duc d'Orléans recalled it to my memory last year, that the Duc de Nemours, then only two years old, persisted in calling Nicholas ' Emperor the Great,' and that nothing would induce him to say ' Grand Duke.' His family at the time said, ' Well, that only shows foresight.'

I am living here quite quietly—fresh air, simple diet, enough visits to keep me informed of what is going on, on good terms with everybody of every shade ; all goes well, except my back.

I have just had a visit from General Baudrand.[3] I could not well avoid it, knowing so well as I do the Orléans family. His stories interested me, but the picture which he drew of his master's situation was far from reassuring. He has to be very careful in his treatment of the Republican party—and of Lafayette, who, although he has recognised the monarchical principle *au fond*, did so with ill grace. The Duc d'Orléans and he were scarcely acquainted, and when the deputies voted him the Lieutenancy (of the kingdom) Lafayette held out for fourteen hours against this general wish—a few minutes longer and the Republic would have been proclaimed.[4] This faction is still very strong, and it will need a good deal of skill to keep it in check. This is a sad lookout. Baudrand

[1] General d'Athalin distinguished himself in the wars of the Empire, created baron after the battle of Dresden. After the Restoration he was appointed aide-de-camp to the Duc d'Orléans, who on his succession to the throne employed him on several diplomatic missions. He was an accomplished artist. There is no ground for Madame de Lieven's suggestion.

[2] Princess Adelaide, daughter of Philippe Egalité and sister of Louis Philippe.

[3] Sent to London to announce the accession of Louis Philippe. He had been tutor to the King when Duc de Chartres.

[4] Marquis de Lafayette, the friend of Washington, served in the American War of Independence, 1777–84 ; took a prominent part in the early stages of the French Revolution ; commanded the Army of the Ardennes, 1790 ; imprisoned by the Austrians ; sat in the Chamber of Deputies 1818–24, and was leader of the Liberal Opposition 1825–30. Died 1834.

ascribes to the Dauphin [1] rather than to Charles X. the blunders which were committed. He entirely disculpates the Dauphine, the only '*man*' of talent in the family, from any share in the catastrophe. Here the Duke of Wellington has received him (General Baudrand) very coldly ; Lord Aberdeen very warmly, consequently very deceitfully. The King was quite correct. He returns to-day with the replies of the King of England.

Here is my letter which I had got ready for the Russian courier. Matuscevitz has played me a trick in not despatching him after having given me notice : last week he sent off one without letting me know—I am somewhat annoyed. What shall I do with my letter ? I will send it, dear Alexander, by the Prussian courier—it seems to me to be домтиеппй,[2] but I will risk it. Let me hear if it reaches you safely and intact. Good-bye, my dear, dear brother. I embrace you most heartily and most affectionately.

[The Greek question, apart from the choice of a king, had been scarcely settled, and the clouds which had collected over the political sky dispersed, when the Belgian revolution threatened to provoke a fresh storm. Belgium (as the Netherlands), essentially Catholic, which until 1789 had formed part of the Austrian dominions, was by the Treaty of Vienna in 1814 united to Holland, a distinctly Protestant Government, with scarcely more than one half its population. Both countries had equal representation in the States-General, but the seat of Government and of the Court was in Holland, the great majority of public officials, as well as of the officers of the army and professors in the Universities, were Dutch, and an effort was made to make Dutch the only language in judicial proceedings. At the same time the Belgians were far more heavily taxed than the Dutch. In the spring of the year the growing feeling of the Belgians against Dutch rule had been shown in Parliament and in the Press, but the elections which followed disclosed no symptoms of immediate disturbance. The events in Paris furnished the necessary impulse to the revolutionary party, and, although some concessions had been made to Belgian feeling, the chance performance of Auber's ' Muette de Portici ' (' Masaniello ') on the night of August 25 gave rise to a

---

[1] Duc d'Angoulême, eldest son of Charles X., whose wife the Dauphine was Marie-Thérèse, daughter of Louis XVI. He died in 1844.

[2] Guesswork.

sudden and unexpected outburst of popular discontent. The mob attacked the houses of the more unpopular Ministers, and in the early dawn the Brabant flag was hoisted on the Hôtel de Ville. The troops were called out, but being left without orders were powerless, and a civic guard was hastily formed by an improvised Committee of Public Safety to protect property and peaceful citizens. Having restored order, they despatched a deputation to the King at the Hague to demand certain concessions to Belgian sentiment. The King replied by sending his eldest son, the Prince of Orange, to negotiate, and at the same time ordered his second son, Prince Frederick, to advance with 6,000 troops against Brussels. On August 31 the two Princes called upon the city authorities to disband the civic guard and to restore the city to the King's troops. This was refused, and barricades were thrown up to prevent the entry of the Dutch troops. The Prince of Orange then consented to enter the city alone, and after various proposals had been rejected, suggested a legislative and administrative separation of the two countries under the same crown. This was generally accepted by both Dutch and Belgians, but the King refused to decide anything until the meeting of the States-General at the Hague, which met on September 13, and for a fortnight did nothing until events at Brussels forced them to endorse an inevitable step.]

C

Richmond : $\frac{\text{August 22}}{\text{September 3}}$, 1830.

As my husband seems to have made up his mind never-more to write to me (since July 22 (O.S.) I have not a line from him), it is to you, dear Alexander, that I turn, beseeching you to give some sign of life. I am sad beyond words at being so neglected, and most eager to know what you are doing, and what you think of the sad and grave events which have happened since we parted. The disturbance at Brussels is more than regrettable ; it is without cause or excuse, and in truth without aim, and this makes me hope that it will lead to no serious consequences. Here this business has aroused very strong feelings. Everybody, without exception, is annoyed with these foolish Belgians, and alarmed at the possible consequences.

It seems, too, that the effect in France has been not less serious, and that no event could have more immediately

affected her Government. I consider she is wholly uncon-
nected with what is passing in Belgium, because it is of the
utmost importance to her that her neighbours should remain
quiet.

The English Ministers have taken themselves off for their
holidays notwithstanding the serious state of affairs all over
Europe. Partridges pass before politics ; Matuscevitz has
followed the fashion.

The King is at Brighton, bathing and promenading.
What is Troubetzkoi about ? [1]   I presume he is promenading
also, for certainly he never travels.

My poor back is still the same, and consequently I am
almost immovable.   My children are in excellent health, they
occupy me and amuse me all day long.

What is Count Tolstoy doing—is he at Petersburg ?
Prevent his forgetting me, I entreat you.   I think too much
about him, and since I have come to know his wit the
English please me less.

Admiral Codrington will arrive with this letter ; he is
determined to go and present himself to the Emperor.   He
will please you at first, and will bore you later.

Good-bye, my dear Alexander, do not forget me, and
believe that I love you most affectionately.

CI

Panshanger : 8/20 September 1830.

Dear Alexander,—Write to me, do ; you know the need
I have of your letters and the pleasure they give me.   I am
still an invalid ; my back does not get well.   I am being
sent to Brighton, to try the effect of sea-bathing ; but before
going I have come here to spend a few days in the country
with Lady Cowper to refresh my spirits a little in the society
of good and true friends.   Matuscevitz is also here, just back
from that sad expedition to Manchester, which began like a

---

[1] Prince Basil Sergievitch Troubetzkoi, general aide-de-camp to Alexander I.,
distinguished himself in the wars against Turkey and France.   Sent to England
as Special Ambassador to congratulate William IV. on his accession.

triumphal procession and ended in a frightful tragedy.[1]   The
Duke of Wellington was also there, to assist at the opening
of an iron-road on which steam carriages were to run.   In
that of the Duke of Wellington were about sixty persons,
Huskisson among them.   Having got out with a dozen
others, including Matuscevitz, he was killed by another steam
carriage running parallel with theirs.   Matuscevitz and the
others thought that they were going to be killed too.   Huskisson's death is a cause of real mourning for all England,
and the cause and occasion of his death add to the vividness
of the catastrophe, which was witnessed by all the notabilities
of the country and 500,000 spectators.   The town of Liverpool is in mourning, the shops closed, and all business
suspended for the whole day ; such expression of regret does
honour to the inhabitants.   There is no one who can take
Huskisson's place, with his capacity for business, his experience, and his enlightenment ; his loss to Parliament will
be keenly felt.   It is more than likely that the Duke of
Wellington intended to take advantage of this chance meeting with Huskisson to make him proposals to join his
Ministry.[2]   The position of the Government is as bad as it
can well be.   There is a general concurrence of opinion that
a change of administration is a necessity.   The union of the
Whigs and the Canningites makes their joint opposition too
formidable for the Government to hold its own in the debates
in the Lower House.   The Whigs, exasperated especially
against the Duke, wish to get rid of him and will come to no
understanding with him.   This is Brougham's tack ; Lord
Grey leans to it a little also, having the ambition to become
Prime Minister himself.   The Canningites would be satisfied,
I think, with the removal of Aberdeen and four other less
prominent Ministers.   This seems to me the only good and
feasible arrangement.   Wellington is a necessity, especially

[1] The opening of the Liverpool and Manchester Railway on September 15,
where Huskisson was fatally injured.

[2] It was said that a mutual friend of Wellington and Huskisson had induced
the latter to get out of the railway carriage, against the request of the company,
in order to bring the two statesmen together and to effect a reconciliation between
them.

at the present moment, and I hope, if things come to such a pass that a change is inevitable, that Lord Grey will range himself with those who wish to retain the Duke, but just now he is furious against him.

So far as our interests are concerned—by which I mean those of the Continent generally—I believe that a Ministry composed of Canningites, such as Palmerston, Melbourne, Grant, one or two Whigs, such as Lord Grey and Lord Lansdowne, with the Duke of Wellington at the head, would be just what is needed to keep France in check, to uphold Conservative doctrines, and to get English democrats to accept them willingly or of necessity. In such a Ministry we should count upon friends to Russia. Notwithstanding my regard for Lord Grey, I would much rather that he stood aloof, because with him would probably enter those whose ideas would not suit us in these critical times. At the same time, it will, I confess, be difficult to form a strong administration without him, and a strong one it must be to keep down English Jacobinism ; and, after all, on becoming a Minister, learning the actual position of affairs, and seeing more closely and more clearly its dangers, its difficulties, and its responsibilities, one adopts very different views. Those who to-day are most decidedly opposed to any intervention in continental affairs may be the first to recognise its necessity when they realise the dangers with which Europe is menaced. God grant, however, that matters may so disentangle themselves that we and the rest of the world may be spared the miseries of a war ; but, of course, a prudent policy always keeps in view such a possibility.

Paul arrived here yesterday from Paris, coming as a special messenger. The picture he gives of that city is lamentable ; disorder, licence, misery on all sides, and very likely worse will follow. A good many of the English Opposition have rushed off thither, and I am glad of it, for they will come back sobered ; but up to the present they hug their illusions. I should like Liberals of countries to go and take note of the fruits of a revolution such as that which France has just gone through ; they would soon slacken their zeal.

I have reason to think that M. de Talleyrand's mission is distasteful to the Duke of Wellington, and I am certain that he did not suggest it. Certainly he would not have M. de Flahault ; [1] but that was because of his dislike for his wife, and I believe that he let drop a clear hint to that effect to General Baudrand ; his own preference, and he expressed it to me personally, was in favour of a Marshal.

The friends and hangers-on of the Duke of Wellington are doubtless disposed in favour of a war ; they think it would strengthen the position of the Government, and would rally the Tory party once more to their side. With regard to the object and consequences of such a war, their talk goes so far as the need for parcelling out France and for rendering her powerless.

If my back allows it, I shall join the Court at Brighton. Meanwhile, I am confident that the King remains and is satisfied with his nullity in all state business. Just now he is fully occupied with his health.

Prince Leopold and his sister the Duchess of Kent are gathering popularity in the provinces. He is much interested in the Regency question, and had a long talk with me about it. Naturally, he wishes it to be given to his sister, but the Ministry wish it to pass to the Queen. The question will be keenly debated, as is only reasonable. After the King's death, the Queen, so far as England is concerned, is a foreigner. As for the Duke of Cumberland, he has no illusions and puts forward no claim, clearly seeing that it would be useless. This question and that of the Civil List will be the first matters debated when Parliament meets.

I am finishing this letter in London, where I am spending the day, superintending our change of house. What a work it is ! Dear Alexander, I want you to do me a great service—it is

---

[1] 'Dined at Flahault's yesterday. He said the other day that he felt there were three persons he ought to have called out—the Duke of Wellington, Decazes, and Dupin, the Advocate-General. The former was too much above him, he said, and the latter too much below him.'—*Moore's Diary*, May 6, 1820.

to entreat Count Nesselrode to grant my son Alexander leave of absence for four months. He has been serving now for five years without a break, with zeal and assiduity, the climate of Madrid at this season is most trying for the chest, and he is anxious to get away for a time. Do try and obtain for him this favour. He is a worthy fellow, attentive to his duties and discreet, and has never been guilty of any extravagance beyond a visit to the Falls of Niagara and a trip to Africa. These are the only distractions he has allowed himself.

Give me some tidings of my boy Constantine ; my husband does not speak of him, and I am getting anxious, for since I left Warsaw I have not heard a word.

Good-bye, my good, good Alexander. If ever the Emperor should have the leisure to remember me, take advantage of the opportunity to lay at his feet my devotion, my respect and my full and faithful attachment. If only you knew how eloquent I get when I speak of him, and how I urge others to go and judge for themselves whether I am not justified in my opinion of him! That I love him with all my heart, I can say with truth, and you know how greatly I admire him. Good-bye again, dear brother.

CII

Brighton : 12/24 September 1830.

I am sending you a line, dear Alexander, by Count Stanislas Potocki. I have not seen him, for he is constantly on the come-and-go, and I as constantly ill or out of town. Consequently he cannot tell you anything about me, which obliges me the more to write to you. Moreover, this is a good opportunity. I came here yesterday. I was too tired to go to Court to-day, but I have had a long visit from the Chancellor, who for the last twelve months has adopted a very confidential tone with me. He is greatly distressed by the Duke of Wellington's obstinacy in remaining at the head of the 'poorest administration which England has ever seen' (take note that these are the Chancellor's [1] own words). He

---

[1] Lord Lyndhurst, whom the Duke of Wellington had not taken into confidence on the question of admitting the Canningites into the Cabinet. (*Greville*, ii. 93.) .

has pressed upon him the fact that the Government must be defeated in the Lower House, and will be treated with contempt ; that rather than submit to certain affront the Duke ought to resign or to ally himself with one or other party ; to get rid of four or five incapables, Aberdeen among them, and to replace them by the Canningites and Earl Grey. The Duke did not seem to like either suggestion ; nevertheless he promised to think over the second alternative, and that he would summon a meeting of the Cabinet for Monday, Oct. 2, to decide upon what step to take. The Duke alone in all England is the only person who fails to recognise the urgency of some change. The Chancellor bemoans his blindness, because, as he says, ' he can only keep in office by means of concessions, and these concessions, always made in the direction of Liberalism, will end by drawing upon England the same ills as have overtaken her neighbours.' In a word, he believes that the Duke is on the way to become a Radical for the sake only of keeping in power ; and this power he wishes to exercise at the head of a parcel of idiots, for he will not brook the idea of a rival.

This is a strong expression, and very curious when coming from a colleague in the Cabinet.

We shall see very shortly the outcome of his advice or of his predictions.

Troubetzkoi has been cordially received by the King, and there have been all sorts of marks of respect and friendship for the Emperor. The (order of) St. Catherine gave great pleasure to both the Queen and the King ; but what most pleased the latter was the sending of Captain Kosavski. In a word, this special mission has been a complete success.

The Duke of Brunswick is,[1] and will be, treated as a Pariah—they would like to have him pronounced mad, and it is in this sense that Münster is working. Just imagine, he has had the imprudence or the folly to represent all that has

---

[1] He went to Brighton to pay his respects to the King, but was not received.

taken place in his own country as proofs of the affection of his subjects.

The King of England is very much displeased at M. de Talleyrand being sent here as Ambassador.

At the moment of writing this, my dear Alexander, we are full of hope that the affairs of Belgium will be settled by the King's authority. Such a solution is devoutly to be desired. In this way this attempt at rebellion may be fraught with good results by putting a stop to the mania of imitation. It is high time indeed—for what is going on around us is truly disgusting. As for *la grande nation!* what a pretty spectacle it is offering to the world just now!

I wish you could hear Paul tell the story of all that he saw, heard, and observed during the few days he was in Paris. He, I will answer for it, is now cured of Liberalism if ever he had the disposition to take the infection.

Good-bye, dear Alexander. I write to you very often—does not that give you a twinge of remorse?

I embrace you tenderly, and your wife and children likewise.

CIII

Brighton : 18/30 September 1830.

As I believe it scarcely likely that a letter will find my husband still at Petersburg, I am writing to you, dear Alexander, requesting, in the improbable event of his being still with you, that you will communicate to him the contents of my present budget.

We are on thorns until we know the result of Prince Frederick's (of the Netherlands) movements on Brussels. Heaven grant that all is over and well over. There is great anxiety on the matter in England, and everyone wishes success to the good cause, for the contrary might set the whole of Europe in a blaze.

M. de Talleyrand has arrived in London. The King proposes to come to town to give him an audience, as this would dispense with the necessity of asking him to dinner—as would be expected were the audience to take place here

As, however, he (the King, I mean) has just been seized by an attack of gout, I do not well see how he is to manage to get to London.

I have just come back from dining with the King. The Duke of Wellington, after an absence of six weeks, had at last come to pay his Majesty a visit. A messenger followed him from town bringing the disastrous news that Prince Frederick had been obliged to withdraw from Brussels. I cannot fully depict to you the impression made upon the Duke by this event. His words to me were : ' It is a devilish bad business—the most serious affair for Europe which could have arisen ! France must explain frankly whether her Government is acting with us ; if not, we shall be forced to oppose her.' Later on he told me that it was certain that Frenchmen had been leading the Belgian resistance : that as a matter of fact a French General had taken up his residence in Brussels, and that diligences crammed with military had been constantly coming from Paris to Brussels. Some Spaniards, too, were mixed up with the movement, among others a Spanish General or officer formerly serving with our troops in the Caucasus, and the author of a book on the methods of defending open towns ; that the method of defence adopted at Brussels was identical with that used with such deadly results at Saragossa—each house being converted into a fortress, and thus making the advance of troops almost impossible. He would not admit that Prince Frederick had blundered ; on the contrary, he thinks that he did everything possible, but that at length, in face of a determined populace with able foreigners to direct them, the Prince could not have held out longer in the confined position which he occupied above the city. Good God ! what a misfortune that things should have come to this pass. How can one foresee the consequences ? [1]

[1] Further disturbances had broken out at Brussels, and the Walloon provinces as well as most of the Flemish towns had declared in favour of separation. Prince Frederick of Orange, on September 23, attempted to take possession of Brussels, but after four days' street fighting had been forced to withdraw his troops. On September 29 the States-General assembled at the Hague voted the dissolution of the union between Belgium and Holland.

The King is much disturbed by this business : but he said to me only yesterday on more than one occasion : ' I am in no doubt at all about the result, and it is sure to be a happy one, because we all hold closely together with a like conservative object in view. I am only grieved at the prospect of the trials through which we may have to pass,' and then he went on to speak in terms of admiration of the Emperor. He and the Queen seemed very much pleased with all that Prince Troubetzkoi had brought with him from our Court. The King did not say a single word in favour of Prince Talleyrand ; he is still angry at his having been appointed to this Court. On the other hand the Duke spoke of him most warmly, and in reply to some observations which I let fall as to M. de Talleyrand's somewhat doubtful straightforwardness he assured me that he regarded him as a thoroughly honourable man. In any case he was convinced that he endeavoured to appear so, and wished to be what he seemed, and that this desire was in itself worthy of praise. I answered that in this object of his ambition M. de Talleyrand had so far been unfortunate.

The King put to me a thousand questions about the Emperor, displaying the keenest interest. He is looking well and strong again ; all things considered, his position is a pleasant one : he is liked by the nation, and might walk from one end of town to the other unattended without meeting anything but greetings. It is only his Minister who is unpopular, and this unpopularity is just now at its height.

I saw the Duchess of Kent yesterday ; she is courted and sought after as much as if she were already Regent. Prince Leopold takes a gloomy view of all that is going on. All the royal princes are opposed to the Duke of Wellington. The King is alone in his determination to support him.

CIV

Brighton : October 4 (N.S.), 1830.

As Matuscevitz has not yet arrived in London, dear Alexander, I think that it would be as well for me to write you just a couple of lines for you to let Count Nesselrode

know that the English Government is negotiating with Lord
Palmerston with the view of getting him to join the Ministry.
Sir George Murray, Mr. Goulburn, and Mr. Herries would be
got rid of, and Palmerston, Goderich, Grant, and Lord
Melbourne would be taken in their place. I am in the dark
as to the answer which Lord Palmerston may have given to
these overtures. He is somewhat difficult to manage, but I
hope that means may be found of coming to an understanding. We should all desire it, as it is to our interest to see
the English Government strong and influential. The Duke
of Wellington having at last recognised the necessity of
strengthening his position, our wishes should be that this
attempt may succeed. If it fails, Ministers have made up
their minds to go on as before. It is more than possible
that they might even then manage to hold on, but in proportion as their difficulties increase their resolution will grow
more feeble, and it is important for us to find an ally who
both will and can act. My next letter will tell you the outcome of these manœuvres. Good-bye. Much love.

1830—(*continued*)

[Belgium, like Greece, owed its existence to a national uprising, or, in the language of that day, to a revolutionary movement. But the integrity of Turkey had not been discussed at the Congress of Vienna, nor guaranteed by that of Aix-la-Chapelle, in the way that the allied Powers had formally ratified the union of Belgium and Holland. This union had been regarded by some politicians as a protection of Germany against French aggression, but it also gave France the right to interfere in any modification of the union, and the fear was aroused that, profiting by the disturbances going on in Germany, she might take possession of the frontier fortresses which had been erected to prevent her advance and to extend her western boundaries. Russia also, taking her stand upon the letter of the Treaty of 1818, was hesitating whether or not the separation of Belgium and Holland did not impose upon the allies the duty of maintaining the union of the two States; while England, regarding the question as a purely internal one, insisted upon observing towards the Belgians the policy of non-intervention which she had laid down at the Congress of Verona and had acted upon in the internal affairs of Italy, Spain, and Portugal. This rivalry of interests and divergence of aims retarded the progress of negotiations and nearly produced the catastrophe which the Great Powers wished to avoid. Early in September Prince William of Orange, who had been entrusted by his father with the conduct of both the military and political affairs, opened negotiations with the Provisional Belgian Government, and so far committed himself as to recognise the separate legislative and administrative independence of Belgium under the House of Orange. This retreat from the position originally taken up by Holland and supported by Russia, that the union of the two kingdoms was guaranteed by the Great Powers in the Treaty of Vienna, upset the calculations of Russia and Austria, and was altogether unpalatable to the population of Brussels. Disturbances broke out in that capital on September 19, Prince Frederick felt bound to intervene, and several days of street fighting ensued. On

September 27 the Dutch troops, finding that they could only occupy the city at a great loss, withdrew to Vilvoorde, and two days later the States-General at the Hague agreed to the dissolution of the Union between Holland and Belgium. The Prince (Frederick) of Orange was thereupon despatched to Antwerp (October 5) to arrange terms with the Belgian Provisional Government, but failed to arrive at an understanding, and on October 25 left that city. On the same day an insurrection broke out and the city gates were opened to the Belgian troops. The Dutch were driven from the arsenal and took refuge in the citadel, whence in conjunction with the fleet they bombarded the city, with serious effect. On the 29th an armistice was concluded, both sides retaining the positions they occupied.

The negotiations between the Duke of Wellington and the Canningites had been resumed after Huskisson's death, and special overtures were made to Palmerston, who was invited to enter the Cabinet. His reply, like that of Lord Melbourne, who had been previously approached, was that he could not enter it alone, but would wish to be associated with Melbourne, Grant, Lansdowne, and Grey. To this the Duke would not assent so far as Lords Lansdowne and Grey were concerned, and Parliament met (October 26) without any change in the Cabinet. The general election which had been held in consequence of the demise of the Crown had resulted in the return of a strongly enforced Opposition.

The Tory magnates had not been altogether strangers to this result, and they looked on with satisfaction at the defeat of the Ministerialists, whose concessions to the Catholics and Dissenters they could not pardon. No Cabinet Minister had stood successfully for an open borough. Of eighty-two county members forty-seven belonged to the Opposition, and only twenty-eight avowed themselves supporters of the Government. The great cities, represented by twenty-eight seats, sent twenty-five Liberals and three Ministerialists, while the other open or contested seats showed seventy-nine supporters of the Opposition to forty-seven Ministerialists. It was calculated that out of the whole House of 658 members only 236 were at that time returned in England and Ireland by popular election. Of these seventy-nine were supporters of the Government, 141 belonged to the Opposition, and sixteen were regarded as neutral. The Ministry, however, had a strong reserve in the close boroughs and in Scotland, and to these they looked for their majority.]

CV

Brighton : $\frac{\text{September 25}}{\text{October 6}}$, 1830.

A good opportunity for writing to you, my dear Alexander, has just offered. I have no fresh news to send you, but I can relieve my mind in discussing the situation with you. All that is happening on the Continent is lamentable, and, what is worse, offers no guarantee for the future. It is not a spirit of giddiness which has infected the nations, but a spirit of reflection. They have learnt their power and they are using it, and experience has strengthened them in the belief in their strength. Governments have shown neither foresight nor vigour. The example set by them is fraught with danger from which the only escape is by the utmost care and vigilance. We luckily have many special grounds for security—our remoteness, the comparative igno- rance of our lower classes, an innate sentiment of religion and of devotion to the throne, and, above all, a monarch at once enlightened, just, strong, and active in mind and body, knowing how to make himself feared and at the same time loved. I have, therefore, no fear for ourselves ; but we belong to Europe and are bound by our treaties—shall we not thereby be dragged into the movement which is disturbing the world ? If this necessity should arise, will not the mere contact of our soldiers with the turbulent populations be a source of danger for the former? These are some of the reflections which force themselves upon me, especially ever since the disastrous result of Prince Frederick's march upon Brussels. What a mistake was that chivalric entry of the Prince of Orange into the city, to be followed by his brother's blundering military exploit. In these days one false step leads to incalculable mischief. Governments no longer dare make mistakes, an in- telligent public criticises and profits by them. Since nations have been allowed to teach themselves, the business of government has become a thousand times more difficult. However, it is not about this that I wanted to talk to you— what is pressing to-day is to know on whom we could count in the event of our being dragged into a war. Do not let us nurse any illusions about the intentions of the English Government. They may be most excellent, but the means of carrying them into action are non-existent. In order for England to take up arms in our interest two conditions are quite indispensable ; first, that England's direct interests are threatened, and, secondly, that its Ministry possesses the absolute confidence of the nation. Failing this we may look in vain for a shilling or for a soldier from this country. To guess what may be expected from the Duke of Wellington we have only to go back a few years in the past. Catholic Emancipation, flouted and opposed by him throughout his life, has been granted solely because he recognised the force of public opinion in its favour. The Grand Seignior, so long supported by all his good will, is now left to our tender mercies. Parliamentary Reform was resisted by him to the uttermost, and Mr. Huskisson was dismissed from the Ministry for having asked that the representation of a rotten borough without house or inhabitant should be transferred to Manchester with 80,000 inhabitants.[1] Now the Duke has taken up this very same proposal, and is prepared to extend it to other towns (for no one for a moment doubts that the Government is prepared to propose representation for Leeds, Birmingham, and Manchester).

Public opinion, in short, rules supreme in England. Its Government, no matter how strong, must needs bend before it, and just now especially the Ministry, so far from being strong enough to guide opinion, weaker also than perhaps any of its predecessors, is obliged to be led by it. There is, too, something else ; the mere reputation of being illiberal forces the present Ministry to make concessions which a Government based upon more truly liberal principles would not attempt. England has taken the measure of the Duke of Wellington ; she does not like his domineering way, she can see in him no other guiding principle than the determination

---

[1] Penryn in Cornwall, but the case was complicated by the further proposal to disfranchise East Retford for bribery. Huskisson, on May 19, 1828, had voted against his colleagues on the transfer of the East Retford seat to Birmingham.

to stay in office at any cost. A Ministry thus constituted cannot nowadays inspire confidence, nor carry away the people with it in its adventures. It does not wish for war and will not have it, and so the Duke of Wellington will never propose it. Let us take our stand on this point, and consider if we can go to war without England. War! Good God! War! it is a horrid word; a horrid thing! and in the present case shall we not be going to wage it against a pestilence? Dear Alexander, may God preserve us from it!

The King strikes me as looking very old and much broken: he is suffering from the gout, which fixes itself nowhere, and thus gives rise to anxiety. He has become very careful in his language and very moderate in his opinions of late; he takes very little part in public affairs, only such as is strictly formal. He leaves everything to the Duke of Wellington, although he has neither regard for nor confidence in him. He acts on the principle that the King's duty is to support the Minister until Parliament by its vote determines that the Minister no longer possesses the confidence of the nation. For this reason he will do nothing to upset him, but he will be at no pains to pick him up when he falls. In the matter of foreign affairs he expresses himself with great good sense. His heartiest wish is that the foreign Powers may remain united, and his strongest belief is that in such a union is to be sought their ultimate triumph over the dangers which are just now threatening all alike.

The Duke of Wellington has at last discovered, what public opinion has insisted upon for a long time, that his Ministry cannot last unless it reforms itself. He has consequently made proposals to Lord Palmerston to admit him, Lord Goderich, Lord Melbourne, and Mr. Grant [1] into the Cabinet, and to get rid of Sir George Murray, Mr. Goulburn, and Mr. Herries. Lord Grey is to be offered the Viceroyalty of Ireland in order to put him out of the way. This is the

---

[1] Charles Grant, whom Brougham pronounced 'the purest statesman he had ever known,' first sat for Inverness burghs, and afterwards for the county; Lord of the Treasury, 1814–19; Secretary for Ireland, 1819–20; Vice-President of the Board of Trade, 1823–7; President of the Board of Control, 1830–4; Secretary for the Colonies, 1834–9; created Lord Glenelg, 1836.

project communicated to me by the Chancellor, who is eager to arrive at some arrangement, being convinced that without a coalition the Ministry must collapse. It is more than probable that this proposal will not be accepted by Lord Palmerston, whose aim is to find himself sufficiently strong in the Cabinet to be able to make his opinions predominate. He wishes, therefore, to see one or two Whigs admitted to it, Lord Grey, Lord Lansdowne, Lord Carlisle, or Lord Holland. Above all, he is anxious to oust Lord Aberdeen, who is generally regarded as the most inept Minister of Foreign Affairs England has ever seen, and who is moreover merely the passive instrument of the Duke of Wellington's orders. Up to to-day not a syllable of anything I am telling you has been breathed to Lord Palmerston beyond the offer of an important seat in the Cabinet for himself alone. He has replied by a polite refusal to consider any proposal which will not give him the power to introduce his friends. The Duke of Wellington has replied that he will confer on the matter with his colleagues. Like a skilled negotiator, the Duke will only advance one step at a time, but I have reason to think that he is aware of his critical position, and if Palmerston is prudent he will obtain all the conditions upon which he may insist. Our interest, as I have already written to you, is to see a strong English Government, and this the present will become by joining with the Canningites and some of the Whigs. There is no need to take alarm at the word 'Whig'; there are no greater aristocrats, and I will answer for it that, once in office, the democracy need no longer go to them for protection. If the pending negotiations should fall through, frankly I do not know what will happen to the present Government. My private opinion (but no one else shares it) is that it will hold on, but only at the price of concessions which will be all to the profit of liberalism. In this case I strongly advise you not to count upon any support, moral or material, from this country, for the Duke of Wellington will not be master enough to offer it to us. For this reason I am anxiously hoping that the negotiations may succeed.

Prince Leopold and his sister are exploring the provinces in pursuit of popularity. The prince assumes the air of a presumptive heir. The regency question will in all probability be decided in favour of the Duchess of Kent, although this is not the wish of the Duke of Wellington ; but the question must of necessity be debated as soon as Parliament meets.

Charles X. has given up the idea of the Continent and wishes to pass the winter in England or in Scotland. Meanwhile he remains at Lulworth, where he receives numerous messages from the South of France which point to a great devotion to the cause of the Duc de Bordeaux ;[1] and his surroundings have no doubt as to the ultimate success of his cause.

The Duke of Wellington is simply smitten by the charms of M. de Talleyrand. You would hardly believe the assurance with which he asserts that he is a most honourable man, and that everything that has ever been said to the contrary is pure calumny. The 'probity' of M. de Talleyrand recalls to my mind 'the cleverness' of M. de Polignac—the Duke of Wellington is not strong in portraiture.

After having spoken of so many things, I must needs say a few words about myself. I am living here quite as quietly as I do at Richmond. I go to Court as often as my back will allow me—this back which is getting better, thanks to sea-water douches. I spend my time with my children, to whom I am having taught Russian, Latin, military exercises, &c., &c. I am, or at least I think I am, on good terms with everybody ; on excellent terms with the Duke of Wellington, and in the confidence of all whom we are accustomed to regard as the friends of Russia.

At the moment of writing to you, I received a letter from Palmerston, and as it throws light upon his attitude I am sending it to you ;[2] make what use of it you like with Count Nesselrode, and at the same time give him many affectionate

---

[1] 'L'enfant du miracle.' The posthumous son of the Duc de Berri, better known by his subsequent title of Comte de Chambord, which he assumed in 1844. He died at Frohsdorf in 1883.

[2] Wanting.

messages from me.   I am brought to suppose that my husband is on his way here, but if so it is due only to my own powers of divination, for he has not written me a line since August 18.

Good-bye, dear Alexander; at least write to me—and assuredly love me.   I know not why one would care to go on living in this world if we did not feel or believe that our life was of a value to someone, and I do believe that you would regret me.   Good-bye, my dear brother.

Make my kindest remembrances to Count Tolstoy.   Stanislas Potocki started a week ago.   Troubetzkoi goes the day after to-morrow ; but it will not be possible for me to see him, for, as I have not been in London a single day, we have had no chance of meeting.   The King spoke to me about him, and said how much pleased he was with him.   Yesterday he gave audience to M. de Talleyrand, who, greatly to the King's astonishment, produced from his pocket a speech, which he read to me.   The Duke of Wellington has told the Duke of Brunswick that he need not look to the King, his master, for aid and abetment, and that he recommended him in the name of the latter to withdraw with good grace from the government of his duchy.   The Duke seemed greatly surprised at this suggestion, and asked for a few days to reflect upon it.

CVI

Brighton : 2/14 October 1830.

Dear Alexander,—A thousand times thanks for your letter of September 10/22. At the same time I received, at last, a few lines from my husband, dated 25th.   His long silence had much disturbed me ; I hope that a few days later he will be able to write, saying when he expects to be back in England.   I expect it will be about November 1, and it is to be hoped that it will be for many reasons, which are not merely personal.

It looks as if Parliament would open without any changes in the present Cabinet.   Public opinion still insists that Wellington is running great risks in not strengthening his

S

Government ; I am not sure whether he is not a better judge
of the situation than the public, and as he has not carried on
the negotiations with Lord Palmerston I infer that he does
not regard the latter joining the Ministry as necessary, and I
feel persuaded that the result will show he (the Duke) is right.
I gather that the negotiations with Lord Palmerston have
ceased, as he has just gone off to Paris. The Chancellor on
his return from London, where he had been for the Cabinet
meetings, tells me that after all the Government can reckon
upon 311 votes in the Lower House, and he is of opinion that
with this number it will be strong enough.

I was dining with the King the day before yesterday. He
could not have been more marked in his attentions to me ;
he spoke in the most flattering way of the union of England
and Russia, and of the impossibility of anything disturbing an
understanding which both Powers had every interest to maintain. He fully recognises the Emperor's merits, and relies upon
him absolutely. He told me the story of M. de Talleyrand's
audience, which was somewhat bewildering. The French
Ambassador on the occasion began a long speech of which
the principal theme was the course of vicissitudes through
which he (M. de Talleyrand) had passed. To talk of oneself
instead of the nation one represents is quite a new departure
in diplomacy. The King asked me my opinion of the Ambassador, to which I replied that in my opinion a man who
had spent seventy-five years in intriguing would not have
forgotten the business in his seventy-sixth year.

Matuscevitz and Paul having come to see me here, the
King was good enough to invite them also to dinner. He
has repeatedly inquired of me if I had news of my husband's
return, as if he was getting impatient to see him arrive.

He is now taking a very keen interest in all that is passing
on the Continent, and his attitude upon the various questions
could not be better. That which is most worrying just now
is the Duke of Brunswick's business. This little Duke is an
ill-disposed madman, who had far better be shut up in
Bedlam.

The Duchess of Berri [1] is coming to Brighton, and will afterwards spend the winter in London. It is rumoured that Charles X. and the rest of the royal family are going to fix their quarters in Scotland.[2]

My health progresses slowly ; I can't walk, and this is discouraging. Good-bye, my dear Alexander, if you only knew what pleasure your letters give me you would write more often. My dearest love to you and your wife and children. Good-bye, dear, dear brother.

CVII

Richmond : $\frac{\text{October } 21}{\text{November } 2}$, 1830.

The latest news from Petersburg, dear Alexander, announces the departure of the Emperor for Moscow. This sublime imprudence—for I cannot express in other words my mingled admiration and anxiety—disturbs me more than you can imagine. God grant we may soon hear of his return ; I shall be in a fever of agitation until that news arrives. I am expecting my husband ; he will find much work has been done and more to be done ; and, above all, he will find a distinct spirit of unrest, for this rich, free, happy, and prosperous England is not by any means free from the dangerous contagion which disturbs Europe. Ireland is on the move : Cumberland and Kent are agitated. In the latter county incendiaries are burning farm buildings and ricks with impunity, just as in Normandy, and the offenders cannot be caught although troops are scouring the country.[3] In London, too,

[1] Caroline, daughter of Francis I. of Naples, widow of Duc de Berri, younger son of Charles X.

[2] The supposed reason for this sudden and secret change of residence was financial embarrassment. The Attorney-General had given an opinion that the ex-King was invested with no special privilege, but it was suggested that within the precincts of Holyrood, a royal palace, he would be protected from arrest.

[3] The practice of rick-burning had been inaugurated in 1828–9 in Normandy and Picardy by the discontented peasantry, and in the winter of 1830 appeared in Kent. It spread rapidly to Hants, Wilts, Bucks, Surrey, and Sussex. The military were called out, and fruitlessly pursued the undiscoverable incendiaries. Large rewards were offered for the apprehension of the offenders, but with very little result, and a Special Commission was sent to the counties most disturbed.

the populace is getting angry—the Duke of Wellington was hooted and attacked in the street. A demonstration was arranged for the night on which the King was to go to the theatre for the first time. The police, warned in time, ordered the abandonment of the performance of 'La Muette de Portici' ('Masaniello') the very same piece which had started the rising at Brussels.

Parliament opens to-day; parties and passions will be arrayed. God grant that interest in the public good and not in private aims may preside over the coming debates. We on our side should wish strength and energy to the Government; but unfortunately, with the exception of the Duke of Wellington and Mr. Peel, none of the Ministers inspire either respect or confidence. Rightly or wrongly, they are looked upon as quite too feeble to hold their own in the struggle which is likely to ensue in both Houses. However, we shall see; things here generally turn out quite differently from what one has expected. It does not seem to me likely that the Opposition will move an amendment to the Address, so the first sitting at least will pass off quietly; the Whig Opposition, it seems, has definitely ranged itself under the banner of Lord Grey, and Lord Althorp will lead it in the Lower House. The Canning party holds aloof, as do also the Ultra-Tories opposed to the Government, but they are none the less hostile to it.

Dear Alexander, write to me soon—tell me that the Emperor has got back in good health. I can only think of him.

I shall remain at Richmond, more or less, until my husband returns, for my children are there, and there also is fine weather.

Good-bye, my dear brother, I embrace you tenderly. I entreat you to write.

[Parliament was formally opened on November 2, and the King in his Speech gave great offence by referring to the Belgians as revolted subjects, and by declaring that he was determined to suppress disturbances at home by all the means in his power. In both Houses it was urged that the actual and impending troubles should be met by reforming Parliament. This demand was met in the two Houses in a way which proved that the Cabinet was hopelessly divided on the subject. In reply to Earl Grey, the Duke of Wellington declared that he had never seen any measure by which the method of representation could be improved, that the Legislature and existing system possessed the confidence of the country, and that he was not only not prepared to bring forward any measure of reform, but would declare that, so far as he was concerned, so long as he held any place in the Government he should feel it his duty to resist any such measures when proposed by others. In the House of Commons, however, Sir George Murray was ready to consider a moderate scheme of reform, while Sir Robert Peel declined to commit himself on either side. The Duke's speech, however, although the actual, was not the proximate, cause of the downfall of his Cabinet. In the House of Commons it was resented by many who were on other questions supporters of the Ministry, but other circumstances combined to make the situation acute. Hume, in view of the prevailing distress, pressed the Government (November 5) to pledge themselves to a reduction of taxation, a pledge which Peel refused to give. Four days later the Lord Mayor elect was expecting to receive the King and Queen as his guests, but in consequence of an alarmist report that the opportunity would be seized by the Radicals to make an attack on the Duke of Wellington the King was induced, much against his will, to renounce his intended visit. On the same night the adjourned debate on the revision of the Civil List, necessitated by the recent demise of the Crown, was renewed, and the motion of Sir Henry Parnell, a recognised financial authority, was met by the Chancellor of the Exchequer, Goulburn, by a decided refusal. The advanced Tories as well as the Canningites supported the motion, which was carried by 233 to 204 votes. The fate of the Ministry was thus sealed, and the Duke of Wellington at once tendered his resignation, which was accepted.]

CVIII

Richmond : $\frac{\text{October 25}}{\text{November 6}}$, 1830.

I cannot say, dear Alexander, whether there will be an opportunity of sending this letter by courier, but I am writing in any case in order to give you a connected account of events here ; for, to judge of the future by the present, England itself may become a point of disquietude. Since my last sure opportunity of writing to you the public has not ceased worrying itself about the question as to how the Duke of Wellington would strengthen his administration. His warmest partisans as well as his adversaries recognised that it was indispensable for him to present himself before the new Parliament with forces proportionate to the resistance he was certain to meet. You know how Lord Palmerston went off to Paris directly proposals had been made to him, which he did not consider acceptable. He came back on October 29, and on the following day, 30th, the Duke of Wellington wrote to him inviting an interview. He accepted it, and thereupon the Duke renewed his offer and further, having understood that he (Palmerston) considered himself pledged to his friends, asked who those friends were. Lord Palmerston replied, 'Mr. Grant and Lord Melbourne'[1] without whom he could never accept office. The Duke said that there was great difficulty in finding places for everybody, but nevertheless he would try : and inquired if on this footing he would join the Ministry. Lord Palmerston in reply asked if he might speak frankly—and added that he could not but regard the Government as very weak, that the opinion of the whole country was in accordance with this view, and that the mere accession of his own party would not strengthen it sufficiently to resist the formidable opposition which was being organised, and, finally, that he could not accept any offer unless it were equally extended to the moderate Whigs. The Duke of Wellington seemed much surprised by this declaration. He, however, made no demur to Lord Palmerston's remark about the weakness of the Ministry, and with reference to the Whigs only said : ' This is all quite new to me, the proposal is altogether unexpected '—and there the conversation ended.

The next day, 31st, the Whigs met to consult ; the peers

[1] William Lamb, third Viscount Melbourne, born 1779 ; entered Parliament as member for Leominster 1805, and as a follower of Fox ; Chief Secretary for Ireland under Canning 1827, and Duke of Wellington 1828 ; Home Secretary under Earl Grey, 1830-4 ; Prime Minister, 1834, July to November, and again 1835-41. Died 1848. He married, in 1805, Lady Caroline Ponsonby, daughter of the Earl of Bessborough.

at Lord Grey's and the members of the Lower House at Lord Althorp's,[1] and settled upon the line they would adopt. They decided to raise no amendment on the Address, because the speech having been delivered by the King it would be disrespectful to oppose him formally. They agreed, however, to prolong the debate from day to day with firmness but without violence, to attack the Ministry and to expose their incapacity of replying (because, with the exception of Mr. Peel, there is not a single Minister in the Commons capable of speaking), to avoid going to a division until the opinion of the House with regard to the Ministers was made clear, and their weakness plainly proved —then to challenge a division on some important question, and to place them in a minority. This programme having been adopted, a deputation was sent to Lord Palmerston inviting him and his party to join the Whigs. While expressing himself flattered by their confidence and ready to support them in all matters which accorded with his principles, Lord Palmerston declined to make any formal coalition. This reply was favourably received, and he was asked only to allow them to keep him informed of all the steps which the Whigs proposed to take.

On the other side the Ultra-Tories, personal enemies of the Duke of Wellington, on the meeting of Parliament were agreed upon no other plan but to upset the Ministry by whatever means seemed possible. This party for the last twelve months has been seeking to come to an understanding with the Whigs, and especially with Lord Palmerston, but so far has only succeeded in establishing friendly relations—especially with the latter, but without any political bearing. By the Ultra-Tories I mean the Duke of Richmond,[2] a young man greatly esteemed for his private

[1] John Charles Spencer, afterwards third Earl Spencer, born 1782 ; entered Parliament for Okehampton 1804-6, sat for Northamptonshire 1806-34. Junior Lord of the Treasury, 1806 ; Chancellor of the Exchequer and cader of the House of Commons, 1830-4, when he succeeded to his father's peerage and practically relinquished political life.

[2] Charles Lennox, tenth Duke of Richmond. As Earl of March he joined the army in 1809, was wounded at the battle of Orthez, aide-de-camp to

character, and for his activity and cleverness in the Upper
House (he is Lord Anglesey's son-in-law), Lord Eldon, the
former Chancellor and Nestor of the Bench, the Duke of
Cumberland, and some others of less prominence.

The late elections showed that there was a strong Liberal
feeling existing throughout the country, and the composition
of the present Parliament proves that the nation at large
looks for some reform of the method of national representation. The reforms mentioned in one of my recent letters
sent by courier were generally anticipated—namely, the right
accorded to Leeds, Manchester, and Birmingham to be represented in Parliament. The seats are to be obtained by the
disfranchisement of certain rotten burghs which exist only
in name, and in which, as I said, there remains neither house
nor inhabitant, and consequently the nomination remains in
the hands of some rich landowner of the neighbourhood.
This transfer of seats commends itself to common sense ; for
years it has been called for on all sides, and no one doubted
that the Duke of Wellington would himself lay the proposal
before Parliament. Quite the contrary, on the very first day of
the session he went out of his way to declare that he was and
always would be opposed to any concession of this kind—an
imprudent, wholly gratuitous protest, for there was no reason
why he should not remain quite silent on the matter. This
profession of faith roused general surprise, which was still
further stimulated the next day when the Colonial Secretary
(Sir George Murray) stated in the Commons that he was
quite prepared to come to an understanding with the promoters of parliamentary reform. This flagrant instance of
disagreement among Ministers, the pitiable attitude of the
Government in the Lower House, the arguments and cutting
sarcasms of twenty members of the Opposition, combined
with the general aspect of the House, where the speeches of
the Whigs are received with loud applause and those of the
ministerial supporters with scoff and laughter—all this seems
to point to at least a partial reconstruction of the present

Wellington 1810–14, to Prince of Orange 1815 ; M.P. for Chichester 1812–19 ; a
vigorous opponent of Catholic Emancipation and of the repeal of the Corn Laws.

Government in a very short time.   At the same time in the Upper House the Duke of Wellington's speech was a lamentable display, while Lord Grey's was really eloquent.   On the following day the latter was greeted with marked favour by the King, who also took care to express through his personal friends the satisfaction which Lord Grey's speech had afforded him. A similar approval was given in the House of Lords by many of the great peers sitting on the ministerial side ; and finally the Marquess of Stafford and some others intimated to the Duke of Wellington that, unless he was prepared to strengthen his Ministry, he could no longer reckon upon their support— so that is where the matter stands.

CIX

London : Same day.

On arriving here to receive the Prince of Orange I hear that Matuscevitz is just sending off a courier, so I hasten to finish this letter.   I have just seen the Duke of Wellington —in the midst of the worries of his position, which I have explained—in spite of his evident disfavour with all classes, for he has suddenly become extremely unpopular even in the City, where his last speech brought about an alarming fall in the Funds ; [1] although he is followed in the streets, hooted, and almost attacked by the mob—in the midst of all this he maintains an impassive demeanour, is wholly undisturbed, even gay and cheerful.   This is to me unintelligible.   The Chancellor [2] told me in confidence that they could not possibly go on any longer, that their position is too humiliating, and, in a word, that the outcry against them is from all quarters.   You see now, dear Alexander, the difficulty in which we are placed between on one side a Government well disposed towards our interests and our political principles, but incapable, absolutely *incapable*, of acting on these principles, and on the other an Opposition which any day may become the Government, enouncing and supporting in Parliament doctrines which are altogether unsuitable to us. In the worst case, however—that is, should Wellington be

[1] The Funds fell on November 3 from 84 to 80.   [2] Lord Lyndhurst.

upset and his place occupied by the Whigs—I should hope that once in power they would amend their ways considerably, and that we should not look upon their advent as the last day of our alliance.

I am on the best of terms with the Duke of Wellington, and in full enjoyment of his confidence and friendship, and at the same time on an equally good footing with the Court.

I have seen the Prince of Orange,[1] and I cannot tell you how deeply grieved I am at his present position, obliged to fly both the country which he has landed in such a mess and his own fatherland—for whatever colour they may choose to give his coming here, this is the real meaning of the situation—and forced by scruples of delicacy to be silent on the encouragement given by his father to the course he adopted—all this combines to make his position most trying.

We talked together for a long time on all subjects. He is greatly troubled by the state of affairs, but externally he maintains a frank and even gay temper. We neither of us could find enough praise for the Emperor. I can see clearly that he (the Prince of Orange) is uneasy as to the view which the Emperor will take of what is going on, for certainly he cannot approve of the present position. In any case, the Prince is in great straits. God grant that things may right themselves, and that he may be able to extricate himself satisfactorily. Our Grand Duchess[2] has behaved splendidly throughout these sad complications, showing her devotion to the royal family and every mark of esteem and affection. She has just passed over to me the whole of her private fortune, which she gives to her husband, and of which she desires me to be the trustee until such a time as he should claim it.

[1] Prince William of Orange, afterwards William II., King of Holland, married Grand Duchess Anna, daughter of Emperor Paul of Russia and sister of Nicholas I. He had come to England in the hope of persuading Lord Aberdeen to consent to the despatch of a British contingent to Holland ; but the Duke of Wellington, while sympathising with the King of the Netherlands, declined to interfere in a question of internal politics.

[2] Grand Duchess Anna, daughter of Emperor Paul, who had been brought up under the care of Prince Lieven's mother.

The King received the Prince yesterday with politeness—
but, as the Prince of Orange said to me, with some reserve,
but on the whole quite properly. I have asked him to dine
here the day after to-morrow, but not in full dress.

I know as a fact that the King is much upset by the
present state of things—that he is convinced that the
Ministry cannot hold on, that the current of public feeling
frightens him, and that the remedy is difficult to find. This
morning the Duke of Wellington again sent to Lord
Palmerston making new proposals, but they were peremptorily rejected, as the Duke's declaration against any
reform rendered it impossible for him to join his Ministry.
Why has the Duke thus pushed things to an extremity ?
Why could he not have held his tongue ? You cannot
conceive how universally he is blamed.

Lord Grey's speech, so far as political principles are
concerned, was detestable—I am sorry for it, and should be
more so should he become Prime Minister—but, I repeat, if
this misfortune should happen England would not withdraw
from her treaties, and, however bold such an assertion may
seem, I believe that she would then fulfil them, whereas now
she is unable to do so.

The news from the provinces is still bad ; the rick-burners
are extending the field of their outrages, which have now
reached to Sussex and Surrey. According to reports received
this morning by the Government from Manchester, public
feeling is highly excited in that town and the neighbourhood.

You will gather from the style of my letter that it has
been written by fits and starts, according as any items of
news have been brought to me. I write as if I were talking,
and I tell you everything without order or thought.

My last visitor has been the Chancellor,[1] who has just
left me. He considers the Ministry lost. This seems a little
strong, but of this you may be sure, that the 16th will be the

---

[1] Lord Lyndhurst, who throughout the crisis and the period preceding it
took so detached a view from that of the Duke and his other colleagues that it was
supposed he was in sympathy with the Reform Party and would hold his office in
any change of the Ministry.

decisive day. The question of Reform comes on for discussion in the Lower House, and if the Government is beaten
it must retire ; but if it is clever, it ought before that day to
secure some adherents. I heartily trust that it will do so, for
its fall at this moment would be most deplorable. On the
other hand, if it can hold its ground it will feel itself
stronger, and will be able to act as we desire.

This is a long letter, but I have not said half of what
I had to tell you.

The Duchess of Kent and her brother hold themselves
very high, as if the throne is to be theirs to-morrow—and
this is most unpleasant to the King. Leopold does not show
himself, but works silently underground.

Good-bye, dear, dear Alexander ; I can write no more—
I am worn out. My drawing-room has never once been empty
throughout the morning. I have been interrupted forty
times at least, so I am off to Richmond as soon as I have
closed this letter, for it is only there that I can get any rest.
I came to town for twenty-four hours just to receive the
Prince of Orange and to dine with the Ministry, but during
this time I have been receiving the confidences of everybody.
I am acting as I told you at Warsaw. I know everything
and say nothing, which means that only on this condition
am I told everything that passes. This I scrupulously
observe, but this principle of reserve does not prevent my
telling you everything.

CX

London : $\frac{\text{October 28}}{\text{November 9}}$, 1830.

We, too, in England, dear Alexander, are just on the brink
of a revolution. For the last two days agitation reigns in
London. It began to show itself on the day of the opening
of Parliament. The Duke of Wellington's peremptory
declaration against any sort of reform has dissatisfied the
upper classes, aroused fear in the middle class, and exasperated the populace. Disturbances have taken place and
troops have been brought up to London. In view, moreover,

of the threatening attitude assumed by the Government, it was asserted that the occasion of the King and Queen's visit to the City to-night was to be taken to make a popular demonstration,[1] of which the object was to assassinate the Duke of Wellington and to create confusion and provoke disorder. Ministers, having been informed of these intentions, persuaded their Majesties to give up their visit to the City, thereby causing general consternation and nervous anxiety.[2] All yesterday was passed in comings and goings, and the public of all classes never for an instant doubted that the Ministry would be dismissed forthwith, on the ground that the King could not submit to be made the victim of the Duke of Wellington's unpopularity. Matters have turned out quite otherwise. I dined last night with the King and all his Ministers. He treated them with greater cordiality and attention than ever. The Duke, for his part, told me that he was quite right in his course, that as for the disorders of the mob he knew how to repress them, and that as for reform it was with it as it had been with the Catholic Question, that it could not be passed without him, and that he would have none of it, therefore it would not pass at all. I have never seen anyone take a firmer and more confident attitude than the Duke. Meanwhile it is generally believed that there will be riots ; but precautions have been taken, and 10,000 troops, who can be relied on, are quartered in London. Moreover, the London parishes have spontaneously offered to provide their own special constables and to answer for the peace of their respective divisions. Permission has been accorded to them, but no arms are to be issued to them.

This is the exact state of things at the moment of my writing to you.

[1] It was expected that the King and Queen's visit to the Mansion House on Lord Mayor's day would be seized as the occasion for a disturbance. Great preparations were made, the King and Queen were persuaded to give up their engagement with the Lord Mayor, but everything passed off peaceably with the exception of trifling scuffles with the mob in Downing Street and Fleet Street.

[2] 'The boldest act of cowardice he had ever heard of,' was the Marquess Wellesley's comment on his brother's letter to the Lord Mayor.

I will not venture upon any prophecy. The Opposition is already shouting victory and allotting posts ; not a soul doubts for a moment of a change of Ministry, except perhaps myself. I still believe the Duke to be very strong, although one cannot hide from oneself that his declaration has caused him the loss of numerous adherents.

I received yesterday, dear Alexander, your letter of October 5—17 from Moscow. A thousand thousand thanks for it ; all that you tell me of the Emperor's reception at Moscow is of the greatest interest to me. How admirable his behaviour is ! what a master is ours ! Here his determination to face personally the danger at its centre has excited general admiration. I confess that my admiration is a thousand times greater now that I know that he is at Tver.[1] May Heaven bless and preserve our Emperor.

The Prince of Orange was present at the dinner at the Palace last night.

The Duke of Brunswick went off suddenly during the night, not wishing to be present at a third revolution.

I am anxious to get back to Richmond ; to-morrow I have to dine again with the King. If it were not for this reason I would not set foot again in London. It is not the business of a woman to despise danger. Good-bye, dear brother. Excuse all the faults of this scribble.

CXI

London : $\frac{\text{October 31}}{\text{November 12}}$, 1830.

Since my Tuesday's letter, dear Alexander, matters have taken a fresh turn. The Lord Mayor is severely taken to task for having given such alarming advice to Ministers, and Ministers are blamed for having listened to it. It is none the less true, however, that they maintained peace and order in the Metropolis ; that the populace was cowed by the forces brought up by the Government, and that now the agitation has so calmed down that the troops are being sent away. The Funds, which had been seriously depressed at the

---

[1] About one hundred miles N.W. of Moscow.

date of my last letter, have now gone up considerably ; even the Reform question has shared in the altered aspect of affairs. On the one hand, it is asserted that the Opposition are unwilling to raise the question frankly ; on the other, if I am well informed, the Government is prepared to make to public opinion the concession I have already mentioned—to allot members to the great towns. How this is to be reconciled with the Duke of Wellington's declaration remains to be seen. Meanwhile Ministers appear infinitely firmer, and the Opposition proportionately downcast. A change of Ministry, which was regarded as sure as the Gospel, is now more than doubtful, and everything will remain as it was. This is extremely fortunate for the interests of Europe.

I dined again last night with the King. He is in good health and spirits ; the Prince of Orange was there also. To-day I am dining with the Duchesse de Berri,[1] a party of three. Her stay in London gives cause for a good deal of gossip. Why is she here ? In her present position she should not be seeking to amuse herself. The Court has taken absolutely no notice of her presence in London.[2]

Admiral Codrington has returned from Petersburg, quite overcome with admiration for the Emperor.

The Court is most attentive to me ; the King and the Queen treat me most kindly. I mention this again because in fact their gracious attentions have been doubled. My husband will be indeed gratified at my relations with everybody ; I am expecting him to arrive next week.

Good-bye, my dear Alexander. I embrace you tenderly ; my poor back does not accommodate itself easily to big dinners, but I am better. Much love to you, dear brother.

[1] Caroline, daughter of Francis I. of Naples.

[2] The Duchess de Dino writes October 27, from London to M. de Barante : ' Madame la Duchesse de Berri promène ici ses royales infortunes ; elle n'intéresse personne et ne fait pas une dupe anglaise ; mais je crains qu'elle n'en fasse en France.'— *Mémoires de M. de Barante*, Vol. v.

CXII

London : 4/16 November 1830.

In my last letter, dear Alexander, I foretold that this would be the day on which the fate of the English Ministry would be decided. I fear that I shall prove to have been in the right—but in a way that we must regret, for anything which involves change or agitation is most inopportune just now, considering the state of Europe. It is only too probable that if a change of government takes place here its first effect will be to excite and encourage the evil-disposed elsewhere.

This reasoning would, however, be erroneous. One has never seen men on attaining power not adopting principles infinitely more moderate than those they professed when in opposition. However, everything depends upon the choice the King may make should the Duke of Wellington retire. If it should be Lord Grey who is consulted by the King, we shall have in his very monarchical, very aristocratic principles ample guarantee that revolution will never receive from him protection or support, and that the maintenance of peace and order will be the aim of his wishes and of his efforts. I am speculating upon an hypothesis which after all may not find application, but it does not appear to me useless to anticipate events.

I have left this letter open until the last moment, but I have nothing to add beyond the fact that the Duke of Wellington has tendered his resignation. It was difficult to foresee any other solution after last night's vote in the Lower House.[1] This clearly indicated what the public had suspected all along, that the recent elections were very unfavourable to the Government. It remains to be seen whether the King accepts the Duke's resignation, and to whom he will commit the task of forming a new administration.

[1] Sir Henry Parnell's motion for referring the Civil List to a Select Committee was opposed by the Ministry, but after a short debate was carried by 233 to 204 votes, some of the advanced Tories voting against the Government. The Duke of Wellington forthwith tendered his resignation and the King commissioned Lord Grey to form a Ministry.

The Government submitted yesterday in the Upper House its plan for a regency. It is to be vested in the Duchess of Kent from the day of the King's decease, if England should have the misfortune to lose him during the minority of the Princess Victoria. The Duchess will govern with the full powers of a sovereign, but the Princess will take the title of Queen. Should the present Queen be pregnant at the time of her husband's decease, she will become Regent on the birth of her child. In this case the Princess Victoria will lay aside the title of Queen, and the Duchess of Kent that of Regent. This plan was unanimously accepted by the House.

All that I know of Lord Grey's policy on the questions of the day is that he strongly approved of the idea of an armistice. I cite his opinion, as in view of the changes in view it is of some importance. By the way, only yesterday he came and told me with tears in his eyes what Codrington had told him about the Emperor. It would seem as if the enthusiasm of the worthy Codrington was contagious. You cannot imagine to what a point he carries his admiration for our master.

Just at this moment the news reaches me that the King has accepted the Minister's resignation, but it is not yet known whom he will send for. My view is that if he consults with anyone besides Lord Grey he cannot look for a strong and lasting administration—possibly one cannot be formed at all, in which case the King would of necessity have to fall back on the Duke of Wellington, who would then find himself strengthened by a number of discontented party-men. Such are my speculations, suggested by a very long experience of parties and individuals in England. Excuse this scrap of a letter, written amid numberless interruptions. I am off again to Richmond, having only come up to London for a few official dinners. Good-bye, dear brother.

T

CXIII

London : 8/20 November 1830.

I have come up to town to dine with the outgoing Ministry, and I hear that a Prussian courier is starting this evening for Berlin. I am taking advantage of him to send this to you.

The new Ministry is now completed, and in all likelihood its composition will be officially notified to the public to-morrow, or perhaps to-night. I send you herewith a list—hurriedly made—which will give you some idea of its members. You will see that the four principal posts are held by friends of Canning's—all the others are Whigs except the Duke of Richmond, a Tory, of whom I have already written to you in one of my previous letters. The tone of the Cabinet will be as moderate as the names composing it foreshadow. It will be Liberal—but very temperately, and I even exaggerate in saying so, for I really believe that it will follow lines altogether satisfactory to us. It will be strong, too—as it seems—for the friends of the old Ministry are leaving town, considering any opposition useless for the moment. The King will support the new Government as warmly and as loyally as he did its predecessor, and it is beyond doubt that this Government meets with public approval. In fact, the Duke of Wellington managed to heap blunder upon blunder, and this, even more than his own incapacity for speaking and the absolute mediocrity of his colleagues (except Peel), rendered his fall inevitable. If he could have made himself strong we should have reason to regret the present circumstances ; but it was obvious that he could do nothing, and from that moment he was of no use to us. We must now endeavour to bring the new Government to our views ; we must take into consideration the position of England as well as that of individuals, and with a little forbearance and gentleness I am certain that it will be possible to manage them.

From what you know of my connections in this country you see, dear Alexander, that the new Ministers of to-day are among my most intimate acquaintances. Without presuming too much on my personal influence, which the actual position of these personages may greatly modify, I think that I may still be of some use.[1] Rest assured of this, dear Alexander, and impress it upon Count Nesselrode, I shall observe an attitude of great caution, so that I may be in a position to see this Ministry retire and the Duke of Wellington return to power without embarrassment or regret. I am on good terms with the Duke, and shall endeavour to be on still better; I am all right with Peel—in a word, with everybody.

I have not forgotten the promise I made to Count Nesselrode at Warsaw with regard to Lord Heytesbury, and I have expressed to Lord Grey the wish that he should remain at his present post—but I am told here that Heytesbury himself wishes to retire next year. Is this so?

It is somewhat curious that twice already I have prevented Lord Lansdowne having the Foreign Office—in Canning's time and again now.[2] Lansdowne would have been preferable to the others, but Palmerston is preferable to him, and we, Russia, will certainly have good cause to think well of him.

The Duke of Devonshire has accepted the office of Lord Chamberlain. Lord Hill keeps the command of the army, and Lord Fitzroy Somerset remains in the same Department. This is the most recent news this evening. Since a change was inevitable, I think the Government is as well constituted as one could have hoped.

Do not make the mistake of confounding the men now in power with the Radicals of the Lower House. Lord Grey

---

[1] At this time M. de Lieven was actually on leave of absence at St. Petersburg. Madame de Lieven had by this time become fully aware that her husband's recall was still under consideration, although no actual steps had been taken to replace him during the sittings of the London Conference. He had, however, started on his return to England before this letter could have reached St. Petersburg.

[2] The grounds for this statement cannot be ascertained. In one or more of the Obituary Notices which appeared on Lord Lansdowne's death in 1863 it was stated that on Canning's death he became Secretary for Foreign Affairs. This was not the case, although his name may have been mentioned in connection with the post. I have authority for saying that nothing is known by Lord Lansdowne's family of the Princess Lieven's intervention on either occasion.— EDITOR.

hates O'Connell and Mr. H.[1] more than the Duke of Wellington does. Their opposition is already made and declared, and for the moment it will, I think, be the only hostile party. I am writing in such a hurry that I cannot even read over my letter. Good-bye, dear Alexander, reply to me sometimes. You see that I am a very chatterbox, but I should like to hear even that I bore you.

Lord Granville will have the Embassy at Paris or at Vienna. Good-bye.

This opportunity is a safe one, and thus I can write with freedom.

(ENCLOSURE)

Members of the New Cabinet

LORD GREY, First Lord of the Treasury.

LORD LANSDOWNE, President of the Council.

LORD DURHAM, Keeper of the Privy Seal. He is Lord Grey's son-in-law, clever, disagreeable, violent, Whig, the intimate friend of Leopold.

LORD MELBOURNE, Home Secretary. Friend of Canning, brother to Lamb, clever, charming, supple, and very lazy.

LORD PALMERSTON, Foreign Secretary. Perfect in every way.

LORD GODERICH, Colonial Secretary. Well suited to the post; his political views are known to me; belongs to the Canning group.

MR. GRANT, India Office (Board of Control). Friend of Canning, a charming man of high capacity.

LORD ALTHORP, Chancellor of the Exchequer. Whig, carrying weight in the provinces, of unblemished reputation in private life, possessing parliamentary qualities.

LORD HOLLAND, Duchy of Lancaster. You know his reputation. I may add, however, that he was the warmest supporter of Russia in the war with Turkey, and now is strong in the interest of the King of the Netherlands.

SIR JAMES GRAHAM, Admiralty. Whig, a man of parts and industry, good speaker, husband of Miss Callender, whom the Emperor saw in London.

[1] Hume (?).

LORD AUCKLAND, Board of Trade. Whig, of some ability, but nothing remarkable.

DUKE OF RICHMOND, Ordnance. Tory, Lieutenant-Colonel, served under Wellington in Spain, of spotless reputation : a man of character exercising a good deal of influence over his party in the Upper House.[1]

LORD BROUGHAM, Lord Chancellor. Democrat transformed into an aristocrat, a tiger whose claws are cut, of wise resolve, although at first apparently violent. He will be dangerous no longer.

CXIV

London : 10/22 November 1830.

I resume my journal, my dear Alexander, as these are lively times, and as I find myself in daily intercourse with the principal actors of the drama I think you will be interested to hear what they say.

The day before yesterday I dined with Mr. Peel. The Duke of Wellington was there. He came up to me at once with 'Well ? ' I found nothing better to retort than ' Well ? ' He replied, ' Bad business, devilish bad business.' 'But, Duke,' said I, 'why did you let it come about unless you wished it to end thus ? ' ' The Devil take me, no'—he replied ; ' I was absolutely surprised when they came and told me we were beaten. I will tell you all about it. I had five parties against me in the Lower House—the Jacobins, the Whigs, the Tories, the Canningites, and *my own*. Fifty of my own followers voted against the Government—I saw at once that this could not go on longer. I took the night to reflect, and in the morning I decided to break up the Ministry. As for foreign policy, my successors have only one course—to continue what I have begun. If they don't, there will be war.'

---

[1] ' As to the Duke of Richmond, people are indignant at a half-pay Lieutenant-Colonel commanding the Ordnance Department, and as an acquisition he is of doubtful value, for it seems the Tories will not go with him, at least will not consider themselves as his followers.'—*Greville Mem.* ii. 67. The Duke of Richmond eventually became Postmaster-General with a seat in the Cabinet, but he declined to draw the salary of his office. Although an Ultra-Tory, he proved far more tractable in the Cabinet than the Ultra-Liberal Lord Durham.

I have not omitted nor added a word, and I have given you his own style of talking.

At dinner I questioned Peel, and here is his reply : ' For the last year the Government has been tottering and has not progressed. We have alienated the Tories without conciliating the Whigs. It was obvious that the collapse of the Government was more or less imminent. The Duke by his declaration against any sort of reform hastened the catastrophe. The head of the Government ought never to allow his secrets to be penetrated. He, however, has imprudently proclaimed them. One may do everything, but one should not say everything. Suppose, for instance, that a Government was opposed to the abolition of taxes ; it might act upon the principle of not revoking any, but to blurt it out once would upset the administration. The Duke, moreover, has the misfortune to be surrounded by women of the most mediocre ability. No man has any influence with him, he is led by women ; the foolish ones envelop him with incense, and he has fallen a victim to this weakness and to his own vanity. My own plan of conduct is settled—I am the enemy of the Radicals only, and the new Government is equally so. In this respect I shall loyally support it. For all the rest I await the Ministers' profession of faith to know whether I shall oppose it or not.'

I have given you the pith of his explanation ; it seems to me of the greatest interest, especially in attempting to understand the man.

Yesterday I saw Lord Grey. This is what he told me of the leading principles upon which the Cabinet as a body was founded. ' In the composition of my Ministry I have had two essential objects in view : the first, to show that in these times of democracy and Jacobinism it is possible to find real capacity in the high aristocracy—not that I wish to exclude merit if I should meet with it in the commonalty ; but, given an equal merit, I admit that I should select the aristocrat, for that class is a guarantee for the surety of the State and of the throne. The second, that I have no wish, like my predecessor, to shine at the expense and to the extinction of my colleagues. On the contrary, my Cabinet is composed of men who have all displayed high parliamentary talents. I have chosen each of them with a view to his special aptitude for the post he occupies, and I leave to each full latitude to manage his department in accordance with his own judgment. Counsel of the Cabinet will then be a veritable counsel, and the dictatorship is abolished.'

These few words will convey a fair portrait of the speaker. I pass now to the subordinates. I will take this hierarchy in order of importance. In the previous one I observed the order of dates.

The Duke of Cumberland is in a great rage, and it has been my misfortune to be in a measure the cause. He believed himself destined, I cannot for the least say why, to play an important part if any change took place here. His unpopularity has been, and always will be, an insurmountable obstacle. However that may be, for a long time he has been endeavouring to draw closer to Lord Grey, and has frequently let fall complaints of the very little eagerness with which his advances have been met. Recently he has dropped more than once hints which I have always pretended not to understand. At last, two days before the last decisive vote in the Lower House he asked me straight out to arrange a meeting between him and Lord Grey at my house. I declined politely, but at the same time distinctly, such a strange proposal, requesting him to remember that in my house plans hostile to the Government could not be allowed to be concerted. This reply, combined with the fact that he has not been made Commander-in-Chief, as it seems he expected, put him in an execrable temper.[1] Certainly his position is a strange one, for, having seen the realisation of his wishes in the resignation of the Duke of Wellington, he suddenly discovers that he has gained nothing—so his ill-temper is vented upon this or that person without rhyme or reason.

There are some slight alterations to be made in the list

[1] He had other grievances also, as he wanted to obtain a grant for his son's education and maintenance, and to be appointed Governor or Viceroy of Hanover in the place of the Duke of Cambridge.

which I sent you the day before yesterday by the Prussian courier. Lord Auckland is not to have a seat in the Cabinet —but Lord Carlisle will, though without office. The Duke of Richmond is to be Postmaster-General, with a seat in the Cabinet—his rank as Lieutenant-Colonel being an obstacle to his becoming Master-General of the Ordnance.[1] The Marquess of Wellesley is to be Lord Steward, and the Marquess of Cleveland Master of the Horse. The former, as you are aware, is brother to the Duke of Wellington and his bitterest enemy. Lord Grey has given the Garter to the Duke of Bedford. The King pressed him to take it for himself, but he declined. The Duke of Bedford quitted Lord Grey and attached himself to the Duke of Wellington, but Lord Grey ignored this fact, remembering only their forty years of intimacy.

The outgoing Ministers deliver up their seals of office to-day to the King, and an hour later they will be handed to their successors. What I wrote to you about Brougham is now the general opinion, and his appointment is approved for the reason I stated. His popularity is gone, and with it the danger also.

Good-bye, dear Alexander, I embrace you with all my heart. I shall probably write again to-morrow.

DOROTHEA.

P.S.—I pressed Lord Grey yesterday upon the Belgian business. He said to me : ' You should understand that, even more than my predecessor, I am interested in preserving peace. Have enough confidence in me to believe that I shall not fail to find the means.' ' These are already to hand, my Lord,' said I, ' if you will follow up what has been begun. A Conference is going on, which proves the union of the five Great Powers on this point—support it, and peace is assured.' ' But at least you must give me time to obtain knowledge of what has been done, and then I shall be able to give you an answer.' ' Lose no time, my Lord,' I interposed : ' the change

[1] ' The Duke of Richmond's appointment was found to be so unpalatable to the army that they have been forced to change it. He is to be Master of the Horse instead, which I suspect will not be to his taste.'—*Greville*, ii. 67.

which has come over England will startle Europe—let Europe be reassured. It is needful that you should speak to her, and that quickly. My Emperor knows you and esteems you. Give me the pleasure of thinking that this feeling on his part will go on increasing.' ' Believe me,' he replied, ' you will be satisfied. I promise you that in the course of the week Lord Palmerston will make such an explanation to the plenipotentiaries as will amply content you. If what has been done so far has had peace for its object, be under no apprehension that I shall not walk in the same path.'

He told me, moreover, that Lafitte had expressed to him the pleasure which the change of the English Ministry had caused him, and that he was quite ready, in the selection of the French Ambassador to London, to be guided by his wishes. He complains to me constantly of M. de Talleyrand, and has recalled to mind that the latter on one occasion had said that the name even of Lord Grey would bring about war in three months—a remark which much annoyed him.

NOTE.—This postscript is written in sympathetic ink (citron). The signature, which is wanting to all the other letters, may have been added on this occasion to mislead the curious.—EDITOR.

CXV

London : 11/23 November 1830.

I have come to town merely to take my letter to the post, but as I have still a few minutes of leisure I devote them to you, dear Alexander. I have just had visits from both Lord Palmerston and Lord Grey. I expressed to both the annoyance which Lord Grey's speech in the Upper House had caused me, as his reference to the relations of England and France was expressed in terms which could not fail to alarm the rest of Europe, although the first portion of his speech aimed at attesting England's desire for peace.[1] I showed

[1] Presumably the passage in Earl Grey's speech alluded to is that in which he took exception to the King being made to speak of the events in Belgium as ' a revolt against an enlightened Government ' and expressed his determination ' to maintain in regard to it those general treaties by which the political system of Europe was fixed.' Lord Grey said that we had no right to praise a Government which the Belgians had thrown off, or to stigmatise them as revolted subjects, but we ought to keep before our eyes the spirit of liberty.

Lord Grey how easily his words might excite the badly
disposed everywhere, and I told him that it was deplorable
that, while professing to wish for tranquillity and order, he
might be suggesting just the pretexts for troubling them.
Lord Grey was quite upset by this interpretation of his speech,
and protested that his sole object had been to warn France
against any deviation from the ways of moderation which
she had so far followed.   Such was the real meaning of the
words he had uttered, and in declaring his hostility to all
ambitious aims he thought he was giving a hint to France
as to the only condition upon which she could reckon on a
hearty union with this country.   With this in his mind, he
believed that he was expressing as much the opinions of
other Cabinets as he was speaking in their interests, and that,
far from anticipating that his words were open to criticism,
he thought that they ought to have earned him praise.   Lord
Grey is a man of too high sense of honour for us not to admit
in its fullest sense the explanation he gives of his speech, and
it only remains a matter of regret that in the absence of such
an explanation his speech is capable of bearing a different
interpretation.

The Prince of Orange has just left me—he is to see Lord
Grey to-morrow.   I pity this poor Prince from the bottom of
my heart.   His position grieves me greatly.   God grant
for him and for us all that the present state of things may
change, and that speedily.

Lord Palmerston is completely in accord with Lord Grey
as to the meaning to be attached to the latter's speech.   It
is impossible to display better judgment, juster views, and
greater propriety than does Lord Palmerston.

Good-bye once more, dear Alexander.   Let me hear if
you get my letters, for I begin to get anxious about all this
scribbling without knowing if it reaches you or if you care
for it.   I embrace you tenderly.

[The revolutionary outbreak in Poland, although stimulated by
what was taking place in France, Belgium, and other countries, was
the natural outcome of the policy of Russia.   In 1815 the Treaty

of Vienna had created the kingdom of Poland, assigning to Russia the Grand Duchy of Warsaw, created by Napoleon out of a district over which, down to 1795, Prussia had ruled. Alexander I. agreed to maintain all Polish institutions, to be crowned King of Poland, and to exercise his authority through a Viceroy. At first the Government was chiefly composed of former partisans of Napoleon, who devoted themselves with great success to improving the material interests of the kingdom. Unfortunately the Viceroy appointed to represent the Czar was his brother the Grand Duke Constantine, a whimsical but ferocious lunatic, whose sole merit in the eyes of the Poles was that he had married a Polish wife and for her had given up the Russian crown. Many acts of violence and illegality were excused, but, notwithstanding the shameless way in which the Constitution granted in 1815 was set aside, the aristocratic party still preferred to submit to the Czar's despotism rather than to expose the nation to complete destruction. The students, however, who drew their hopes and aspirations from France and the Revolution, wanted open strife, and these views were endorsed by the democratic party. The idea which Nicholas entertained momentarily of sending Polish troops to sustain the cause of absolutism in France and Belgium furnished the occasion for a national rising, and the threat of punishing the cadets of the military school for drinking to the memory of Kosciuszko gave the signal. A body of young men forced their way into the palace of the Grand Duke, who fled for his life. A great proportion of the national troops sided with the students and their leaders. Constantine, having proved his incapacity, withdrew from the city (November 30) and shortly afterwards was forced to leave the kingdom. A Provisional Government was formed by the aristo-cratic party and the command of the troops given to General Chlopicki, who subsequently took the dictatorship 'in the King's name' in order to hold in check the more revolutionary party. Attempts were made to negotiate with Nicholas, who replied by a manifesto demanding submission or death. The conciliatory party (the 'Whites') thereupon withdrew from the Provisional Government. Prince Adam Czartoryski was placed at the head of the Government and Prince Radziwill in command of the army. The Diet, at the instigation of the 'Reds,' proclaimed the union of Poland and Lithuania and renounced the Romanoff Dynasty (January 1831). Attempts were made to obtain support from the Western Powers, but without success. Lord Palmerston took the line that under the Treaty of Vienna there was no clause which guaranteed the Constitution of Poland, and the French Ministry, although strongly urged by repeated demonstrations of popular sympathy with the Poles, after some hesitation declined to take any active part, owing chiefly to the restraining influence of M. Casimir Périer.

The Polish army—which was wholly distinct from the Russian and wore a different uniform— thereupon took the field, and Diebitch, who had successfully brought about the conclusion of the war with Turkey, was entrusted with the command of the Russian army. The Poles, who had advanced into Lithuania, fell back to the line of the Vistula, but after five bloody and indecisive battles, including that at Ostrolenka, the Poles found themselves closely hemmed in round Warsaw. Cholera, which had followed in the track of the Russian army, spread to the Polish, and for a time paralysed all operations. Marshal Diebitch fell a victim to it at Pultusk, and in the same week the Grand Duke Constantine and his Polish wife. There was a temporary pause in the progress of the campaign, caused as much by the critical state of European politics as by the ravages of the cholera. Marshal Paskievitch, who had reaped renown in the Caucasus, assumed command of the Russian army. With the connivance of Prussia he was enabled to obtain supplies through that country, and thus his plan of advancing on Warsaw from the west was rendered feasible. On July 7 he crossed the Vistula at Plock, and, abandoning his communication with Russia, advanced steadily against Warsaw. He offered amnesty to the Poles, whose Generals advised the people to accept; but the democratic party, whose rule had been marked by acts of barbarous cruelty, refused to treat with the Russians. Warsaw, after two days' bombardment, capitulated September 8. The Charter of 1815 was abolished, and Paskievitch, appointed Viceroy, with Russian officials and officers, ruled by martial law.]

CXVI

London : December 9–13 (N.S.), 1830.

I am writing this to you, dear Alexander, on St. Nicholas' Day. Although my religion [1] does not prescribe respect for the saints, I am prepared to invoke them all, and especially this one, to shower benedictions on our beloved Emperor, and that he may gloriously triumph over the difficulties which surround him.

This revolution in Poland distresses me for more than one reason—public as well as personal ; personally on account of my poor Constantine, of whose fate I am and probably shall

---

[1] Madame de Lieven was a Lutheran.

long be ignorant, and I entreat you on my knees to let me have the news as quickly as possible ; publicly because to quell this revolution great sacrifices will be necessary, because our army is separated from Poland by many weeks' march, and because the Emperor may throw himself into the field just as he did into the midst of the plague, and that, while admiring him for his noble courage, I tremble when I think he is in danger.

This news has caused the greatest surprise here, and to Lord Grey the greatest alarm, for, notwithstanding the indiscreet words he may have uttered before becoming Prime Minister, since he has come into office he has been the most pronounced enemy of revolutions, revolutionists, and of disturbance in general, wherever it shows itself. He recognises that force is the only course open to the Emperor to adopt, and he trusts that it will speedily give him the mastery over this turbulent Poland. Nevertheless he advises me to brace my nerves in order to bear with insults on one hand and sympathy on the other ; for there is too much ill-will in England, as elsewhere, not to foresee that the Poles will find many sympathisers.

It must be allowed that Europe just now presents a scene of incredible confusion. What will be the outcome of it all ? The man who can solve that question certainly does not exist. I believe, however, that if we emerge with glory, as I doubt not we shall, from the struggle which is about to begin with Poland, our strong position, posted as we then shall be on the frontiers of both Prussia and Austria, will impose tranquillity upon the rest of Europe. From this advanced post we shall reassure the well-disposed and shall make those who dislike us tremble. England will be with us so long as we remain within our own limits ; if France should stir she will have all the Powers against her, England included. The least sign of ambition on the part of France would raise all the English against her. Let her put herself in the wrong, if she dares. My poor judgment tells me that this line agrees with our dignity as well as with our interests, and with the tranquillity desired by all, except perhaps by France, and even in saying by France would it not be more correct to say by M. de Lafayette ? You have no idea of Lord Grey's distrust of France, nor of the nice little ' services ' which I may be able to render to the French faction when the occasion offers. Dismiss from your mind the idea, if you ever had it, that Lord Grey is a Liberal. He is so near to becoming the very opposite that only yesterday he told me that his only wish was to be dictator for six months. His greatest fear is Italy, and the mere thought of troubles in Piedmont gives him the stomach-ache. If Austria interferes France will intervene, and England will throw the blame on Austria— even Castlereagh was forced to do the same.[1]

I am writing by the Prussian courier. My husband, however, is going to send you one shortly—he is up to the eyes in conferences. Matuscevitz is gone a-hunting. The King goes to Brighton to-day ; he is now on excellent terms with his Ministry, especially with Lord Grey, in whom he has the utmost confidence, and Grey adores his master. He wishes to let the English heads get cool, and so puts off the Reform question. When it becomes necessary to take it up he will do so, but as gently as possible ; in all probability the Radicals alone will object to his proposals, they want to get everything. The Tories will not have the folly to oppose them for the sake of opposition, for the upsetting of the actual Government would mean O'Connell or Cobbett Prime Minister.

Good-bye, dear Alexander ; I have a thousand things I should like to write, but you have not the time to read them. Heaven knows where this letter will reach you.

The Prince of Orange is still here. I hope for his own sake that he will go back to Holland—that is his proper place.

I embrace you with all my heart ; all my wishes and all my thoughts are with you.

---

[1] Lord Grey's anticipations were not realised until the following spring, when Central Italy rose against its rulers, and Austria and France, brought face to face, were with difficulty kept from flying at each other's throat.

CXVII

London : 10/22 December 1830.

Dear Alexander,—My husband is preparing for the courier's bag, and so I will get my letter ready also ; therefore, not to waste your time, I come to business at once.

The London Conference has taken a very serious and important step.[1] Exactly three weeks, day for day, after my husband's return he has put his signature to an Act which paves the way for the independence of Belgium.   If any-one had foretold him this on the day of his arrival he would have regarded him as a lunatic.   This, however, is what he has been brought to by force of circumstances ; it was imperative to move with them, or to see Belgium lost to Europe.   He (M. de Lieven) has moved—but he was the last to do so ; the union of the five (Powers) subsists, and the union of four is assured, and now, unless we do not care to have her on our side (which is not likely), we have England with us.[2]   The new Ministry has acted wisely, with distrust of France and with confidence in us.   You may take my word that it is very far from approving the doctrines and the events of the day.   Its position, like that of each individual Minister in the Cabinet, prevents England supporting contrary views, but you will not find it favouring, as France will probably, a system which would run counter to our interests and our principles. We must avoid discussing principles with it, but act upon Peel's maxim which I repeated to you the other day, that

[1] The London Conference, at which Palmerston had replaced Aberdeen, agreed (December 20) to recognise 'the absolute and entire separation of Belgium from Holland as an irreversible fact.'

[2] 'The Belgian question is approaching a crisis. The Provisional Government, as I understand, have made two proposals with the sanction of Lord Ponsonby. The first is that Prince Leopold should be Sovereign with a French princess as his wife ; the second is that a French Prince should be Sovereign and that he should marry the daughter of the Duke of Cambridge.   I have long suspected that Leopold was deeply engaged in this affair, but he is strongly objected to by Lieven, both in consequence of his conduct towards the Emperor and the creation of a French influence, as well as in consequence of the hopes which had been held out by Russia to the Prince of Orange.'—'Earl of Aberdeen to Duke of Wellington,' *Dispatches*, viii. 385.

'here you may do anything, but you must not say everything'—that is England's maxim.

In his foreign relations Lord Grey's chief desire is peace, a good understanding with all—but especially with Russia—and this political principle is endorsed by all the Whigs. They have a natural antipathy to Austria, a decided aversion to Metternich—and this feeling is especially marked in Lord Grey, whose straightforwardness has never been able to accord itself to the tricks of the Chancellor of the Court and Empire.

At the same time he admits in principle that this phantom of Austria must subsist in Europe. He has, however, something like a real veneration for the King of Prussia, and a sort of liking for that Power, a feeling dating from the last manœuvres in Silesia under Frederick the Great, at which he was present. He looks upon France as stricken, but stricken with a dangerous and contagious disorder; he is grieved at the warlike feeling exhibited there, and fears lest this feeling may carry the Government away with it. In this case, and if France should become aggressive, she will have to reckon with England, which, however deep in debt and desirous to retrench, will always be able to find means for going to war. By no other hypothesis can we reckon upon this country, so let us leave to France the privilege of putting herself in the wrong.

With regard to home affairs here, the restless spirits are on the move; the Government will have a good deal of trouble in keeping within the limits of the very moderate reforms it proposes to offer. God grant that it may be able to do so, and the Tories, if they are wise, will lend their help; otherwise the democracy will seize upon the reins of power, and King William will be packed off to Hanover. My husband was greatly struck by the change which had come over England during his absence. The weakness of the late Government allowed everything; it only lived by its concessions, and in this way fostered every hope. Just now there is a belief in universal suffrage—imagine what would become of England if it were obtained! At the same time it is quite certain that the wrongs of the lower classes need a remedy.   The aristocracy rolls in wealth and luxury while the streets of London, the highways of the country, swarm with miserable creatures covered with rags, barefooted, having neither food nor shelter.   The sight of this contrast is revolting, and in all likelihood were I one of these thousands of poor wretches I should be a democrat.   How is it that no Government seems ever to have been able to find a remedy for this evil ?   The Poor Laws raise funds for them ; a pauper goes to the parish for relief, if he is unmarried the pittance is quite inadequate, if he marries he gets twice as much—so he gets married, begets ten children, draws double relief for himself, and allows his children to die of starvation. The intention of the law is doubtless philanthropic, but its result is inhuman—but I am getting involved in details. I must get back to the situation at large.

It will be a critical moment when the Government takes up the Reform question next session, which is now fixed for the day when Parliament resumes its sittings in February— no further respite will be allowed.   What will be the state of Europe then ? for really with the pace at which events move nowadays a dozen catastrophes may have occurred in six weeks' interval.

You may imagine with what impatience we are awaiting news from Petersburg and the decision taken by the Emperor with regard to the revolution at Warsaw.   I cannot, however, in truth say that I am disturbed ; my Emperor will know how to read a lesson to kings and peoples, and my heart, wholly Russian, swells with pride at the thought.

The King is at Brighton, worried and anxious, seeing democracy advancing and finding no remedy.   Ministers also are disturbed.   Hunt's election to the Lower House is the most ugly symptom so far—the sureties required were deemed satisfactory.[1]   Ireland is more than disquieting— O'Connell has gone over there to arouse public opinion against

[1] Mr. Stanley, having accepted office as Chief Secretary for Ireland, vacated his seat for Preston.   His re-election was opposed by ' Orator ' Hunt, the hero of Peterloo, who ten years previously had been imprisoned for seditious speeches. He made no mark in the House of Commons, where, however, he was well received.

Lord Anglesey. O'Connell's one device is the separation of Ireland from England. God knows if he may not be successful—a general rising of the country is quite on the cards. There is an army of 25,000 soldiers there, but with a population of 7,000,000 that counts for little.

If there should be any disturbance in France, as people seem to fear, I do not for one moment doubt that there will not be the like in England. The Duke of Wellington has gone to take his part in the proceedings of the county of which he is Lord-Lieutenant.[1] From his place in Parliament he gives himself out as a Moderate, but he is full of bitterness and aims only at upsetting the Ministry—a terrible temptation, and if it were for his own advantage well and good, but there is not a single person who does not see that it would be wholly to the advantage of the Jacobins. However, should the Lower House consent to humour his fancies I have little doubt that the Government would dissolve it. So you see, my dear Alexander, that in one way and another we are not looking for quiet times here ; will they be more so elsewhere ?

My relations with the Ministers are excellent and most friendly. Lord Grey continues to pay me his daily visit and to listen to what I say. He is most chagrined by all that is happening, and wishes he were strong enough to prevent it ; but that strength has still to be sought, for the disorganisation of parties is such that it is impossible to make any forecast.

December 12/24.

I am closing my letter to-day, my dear Alexander. Our news from Paris just received comes down to 22nd. Sentence has been pronounced against the ex-Ministers.[2] Paris greatly excited, and Lafayette not sufficiently liberal. Well, that seems promising. There is, then, something more democratic still than Lafayette. I am curious to know what.

[1] Hampshire, in which much unrest and dissatisfaction had been caused by the proceedings of the rick-burners.

[2] Prince Polignac and his colleagues. He was sentenced to imprisonment and confined at Ham until 1836, when he was amnestied and came to England. The conclusion of the trial was marked by serious disturbances in Paris, which were happily and promptly appeased by Louis Philippe and his son riding through the streets at night.

Lord Grey expresses himself most correctly about our affairs in Poland. He earnestly and sincerely wishes that we may promptly repress this revolution—for my part I have no sort of doubt about it. Here they are going to have a special form of prayer for deliverance from the calamities which afflict England. I confess I don't altogether understand this, for these calamities come from the disturbers of peace. Let these be repressed, this would avail more than prayers. It is true they are doing this also, for a fair lot of people are going to be hanged.

Leopold is again upon the scene. Lord Grey is thinking of him. I do not let a day pass without telling him that it is a folly, that it is the Prince of Orange alone who will suit everybody, for in spite of everything that there is in his disfavour—it is frivolity, but nothing else [1]—I cannot conceive how the Belgian business can have a solid foundation without him. These two words don't go well together—yet what I say is true ; but I am too idle to explain.[2]

Let me know, too, my dear Alexander, if you were able to decipher all my previous citron,[3] and in future do not fail to take notice if my Christian name appears at the end of my letter. It may be that I shall have occasion to make use of it.

I am happily reassured about Constantine. God grant that he find an opportunity to distinguish himself.

My husband sends his love ; he wanted to write to you, but he has no time—I tell him, moreover, that it is needless. You have plenty to do to get through my long letter. Give Count Tolstoy my best regards. How right he was in all that he told me at Warsaw. I constantly recur to it. Good-bye, dear, dear Alexander ; where are you ? What is the Emperor doing ? How I wish I could know. I embrace you.

[1] 'He made a great fool of himself here, and destroyed any sympathy there might have been for his political misfortunes. Supping, dining, and acting, and a little (rather innocent) orgies at ladies' houses formed his habitual occupation.' (*Greville*, ii. 133.)

[2] The antithesis is between *léger* and *solide*.

[3] This refers to the postscript to the letter 114 written in sympathetic ink (citron).

1831

[In the interval between the date of the preceding and the following letters Belgian affairs had been the chief source of anxiety, and
at several junctures threatened the peace of Europe.   The Russian
and Prussian Governments, for family as well as for political reasons,
actively supported the claims of the Prince of Orange, and Lords
Grey and Palmerston were not disposed to offer any serious opposition if the other Powers concurred.   Baron Stockmar, who was
eminently qualified to speak with authority on this matter, says that
the endeavours to render the Belgian revolution less disastrous to the
House of Orange were defeated by the obstinacy of the King of
Holland and by his jealousy of his son, the Prince of Orange.
There was every prospect of a reaction of feeling among the
Belgians in his favour, and it was not until every prospect of a more
desirable arrangement had been destroyed that the British Government countenanced the candidature of Leopold.   One of its reasons
was to counteract the designs of Louis Philippe, who wanted Belgium
for one of his own sons, and thereby to pave the way for its annexation
to France.   Metternich was equally opposed to any restoration of
the Orange family, and he was not prepared to see the line of forti-
fication erected by the Allies on the south-western frontier of Belgium
with the express object of keeping France in check pass into the hands
of a ruler under the influence of that country.   Moreover, in the
Archduke Charles he had a candidate of his own, who, if accepted,
would virtually restore the situation as it existed before 1795.   The
French party in the Belgian National Congress were divided in their
sympathies, one section, representing the French Court, holding for
the Duc de Nemours, son of Louis Philippe, while the other,
more Republican and Bonapartist in feeling, favoured the choice of
the Duke Augustus of Leuchtenberg, son of Eugène Beauharnais and
grandson of the Empress Joséphine.   At the outset the London Conference had agreed that the wearer of the Belgian crown should belong

to neither the French nor English reigning house, and Louis Philippe, in anticipation of the proceedings at Brussels, had declared that he would not consent to the nomination of the Duc de Nemours.   The Belgian representatives were nevertheless assured by interested persons that if the Duc de Nemours was actually elected his father's scruples would vanish.   The three names were put to the vote on February 21, when it appeared that Nemours had 97, Leuchtenberg 74, and Archduke Charles 21 votes.   Talleyrand, who at that time represented France in London, at once perceived that unless Louis Philippe stood firm to his promise war would ensue and his crown would be in danger.   He therefore finally declined to accept the nomination for his son, but before the vote was taken the name of the Prince of Naples, brother of Ferdinand II. and nephew of Louis Philippe, had been put forward apparently with the assent of England.[1]   The Belgians, however, refused to entertain the idea, and the French Ministry of M. Casimir Périer, which had succeeded that of M. Lafitte, allowed the matter to drop, and the Belgian Congress elected a Regent, Baron Surlet de Chokier, to act until the Powers should agree upon a candidate.   France and England were now in complete accord, and notified to the Belgian Government that the *bases de séparation* agreed upon by the Five Powers were irrevocable, and if not accepted before June 1 diplomatic relations with Brussels would be suspended.   They, however, intimated that they were willing to open negotiations with the King of Holland on the question of the Grand Duchy of Luxembourg. Meanwhile Prince Leopold of Saxe-Coburg, the widowed husband of the Princess Charlotte, had been approached by the Belgian delegates, and, his candidature receiving the support of both England and France, he was elected on June 2 by 152 to 44 votes.   His election, although it did not remove all the difficulties of the situation, induced the Powers to recommend a modification of the terms of the separation of Belgium from Holland, and these having been accepted by the former, the Powers undertook to obtain the acquiescence of the Dutch Government.   But this was not attained without difficulty and even danger to the peace of Europe.

There is little to be added to Madame de Lieven's remarks on the Reform Bill.   It was introduced (March 1) by Lord John Russell, who held the office of Paymaster of the Forces and was not a Cabinet Minister, but had taken a prominent part in previous agitation and in framing the ministerial measure.   Its secrets had been well preserved up to the last moment, and when revealed its provisions were found to be more drastic than had been generally

---

[1] *Mémoires de Barante*, iv. ; letter of M. Guizot, February 13. 1831.

anticipated. Its leading principle was the substitution of election for nomination in the return of members to the House of Commons. Sixty boroughs having less than 2,000 inhabitants were to be wholly disfranchised, and forty-six having less than 4,000 were to lose half their representatives, including Weymouth, which had hitherto returned four members. By this arrangement 167 seats were made available for distribution, but as the Bill proposed also to reduce the total number of members from 658 to 596 only 110 seats were to be allotted. These were to be distributed on the basis of the representation of all towns of 10,000 inhabitants and upwards, and of an additional member to all counties with 150,000. Thus the English counties obtained 55 in addition to their actual representation, Scotland 5, Ireland 5, and Wales 1. Four fresh metropolitan boroughs returning eight members were to be created, and the large provincial towns, hitherto unrepresented, were to send 36 members to Westminster. At the same time the franchise was extended to all 20*l.* leaseholders in boroughs and to 10*l.* copyholders and 50*l.* leaseholders in counties.

The debate on the introduction of the Bill extended over seven nights, but by a tacit understanding no division was to be taken on the first reading. The second stage was fixed for March 20, and after two nights' further discussion the Bill was read a second time by 302 to 301 votes, making a House of 608 members, one of the fullest divisions on record. The Committee stage was postponed until after the Easter holidays, and on the second night (April 14) the Government was defeated by 299 to 291 on the point of reducing the number of members of the House. Two days later the Ministry was again defeated on a question of Supply, and thereupon tendered its resignation, which the King refused to accept. His reluctance to dissolve a Parliament in its first Session gave way before his desire to see the Reform question settled and his irritation at the line taken by the Tory peers. Under circumstances of almost unparalleled excitement, he suddenly appeared (April 22) at Westminster and prorogued Parliament with a view to its immediate dissolution].

CXVIII

London : $\frac{\text{February 17}}{\text{March 1}}$, 1831.

At length the great day has arrived on which the Reform Bill is to be laid before Parliament. The Ultra-Tories and the supporters of the late Ministry met the day before yesterday to decide upon the course of action to follow. It is

understood that they will not oppose the introduction of the
Bill, but will throw it out on the second reading, which will
most probably be taken a week or ten days later, so that my
calculation that the real crisis will be about the 15th holds
good.   The Opposition is quite sure of the result and counts
upon a majority of 80 or 100 against the Bill.   But this
achieved, if it be achieved, the opponents of the Government
will find themselves somewhat embarrassed by their victory.
Will the country quietly submit to the loss of the hope of
reform?   Will it suffer itself to be governed by men opposed
to the idea?   Would the King care to have them? and,
supposing all these conditions admitted, how would the
new Ministry be composed?   The Ultra-Tories will have
neither the Duke of Wellington nor Mr. Peel at the head of
the Government; they have not yet condoned the emancipation of the Catholics.   In all their anticipations of a new
Government they assert great pretensions and claim a large
share of power.   The Duke of Wellington will give nothing
to any of those who helped to upset him, and yet without
these he cannot count upon any following.   On the other
hand, the Duke and Peel are not in accord.   Peel wishes to
be Prime Minister—will the Duke consent to be merely a
member of the Cabinet?[1]   Such are the difficulties which
face us in the future.   It remains now to ask what should be
Lord Grey's course.   We have talked together much upon
the subject.   My opinion is that for him the question of
reform is not one of life or death.   He might admit alterations
in his Bill, and in that case will not regard himself at the
end of his tether unless the Bill is absolutely rejected.   In
this case he would have to consider whether he should or
could dissolve Parliament.   For my own part I should say he
should not, for dissolution would provoke a dangerous agitation throughout the country.   I am quite ignorant of the
decision of the Cabinet on this point, and I am equally
ignorant whether the King would give his consent.   It would

---

[1] ' Everybody inquires what line Peel will take, and though each party is
confident of success in this question, it is thought to depend mainly upon the
course he adopts and the sentiments he expresses.'—*Greville*, ii. 122.

depend a good deal upon public opinion, for I believe that the King would not act in opposition to it. My wish is that certain amendments should be made to the Bill which would allow Lord Grey to remain and would force Lord Althorp and some Radical members of the Cabinet to retire ; that then advances should be made to Wellington and Peel, and that places in the Cabinet should be found for them and some of their adherents. This would be the most favourable arrangement, and I do not think it at all impossible. A very few hours, however, will show whether such a scheme is realisable. For my own part I think Peel will not show himself opposed to a moderate measure of reform. In connection with these eventual arrangements for a new Ministry the Duke of Wellington is talked of for Foreign Secretary.

March 2.

I was absolutely stupefied when I learnt the extent of the Reform Bill. The most absolute secrecy had been maintained on the subject until the last moment. It is said that the House was quite taken by surprise ; the Whigs are astonished, the Radicals delighted, the Tories indignant. This was the first impression of Lord John Russell's speech, who was entrusted with explaining the Government Bill. I saw Lord Grey when the first report of what had passed in the House was brought to him. He believed—or said he did—that it was a great triumph, and repeated with self-satisfaction, ' I have kept my word with the nation.' It was impossible for me not to express my regret. The Ultra-Tories, under the presidency of the Duke of Cumberland, have just been called together. The Duke went with the determination not to consent to any amendment, except such a one as would absolutely destroy the Bill. I do not yet know what line the late Ministers propose to adopt ; I shall only hear this evening, too late to tell you in this letter. Everybody is lost in amazement and dumbfoundered, the friends of the Ministry included—but it is admitted that the Bill bears examination and contains many useful things. I have had neither the time nor the courage to read it. Its leading features have scared me completely: 168 members are unseated, sixty boroughs disfranchised, eight more members allotted to London and proportionally to the large towns and counties, the total number of members reduced by sixty or more, and septennial Parliaments maintained— the two last being the only good features of the Bill.

Good-bye, my dear Alexander ; the Emperor's manifesto, dated January 25, has caused a sensation in the Ministry, and its last words have frightened it. However, to-day everyone is absorbed in the Reform question and thinks of nothing else. The debate will be continued to-day and probably to-morrow.

I hear from a good source (but not from himself, for he would take care not to tell it to me) that Lord Grey leans towards war with France,[1] but that he has met with resistance in the Cabinet from Lord Althorp and other Liberals. Grant will quit the Cabinet as soon as the Reform question is passed—if it is passed ; if not, he will make the plunge with all the rest. There is some talk of recalling Gordon from Constantinople and sending in his place Adair, an old diplomat of the days of Fox and a great friend of Pozzo. Frederick Lamb is named for the Embassy at Vienna. Lord Grey counts upon a majority of seventy votes.

CXIX

London : May 3 (N.S.), 1831.

I sent you by Baron de Krüdener [2] the money you required, dear Alexander, but there was no time to send a letter with it—so I am writing to-day to repair my omission.

The elections in England have taken a startling turn ; for the most part they are Radical, and go infinitely beyond all

[1] Louis Philippe was very indignant with the English Government and they with him ; he because they betrayed him to follow the views of the continental Powers, and they because of his duplicity in regard to the election of the Duc de Nemours. General Sebastiani, Foreign Minister in M. Lafitte's cabinet, had instructed Talleyrand to dissent from the decisions of the London Conference and backed up his remonstrance by making warlike preparations. The fall of the Lafitte Ministry (March 12) was followed by a complete change in the attitude of France to England.

[2] A member of the Russian Diplomatic Service and son of the husband of the well-known Egeria of Alexander I. and the author of *Valérie*.

that either the lovers or even the authors of Reform could ever have anticipated. The reaction against the Bill, which every-one imagined would spread rapidly, was suddenly cut short by the dissolution of Parliament. Then from the moment that the country saw that the King lent himself to the measure, and regarded it with favour, there was no way of raising a cry against Reform. It was long doubtful whether the King wished for Reform à *outrance*, but there is no longer any room for doubt, and this has inspired the Liberal party with fresh energy.[1]

I am greatly concerned at all that has happened; and I could not forbear to say to Lord Grey, in reply to some words of triumph of his on the elections, that he would long for his enemies when he found himself face to face with his new friends. Lord Grey is possessed by a demon of incredible madness. Very few persons of weight share his illusions, and quite a string of the Whigs themselves are taking steps to prevent the Bill being presented again in the same shape as that of the rejected measure. There is, too, serious alarm at the Jacobin tendency displayed in some quarters; it is easy to rouse such a feeling, but·very difficult to keep it in check later on. Ministers wanted to gain popu-larity for themselves and for the King; they have got it, but at the expense of England's happiness. I send you herewith a letter from the Duke of Wellington which touches slightly on this subject as well as on our operations in Poland. You can hardly believe what harm this prolongation of our war is doing us here and everywhere, or how difficult it is for me to conceal the feelings of vexation and anger which are aroused by many inconsiderate acts and idle remarks.

Lord Grey has received a letter from Adam Czartoryski, dated March 20, brought to him by a certain M. Bière, a

[1] The general election, which gave the Government a majority of 104 votes, showed the following results :

	Reformers	Anti-Reformers
Counties	70	6
Cities	42	8
Boroughs not scheduled . . .	126	46
Boroughs to be disfranchised . .	28	76
Boroughs to be partially disfranchised	31	53

Frenchman residing at Warsaw,[1] who was detained ten days at Breslau. The tone of the letter is very moderate, according to Lord Grey ; I should like to know what he calls moderate, for I know that on this subject I am not at all so. This M. Bière called upon Lord Brougham, who, however, told him that he could listen to nothing and say nothing on Polish matters. I repeat what he boasted to me, but I will not answer for its being the truth. For the moment, however, he represents what is called the moderate element in the Cabinet, which means that he does not like the Reform Bill.

The King has been greatly annoyed by the disturbances which marked the illuminations for the dissolution of Parliament. The Tories refused to illuminate—so all the windows of their houses were broken by the mob, and they were forced to sleep in fresh air. This is a nice state of things.

Good-bye, my dear Alexander ; send us some good news, with which I may annoy some of my friends. Lord Grey has behaved well in the French intrigue against us at Constantinople, and it is most certainly to him that we owe the reparation made to us by the recall of M. Guillemenot.[2] He is sorry, however, that it is he and not Sebastiani who has been made the victim on this occasion.

(ENCLOSURE)

Hatfield Park : May 1, 1831.

Madame la Princesse,—It was only yesterday that I received the letter which you have done me the honour

---

[1] This is apparently a second letter, for according to Greville a letter from Prince Czartoryski was delivered in January by an ' Envoy,' whom Mr. Henry Reeve identifies as Count Alexander Walewski, a natural son of Napoleon I. He remained in London, and in the course of the year married Lady Caroline Montagu, daughter of the Earl of Sandwich. (*Greville Mem.* ii. 104.) It is, however, elsewhere stated that the Marquis Wielopolski was deputed in March 1831 by the National Government of Warsaw to present a memorial to Lord Palmerston praying for the good offices of England. No notice was taken officially of the appeal.

[2] The French Ambassador, who had been intriguing against Russia and encouraging the Turks to resistance. Sebastiani was Foreign Minister.

to write to me, and I am much obliged to you for the interest you take in the misfortune which has befallen me.[1]

It is difficult to form an opinion of military affairs in Poland from the meagre and untrustworthy reports which reach us from Warsaw through Paris, and are often concocted in the latter city. It seems now that the Polish force which was at Zamosk has pushed forward into Volhynia. I infer therefrom that Marshal Diebitch, having been able to recommence further operations, has thought it advisable to recall to his own control the detachments which were holding this corps in check and to employ them elsewhere. If so, we shall very shortly hear the result of these operations. One must never lose sight of the topographical difficulties in which the Marshal finds himself. I passed through Warsaw in mid-April in 1826 ; the season was an early one, but I can assure you that an army could not have commenced operations at that season in Poland—certainly not an army encumbered by wagons, as is the Russian. So you must have patience. You should also bear in mind that the Emperor Napoleon, who never had any time to throw away at such a distance from Paris, opened the campaign which ended in the Peace of Tilsit only towards the month of June.

You are aware that I have always held a very clear idea of the importance of a successful issue to these affairs in Poland, and that I regretted their unseasonable beginning because it made their ending hazardous. I think now, however, that the danger is past and that we shall shortly receive good news.

But your troubles in Poland are not a half so serious even for the Russians or for the world as are affairs here. I know this country well, and I am sure that I do not deceive myself. If those who guide us do not know how—or unfortunately are not able—to stop themselves, there will ensue troubles such as the world has never yet seen, and will in the end submerge everything.

[1] His wife died on April 25. She was the Hon. Catherine Pakenham, daughter of second Lord Longford, and was married to the Duke (then Hon. Arthur Wellesley) in 1806 after his return from India.

But this is too big a subject to discuss in a letter like this. I am sorry to learn that the Grand Duchess is forced to take sea baths. As soon as I hear of her arrival, I shall go and pay my respects to her.

Believe me, Madame la Princesse,
Your faithful servant,
WELLINGTON.

CXX

Richmond : $\frac{\text{April 29}}{\text{May 11}}$, 1831.

I have nothing to tell you to-day, dear Alexander, because Diebitch has not yet defeated the Poles, and without this preliminary I can neither think nor write letters.

The elections in England have gone Liberal as if under a spell. Ministers have already a majority of one hundred in favour of their Bill and the county elections are not yet over. These will certainly go in their favour. Therefore they are the masters. Will they use or abuse this situation ? The former implies moderate Reform—the latter a Bill on the lines of that already brought forward. The King has intimated his wish for some changes in the measure, as proposed. A section of the Cabinet desires them ; the majority of the great Whig Lords have made representations to Lord Grey in the same sense. We shall see what comes of it. There is a curious point to be noted in what is passing now in England. On the Continent the source of all Radical ideas are the schools—the universities and their students propagate republicanism ; while in this country the only resistance which the proposals for Reform have met with comes from the three universities of the Empire—Oxford, Cambridge, and Dublin. The universities have unanimously elected anti-Reformers.[1] One would say, then, that here it is the most educated party which repels any so-called improvement of the method of representation. This fact has made a strong impression. The King himself, among others, had said when giving his assent to the new elections that he would regard

[1] The only change was at Cambridge, where Lord Palmerston and Mr. Cavendish were defeated by Mr. Goulburn and Mr. R. Peel.

the choice made by the universities as the touchstone of the saner portion of his subjects.

May 1/13.

This is Petersburg's joyful and brilliant fête day. Will Diebitch have given you cause to celebrate it with a happy heart? You see that all my thoughts are centred on his big head—I thought it a clever head, too, in the few talks I had with him at Warsaw. But why has he not yet finished with Poland? Do you know that this Poland was the final argument used to obtain the King's consent to the dissolution of Parliament? Lord Grey represented to him that it was the spirit of the times which was triumphing; that to withstand it was to court certain destruction; that nowhere would the King find any support for a backward step, that Russia even—that immense and great Empire— was unable to repress a handful of rebels, how then could the King hope to maintain himself with a few Ultra-Tories against Reforming England? So the King gave way. This poor King is never tired of talking to my husband and to me about Poland. Only yesterday he said to me, 'Madame, you cannot desire more than I do the triumph of your Emperor, for it concerns me very closely.' Leopold is very prudent and very close, very chary of his feelings, very cowardly and very depressed. He will not be King, that cannot be— Belgium will end by resuming its natural course (with) Holland.

Michael Woronzow has just arrived with wife and children. Good-bye, dear Alexander, I embrace you heartily, and all your family and our own also. A thousand kind things to Count Tolstoy. My son, the Spaniard, has just arrived. He is a fine good fellow. He came by way of Lisbon—where they don't adore Dom Miguel, but are resigned to him. I embrace you a thousand times, and entreat you to love me and to beat the Poles.

CXXI

Richmond : June 24 (N.S.), 1831.[1]

It is just a year ago, my dear Alexander, that I was with you in that same Warsaw which to-day is causing so much harm to Russia and to all Europe.   Even then we heard the rumblings of what has become a terrible revolution.   I never like to dwell upon the past—it is beyond remedy ; but how can one dismiss the thought that if at that time the fatal powers of Grand Duke Constantine had been restricted, Poland would have remained faithful ?   How well can I recall the many hints let fall by all those Poles, mere casual acquaintances : 'We are devoted to the Emperor, but we abhor his brother.'   This hatred had become an instinct— without a future, without hope.   We are now reaping the consequences.   A good deal has been done since I last wrote, but so far as I can judge the state of things is worse.

This Belgian question affects the honour of the Powers. Possibly in the interests of peace this sacrifice is necessary ; but what a sacrifice it is, and, after all, have we done well to submit to it ?[2]   I am greatly annoyed, but with the feeble position of the French Government, the pitiable cowardice of Lord Grey, and our powerlessness for the moment, probably there was no other course possible.   At any rate, the Great Powers are looking exceedingly small—it is an eclipse, and a disgraceful one, but one which, I trust, will not last long.

The opening of Parliament has caused me a lot of worry and trouble.   Lord Grey came here and read me the para-graph in the King's Speech referring to Poland.   He would not speak of the Poles as rebels—it was more in his way to go round about the word.   I did not for a moment deceive myself that I should get him to make use of it, and I do not attempt the impossible.   All my efforts, therefore, were

[1] This letter appears to have been written on a later date than that given, probably on 26th.

[2] The Belgian delegates had made the offer of the crown to Prince Leopold, and in the King's Speech a paragraph was introduced conveying his approval of their choice.

directed to getting him to change the word 'war' for that of
'struggle.' The request was a small one, nevertheless it
cost me much trouble to obtain it. I send you our two last
respective letters on this subject. The paragraph in the
speech referring to Belgium is most unseemly,[1] and Lord
Grey's speech in the Upper House on the 24th inst. was even
more unbecoming. However, the debate on that occasion
was most satisfactory in that it forced Lord Grey to give up
what I know was his fixed purpose on the very morning of
that day—namely, to break up the Conference and to recognise
Leopold as King off hand.[2]   It seemed to me that there was
not a moment to be lost, knowing the character of the man
and being sure of my facts.   I therefore allowed the Duke of
Wellington to guess that we were not satisfied ; and on this
inference he founded the appeal he made to Lord Grey in
the House to go hand in hand with us, commending highly
the settled course which had been so far pursued by both
Powers.   Lord Grey was furious, as you will see by a letter
he wrote to me on the very day—but at the Conference he
gave way.   It will not be broken up, and we shall keep
England within bounds.   All this is so confidential that I
have not dared to speak of it to my husband.   He is delighted
with the result, but that is only because he is ignorant of
the author—Lord Grey's suspicions are divided between the
Spanish Minister and M. de Zuylen,[3] but they will wear off.
Let Count Nesselrode see my letters, they will teach him to

[1] It was as follows : 'The principle on which these Conferences have been
conducted has been that of not interfering with the right of the people of Belgium
to regulate their own internal affairs, and to establish their Government according to their own view of what may be most conducive to their future welfare and
independence under the conditions . . . that the security of neighbouring States
should not be endangered.'—*Hansard's Debates*, ix.

[2] Lord Grey's opinion as expressed to Madame de Lieven was that the Dutch
King seemed determined to do everything in his power to prevent an arrangement.
In his speech in the House of Lords he asserted that 'the interests of the King of
Holland had occupied a full share of the attention of the other Powers of Europe,'
adding, with reference to the pending negotiations with Prince Leopold, that ' his
elevation to the throne of Belgium would be a fortunate circumstance for the
country he was called on to govern.'—*Ibid*.

[3] Señor Zea Bermudez. M. de Zuylen was Dutch Plenipotentiary at the London
Conference.

know Lord Grey—out of such details one can construct the whole. I am always on the best terms with him. I shall see him to-day ; he listens when I am speaking, but it only lasts twenty-four hours, for then his accursed son-in-law Lord Durham comes along, and carries him off, and he becomes either a Jacobin or a child as it suits the other.

Palmerston is in the most trying position ; he cannot take his seat [1] for the next few days, Parliamentary forms make this delay inevitable. Until then he cannot enjoy any independence in the Cabinet, because his seat depends upon the Government. He has therefore been forced to bend, to give way, and to obey. He will not take up his position as Minister of the Crown until formally seated in Parliament : his bondage has thus occurred just at a most critical moment. This is one calamity, but worse follows. Durham aspires to take his place—good Heavens ! if he should succeed in driving Palmerston out and putting himself at the Foreign Office, we may expect anything. He is a Pole *enragé*, and I know that on three occasions already he has put forward at Cabinet Councils the proposal to recognise the independence of Poland, asserting that this announcement would be received with acclamation by the Lower House and by the country at large. Unhappily this is true up to a certain point ; the Cabinet, however, on each occasion rejected the proposal.

Lord Grey was much disturbed on learning that Dom Pedro and Donna Maria were in the power of France.[2] He recognises that these two may be used as instruments fatal to Dom Miguel, but he does not want France to reap the honour and profit of having turned them to this purpose. I suspect that the visit of Dom Pedro to London was due to some indirect invitation on the part of the English Government.

The Opposition is very strong in the Upper House [3]—and

[1] For Bletchingley, one of the boroughs scheduled in the pending Reform Bill for extinction.

[2] The French fleet was blockading the Tagus in consequence of the ill treatment of French subjects by the Portuguese Government and its refusal to give redress. Dom Pedro had just arrived in Europe.

[3] The followers of the Duke of Wellington and the old Tories had made up their quarrel, and were united in opposing the Ministry.

X

its ranks are well-filled and well-disciplined, but in the Lower House the Government has a large majority. The Reform Bill will be passed there without doubt by a large majority ; the struggle in the Lords will be very keen—they will try to worry Lord Grey to death with pinpricks, and they might be physically successful, for he is the most sensitive man I know.

The King sent his greetings to the Grand Duchess by Sir Whalley,[1] one of his gentlemen in waiting, and gave him a letter for her ; and both the King and the Queen expressed to me their sincere wish that she would pay them a visit at Windsor before leaving England.

I am told that Prince Paul of Würtemberg recently passed through London on his way to Sidmouth, where we are going to-morrow. The reception of the Grand Duchess at Plymouth was most correct, and at Sidmouth most enthusiastic. The inhabitants subscribed to have cannons, music, triumphal arches, &c., and shouted deafening hurrahs— Russia, at all events, is popular in Devonshire.

Good-bye, dear Alexander. I entreat you never to make the least allusion in your letter to the iniquities I confide to you. My only confessor is 3,000 versts away—remember that. We await with impatience to see what Diebitch's successor will do. By the way, Wellington greatly regretted the death of our Marshal.[2] He and all his party always show the greatest interest in our affairs, and express best wishes for us.

(ENCLOSURE IN LETTER NO. CXXI)

To Earl Grey

June 18.

The word I had to say to you, my Lord, really refers to the single word ' war,' which you propose to use in speaking

---

[1] Presumably Colonel Sir Joseph Whalley, K.C.H. The Grand Duchess Helena had come to England for the benefit of her health. She frequently visited this country, staying at Sidmouth, Torquay, and other places on the South Coast.

[2] Marshal Diebitch died of cholera on June 9, a fortnight after the indecisive battle of Ostrolenka, and in the same week as the Grand Duke Constantine and his morganatic wife. General Paskievitch was appointed Commander-in-Chief.

of Polish affairs.   In reflecting on the sentence which you
told me in confidence, it seemed to me that this word, coming
after the term of ' civil commotions ' employed with reference
to the affairs in Italy, implied a different meaning, while the
case is identical—for it is an insurrection in Poland just as it
was an insurrection in Italy.   The word ' war ' has never been
employed in any official document dealing with the affairs
of Greece ; strictly speaking, this term can only be applied to
two belligerent Powers, and this relative position cannot
exist between the Emperor of Russia and Poland, because
the former has been recognised by treaty as sovereign of that
country.   In strict accuracy, therefore, the word ' war ' does not
apply to the present circumstance.   Moreover, it is important
to furnish your opponents with no pretext for quibbling, and
this expression would certainly be seized upon by them with
avidity in order to draw you into an embarrassing discussion.
I think that it is more to your interest to avoid it.   The
word ' struggle,' or the more general expression ' unfortunate
events,' ought to be substituted for ' war.'   ' Struggle ' would
convey the same idea, and would not involve the same
objections.   Pardon me, my Lord, if I dare thus to express
to you my opinion.   I was so much touched by the trust and
friendliness with which you spoke yesterday that I do not
hesitate to tell you my thoughts.   I assure you that it is
impossible to appreciate more truly than I do the delicacy
and consideration of the confidence you have shown me, and
I regard it as one of the most precious proofs of your good
intentions towards us.   Grant me the word ' struggle ' instead
of ' war,' and I shall be thoroughly grateful.[1]

[1] Lord Grey's reply is missing, and by a curious coincidence (from which
the reader may draw his own inference) it is also missing from the Princess's
correspondence with Lord Grey, edited by Mr. L'Estrange ; vol. ii. 245.

The actual words of the King's Speech were : ' The assurances of a friendly
disposition which I continue to receive from all foreign Powers encourage the
hope that notwithstanding the civil commotions which have disturbed some parts
of Europe, and the contest now existing in Poland, the general peace will be
maintained.'   Madame de Lieven, in thanking Lord Grey for his letter and its
contents (missing), merely says : ' The fact is a great satisfaction to me, and it is
enhanced by my being indebted to you for the same.'

The word employed by Madame de Lieven which she wished Lord Grey to

CXXII

Richmond : 10/22 July 1831.

Dear Alexander,—You no longer write to me. Events are getting more complicated than ever, and press for settlement. I am most anxious for news from you—the *cholera morbus* in our country fills me with terrible alarm, and occupies my thoughts so much that I have almost forgotten the Vistula. Yet it is on that river that our attention and that of the world at large should at this moment be fixed. Has Paskiewitch crossed it? I cannot fail to see in the unexpected and closely following deaths of Diebitch and the Grand Duke Constantine two striking signs of the will of Heaven, which bids us prepare for a speedy ending to this terrible revolution in Poland. Diebitch could never have brought it to an end, for in truth it looks as if he had never made a beginning. The Grand Duke is no longer there to blight the future of the Poles, for the chance of falling back again under his rule exercised a terrible influence on the minds of the people—at least, such is the impression which the agents of that country have managed to spread in France and England. Paskiewitch comes to the front, and at last the Russian army has an object in view. It is marching on Warsaw—may Heaven help it and lead it! There is something in me which tells me that it is done—that we are there. I am filled with hope, almost with certainty—but the cholera may destroy it. Write to me then, quickly, and tell me that all I love are safe.

The Government here still stands out bravely against the perfidious steps which France is taking against us.[1] Up to yesterday, at all events, everything was going well here in

substitute for 'war' is *lutte*—the word introduced into the King's Speech is 'contest.' In the absence of direct evidence, it seems not improbable that Lord Grey may have adopted this word as a compromise between his original word 'war' and Madame de Lieven's *lutte*, which I have translated 'struggle.'—EDITOR.

[1] The French Government made overtures to Russia to bring about negotiations between that country and Poland, but the only promise which could be obtained was that on order being restored a general amnesty should be proclaimed.

this respect ; but British virtue is tottering—Paskiewitch must support it, and promptly, for otherwise it will succumb. The English papers daily become more hostile and insulting to us ; but their hostility does us little real harm if eight months' abuse have ended only in the rejection of the proposals of France. One is almost inclined to think that these have only been put forward to amuse the public, for, after all, the upper and more intelligent classes do not share the wild aspirations of the ' Times ' and the ' Courier.'

Our poor Grand Duchess is not going on well. Crichton considers her case very serious, and suggests a change of residence in England. I am grieved for her on account of the Countess Nesselrode's anxieties, which under the circumstances are only natural, for to lose the only person in whom she has confidence and affection here in a foreign land and in her wretched state of health is terribly sad. No one can better sympathise with those who are ill than I ; but I will not talk of myself, dear Alexander, for I do not wish to weary you—but I am pining and withering away. I have no strength left, and at my age one does not recover from premature decrepitude.

Dom Pedro leaves the day after to-morrow for France, and is taking back his wife and daughter with him. He said to me yesterday : ' Donna Maria shall remain in Portugal, or my name is not Pedro.' He has no other thought. He has, I think, cooled down marvellously on the subject of a Constitution. My own idea is that he wants to establish his daughter and to get back to Lisbon—nothing more. The Government here treats him with all deference, but gives him nothing. His manners are captivating ; he speaks freely, straightforwardly and hopefully, and is well received in all quarters. Dom Miguel entreats England to assist him against France, but the English Cabinet refuse and decline to have any dealings with him. They believe that a serious revolution is pending at Lisbon and secretly rejoice at the prospect, but externally they maintain an attitude of stern indifference

Lord Grey is going to take a house in the country near us, and the other Ministers come to see us. They meet at

our house the leaven of the Opposition.   This is as it should
be, for it proves that we are as intimate with one side as with
the other.

What have you to say about this Belgian business ?   What
a disgraceful page in the history of the Great Powers !   No
argument has yet conquered my repugnance to what has
been done.

Good-bye, my dear Alexander.   I hope in my next letter
to be able to rejoice with you over the capture of Warsaw—
I shall then indeed be proud and happy.   I embrace you
with all my heart, and all belonging to you.

CXXIII

Richmond : 17/29 July 1831.

We are expecting from hour to hour, dear Alexander,
important news from Poland.   You can imagine my state of
anxiety.   I can think of nothing else but of it and of the
cholera at Petersburg—may Heaven protect all who are dear
to us.

King Louis Philippe's speech has greatly annoyed both
the English public and the English Government.[1]   Lord Grey,
who came to see me here yesterday, said to me that, after all
the sacrifices he had made to support the Périer monarchy in
the interests of peace, he had some ground for surprise at the
insulting words which this Ministry had thought fit to put into
the King's mouth.   There was not a Power nor pledge which
it had not treated scandalously, and he had consequently

[1] King Louis Philippe's speech delivered at the opening of the French Chambers
contained the following passages : ' The kingdom of the Netherlands as constituted
by the treaties of 1814 and 1815 has ceased to exist.   The independence of Belgium
and its separation from Holland have been recognised by the Great Powers.
The King of the Belgians will not be a member of the German Confederation.
The fortresses erected to threaten France, and not to protect Belgium, will be
demolished.   A neutrality recognised by Europe and the friendship of France
insure to our neighbours an independence of which we have been the chief
support.   The Power which governs in Portugal had insulted French subjects . . .
our ships of war have appeared off the Tagus . . . they forced the entrance . . .
the Portuguese men-of-war are in our power, and the tricolour floats on the walls of
Lisbon.'   With reference to Eastern Europe the King spoke of ' the sanguinary and
inveterate struggle which is prolonged in Poland.'

made the French Government understand that the patience of the European Cabinets might come to an end. He also told me that he had requested France to recall her fleet from the Tagus, as, having obtained from the Portuguese Government all the satisfaction which had been deemed necessary, the French ships had no longer anything to do in Portuguese waters. I warmly congratulated Lord Grey on these resolutions, and in his present humour I have no doubt that his dealings with France will be most correct.

Did I tell you that Dom Pedro had asked the Queen of England to receive Donna Maria into her family, and that he wished her to undertake his child's education ? The Queen, as she herself told me, replied that she did not see how it was possible for a Protestant Queen to bring up a Catholic one. All this passed in writing and in the most official terms.

I have so little leisure to-day that I cannot write to you much that I have been keeping in my head for you. By the next courier you shall have a longer letter. Meanwhile, good-bye, dear Alexander. May Heaven protect you and all of us.

[The interval in the Princess's correspondence was so crowded with important events that it suggests the loss or miscarriage of more than one letter. Prince Leopold having obtained more favourable conditions for Belgium, the Belgian Congress had accepted the amended terms, and Leopold had left England to take possession of his throne. The King of Holland, however, refused to be bound by the decision of the London Conference, and, having assembled an army on the frontier, marched on Antwerp. Leopold appealed to the Powers for protection. France immediately ordered the advance of Marshal Gérard and the troops under his command, while Sir Edward Codrington with the English fleet entered the Scheldt. These steps did not stop the King of Holland, and a battle took place (August 11) near Tirlemont in which the Belgians were defeated, but on the intervention of Sir Robert Adair, the British Minister at Brussels, an armistice was proclaimed. But a French army was on Belgian soil, and although the French Government promised its withdrawal as soon as the decisions of the London Conference were carried out, this assurance, having regard to public feeling in France, was regarded with considerable doubt. After strong representations from Lord Palmerston, however, and in view of the danger of a general war, France withdrew (August 18) 20,000 men, and undertook to withdraw the remainder on the evacuation of Belgium by the Dutch troops. This took place a month later. The Belgian Government then opened direct negotiations with Holland, which ended in a further modification of the terms settled by the Powers at the London Conference. Neither country professed itself satisfied with the new arrangements, but the articles were signed on October 14 and subsequently embodied in a formal treaty. At the instigation of the King of Holland, however, his brother-in-law the King of Prussia promised to delay his assent, and the Emperor of Russia, whose sister had married the Prince of Orange, agreed to do likewise ; but France and England having on January 31, 1832, ratified the treaty, Count Orloff was despatched to the Hague to induce the King of Holland to recognise the independence and neutrality of Belgium. His mission was unsuccessful, and he then came on to London, where his instructions were to show that Russia was acting fairly towards the Conference. After much hesitation, Austria and Prussia announced their intention to ratify the treaty, with certain reservations of the rights of the German Confederation in Luxemburg, but it was not till May 4 that Russia finally gave her adhesion, and then only with important exceptions with regard to the navigation of the Scheldt which rendered it almost nugatory.

The popular risings in Germany and Italy, and the consequent armed intervention in the latter country by Austria and France, although indirectly affecting the British Government, were matters with which the Russian Embassy in London was not immediately concerned, and evidently presented no features of interest to the Ambassadress.

With Portuguese affairs it was otherwise. Madame de Lieven had shown lively satisfaction with the policy by which Wellington in his desire to recognise Dom Miguel had roused popular feeling against himself. The King of Portugal—as he certainly was by the vote of Cortes—had more than once given the promise to abate the cruelties and persecutions by which his accession had been followed. On each occasion he had been false to his word, and with the fall of the Wellington Cabinet Dom Miguel's tyrannous conduct to British residents, as well as to his own subjects, recommenced. The ships which had been sent to reduce the Açores to submission seized British trading vessels, and sent them to Portugal to be adjudicated on. Lord Palmerston, on April 15, sent to the British Consul at Lisbon (no Minister having been accredited to the Court) a detailed list of British grievances and claims, allowing ten days for their settlement, with the alternative of a visit from the British fleet to the Tagus. Satisfaction was given without delay, but almost simultaneously French subjects were made the objects of Portuguese ill-treatment. A French fleet at once (May 15) appeared in the Tagus, and for two months Dom Miguel attempted to temporise, relying upon the jealousy of England to prevent overt action by the French. The event proved him to be wholly mistaken as to the relations existing between the two Western Powers. The French fleet advanced up the Tagus on July 11, and captured the Portuguese ships under the guns of their own forts. Meanwhile Dom Pedro, forced to abdicate his Brazilian crown, had arrived in England to support his daughter Doña Maria's claims in Portugal at the very time that the French fleet was blockading the Tagus. His presence in Europe stimulated the young Queen's partisans, but for several months no active measures were taken to support her rights or to drive away Dom Miguel from the throne he had virtually usurped.

In Poland the end had come more swiftly than had been anticipated even by the Russians themselves. Early in September the revolution was practically at an end, and order reigned in Warsaw.

Parliament, after the general elections, had re-assembled on June 21, and three days later Lord John Russell, who had recently been taken into the Cabinet, introduced the second Reform Bill, which differed very slightly from that originally explained. The Tories, recognising the hopelessness of a frontal attack on the Bill, allowed it to be introduced and to pass the second reading (July 8) with slight resistance, the ministerial majority on the latter occasion being 136. In Committee, however, different tactics were employed, and it was only after forty nights that, on September 7, the Bill was reported to the House, on the eve of the day on which the coronation of William IV. in Westminster Abbey took place.[1] Several more days were spent in discussing the Bill as reported, but it finally reached the House of Lords (September 22) very slightly altered in word or in spirit from that in which it had been originally proposed. In the House of Lords the Bill met with very different and far more prompt treatment. The debate on the second reading occupied five days of the week, and the division, which took place at 6 A.M. on October 8, showed that the Bill was rejected by 199 to 158 votes. The excitement and angry feelings produced throughout the country by this refusal of the Peers to recognise the popular demand were unbounded, and in many places

[1] It is perhaps worthy of remark that, unless the letters should be missing, Madame de Lieven, although resident in England at the coronation of both George IV. and William IV., makes no reference to either ceremony.

gave rise to serious disturbances. The announcement of the Ministry that after a short prorogation Parliament should be again summoned and the Bill re-introduced, pacified, if it did not satisfy, the most ardent reformers.]

CXXIV

London : 9/21 October 1831.

Do not expect more than a few words from me, my dear Alexander. The Grand Duchess Helena is still here, and it is only respectful on my part not to die until after her departure. Beyond that I cannot make any promise. Ouf! what a weary business! However, everything has passed off admirably ; she is entertained and treated with the utmost respect, and the King received her with the greatest cordiality. In fact the King deserves some small mark of the Emperor's appreciation, for it would be impossible for him to show greater marks of attention and regard for the Grand Duchess, or to express greater admiration of and attachment to the Emperor. So, my dear Alexander, if you see your way, try and get the Emperor to write a letter of thanks. The Grand Duchess has met at our house all the big-wigs of English society, and they are nearly all delighted with her ; she came with the intention of pleasing, and has succeeded to the uttermost. Her idea of returning by sea to Petersburg has met with insuperable obstacles. The Admiralty Board declares that the voyage at this season is full of serious danger ; it has rejected the ships offered by the King, and implored the Grand Duchess, for her own security, to give up the idea. After the expression of such competent authority it was impossible to encourage her ; but she is much disappointed, and will now go to Biebrich.[1] Countess Nesselrode, with true Roman courage, has embarked to-day in a sailing ship. I shall be most anxious until I hear of her safe arrival on dry land.

The Conference has concluded its labours ;[2] Parliament

---

[1] On the Rhine, where the Duke of Nassau had a residence.

[2] These were the new conditions, known as the twenty-four articles, differing from the original eighteen articles of January and the amended proposals of June. It was now arranged that the western portion of Luxemburg should be

is prorogued ; the public is quieted ; the Opposition is off shooting and hunting ; and Ministers are gone away too—in a word, we are in full holiday.   Don't believe in a revolution in England until you are informed of its having broken out— not a soul now even thinks of such a thing.   Excuse this short letter, my dear Alexander, I can't write any more, and have only strength left to embrace you.

CXXV

Richmond : 3/15 November 1831.

I have been writing such a long letter to Count Nesselrode to-day, my dear Alexander, that nothing remains to tell you— unless it be that I am still full of anxiety about Constantine. Where is he ?   Who is his chief ?   Can you recommend him to the care of the latter ?   And can you get reports on his conduct—which, if good, may be passed on to my husband ? Do keep an eye on him a little now and in the future.   All this, dear Alexander, lies very close to a mother's heart—enter into my feelings, and render me the great service I ask.

Ministers here are struggling with all sorts of questions in a spirit of hesitation and timidity.   They seem unable even to more than half-do anything, good or bad.   They retrace their steps a score of times ; this cowardly policy strikes every- one, and never was a Government held in less esteem than the present.[1]   They have actually given encouragement to the patriotic clubs or associations—but only out of hatred for the Tories, whom they expected to frighten by so doing.   Now it is they themselves who are in a fine fright.   Lord Grey has often agreed with me that no Government could hold its own against these associations.   He resorts to every possible

assigned to Belgium in exchange for the Eastern portion of Limbourg, retained by Holland, that the navigation of the Scheldt and of the waterways connecting the Rhine with it should be free to Belgium, and that the latter's share of the annual charge of the debt should be reduced to 8,400,000 florins.

[1] The policy of the Government in their dealings with the National Political Union and its branches was judged in a different spirit by the majority of English- men.   Instead of provoking conflicts with the military, Lord Melbourne, as Home Secretary, interviewed the leaders and pointed out to them the dangers to which their designs exposed them.

means to ruin them, and the press is especially used with this object—the same press which had done so much to call them into existence. You can see the consequence and infer the danger. Nevertheless, in the present state of affairs and of men's minds it is not the less true Lord Grey is the only possible Minister, but neither affairs nor opinions are stationary, and although the chance of change is beyond calculation, it is not, therefore, less possible.

The Cabinet wants to get all its political programme settled before Parliament meets. As for Portugal, it will as readily recognise Dom Miguel as Donna Maria in four and twenty hours—and on my honour I firmly believe that at the moment I am writing Lord Grey himself does not know which of the two it will be. As for Belgium, they are pressing for the Treaty to be signed![1] Alas! why sign it? Greece for the last few days has been put aside, but in default of anyone else Grey rather leans towards the Prince of Würtemberg.[2] We certainly do not lean in that direction; but, after all said and done, who can say that he might not be better than another from the moment that Frederick of Orange has no desire for it?

The Queen is made ill by the worry which Ministers are giving her, and the King's inside is much upset by the same annoyances. His wife and sisters are sworn foes to the Government.

Lord Grey threatens to create a crowd of peers to carry his Bill. He is quite within his rights, that cannot be denied. I expect that among others he will call to Westminster all the Scotch and Irish peers who have now no seats there. The Bishops, it is expected, will not vote at all. They are really dismayed at the disfavour with which they are looked upon by the public. The actual date of the meeting of Parliament is not yet fixed, and I still hope that it may not

[1] The twenty-four articles were to be embodied in the form of a treaty to be signed by both Belgium and Holland, and the Five Powers, having first formally ratified the treaty, undertook to enforce its acceptance on either country which refused the prescribed terms.

[2] Capo d'Istria, the President of Greece, had been assassinated on October 9, and the question of a ruler for Greece was again mooted.

take place before the end of January.   The cholera is **very**
like the Ministry here—it has no decided course of action.
One day we are frightened, the next day we are reassured ;
meanwhile there have been but few cases besides those at
Sunderland—300 miles away from London—that, however, does not free me from mortal dread of it.   The
newspapers announce the departure of the Court for
Moscow ; I wish you would write me your impressions of
that city—I am sure that the Emperor will be received there
with enthusiasm.   I am indeed glad to have to speak no
more about Poland, except to annoy Lord Grey when he
provokes me.   What a strange aberration of judgment he
shows in his manner of interpreting the Treaty of Vienna.
If I had my choice there would be quite a new way of
explaining it.   The Treaty says : '(Poland) shall be bound
irrevocably to Russia by its Constitution.'   This bond has now
been recognised as faulty—and it is just on account of this
Constitution that the bond could not hold—so another must
be found.   This seems to me a most fair reasoning.   You
may, however, think it a bad joke perhaps, but what is not
so is that to the Emperor belong both the right and the duty
to take away from Poland the means of revolting again—
whoever says the contrary is a fool.

I have just learnt that the Duke of Wellington has written
a long and pressing letter to the King, representing to him
the dangers which threaten this country.[1]   He points out that
the lower classes are getting together a considerable quantity
of firearms, and declares that by tolerating this state of things
longer he is risking his crown, and may plunge England into
awful anarchy.   The King forwarded the letter to Lord Grey,
who forthwith entered into correspondence with the Duke on
this subject, inviting him to furnish the Government with
all information bearing on the question of public safety.   The
correspondence is still going on.   Take care, however, to
make no reference to anything I tell you about the affairs of

---

[1] From the Trade Associations and political societies which, under the pretext of
discussing the Reform Bill, had become centres of opposition to the economic
policy of the time.

this country, because if Grey should learn from Heytesbury that I repeat to you what the former tells me he will never again give me his confidence. This is therefore in the strictest secrecy.

Good-bye, my dear Alexander, I embrace you with all my heart. Write to me and tell me all you hear about my boy. My heart is very heavy on his account, and I can only calm myself by the thought that you love me enough to make you take an interest in him.

1832

[Parliament, after a short recess, re-assembled on December 6, 1831, and on the 12th Lord John Russell introduced the third Reform Bill. Since the close of the previous Session the Ministry had not increased in reputation by its attempts to put down political unions by proclamation, after having hitherto tolerated them. The threat to create new peers in order to pass the Reform Bill had caused dissensions in the Cabinet, but at the same time a section of the hitherto obstructive peers, who became known as the 'Waverers,' showed a preference for yielding to avoid being swamped. Of these Lord Wharncliffe, and after him Lord Harrowby, were the most active. Negotiations with the Ministry were set on foot, and the result depended upon the concessions to be made in the new Bill. These were not very apparent from Lord J. Russell's speech, but they were not expected to be disclosed until the Bill reached the Lords. Its passage through the Commons was at first easy. No division was challenged on its introduction, and the second reading, after two nights' debate, was carried on December 18 by exactly two to one—324 to 162 votes. The Committee stage lasted from January 20 to March 9, and finally the third reading, after three nights' debate, was passed on June 22 by 355 to 239—a majority of 116. Without delay the Bill was sent to the House of Lords, where the debate on the second reading was commenced on April 9 and the intentions of the 'Waverers' at once became manifest ; but four days elapsed before the discussion closed, and at 7 A.M. on April 13 the Bill was read a second time by 184 to 175—a majority of nine for the Ministry. But their triumph was of short duration. On May 7 Lord Lyndhurst moved : 'That the question of enfranchisement should precede that of disfranchisement,' and this was carried against the Government by 151 to 116 votes. Thereupon Lord Grey proposed to the King to create fifty new peers. After a few hours' consideration the King refused. Lord Grey at once tendered his resignation, and Lord Lyndhurst was commissioned to form a

Cabinet in conjunction with the Duke of Wellington; but Sir Robert Peel declined to take any share in the Government, of which one of the necessary duties would be to pass the Reform Bill in some shape. The Speaker, Mr. Manners-Sutton, was then tried, but without success, and the attempt to form a Tory Government had to be abandoned. Outside Parliament great excitement prevailed; meetings were held and petitions in favour of reform were drawn up in all important centres, and the City of London petitioned that the House should refuse to vote supplies until Reform was granted. On May 15 the Duke of Wellington informed the King that he was unable to form an administration, and Lord Grey was invited to retain office with full powers to secure a majority by the creation of new peers. On the re-assembling of the House of Lords the debate on the Reform Bill was renewed, and the Duke of Wellington, after explaining the transactions of the previous week and recognising that the King's Government must be carried on, left the House, followed by about a hundred other peers, who with him absented themselves during the remainder of the discussion on the Bill. The opponents of the Bill were now reduced to thirty-six, and these dwindled as the days passed in Committee, only eighteen peers recording their dissent from the report. Finally, on June 4, the Reform Bill was passed by 106 to 22 votes, and three days later received the Royal Assent by commission.]

CXXVI

London : $\frac{\text{December 24, 1831}}{\text{January 5, 1832}}$.

What thanks do I not owe you, my good Alexander, for the letter you have written to us about Constantine. You have entered heart and soul into the appeal I made to you, and I cannot sufficiently express my gratitude.

My husband is much touched and made supremely happy by the Emperor's remembrance of him, of which you speak. He is more especially grateful to receive fresh proofs of this at a moment when his master may not have altogether approved of what he has done here. It is a topic, however to which I will not revert. You know all that I, for my part, thought about it—and it is no small honour for me to find that my Emperor is of my opinion on the matter, and, after all, the Emperor has known how to come to a decision which, thank God, makes everything smooth. He maintains his own views and at the same time satisfies his allies. Our last despatch of December 4/16 has been well received here. The reception given to Czartoryski annoys me excessively, and I have not scrupled to say some unpleasant truths. Ask Count Nesselrode to send documents to justify me. At the present moment my private opinion is that all this fuss is the result of sheer stupidity and ignorance of good manners. The English learn Latin—but they don't learn the art of living.[1]

The Duke of Wellington is very ill, and for a long time will not be in a state to take part in public business—the Tory party is thoroughly disorganised. The Reform Bill will pass without a shadow of doubt; but that accomplished, the present Ministry cannot hold together—it is regarded as too incapable and ignorant in general affairs. Who will take its place? That is not so easy to foresee. A coalition perhaps, for a purely Tory Government is out of the question.

France and England are coquetting together, and Lord Grey's surroundings are distinctly democratic. He is weak and easily led, so that everything is not going on well.

I am going to reply to a charming letter from our dear delightful Empress. Her letters are like herself—full of grace, good taste, and kind feeling. I should like to kiss her after reading them. This is a horrible familiarity, but in spite of all the respect which I owe her and feel for her I cannot refrain from loving her with an idyllic love.

Good-bye, my dear Alexander. I won't say a word about politics, they vex me and bore me, and moreover there is nothing to say. You must keep your eye on what the King of the Netherlands is going to do; the whole matter rests with him, and no longer with others.

I embrace you and love you very dearly. What are all your dear children doing? A thousand loves to my sister-in-law and to Masha. Good-bye again, dear brother.

[1] Prince Adam Czartoryski dined with Earl Grey on New Year's day, the only other guest being Lord Palmerston. Prince Lieven had an interview with the latter on the ground that the Prime Minister had entertained a 'State criminal.' The Princess also wrote several angry letters to Lord Grey on the same subject, but without obtaining any official or non-official apology or expression of regret. (*Lieven Corresp.*, ii. 316–322.)

CXXVII

London : January 9 (N.S.), 1832.

I find by a letter of Constantine's from Warsaw that your protection, dear Alexander, had not been without result. A thousand thanks for all that you have done for my son.

Ministers are so much divided in opinion on the question of increasing the peerage that Lord Grey has not been allowed to submit more than half a dozen names in the first instance.[1] As, however, the only motive for increasing the numbers of the Upper House is to ensure the passing of the Reform Bill, and since without at least thirty more votes the Government cannot flatter itself that it will find itself in a majority, this small sample of its power is the most ridiculous thing imaginable. People who wish to make an outcry will do so quite as shrilly if one peer is created—or forty. There is, moreover, this difference, that an unusual act done in a grand way sometimes carries conviction, while if frittered away in little doses it only excites ridicule. At the same time even in its reduced form the King by no means fancied the Prime Minister's proposal. He requested each member of the Cabinet to present his own opinion in writing, and his own reasons for the step. The public will draw the conclusion that the King is not satisfied, that Ministers are not united, and that the Cabinet as a whole is nerveless.

There are two very distinct factions in the present Government—the moderates and the extremists. Among the former are Palmerston, Melbourne, Goderich, Carlisle, Lansdowne,and the Duke of Richmond ; all the others belong to the second category.[2] These are in favour of an alliance with France, while the others desire at any price to hold to their engagements with the other Powers. Grey allows himself to be led

[1] Lord Grey and the extreme reformers wished to make a dozen peers, the moderates only five or six. (*Greville Mem.*, ii. 230.)

[2] According to Greville, Mr. Stanley was also among the moderates, and the King had asked for only Lord Palmerston's reasons in writing for making five or six peers instead of a dozen, as suggested by the Ultras. Among the latter the most prominent was Lord Grey's son-in-law, Lord Durham, who was most eager to take Lord Palmerston's place at the Foreign Office.

by his son-in-law, who under the most haughty and aristocratic manners is a thorough democrat.   Brougham is shifty ;
he stays away from the Cabinet, but when forced to deliver
his views they are generally on the side from which the wind
—that is, public opinion—blows.   Such is the administration
which rules over England.   The Duke of Wellington is getting
better.

Good-bye, my dear Alexander.   The Emperor's stay at
Moscow was superb, its effect will be felt far and near.   I
embrace you and love you with all my heart.   A thousand
thousand thanks again for what you have done for Constantine.
I count upon you in the future as I have had good cause for
counting upon you in the past.   Good-bye, dear brother.

CXXVIII

London : 18/30 January 1832.

A courier is starting, dear Alexander, and you will be
expecting to hear what is going on in this corner of Europe,
a corner whence, after all, great things are prompted ; and if
we can manage to keep England in line with us all will be
well, whatever happens.   If she escapes us, good-bye to the
peace of Europe—this contingency is quite on the cards.   At
the point to which things have come England cannot
abandon Belgium without dishonouring herself, and this
would be the line which the Duke of Wellington himself
would adopt were he Prime Minister to-morrow.   It is
perfectly certain that the King of the Netherlands will refuse
to recognise a treaty which dispossesses him of the kingdom
of Belgium.   Last winter he prevented his son from accepting
the throne, therefore with all the more reason will he have
nothing to do with a stranger.   Can you really suppose that
England, having once recognised Leopold, will leave him in
the lurch ?   It is impossible.   Will the Emperor personally
vindicate the pretensions of the King of the Netherlands ?   I
don't believe it for a moment.   In that case all will go
smoothly ; we shall keep friends with England, and under
no conceivable condition is she likely to become the enemy
of Holland, which, strengthened by our union, will always

remain at heart the enemy of France, or at least will always look upon her with watchful suspicion. If we are going to take up the personal interests of King William we shall lose England, who, unwilling to remain without allies, will throw herself into the arms of France, and Europe will be handed over to the united influence of these two Liberal Powers, and then—we shall see what we shall see. Europe is still in an unsettled state, the tone of public opinion bodes no good, and a war at this juncture might find the people in many countries very ill-disposed to uphold the throne. This is a consideration which deserves attention, and even some sacrifices. You see that at this end of the world we are somewhat given to reasoning, for when one sees such disturbance abroad one cannot help trying to examine closely and seriously its causes and its possible consequences.[1]

The English Ministry holds on, notwithstanding the very little esteem it enjoys. It is needed to pass the Reform Bill, but that once effected there will be little scruple in bringing about its fall, for it is recognised that it is wanting both in the experience and foresight necessary for carrying on the business of the State. Whoever may be its successor, however, I doubt much the stability of any Government in England. The art of governing has become too difficult ; the students are ill-taught, the newspapers too insolent. Things cannot go on thus always. Everybody here is anxious, and Ministers more than anybody. The King says to himself : ' It is no fault of mine,' and with that allows nothing to trouble his digestion or his night's rest.

January 22
February 3*

My letter will not go off until to-day, and three days have sufficed to change the outlook completely. England is clear of her embarrassment, Austria and Prussia declare themselves on her side. This is good, for at all events it renders use-

---

[1] In the House of Lords Lord Aberdeen moved (January 26) a resolution which practically censured the Ministry for assisting and guaranteeing the execution of the treaty by which Belgium should enjoy free navigation of the Scheldt and for forcing upon Holland a treaty distasteful to her. The motion was rejected by 132 to 95.

less the alliance of France and England. At the same time our position is not a pleasing one ; it leaves us altogether out in the cold, and our self-esteem must submit to a very decided rebuff.[1] This is a situation to which Russia is not accustomed, but the Emperor will extricate her. The King of the Netherlands has made an unfair use of the protection offered him, and found in it an encouragement to resistance, which forces the other Powers to declare themselves in favour of the treaty. After all, the chief interest of all is to preserve peace, and in order to preserve it England must be kept in the ranks of the Alliance, and to keep her there it is absolutely important for all to associate themselves in an act which it is no longer humanly possible for England to repudiate.

Send us, therefore, good news, dear Alexander ; let us remain united, for in this union each will find safety. Let justice be done by all means to the King of the Netherlands, but there is no need that for his personal interests the Powers should quarrel and the peace of the world be brought into question.

We have been attacked in Parliament over the Russian loan.[2] The Ministry defended itself bravely, and yesterday Brougham made himself our champion and won a great triumph. This has given courage to the Ministers and put them in a good humour. Lord Grey came to see me to-day, and in a marked way asked for good news from Petersburg, for with this everything will tend to make the peace question firm and lasting.

Here are some patterns of silk for hangings. You shall

[1] Count Orloff's efforts to bring the King of the Netherlands to accept the Treaty of London had failed, and Russia found herself unsupported by Austria and Prussia in refusing any longer to sign the treaty.

[2] During the long war Russia had contracted with an Amsterdam house a loan of 90,000,000 florins. After the war two-thirds of the charge was transferred to Great Britain and Holland on the stipulation that the charge should cease in the event of the Belgian provinces being at any time separated from Holland. Lord Palmerston refused to take advantage of the new situation, and admitted the liability of England for its portion of the loan. When the matter came before Parliament it was vigorously attacked by both the Tories and the Liberals, who distrusted Russia, and the Ministry narrowly escaped defeat by a majority of only twenty-four votes.

have some more the day after to-morrow by the Prussian courier—and in a better condition.

Good-bye, my dear brother. Write to me and tell me about the Emperor and the Empress, and their health. How the Grand Duchess, and how does her household get on ? Be less sparing of your words—you know how everything interests me. A thousand kind things to you and all yours and ours.

CXXIX

London : May 3 (N.S.), 1832.

Dear Alexander,—Herewith goes your Orloff,[1] who is become somewhat mine also. Although I hardly expect that you will pay much attention to my letter when you have him and his stories to regale you, I do not consider myself less bound to write to you a few lines to ask you to thank the Emperor for his excellent idea of sending him here. You can have no idea of the good his presence has done. He seemed to represent Russia in his own person. His square shoulders and towering head well typified our great empire. His frankness and his acuteness pleased everyone, and his grave demeanour and his peals of laughter delighted everybody. He is marvellously witty, with an easy cordial politeness before which the iciness and awkwardness of the English melted in a moment. He is a clever man is our Orloff ; he upsets the old diplomacy, and his school seems to me the best.

I will say nothing about public affairs—Orloff knows everything, and will tell you about them better than I can. He was able to make himself acquainted with English questions in a wonderful way. I should think that he is going back full of good will towards England. He was everywhere received and treated with the greatest distinction. Everywhere he met with attention for Russia, and friendliness for

---

[1] General Aide-de-camp to the Emperor. He had previously signalised himself in concluding the Treaty of Adrianople, and had been sent on a special mission to the Hague, whence he came to this country. He remained five weeks in London, and returned to St. Petersburg with the ratification of the treaty dealing with Belgium and Holland.

himself. All parties of every shade and condition were anxious to do him honour. He has but a poor opinion of the Ministry. He has some esteem for Lord Grey, wishes Lord Palmerston well, but considers him mediocre. He believes, and with reason, that they wish to be and to remain on good terms with Russia; that they blunder through weakness or ignorance, but that their intentions are good. It's a poor Government, but God knows if others would make a better. For my own part I have my doubts, and for reasons which Orloff will explain. However, one must put up with what one cannot alter, and try to make the best of things until circumstances open up another course. I believe that to remain on good terms, with some reserve, with England is the best way of keeping the rest of Europe in peace and in order. For this reason, until I receive notice, which I beseech you to communicate to me, I shall continue to cultivate Lord Grey, although he bores me not a little.[1]

How much I should like to be at St. Petersburg and listen to Orloff. I am sure he will make you laugh quite as much as he made me. By the way, he treated me rather cavalierly. He found me such a good customer for his mystifications that scarcely a day passed without trying his hand on me, and from the day he announced his departure I received a double allowance.

Good-bye, dear Alexander; beside Orloff my letter will count for little; you will set a better price on me when I present myself alone.

I embrace wife, sister, and children most heartily. Here are some more patterns for dresses—I will send those for the furniture by the next opportunity. Good-bye, dear brother.

CXXX

My dear Alexander,—I have written so much to-day that I have only strength enough left to ask you to read my letter to Count Nesselrode, in which I have exhausted myself on

---

[1] 'I am quite annoyed at seeing that you no longer think of me.' (Madame de Lieven to Earl Grey, May 1, 1832.)

the subject of Lord Durham.[1] I do not hesitate to say that his mission torments me, for I foresee what unpleasant thoughts the name will suggest to you. To say, however, that I augur well of the results of this embassy would be premature, more especially as these consequences depend wholly upon the Emperor's will and pleasure. But of this there is no doubt, if he wishes he may, through Lord Durham, direct the policy of the English Cabinet. Let only the Emperor accord him half the attention which met Orloff here, and he is ours, both by conviction and inclination—and for the moment he governs England.

He is leaving on Monday next, July 2 (N.S.), will stop two days at Copenhagen, and hopes to reach Petersburg on the 13th—I have my doubts. He proposes to make a visit to Moscow, and will leave Petersburg in the month of September. The ostensible motive of his journey is health— and nothing more.

The man's vanity is proverbial ; he is the haughtiest aristocrat. Only yesterday he assured me that he traced his descent from the kings of England ! He insisted upon being made Lord Privy Seal in the Ministry, because this post gave him precedence over all English Dukes—and in such puerilities he takes real delight. Here he is cordially and universally disliked. The King in speaking of him never alludes to him otherwise than as 'Robert le Diable.' Yesterday, with a big sigh of relief, he said to me : 'Thank God, we've got rid of him for some months.' 'That is all very well, Sire, but why should it be at our expense ? ' 'Well, Madame, take my word, this may be turned to good account ; he has so much vanity that he will make up his mind to please and to succeed, and with very small marks of attention you will gain him over, and this will be most fortunate for both Empires.' This is the exact truth.

[1] He was sent to St. Petersburg, as a member of the Cabinet, on a special mission to persuade the Russian Government to give its complete assent without delay to the Belgium Treaty, and to discuss the means of giving effect to its provisions. He was also instructed to intercede for the Poles and to obtain for them milder terms. In both objects his mission was unsuccessful, but he pleased the Emperor, who conferred upon him the highest Orders.

In any case, my dear Alexander, I entreat you to show every politeness in the form of a visit at least to Lord and Lady Durham. Lord Grey has scarcely a thought for anyone but this daughter.

I have just been reading yesterday's disgraceful debate in the House of Commons, and I have just written to Lord Grey a bit of my mind.[1] It is scarcely credible at the moment our Emperor was being attacked in the most odious manner in the Lower House that the King at a dinner table where I was one of the guests (my husband being detained by a Conference) turned to me and drank the Emperor's health as that of his old and best ally. That Lower House makes me choke with rage.

Good-bye, dear Alexander. I embrace you all, and I have need to think of you all to cool my blood. A thousand loves to your children, your wife, and to Masha.

CXXXI

Richmond : $\frac{\text{July 21}}{\text{August 2}}$, 1832.

Dear Alexander,—I am only sending a line in answer to the letter which the last courier brought me from you. I am writing such a long letter to Count Nesselrode about things in general that nothing remains for me to tell you, and I know that my letters to him are common to you both.

The Emperor was admirably inspired to give such an excellent reception to Lord Durham. The man is gained to our side, and should his cross, intractable humour lead him to commit some folly he alone will have to bear the odium. Lord Grey is extremely delighted at his son-in-law's good start.

The opinion here is that the Belgian business will be settled pacifically in the next three or four days. Ministers

---

[1] The Russian policy in Poland had been condemned in strong terms on the Liberal side of the House, and O'Connell and Hume had indulged in very violent language, the one calling Nicholas 'a miscreant,' the other 'a monster in human form.' Madame de Lieven's protest to Lord Grey turned mainly on Lord Palmerston's silence. Lord Grey in the House of Lords expressed his regret that such language towards an ally should have been used. (*Lieven Letters*, ii. 359.)

who go about with the word 'war' in their mouths are those who least of all wish it to come about. I fancy that the state of affairs in Germany has not been without effect on them. The attitude taken up by the three Great Powers is a wall of brass which makes France and England hesitate. This business has been concerted and arranged with so much quiet, reflection, and prudence that it gives no handle for attack, and absolutely prevents anything being done. Here there is an appearance of respect for this imposing sight. If Lord Durham has eyes in his head, as I believe, his reports will not lessen this feeling. My own impression is that on his return I shall find his Liberalism considerably cooled down.

My husband is well in health and greatly encouraged, the St. Andrew in brilliants having given him great satisfaction. Good-bye, dear brother.

I have always forgotten to tell you that Lord Durham is brother to Mrs. Howard, the Emperor's first 'flame' in London ; she has since married a cousin of the Duke of Devonshire.[1]

[The protracted negotiations relating to the Belgian question had entered upon a fresh phase. Belgium had accepted and Holland had rejected the amended treaty, and the armistice terminated. Personal and family influences quite as much as political considerations separated the aims and wishes of Russia from those of the Western Powers. The Dutch Government relied on the support of the three autocratic Powers, especially of Russia, but although she had signed the Treaty of London she had done so under restrictions with regard to the navigation of the Scheldt and the maintenance of Dutch forts which rendered the free commerce of Belgium impossible. England and France endeavoured to persuade Russia to withdraw her opposition, but the possibility of a change of Ministry in England and the return of the Duke of Wellington to office had encouraged the Tsar to persevere in his attitude of non-interference in Dutch affairs, and he urged the Western Powers to exercise

---

[1] Miss Frances Susan Lambton, daughter of W. H. Lambton, M.P., married, 1811, Colonel the Hon. Henry F. Howard, son of fifth Earl of Carlisle ; he was killed at Waterloo ; and secondly, 1819, Hon. H. F. Compton-Cavendish, third son of first Earl of Burlington.

upon King Leopold the pressure which they wished him to adopt towards the King of Holland. Lord Durham, Lord Grey's son-in-law, was therefore sent as a Special Ambassador to St. Petersburg to induce the Russian Government to reconsider its policy. Meanwhile the marriage of the Princess Louise d'Orléans, daughter of Louis Philippe, to King Leopold had increased the distrust of Prussia of the probable neutrality of Belgium in the event of a war, and drove the Government of that country, as well as that of Austria, to secretly support the policy of Russia. The death of M. Casimir Périer, moreover, had brought about a change in the French Ministry, and the strength as well as the policy of his successor was unknown. The advent to office of Soult's Ministry changed the aspect of affairs. Lord Durham's mission produced no results; but the arrangements respecting the Russo-Dutch loan proved a useful lever in the hands of the English Cabinet. Lord Palmerston drew up a modified treaty which was submitted to both the Dutch and Belgian delegates. The latter accepted it, but the former declined even to discuss it. On this being communicated to the London Conference (September 30) the French Plenipotentiary, Talleyrand, proposed that the treaty should be enforced on Holland, and this was supported by Lord Palmerston, the three autocratic Powers pleading for still further delay. To this the Western Powers would not consent, and Holland was notified to withdraw all her troops from Belgian territory by November 12, and a convention pledging Great Britain and France to carry out this decision was signed (October 22). Holland, however, obstinately refused to submit, and still held Antwerp and the forts on the Scheldt. On November 15 Marshall Gérard crossed the frontier and marched upon the city, which after a brave defence finally capitulated (December 23), but many years elapsed before Holland would formally recognise the new kingdom of Belgium.]

CXXXII

Richmond : 6/18 October 1832.

I have nothing new to report to-day, my dear Alexander, but my habit not to throw away a good opportunity induces me to write. England continues bellicose. M. de Talleyrand declares that if the best possible Ministry for France—Broglie & Co.—is to maintain itself it can only be by making a striking *début*. Thus war is wanted to keep in office a set of new men who have done nothing to merit any help from

Europe, and who have as their leader the man whom Lord
Grey and M. de Talleyrand qualified only a few months
since as the Minister-Conqueror.   This is all stuff and nonsense, good enough for children or for the imbecile.   As we
are neither the one nor the other, I see no reason why we
should allow ourselves to be moved.   If it needs so much
contrivance and so many sacrifices to prevent a new upset in
France—well, let her be upset.   I don't see what we shall
lose thereby.

Lord Palmerston is a poor, small-minded creature, wounded
in his vanity, who wants a great warlike demonstration
behind which he hopes to conceal his blunders.   As for the
other Ministers, some allow themselves to be carried away,
and others rush with pleasure and without reflection to
start upon a road which to them is attractive, short, and
devoid of danger.   Lord Grey alone seems to me very
troubled, but he is started—and he is weak.   Lord Durham
is also, I believe, of the war party, because decided views suit
his disposition ; nevertheless, I can see that he is bitter and
discontented with English diplomacy, and I also see that he
is quite at variance with Lord Palmerston.   From this I
conclude that he severely judges the way in which the latter
has brought matters to the catastrophe which is apparently
imminent.   I have nothing but praise to give to the terms in
which Lord Durham expresses himself to us, and not for a
few days shall I know what language he holds with others.
He professes an extreme admiration for the Emperor ; he
thinks that he is a man who in whatever position he had
been born would have made himself conspicuous, but considers that he is specially fitted to govern an Empire like
Russia by the energy and strength of his character, the
breadth of his intelligence, and by his extraordinary capacity
of grasping all the possible sides of his exalted position.   I
am repeating to you textually the words which he used in
talking to me.   He is touched, flattered, and grateful for the
kindness and confidence with which he was treated by the
Emperor.   His last interview with the Emperor left a deep
impression on him, of which he will for ever preserve the

recollection. On every occasion he will consider it an
honour and a duty to express loudly his devotion to and his
admiration of the Emperor, and his complete confidence in
the good faith of this Cabinet. The last is his own personal
opinion, which is not shared by everybody, 'for even in the
Cabinet I meet with opposition'—such is the warning which
he thinks fit to give me.

He displays his Russomania in a thousand ways and
make himself very amusing. He wishes to live *à la Russe*
—drinks *shale* (skaal ?), dines at five o'clock as in our
country, enters the room in single file as at Court—in a word,
he is a delightful dear of an Englishman. He has only seen
two things in the world which surprised him, Petersburg and
the Simplon. This is about all that I can say concerning
him.

7/19 October.

As everything here is like a weathercock, my letter must
follow the fashion if I wish to give a correct idea of what
is going on. The day before yesterday I believed im-
plicitly in war ; to-day I believe in it less, but to-morrow
I may revert to my former belief. It seems that Ministers
are seized with irresolution—that they do not see how
to withhold France or how to let her go her own way.
There is constant coming and going ; sighs from Lord Grey
(I adore those sighs, for they show that his affairs are going
badly), fears of the Court, fears of the press—altogether a
wondrous show of valour. We, however, are quite easy in
our minds, although I cannot say what news this courier may
take with him, as I hear that the Conference has just been
summoned.[1]

Good-bye, my dear Alexander. I am thinking more of
the Empress's confinement than of the Belgian question. I
pray God for her and for the happiness of our dear Emperor.
I embrace you with all my heart.

Read the letter which I have written to Count Nesselrode.

[1] 'Nothing has damaged this Government more than these protracted and
abortive conferences.' (*Greville*, ii. 321.)

1833

[Parliament, which had been prorogued in August, was dissolved
in December, and a general election was held for the first time
under the provisions of the new Reform Bill.   The relative strength
of the two parties in the House of Commons was little changed,
although the tone of the Tories, as expressed by Peel, was considerably altered.   At the same time, the Ministerialists were more
acutely divided than before the passing of the Reform Bill, the
Whigs being content with what they had achieved, the Radicals
being eager to use their victory as the means of carrying out still
wider changes and reforms.   This division of opinion was reflected
in the Cabinet, which on more than one occasion seemed on the
point of collapse, the government of Ireland being the chief question
of dissension ; but the only actual withdrawal was that of Lord
Durham, who resigned the Privy Seal and was created an Earl.
His post was given to Lord Goderich, Mr. Stanley succeeded to the
Colonial Office, and Mr. Littleton (afterwards Lord Hatherton)
became Chief Secretary for Ireland.

But a more important matter so far as concerned the relations of
Great Britain and Russia was the selection of an Ambassador to
St. Petersburg in the place of Lord Heytesbury, who was forced to
retire on account of health.   When Lord Durham had been
despatched on his special mission the Embassy was in charge of
Mr. Bligh, and it was Count Nesselrode's wish that Lord Heytesbury should return.   Madame de Lieven, according to Greville
and others, was commissioned to bring this about, and she obtained
from both Lord Grey and Lord Palmerston the promise that he
should do so.   Lord Heytesbury, however, insisted upon retirement,
and Madame de Lieven learnt that the choice for St. Petersburg lay
between Sir Stratford Canning and Sir Robert Adair.   Nesselrode
wrote at once to Madame de Lieven to prevent the choice of the

former on the ground that he had been guilty of some incivility towards the Emperor when Grand Duke, and also because he was *soupçonneux, pointilleux, et défiant*—in other words, that he was not *persona grata.* Madame de Lieven represented this to Lord Palmerston, and she understood from him that Canning should not be sent, Lord Durham having previously, but apparently without authority, given a similar assurance to Count Nesselrode. Shortly afterwards Palmerston informed Madame de Lieven that Canning would be sent to St. Petersburg, his appointment was gazetted, but Nesselrode positively refused to receive him. Madame de Lieven appealed to Lord Grey, Lord Durham supported her, but it was without immediate results, and the blow given thereby to Madame de Lieven's prestige was such that the invitation to Peterhoff was well-timed, giving her the opportunity of explaining more fully the difficulties which she had failed to overcome. It may be added that it was not until 1835, and after the withdrawal of Prince Lieven from London, that an Ambassador was accredited to the Russian Court. Sir Stratford Canning never admitted that he had acted uncourteously to the Grand Duke Nicholas, and his omission to pay the latter a formal visit fifteen years previously would scarcely have been sufficient to explain the decided objection of the Emperor to receive him as an Ambassador. It is possible that the turn which affairs were taking in the Levant may have had something to do with Nicholas' unwillingness to have at his Court a statesman so thoroughly conversant with Turkish affairs as was Sir Stratford Canning. Mehemet Ali, who had come to the aid of the Sultan his master in his attempt to put down the Greek revolution, had withdrawn to Egypt on the evacuation of the Morea. In 1831 the Pasha of Acre, who, like Mehemet Ali, was a tributary of the Sultan, gave some occasion of offence to the Pasha of Egypt. Mehemet, without waiting for the Sultan's permission, at once despatched his son Ibrahim to attack Acre. A force was sent from Constantinople to relieve Abdallah Bey, but Ibrahim quickly routed it, and after five months' siege Acre fell (May 27, 1832) into the hands of the Egyptians. A week or two later Ibrahim entered Damascus after a series of engagements in which the Turks were uniformly defeated. By the end of October the whole of Syria was in his hands, and after the battle of Konieh (December 21, 1832) nothing stood between them and Constantinople. In his extremity the Sultan appealed to Great Britain for help and then to France, but the Belgian question was still unsettled, the British fleet was lying off the Scheldt, and Marshal Gérard was marching upon Antwerp. In despair the Sultan turned to the Tsar, who at once despatched 6,000 men to the Bosphorus, but with orders to with-draw as soon as the Sultan expressed the wish. Almost simulta-neously the French Ambassador to the Porte, Admiral Roussin, arrived (February 17, 1833) at Constantinople. He at once assured the Sultan that there was no need for Russian intervention, that he would undertake to make terms with Ibrahim Pasha, and insisted that the Russian fleet should at once be requested to with-draw. The Sultan acquiesced, and the Russian ships sailed away without having landed any troops. But the price of this complais-ance had still to be paid. England was unrepresented by either a fleet or an Ambassador at Constantinople, and Russia, taking advantage of her opportunity, concluded (July 8, 1833) with the Porte the Treaty of Unkiar Skelessi, which closed the Dardanelles against the ships of war of any foreign nation but her own.]

CXXXIII

London : 17/29 March 1833.

It is a very long time, dear Alexander, since I last wrote, but I have nothing very agreeable to say. Everything here is going on wretchedly. Ineptitude and bad manners in foreign policy ; radicalism at home and abroad ; flirtations with France ; suspicion, animosity, almost hatred of Russia—such is, roughly speaking, our daily bread.[1] This Government is after all a very poor concern ; it has only one good quality —stupidity—and this is leading it each day nearer to its destruction. What a change has come over the scene since this time last year ! Then it was popular, now it is despised and almost universally hated. The more prudent are quitting it. Durham, whose keen nose detected decay, left the Government so as not to fall with it. His withdrawal gave warning to the public, and now there is no one who will bet that the Ministry is in office this day three months. But after ? That is the great question, and it is apparently insoluble. Would you care to know what the King thinks, and of what he has firmly persuaded himself ? That before long Mr. Stanley and Sir R. Peel will form a Ministry.

---

[1] It was the general feeling in English and French diplomatic circles that Russia, feeling herself unable to go to war with either of the Western Powers, was trying to get up a war anywhere.

Stanley is the most Tory member of the actual Government—
Peel the most moderate of the Tories. A combination such
as this would be a real blessing for England, but it is not
given to others than the King to believe it to be so easy
or so near at hand. Meanwhile the shuffling of offices in
the Ministry which took place this morning is not wholly
a matter of indifference, for in the subordinate changes
resulting from it certain useful elements of embarrassment
may arise. By the word ' useful,' I mean anything which may
cause misunderstanding among Ministers themselves. You
see I am in a charitable mood.

Lord Durham assures me that he will now be able to
render us greater service than he could when he was in
office—and I believe that he tells the truth. His good will
is not to be despised. As for his view of the political position in England, it can be briefly summed up. He regards
himself as the Chief of the True Believers—that is, of those
who desire reform, but not a republic ; whereas in his
opinion his father-in-law's course leads straight to the latter
result, on the one hand by the resistance which he displays
to the reform party (as witness his Irish Coercion Bill), on
the other by the bids for support which he makes to the
Radical faction. Lord Grey has become such a thorough old
woman that it is scarcely worth while mentioning him.

What has been going on at Constantinople stirs my
blood. I am eager for news from Petersburg of our reply to
French insolence,[1] and all Europe also shows its curiosity by
its anxiety. The Duc d'Orléans is expected here, but what
to do I cannot imagine.

Good-bye, my dear Alexander, I commend warmly to
your friendliness the bearer of this letter, Matuscevitz. He
is a trusty good fellow, a devoted servant of his master, and
a firm friend. I am looking after your plants and seeds,
which shall be sent direct to Revel by the first vessel which
is sailing for that port.

I embrace you most heartily, dear, dear brother ; I am
already looking forward to my visit to Peterhof this summer.

[1] The action of Admiral Roussin at Constantinople.

Z

It is a great undertaking, for my courage breaks down at the thought of a sea voyage. I am always ill, and generally half dead ; but the happiness and pleasure of seeing the Emperor again would make me cross Europe. Remember, however, that it is important that I should find him when I arrive, for if by chance it should happen that he is going to absent himself from Petersburg this summer I look to your kindness to give me private warning.

CXXXIV

London : 7/19 April 1833.

Dear Alexander,—Here is a packet of seeds, and a list of the names. Let me know if your gardener is satisfied with them, and if you want any more send me your own list, so that I may not be altogether in the dark as to your wants.

I am writing a long letter to Matuscevitz to-day, so if you want to know what is going on here ask him to show you my letter. Although Europe seems to me to be in greater confusion than ever, I have ceased to disturb myself ever since we have taken such effectual and good measures in the East, and France makes such a pitiable display in the West. This contrast, and the political spectacle it affords, is most lively and entertaining. My impression is that the English Ministers are awfully ashamed of themselves for the position in which they find themselves placed—looked on suspiciously, or at least coldly, by all the Conservative Powers, which alone are firmly established, and having no ally but France, whom they distrust—for they do distrust her, I can vouch—hated or counted as nothing by those whom they insist upon protecting—Leopold and Dom Pedro. And what, after all, have they done for even these ? Truly this is not a pleasant predicament for a Great Power. In home affairs their attitude is no better ; they wobble from the Tories to the Radicals, despised by both parties. How are they to last in office ? It is, therefore, not surprising that there should be a general presentiment of approaching change. But what change ? I will not venture to prophesy, and, happily for us, it does not matter.   First, because the Emperor has made his own policy so safe that he can afford to do without England ; secondly, because England has so well managed her affairs that she has become powerless ; and, lastly, because Lord Palmerston has acted in such a way that we might even accept Mr. Cobbett as his successor without repugnance.   I think I have fairly stated the reason for my philosophic indifference.   We cannot, however, speak too highly of the King and Queen—both have been perfect in all that regards us.

The Duc d'Orléans has announced his arrival for May 7. This visit is unwelcome to everybody—to the Court, to the Ministry, and to the French Embassy.[1]   Ministers do not conceal their ill humour, which goes badly with their tenderness for the new alliance.

Good-bye, my dear Alexander.   Everybody here is suffering from influenza.   All my household is down with it—all the children, and two adults.   In London it is said that there are eighty thousand persons laid up ; the theatres have been closed for the last three days, such a thing has never been known, not even during the cholera ; but actors and audience are alike on their backs and in bed.

[Dom Pedro, with the connivance of the British and French Governments, had fitted out an expedition in the winter of 1831 and had sailed for the Açores, where Doña Maria was still recognised as rightful Queen of Portugal.   In July 1821 he sailed for Portugal and occupied Oporto, from which the troops of Dom Miguel were unable to drive him ; but he failed to extend his authority, and for more than a year the relative position of the two kings underwent little change.   In June 1833 the Duke of Wellington carried by 79 to 69 votes an address pledging the House of Lords to neutrality, but 'nobody out of the House of Lords cared either for Dom Miguel or Dom Pedro.'   A change in the command of Dom Pedro's fleet gave Charles Napier his opportunity, and in one

---

[1] 'The Duke of Orleans is here, and very well received by the Court and the world.' (*Greville*, ii. 373.)   'Le voyage du prince royal a dû le satisfaire entièrement sous le rapport social, mais moins sous le point de vue politique, car malgré quelques efforts, trop peu déguisés peut-être, le roi d'Angleterre ne lui a parlé que de la pluie et du beau temps.' (*Mémoires de Barante*, v. 60.)

engagement he captured every ship of Dom Miguel's fleet off Cape St. Vincent. The Portuguese question was promptly settled ; every port was blockaded, Lisbon was surrendered, and Doña Maria proclaimed Queen. Dom Miguel, after a brief campaign, in which General Bourmont took the command but gained no success, retreated over the Spanish frontier and joined himself to Don Carlos, who claimed the Spanish throne to the exclusion of his niece Isabella.

The question of the choice of a king for Greece had meanwhile been postponed by common consent, while that for Belgium was still unsettled. The assassination of Count Capo d'Istria, however, had forced the former matter to the front, but there was comparatively little difficulty in arriving at some kind of result. In the selection for Greece, as for Belgium, Russia was ready with a member of the House of Orange, Prince Frederick, but he was strongly opposed by both France and Great Britain and his candidature was not pressed, and finally Prince Otto of Bavaria was adopted with the consent of the Powers, but in consequence of the disturbed state of the country he did not assume its sovereignty until two years later.]

CXXXV

London : 10/22 August 1833.

Dear, dear Alexander,—How am I to manage to enjoy my happiness in Russia and at the same time my happiness in England ? For I am truly glad to find myself back with my husband, my daily life, and my good friends. Yet if you knew how much of my heart I have left behind, and much as I loved and admired the Emperor at home, I adore him a thousand times more now that I am here. I recall his every word, and remember his every gesture, and I almost cry when I think of what I have lost—I did not think that I was so soft-hearted. Do not let him forget me ; tell him of my respect, my enthusiasm, and my devotion—but don't bore him with all this, but tell him briefly once for all that my fidelity, my gratitude, and my passion for him can never be equalled.

I find nothing new here—the same Ministers, the same stupidity and insolence, the same powerlessness. Ah ! our good Russia, how much better is she governed ! Of the Ministers I have as yet only seen Lord Grey, and I am sending my report to my chief. He is anxious about the state of affairs, but he will be very soon free from his parliamentary worries. His Portugal, since the taking of Lisbon, is in a greater mess than ever, and certainly the English Cabinet finds itself there at loggerheads with everybody ; on bad terms with Miguel, on worse with Dom Pedro, whom it dislikes more than his brother, and almost on as bad terms with Donna Maria, because she has taken it into her head to marry the son of Eugène Beauharnais.[1] This is a nice kettle of fish, but I confess that it makes me laugh. In a few days, however, we shall know which one has swallowed the other.

Everybody here is furious at our treaty with Turkey [2]— the idiots. As Grey did not allude to it I said nothing about it, but I cannot understand the excessive stupidity or excessive pretension which induces the English Government to say that in their eyes our treaty is null and void. It does not matter to us what they think, for us it is binding—and if they challenge it, it must be with arms. There would be some meaning in that, but for my part I like gentler ways— but what then ? Just what makes Europe shake in her shoes ; Russia once again at Constantinople would never withdraw—that is my idea of this 'null and void' treaty. However, all that they say is sheer stupidity ; they are half dead with fright, and all we need do is to jeer at them. You can see now how a stay within touch of the Emperor revives one's feelings, and how I have come back here quite tranquil and serious, and able to regard with pity all these petty diplomatic storms and petty disputes. I feel that I have learnt much during the last six weeks ; my husband was very delighted to have me back again. He has not the divining spirit which marks the Emperor, for he was not at Richmond, at home, nor even in London. You may guess my temper and annoyance—I had a good mind to close

[1] She eventually married him, but he died a few months afterwards at Lisbon. Doña Maria was subsequently married to Prince Ferdinand of Saxe-Coburg. Her father, Dom Pedro, had married, in 1829, Amélie, daughter of Eugène Beauharnais, Duke of Leuchtenberg.

[2] The Treaty of Unkiar Skelessi.

the house and to return to Russia, where you had treated me so well, and of which I brought back such pleasant memories.

I have not said anything as yet of the Emperor's journey—of which nothing is at present known here—and for two reasons.[1] We are not called upon to render an account to these people of all that we do, and also I shall not be sorry to see this bomb burst over them unawares (for it will be a bomb, I assure you). Moreover, my husband would not have liked the news to have come from anyone but himself. Is not this showing respect for a husband's wishes ? I kept silence also on everything concerning Turkish affairs, although I well knew how furious the Ministers were about them. Well ! let them digest our policy if they can ; it will do their stomachs good, after all. When they know the contents of the treaty they will be satisfied—if they are not idiots, and until that time I enjoy their mulligrubs, for I feel that, considering all things, we have nothing which needs justification, and least of all this really noble page of our history.

My dear brother, I am full of good spirits and gaiety the result of having been in the company of that dear master.

I am not going to Court for a few days, but meanwhile I have received a most amiable letter from the Queen, showing much interest and curiosity about the details of my journey. When I am talking of the Emperor my tongue never tires.

Good-bye, my dear Alexander ; write soon and love me always. I am sending you herewith a travelling inkstand, which will, I think, be useful to you ; press the spring, and

---

[1] To attend a meeting with the King of Prussia at Teplitz and with the Emperor of Austria at Münchengratz. A manifesto was drawn up by the three Sovereigns, but the King of Prussia, on the advice of his Ministers, declined to sign it for fear of being entangled in a war. In its place a secret treaty was signed at Berlin (October 15) 'in view of the dangers with which the order of things established by public law and treaties is threatened.' The three autocratic rulers recognised 'the right of every independent Sovereign to call to his aid in domestic troubles as in the external dangers of his country such other independent Sovereign as seems to him most fitted to assist him.' This was an engagement to maintain the doctrine of intervention formulated at Troppau in 1820, and to confirm the union of the three Eastern against the two Western Powers.

do not fill the inkpot to the full. Here, too, is the programme of the ballet which Prince Wolkonsky asked me to send him. I will follow it up by a more detailed description of the groups and dances. Meanwhile this will give some general idea of the performance.

CXXXVI

Richmond : 17/29 August 1833.

Dear Alexander,—I have been writing a long letter to the Empress to-day, and a long one to Count Nesselrode, so that there is not left a single novelty for your share ; yet I cannot allow the packets to be closed without slipping in a line for you. Here I have all my time to love you ; I do not go every morning to reviews and every evening to a ball, and I have not to dress three times in the interval. Here I can rest and think ; can think with fondness of all that I have left behind me, even the fatigue of the journey. I never thought that it would come to this ; but if I had known how much I loved the Emperor and all of you I could never have torn myself away from Peterhof. I often think of my last hours there, and of your absence.

The article in our Gazette upon Poland is admirable. Everybody who is not either a fool or a Jacobin thinks so too. Make your mind easy, however, for Poland is dead to England for the next six months. Parliament is up. It seems to me, therefore, that it is all the more opportune to enlighten Europe a little on this subject. Your view is the true one, and I wish others would share it. Since the Press has become a power, one cannot do better than make use of it. What is the good of leaving an open field to falsehood ? It is right to confront it occasionally with the truth—briefly and cogently. If the ill-disposed are not converted, at least the well-disposed are supported and encouraged.

I have not seen enough of the various parties here to be able to express an opinion of what is going on. To-morrow I am going to Windsor for a few days, and I shall be able to find out something from the Queen and from some others of the right colour. The Ministers whom I have seen fancy themselves fixtures ; but one of them, Lord Melbourne, whose candour is delightful, cannot understand why they should be. After having proposed so many foolish things in Parliament, they must now proceed to their application. Never have so many Bills been passed as during the last session ; we shall see how they work. Lord Grey will leave this part of the business to others, for he himself is off to his country-seat on the borders of Scotland. He has strongly urged us to pay him a visit, and I am tempted to put forward as a reason for accepting that the Emperor thought it ridiculous that my husband should have been one and twenty years in England and never found an opportunity to see Edinburgh.

The news of the Emperor's journey has made a great sensation. If this were the only result it would be something to the good, but I trust that, besides the dread which it causes our enemies or our quasi-such, it will give courage to our friends. There is no use in going to sleep on our virtue, as some of our neighbours seem inclined to do ; one should know one's strength and show oneself ready to make use of it. Oh God ! a quarter of an Emperor Nicholas on the right and on the left, and how very differently the world would move ! [1]

Meanwhile it is the Peninsula which occupies men's minds. If the King of Spain should die just now, the whole country would be in a blaze. Don't you think that anyhow this will be the case sooner or later? This is a question which has worried me ever since I got back to England. These people seemed to have picked up their courage so much that I should like to see an end of them. By blundering,

[1] (August 29, 1829.) The state of politics at home and abroad remains unaltered, the Belgium question is still unsettled, civil war continues to rage in Portugal. The Russian troops, it is true, have quitted Constantinople, as pledged to do, on the retreat of the Pasha into Asia, but not till a treaty, offensive and defensive, was signed between the Emperor and the Sultan unknown to the other Powers, by which means the influence of the former in Turkish affairs is rendered more decisive than if a Russian army of occupation had attempted to prolong their stay in the Turkish capital. Stratford Canning is returned from Madrid to England, his mission to the Spanish Court having proved abortive. Otho is established King of Greece, and little attention is excited by his proceedings. Austria and Prussia remain *in statu quo*, watching with a jealous eye the proceedings of France and England in Portugal. (Raikes' *Journal*, i. 114.)

if not intentionally, they have brought things to such a pass that a conflict might become unavoidable. Why should not we try to disunite France and England ? England is in the hands of incapable and incompetent creatures, hostile to us, who imagine that they have to avenge some affront to their self-esteem—always the most difficult to treat. France, it must be admitted, is governed by more satisfactory men— eager to get into good society ; a few words of politeness from us would bring them over at once. You see that I let go the reins when talking to you.

August 18/30.

I am finishing this letter in London, where I have just arrived. Lord Grey has this moment left me. He spoke of the meeting of the sovereigns, but merely as a piece of news, and I did not allude to it otherwise. He then talked about Portugal, saying that his patience was exhausted, which means that Miguel and Bourmont [1] are still worrying him, and that he threatens to intervene in the matter. Moreover, since they see that Dom Pedro is not going to allow himself to be sent away, Lord Grey seems disposed to resign himself to endure him—but they are terribly annoyed. Leuchtenberg has found means to get into France with a passport from the French Consul at Genoa ; he is going to join Donna Maria at Havre.[2] The French Government is furious at this, and Lord Grey laughs at it. This is my latest news. I embrace you, dear brother, most tenderly.

[1] General Count Bourmont had deserted Napoleon previous to the battle of Waterloo. He was Minister of War in the Polignac Cabinet, and subsequently commanded the French expedition to Algiers and captured the town in 1830. At the Revolution he refused to take the oath and was struck off the lists of the French army, and in 1833 Dom Miguel placed him in command of his forces, with which he marched on Lisbon, but was unable to capture the city and to reinstate his master.

[2] The Préfet, acting under the law excluding Napoleon's family, refused him permission to remain at Havre, upon which he demanded to have his passport *visé* for Munich.

London : August 25 (O.S.).

By the next courier it is to you, dear Alexander, that I shall write my first letter, and this means that you will have one of proper proportions. My first always contains all my gossip, and this goes to Count Nesselrode ; there generally remains but little for my other clients. I refer you, therefore, to him to-day, and the next time he will apply to you for news.

We are fairly satisfied with the humour here, it is pacific in principle and mild in expression. I really think that my good temper had something to do with Lord Grey's. The ill-feeling against France amuses us greatly, as you may well imagine.[1] In talking, I side with Louis Philippe in the Leuchtenberg affair, if only for the pleasure of seeing Lord Grey's irritation, and to hear him magnify the offence in order to bring me over to his views.

Good Heavens ! how funny my visit to Windsor seemed and what a king compared with our Emperor, what a queen compared with our Empress, what a Court compared with ours. How time dragged on here, and how it slipped away with us. Then the King's talk ! I had to drive with him *tête-à-tête* packed for three hours in his carriage. His questions are really incredible. His mind seems to be attracted, at first, by the most trivial details—and he goes straight to the question. He wanted to know where the Emperor sits at table, how long the dinner lasts, if, at dessert, ices are handed first, as in England, or whether they are brought round later—he cannot understand why they should come at the end. All this occupied at least half an hour. Then came another series. ' Is the Emperor given to gallantry ? ' Yes, Sire.' ' Is the Empress jealous ? ' ' No, Sire, because the Emperor always makes her his *confidante* when his heart has been singed.' (This is really the expression used by the Emperor to me.) ' Ah ! I quite approve of

[1] In consequence of the desire of the French Government to intervene more actively in Portugal.

that.' I give you a short abstract in order that you may judge of the style. We talked, however, on many other things, and what he said upon less important topics proved to me his good sense. His principles and our own are identical on most points ; respect for royalty, hatred of new ideas, confidence in the old policy which united the two Courts, great dislike for France at all times, and a positive repugnance to the France of to-day. With regard to things at home he did not seem so clear in his mind ; he had not a word of praise for his Ministers, but greatly appreciated the conduct of the Tories and was extremely annoyed by that of the Duke of Sussex.[1] I think I told you that the King had forbidden him to come to Court after his detestable speeches in public about Poland and Portugal. In a word, this dear old King leaves us to wish for nothing more in him than a little more intelligence and a little stronger will. But as these are wanting, what is to be done with him ?

The Queen is most delightful ; I am writing about her at great length to the Empress and to my chief.

We had here on 18th and 19th inst. (O.S.) a most frightful storm. You cannot believe how terribly frightened I was. The Emperor at the time must have been at sea. This thought pursues me, and I shall not be reassured until I hear of his safe arrival at Stettin—I am constantly thinking about him on all occasions. The other day I was talking to M. de Talleyrand, and was exchanging with him reminiscences of the Emperor Alexander. In the course of conversation he remarked : ' The Emperor Alexander wanted to show his power—a bad plan ; the Emperor Nicholas holds his fist closed—that is how it should be done.' I pass on this story to you because it seems to me to be true and well said. I like talking to everybody about the Emperor, especially to people of intelligence. They can understand me, and listen with interest as well as curiosity—I can talk well when I talk of him. Good-bye, dear brother. I run the risk of wearying you by always repeating the same thing, as my mind is too

---

[1] The Duke of Sussex had recently supported the Bill for the Emancipation of the Jews, which the Duke of Gloucester had vehemently opposed.

closely in touch with your own.   By the way, write to me, for
I will not always go on writing without payment from you.
I embrace you with all my heart.

CXXXVIII

Panshanger : $\frac{\text{August 31}}{\text{September 12}}$, 1833.

Dear Alexander,—I am writing in the greatest anxiety.
You had not reached Stettin on the evening of September 4,
although you had left Kronstadt on August 28.   We have been
having a week of frightful storms—how do you imagine that I
can either sleep or eat ?[1]   Never have I been in such mortal
terror—and our dear Emperor !   I think only of him, and
of you, dear brother.   When shall I be relieved from this
agony of mind ?   I try to distract myself, but it is a dismal
failure.   The most startling events would not disturb me, so
completely are my thoughts fixed on the Baltic.

I thank you deeply, dear brother, for your letter from
Peterhof.   I read it over and over again in order to persuade
myself that you are all safe, as well as prudent, and that you
have taken shelter at Bornholm, at Rügen, or anywhere
else to be out of the reach of danger.   Off the coasts of
France the shipwrecks have been awful, no one can recall the
like ; thousands of lives have been lost—it is too terrible for
words.

Donna Maria and her mother-in-law have arrived at
Portsmouth, after having to submit to the coldness and ill-will
of the French Government (one cannot understand the gist of
Louis Philippe's policy).[2]   The King of England, who holds
the little Queen's cause in detestation because it smacks of
radicalism, had no sooner learnt that she had been badly
treated by the French than he took her under his protection,

---

[1] ' Awful storms these last few days and enormous damage done, the weather
like the middle of winter.' (*Greville*, iii. 30.) Madame de Lieven's anxiety was,
however, unnecessary.   The weather was so bad that the Emperor was unable to
leave Kronstadt and had returned to St. Petersburg, whence he travelled by land
to Schwedt, where he was met by the King of Prussia.

The presumed cause was Dom Pedro's refusal to entertain Louis Philippe's
proposals for Doña Maria's hand, first for his son the Duc de Nemours, and then
for his nephew Prince Charles of Naples.

and loads her with honour and attention for no other reason than to be a contrast to Louis Philippe.[1] She is now at Windsor, where she is fêted and petted. She will stay there some days, and on Monday, September 4/16, embarks for her kingdom, which somehow does not seem to much belong to her. However, these demonstrations involve the English Government in her cause, and supposing—which is quite possible—that she meets with some reverses it will be obliged to support her in some way. Possibly that is what Ministers want, but what afterwards?

The King invited Prince Esterhazy to Windsor to meet Donna Maria, but he declined to go. The Duke and Duchess of Cumberland are leaving England with their son [2] for Berlin, where they are going to place the poor child under a German doctor. I think they are well advised. I have no news to send you. There is much talk of what is going on at Friedland.[3] This causes some worry here, but in France it seems that the obliging and polite forms in which we announced the meeting have caused its grounds to be accepted with less suspicion than in England. M. de Talleyrand, in speaking to me of this communication, told me that his Government was greatly flattered and pleased with the agreeable tone of the despatch. It was regarded as quite an event, every word of it seeming to have its weight and value. Good-bye, dear Alexander. May Heaven preserve our dear master—I would that I knew him to be safe again in Petersburg. I embrace you.

CXXXIX

Panshanger : 6/18 September 1833.

My delight in learning that the Emperor was safe and sound at Schwedt [4] was in proportion to my anxiety ; that

---

[1] This is confirmed by Greville, iii. 33.

[2] Subsequently George V., the blind King of Hanover, 1851–78.

[3] Friedland was originally chosen as the meeting-place for the three Sovereigns, but Münchengratz was afterwards selected. The Emperors of Russia and Austria and Crown Prince of Prussia met there in September. Lord Palmerston, writing to his brother (September 3), suggests that an eventual partition of Turkey was one of the topics most discussed between the two Emperors.

[4] The meeting with the King of Prussia had originally been arranged to take place at Teplitz in August, but the Emperor Nicholas delayed his departure so

will tell you, dear Alexander, how deep and real it was.   I can imagine what must have been the raptures of the Prussian Court on his arrival.   I shall not, however, be completely re-assured until I hear all are back in our own country.   This too, will tranquillise me the more as I shall know where to find you.

I hope the interview passed off well, and that on each side there was a more complete understanding that both were standing shoulder to shoulder together, and that they could afford to look with pity on the extravagances of this side of Europe.   Really one loses patience when one lives long with these people, yet until one has given them a thrashing it is better to laugh at them than to be angry with them.   They are still deep in their Portuguese perplexities ; the struggle seems to have reached its last stage, my latest news reporting Bourmont at the gates of Lisbon.[1]   Everything is still possible, but the good arrives so rarely that I sadly fear all Dom Miguel's chances are gone.   A strange outcome, for one has to repent of both the wishes that one made for him and for those one made against him.   For, after all, he was a detest-able man, but the triumph of his rival is a moral catastrophe. What is more, it will be a British triumph, and this decides me—I am for Dom Miguel.   Donna Maria is, they say, hideous ; she is off now.

I had a letter from the Prince of Orange which proves to me that he is not going to visit the Emperor.   It seems as if English diplomacy fishes for news in a strange way, for it was Lord Palmerston who informed us officially of this decision.   I have been spending my time here in the society of that amiable Minister, with the result that I hate him a little more than I did ; but outwardly we are on the best of terms.

London : September 8/20.

I am finishing this in London, where I came yesterday in order to dine with the King.   He showed the greatest

long that King Frederick William had to leave to attend the autumn manœuvres of his army.   He had, however, a meeting with the Emperor Francis of Austria at Theresienstadt, and afterwards with Nicholas at Schwedt.

[1] General Bourmont had defeated the troops sent against him by Dom Pedro, and advanced rapidly on Lisbon ; but his further progress was stopped, and he ultimately was obliged to retire with his forces.

sympathy with us in our anxiety for the Emperor, and in our joy at getting good news. He is always most charming when not under the eye of his Ministers, and yesterday he was quite free from them. He did not cease laughing at Portugal and its Queen, who, he says, is hideously ugly and rather stupid.

I have been somewhat excited about certain Belgian deputations concerning which you will hear more.[1] The Belgians are becoming rebellious, the Dutch more loyal than ever—both excellent symptoms in my eyes. God grant that we may see their alliance. Have I ever told you about Leopold's melancholy letter to the Queen of England? No, I think that it was to the Empress that I spoke of it; the circumstances of to-day explain that letter. Good-bye, dear Alexander; I am writing very briefly to-day, but there is really nothing fresher to report. Tell Count Blome that I have made his niece's acquaintance and think her delightful. I will do my best to make myself agreeable to her as well as to her husband, and all with the object of being agreeable to the Count.

I embrace you heartily.

CXL

Richmond : 12/24 September 1833.

We are anxiously looking, dear Alexander, for news from Münchengratz, as we have been kept on short rations for a very long time. Here nothing has happened which is worth while repeating. The Conference naturally bowed out the Belgian deputation—it could not have done otherwise. If however, their statements are to be believed there is something which threatens danger to the Leopoldian edifice. Talleyrand is off to Paris with Belgium uppermost in his thoughts. On this point his interests and those of the Whig Ministers

---

[1] M. Goblet and M. Sylvain van de Weyer had come as a deputation to London to urge the members of the Conference to insist upon Holland's carrying out the treaty founded on the twenty-four articles. The delay in the execution of the treaty had led to rioting in Ghent and Antwerp, where the Orangeists were strong.

have nothing in common. As a matter of fact, I doubt if there is any question upon which it is likely that they agree completely. It seems to me very doubtful if M. de Talleyrand returns to England. His arrangements would seem to indicate that he has in view either death or the Presidency. As good company I shall regret him vastly, but politically it is most difficult for me to believe that anyone else will have so much influence with English Ministers, and for this reason we can do very well without him. Just now everyone is for love and fealty to France, except the King, who often disconcerts his Ministers by his political flights. For instance, quite recently at a great military banquet at Windsor he said, in the presence of a hundred officers : ' In spite of the accidental union now existing with France he should never cease to regard that Power as the natural enemy of England, or to resist by every possible means her encroachments.' Naturally this gave great offence in ministerial headquarters, and as a penance the King was forced to invite M. de Talleyrand to spend a day at Windsor before leaving for France. This is a little sample of domestic harmony.

Lord Lowther [1] and Lord Ranelagh [2] have been sending home letters full of enthusiasm for the Emperor, and of appreciation of the manner in which he received them. I am rejoiced to hear it, for both are men of notoriety here, and the former of considerable talent and importance.

There is no daylight as yet in Portuguese affairs. Lord Grey tells me that he fears that a Vendean war may go on there for a long time, and that he is greatly tempted to intervene at once to put an end to it. There is no doubt that some such step is under consideration, but I much doubt if

[1] Lord Lowther, son of Earl of Lonsdale, sat in the House of Commons for Cockermouth, 1808–13 ; Westmorland, 1813–31 ; Dunwich, 1831 ; Westmorland, 1831–4 ; Lord of the Admiralty, 1809 ; Commissioner for Indian Affairs, 1810–18 ; Lord of the Treasury, 1813–27 ; Chief Comissioner of Woods, 1828–30 ; Vice-President of the Board of Trade, 1834–5 ; Lord President, 1852.

[2] Thomas Heron, seventh Viscount Ranelagh, born 1820; entered 1st Life Guards, was present as a volunteer at the siege of Antwerp, and served with the Carlists in the Spanish War of Succession 1833–6 ; was one of the earliest promoters of the Volunteer movement in England, and Lieutenant-Colonel of the South Middlesex Volunteers, 1860–85.

the Ministers have courage enough to take it. Buchanan, the American Minister at Petersburg,[1] has been staying some days in London ; Palmerston has been most attentive to him. He is a good fellow, who speaks his mind freely about us, and what he says is that our Emperor is a great and powerful monarch and 'a very clever and a very honest man.' I repeat these republican sentiments ; they are not elegant and refined in expression, but I like them all the better for that.

By the by, Lord Lowther in his letters expresses the greatest surprise at the Emperor's intimate knowledge of English home affairs, the position of individuals, &c. &c., and at the correct estimate he forms of them.

Good-bye, dear Alexander ; write to me and tell me lots of things, with plenty of details—I like to know everything, and everything interests me. I am writing this letter the day before the courier starts, as to-morrow I am going on a jaunt to the country with the King and Queen, and shall consequently have no time for anything else.

CXLI

Richmond : $\frac{\text{September 20}}{\text{October 2}}$, 1833.

Not a single scrubby line have you written to me during the whole of the time you have been away from Russia. How badly you treat me, dear Alexander ; it is really atrocious. I must indeed be of exceeding good alloy to continue to write to you. We are impatiently awaiting the decrees of Münchengratz. From here there is little news to send you. From a few ministerial remarks which have reached me I gather that before deciding upon the supreme folly of supporting Dom Pedro materially they are making a last effort to come to an understanding with Spain. If this should fail

[1] James Buchanan, a prominent American statesman employed by General Jackson as Minister to Russia in 1829-32 to negotiate a commercial and maritime treaty ; became Secretary of State to President Polk, 1844-8 ; Minister to England, 1853-6 ; President of the United States, 1856-60. His opinion of Russia as expressed in the pamphlet referred to was : ' There is no freedom of the Press, no public opinion, and but little political conversation, and that very much guarded. In short, we live in the calm of despotism, though the Emperor Nicholas is one of the best of despots.'

they will reconsider the matter ; meanwhile, Lisbon is much in the same state as Oporto. One side is busy watching the other and preparing to attack, but nothing comes of it. Grey in his last letter to me suggests that we should send Dom Miguel to Siberia, while he would embark Dom Pedro for St. Helena. I mention this just to show you how unsettled are the views of this Government on the subject.

As for the King of the Netherlands, they despair of his ever agreeing to any definitive arrangement, but they seem to be more resigned to a provisional condition than they were last year. In fact, all political questions for the last three years have been in a strange state. Scores of times people have said that this could not go on, nevertheless the three years are there to prove the contrary. Leopold is not going to Paris, as was announced ; he has his hands full in keeping his loyal subjects in order.

The Duke and Duchess of Cumberland have gone to Berlin with their boy ; for ever at least as regards the Duchess, but her husband wants to be back here on October 4 for the meeting of Parliament. I have absolutely nothing to add to this letter. We are literally famishing for news ; we ought to know everything about the interview, and as a matter of fact we have not heard a word. I am delighted, however, to think that the Emperor is safe back again. I have him always before me, that dear Emperor—the little bust of him accompanies me everywhere. Tell this to Prince Wolkonsky, to whom I am indebted for this charming clock.

By the way, I am sending to the Emperor by this occasion a collection of views of English scenery and a small supply of pretty women. He gave me permission to send such things to him from time to time, so I pray you place these at his feet ; would that I might place myself there also. You will give me much pleasure by assuring me that he has not forgotten me.

Good-bye, dear brother—I embrace you heartily. I will write to you only to-day ; nobody replies to me, and you see I am in the last stage of destitution—not a single rumour or bit of news to send you. A thousand loves.

[Portuguese affairs were still unsettled, and the respective chances of Dom Pedro and Dom Miguel hanging in the balance, when Spain was once more brought into the field of international politics. Ferdinand VII.'s death (September 29, 1833) had opened the question of succession to the throne.   According to the Spanish law females in direct descent could succeed to the crown, but since the accession of the Bourbons the succession had been through the male line exclusively.   In 1789 a decree had been prepared, though never promulgated, restoring the old order of female succession, but in 1830 Ferdinand, then childless, promulgated the decree without notifying the Council of State or his brother.   In the same year Ferdinand married for the fourth time, his wife being his niece Princess Maria Christina, daughter of Francis, King of Naples and Sicily, and two daughters were born to him. Subsequently, in 1832, Ferdinand, believing himself on the point of death, and acting under the influence of the clergy, revoked the decree of 1830 ; thus Don Carlos again found himself in the position of heir to the throne.   But Ferdinand recovered, dismissed his Ministry, and placed the government in the Queen's hands, who at once obtained a royal Act annulling the Act of 1832, and in June 1833 the Castilian Cortes, convoked in due form, were sworn to recognise the Infanta Isabella Queen presumptive. Don Carlos, invited, to take the oath, refused, and addressed his protest to the Sovereigns of Europe.   On the King's death Queen Christina assumed the regency with Señor Zea Bermudez as her chief adviser.   France at once recognised Isabella and England followed suit, while the three autocratic governments recognised Don Carlos.   Zea, although opposed to Don Carlos, was in favour of autocratic government, and in Portugal was anxious to support Dom Miguel against Doña Maria.   Christina promptly realised that to resist the Carlists she needed the support of all the Liberals, and summoned Señor Martinez de la Rosa to the head of the Government, her partisans being known as Christinos.]

CXLII

Richmond : 2/14 October 1833.

Dear Alexander,—Your letter from Münchengratz is the most interesting and the most amusing you have ever written to me.   It reached me two days ago by the Russian courier from Berlin ; I thank you for it most sincerely.   I am extremely delighted and not a little vain of the success of the interview between the two Emperors, and of the good

A A 2

impression which one has brought away with him. You will recollect that I did not hesitate for a moment to support warmly the idea of the meeting, and that, even if it led to nothing, it could not but be otherwise than good and useful in itself, because the mere fact of the two Emperors meeting would inspire the rest of Europe with respect. This impression has been amply produced, and, over and above, a number of other good and useful things have been achieved—so the journey has gained its end. From Vienna I get letter after letter full of enthusiasm for the Emperor ; everybody has some anecdote to relate, every word and gesture was noted, and he struck, astonished, and carried away all who came in contact with him. I laugh to myself when I remember that the Emperor once said to me that he was afraid of Metternich ; ask him, if now he does not laugh at himself for harbouring such a thought. Do you know what has happened ? Merely the Emperor has learnt to know himself better, and that he has discovered, what I took the liberty to discover beforehand—namely, that he knows more than all the potentates and statesmen of Europe together. In a word, dear Alexander, our Emperor is like our Russia, greater, stronger, more exalted than all the rest, and, to crown all, we have the handsomest man in Europe, which is something also. I have now received his portrait, and you should see my delight ; I have my magnifying glass beside me, for the miniature is very small, but admirably painted, and both his portrait and that of the Empress are marvellously good likenesses. Everybody throngs round me, friends and enemies, to examine and admire this beautiful and precious bracelet.

It seems, then, that we too have now plunged into Spanish affairs. I cannot in truth say that we have done wrong when I see the sorry mien of Ministers here. They are frightened to death, and absolutely motionless. The amusing part of the business is that it is Lord Grey from his remote country house who is the most bellicose. The Home Secretary,[1] with whom I am on very good terms since the

---

[1] Lord Melbourne.

departure[1] of his sister Lady Cowper, confided to me (he confides strange things, the Minister) that Lord Grey on hearing of the death of Ferdinand wrote at once to Palmerston to advise him to strengthen the army. The other Ministers look upon this as folly, and cannot conceive what possesses Lord Grey. Indeed, if England has done nothing, at all events openly, for Donna Maria why should it bother itself about Donna Isabella with the possible complication of French intervention into the bargain? As for us, let things take their course, and I firmly believe that they will turn out to be favourable to good principles. This is the way in which, with all humility, I put the matter. If France does not interfere Don Carlos will have an easy triumph in Spain, and the reaction will be felt throughout the Peninsula. If she does interfere, she will be by so much the less embarrassing and formidable to the rest of Europe, and her troops will find a grave in Spain more certainly than did Bonaparte's, for he is no longer there.[2] Is my argument faulty?

Thursday, 5/17.

I have nothing to add to the foregoing. I have received a letter from Lord Grey, who is evidently in a bad humour. We had half promised to pay him a visit, but the prolongation of Count Nesselrode's stay at Berlin obliges my husband to await his last instructions in London. He therefore cannot budge, so· we have given up the visit. Lord Grey is much annoyed, and that makes him snappish about everything. With regard to Spain he writes to me that he has made up his mind, and that he will take his own course, whatever the others may do. This is somewhat enigmatic, for he does not say what his course will be; but his intention is to frighten me, and to make me believe in mere promises. I replied by applauding his decision, which I had seen developed in an article in the ' Globe' (a ministerial

---

[1] For the Riviera.

[2] This seems to be an echo of Pozzo di Borgo's opinion as expressed to Raikes and transmitted by him to the Duke of Wellington, whose comment on it was that the Russian Ambassador at Paris had left one element out of his calculation—namely, Portugal. (*Raikes' Journal*, i. 121.)

paper), which said that England had nothing to do with this business. In fact, so clearly is this the intention of the Ministers here that the day before yesterday, at a dinner party where several were present, a lady of the company having asked if they were to drink the health of the King Don Carlos or the Queen Isabella, Lord Palmerston replied : ' For my part, I drink to the health of the one who gets the better of the other.' This, at any rate, is neutrality. I have repeated his words because they seem to me to be worth attention at this moment, and because all this shows that Lord Grey and Lord Palmerston do not think alike.

Matuscevitz, who has been away hunting, is back for a few days. Happily, he has broken neither legs nor arms ; I am always glad to see him, and it is a pleasure to talk with him. I am delighted with the Emperor's journey through Poland : it must have been an imposing sight. I am forwarding to him to-day a volume of Devonshire views, and as he has travelled through that county they will have some interest in his eyes ; those of Scotland, and of Edinburgh especially, will follow by the next courier. You will be doing me a kindness if you can tell me whether these little offerings afford the Emperor any amusement. I must ask you, too, if a certain rose-coloured dress which I have taken the liberty to send to the Empress is to her taste. Take the trouble to make a note of this, and tell me in your next letter.

Buchanan (it is my firm conviction) has written an admirable pamphlet on Russia and the Emperor. This good man only just escaped a tender embrace from me, for in spite of his incognito I should not have hesitated to have embraced him heartily, if he had not gone off to America the very day on which his pamphlet appeared. It is impossible that he is not the author—it bears the mark of absolute truth. Good-bye, dear Alexander. I embrace you a thousand times ; my husband joins me, for he too loves you much. Write to me often, for you know that everything, great and small, interests me, but what pleases me most is to feel that I am not forgotten in the spot where my heart and soul are constantly fixed.

Tell the Empress that the King of England is coming from Windsor to-day to dine with one of his daughters, where we are invited, expressly to see my bracelet, of which the repute has travelled over England.   He sent to ask me to wear it and to bring a magnifying glass, so as to be able to examine the portraits.

CXLIII

London : 13/25 December 1833.

This courier, dear Alexander, brings somewhat more pacific news than the last. Ministers have changed their tone—they are desirous of explanations ; they profess to desire peace, and to make it dependent upon our will and pleasure.   These are fine words ; what we want are deeds, perhaps they will follow. Meanwhile, either because they have a clearer idea of our intentions, or because France holds them back, or that public opinion does not seem so very hostile to us, there has certainly been a considerable change in their ways and tone.   My husband has behaved very well in all this business. He has waited for others to approach him, having at first adopted a cold and indifferent attitude— more recently he has been frank and dignified, but quite firm. We have, moreover, given no little annoyance to the Government by a visit to the Duke of Wellington, which I had planned with him. I can assure you this trivial matter has been of real value ; for the Duke, when sure of our coming, had invited (the Ministers of) Austria, Holland, and even of France to meet us. This, as you may imagine, caused a hubbub at headquarters ; but there was nothing to be said, for it was not one Power but Europe collectively which was conspiring with the leader of the Opposition.   It has given some relief to the Tories and subject for thought to Ministers. My husband informed the Duke of Wellington of the actual state of our relations with his Government, and I on my side discussed with him the best means to be adopted for enlightening public opinion and for counteracting the obvious ill-will of the ministerial papers. He was quite ready to fall in with my views, and Matuscevitz is already hard at work. When finished I shall hand it over to the Duke, who, in turn, will pass it on to a trusty henchman, devoted to his party and very competent.[1] So far as the Duke is informed, my husband knows nothing of all this—although it is with the latter's assent that I have made this little arrangement. Matuscevitz shows as much zeal as ability in the business, and that says everything.[2] I fancy that between now and the meeting of Parliament the public will learn what is to be believed of these artful Ministers, if they persist in their hostile attitude towards us ; but my idea is that they will soon change, because France is not really supporting them—at least, not at this moment. Talleyrand has come back, strong in his master's full confidence and in their common dislike for M. de Broglie.[3] Talleyrand has two words constantly on his lips, ' the *status quo* ' and ' peace.' Talleyrand is well aware that Palmerston dislikes him, and he frames his conduct in consequence. His object is to influence other Ministers who have a greater liking for him. Talleyrand is a trickster—but he really wants peace. He does not wish to bring about a quarrel with Russia, so for the present we have reason to be satisfied with Talleyrand.

December 15/27th.

There is nothing, I think, to add to this letter, dear Alexander. We continue to turn in the same circle of thought, and to be constantly asking : Is it to be peace or war ? The answers to be given to the despatches sent off to-day will probably settle matters, one way or the other. I firmly believe that Ministers here do not want war—but, the idiots! they have given the tail end of the story first. They start with an insulting despatch, and then

[1] Presumably Croker, as an article by him appeared in the *Quarterly Review* shortly afterwards.

[2] Greville's account of his visit to Belvoir Castle just after the New Year (1834), and of the conferences there between Wellington and Matuscevitz, would point in the same direction. (*Greville*, iii. 46.)

[3] The French Cabinet was as much divided on the Spanish question as the English. Thiers and Marshal Soult were in favour of intervention. but M. de Broglie was opposed to it, owing to the readiness with which the three northern Powers had acceded to it.

express (as they should have done sooner) a polite wish to explain their meaning. Would you believe it? They are possessed with the idea that it is we who want to begin the war—that, for example, we want to turn them out of the Ionian islands, and then to turn them out of India. All this they believe and repeat among themselves even in private.

What amuses me most is their great anger at our reply to their despatch. From this one would infer that they threatened before we were, as they term it, insolent. Logically they should now become a thousandfold more menacing —at least one would think so ; but no, they are now quite civil and polite. How well the Emperor understands and treats them, and how he dominates them by his greatness and dignity! Good-bye, dear Alexander; I embrace you with all my heart, and all yours and ours.

Present my compliments to the Comte de Blome, and tell him that all his belongings here are well. M. and Madame de Blome [1] are going the day after to-morrow on a short visit to Lord Palmerston's in the country. They are very pleasant people and everybody here likes them.

By the way, the Swedish Minister is detestable—a wild Pole !

Good-bye once more, and a thousand thousand loves.

[1] Madame de Blome was a daughter of Metternich.

1834

[The change in the attitude of Great Britain to Russia had been
gradual but continuous. In 1827 the Russian policy towards
Greece had attracted the support of the Whigs, and for a while, both
before and after his joining the Ministry, Palmerston had favoured
an understanding with Russia, and had been consequently treated
with attention by Nesselrode. On Palmerston's advent to the
Foreign Office he found, however, that Russia lost no opportunity
of throwing obstacles in the way of British policy in Holland,
Greece, and Portugal. The savage repression of the Polish revolt
further alienated Liberal opinion from Russia, and on the announcement in the 'Morning Herald' (August 21) of the signing of the
Treaty of Unkiar Skelessi there was a general explosion of public
feeling against Russia. Palmerston induced the Government to
strengthen the Mediterranean fleet, persuaded the French Government to join in a protest against the treaty, and notified to Nesselrode
that if circumstances arose leading to an armed interference of Russia
in the internal affairs of Turkey the English Government would
consider the treaty as *non avenu*. Nesselrode replied that the
treaty was purely defensive, but according to Baron Stockmar
(vol. i. p. 347) Nesselrode's actual reply was that Russia would consider
England's protest as *non avenu*. Greville, moreover, amply confirms
the warlike rumours which were current at the close of the previous
year. According to him, Madame de Lieven spoke in a lofty tone, that
Russia neither desired nor feared war ; that our tone had latterly been
so insulting that they had no option but of replying haughtily. She
said that we must not imagine that in conjunction with France we
could hold the rest of Europe in check, and that the first result of a
war would be the downfall of Louis Philippe. She complained also
of the language used in Parliament and in the newspapers respecting
Russia, which had greatly incensed the Emperor and his Court.

There would appear to be some truth also in what Madame de Lieven says of the action of the British Cabinet. Palmerston's despatch was written without due appreciation of what had occurred at the signing of the Treaty of Adrianople ; and subsequently we had practically divested ourselves of the right of interfering with Russia's policy towards Turkey, provided it did not interfere with our own interests. The protest against the Treaty of Unkiar Skelessi, therefore, could only take the form of a notice that we should not submit to its stipulations if enforced against ourselves. Meanwhile the relations between the two Powers had not been smoothed by the persistent refusal of the Emperor to receive Sir Stratford Canning as Ambassador, upon whose acceptance Lord Palmerston wished to insist as no adequate reason for his rejection had been put forward, and Sir Stratford Canning had denied having omitted to show proper civility to the Emperor when Grand Duke. Nicholas was, however, obstinate, and Palmerston had to give way and cancel the appointment.

Thus the last year of Prince Lieven's Embassy to London opened under unfavourable auspices. Lord Palmerston fully shared the distrust of the Russian Ambassador and his wife which the Duke of Wellington had expressed in his correspondence five years previously. Whatever the cause, the relations between the two countries had grown steadily worse, and M. de Lieven was charged with having intentionally done his utmost to embroil them. In the Belgian business Russia had been forced to give way in consequence of the combined action of France and Great Britain, to which M. de Talleyrand attached the utmost importance. In the matter of Spain and Portugal the action of the three autocratic Sovereigns had again brought the two Western Powers into apparent accord, and France was bound to follow up Admiral Roussin's exploit at Constantinople by a note on the Treaty of Unkiar Skelessi; but all the time doubts were growing as to the value of the French alliance, and more perhaps as to the stability of the French throne. Lord Palmerston was meanwhile making himself unpopular in nearly all the Chancelleries of Europe by adopting a haughty, supercilious tone, and affecting to regard without apprehension the isolation of England.

At the same time, the Cabinet was divided upon the question of sending troops to Portugal to support Doña Maria, a course to which Lord Grey was so strongly opposed that he threatened to resign, but the King desired him to come to some arrangement with his colleagues. Soon after the House met the Government found itself in difficulties chiefly arising out of Irish questions and O'Connell's hostility. A motion to remove Mr. Baron Hill from the Irish Bench, which the Government resolved to oppose, Lord Althorp, the Irish Secretary, and the Solicitor General agreed to accept with some slight alteration. This their colleagues refused, and the Ministry were defeated by six votes. On the Pension List Bill, which involved a question of the King's prerogative, they obtained a bare majority of eight. The Irish Church Bill brought matters to a crisis : Mr. Stanley and Sir James Graham, refusing to support the Appropriation Clause of the Bill, which they denounced as spoliation, resigned, and were followed by the Duke of Richmond and the Earl of Ripon. Their places were filled forthwith by the Marquess of Conyngham (Postmaster-General), the Earl of Carlisle (Privy Seal), Lord Auckland (First Lord of the Admiralty), and Mr. Spring Rice (Colonial Secretary); but the general opinion was that the Cabinet in its new form could not last, and six weeks later Lord Grey resigned, Lord Melbourne succeeding to the premiership.]

CXLIV

London : January 6/18, 1834.

Dear Alexander,—Your letter of November 2 only reached me by the courier on January 3/15. Find out where the blame lies, on your department or on that of Foreign Affairs. I am sorry that the excellent news you had to give was so much delayed. Your interview with Bligh[1] is on my table—I shall know how to make good use of it. Your estimate of English policy is very true, and your summary of its days of glory and of shame is the best picture I have ever seen.

January 12/24.

I sent a line by the last Prussian courier to Count Nesselrode to advise him of the great ministerial crisis which was going on here last week. What I have since learnt is worth while repeating to him. It was Lord Melbourne who in the Cabinet took his stand upon the ground of principle (to make use of Metternich's expression), who defended the principle of non-intervention, and who proved from the words of the treaty that they could

---

[1] Hon. Sir Robert Bligh, K.C.B., son of Earl of Darnley ; *chargé-d'affaires* at St. Petersburg during the prolonged absence of any British Ambassador, no substitute for Sir Stratford Canning having been named. He was afterwards Minister at Hanover.

not without startling bad faith invoke it now to intervene by force in the Portuguese business. He argued that Dom Pedro's Government, in asking for English troops to be sent, was explaining the treaty by sophisms, and that for his part he (Lord Melbourne) would never take upon himself the responsibility of having agreed to a step which neither the honour nor the interests of England demanded. Eight members of the Cabinet endorsed this view—and Lords Grey, Holland, Palmerston, Brougham, and John Russell were left in a minority, and furious with rage. Grey started off at once to Brighton to tender his resignation ; but his party, alarmed at this violent decision, sent with him his brother-in-law, the Minister at War, who has not a seat in the Cabinet, but who has great influence with him. He is one Ellice, surnamed 'the Bear,' because he has the appearance of that animal.[1] During the journey he managed to make Lord Grey change his intention and persuaded him simply to lay before the King the unfortunate disagreement in the Cabinet. The King asked him if he intended to make a ministerial question of it ; in other words, if Lord Grey thought it obligatory on him to pass the resolution to send troops to Portugal—or, failing that, to leave the Ministry ? Lord Grey replied : ' No, it was a matter of opinion.' Thereupon the King thought that the best advice he could give was that Lord Grey should bow to the views of the majority, and this he has done.

You can picture to yourself easily the ill-feeling this has given rise to, and the strange position of Ministers towards each other. Here are two patent facts—a division in the Cabinet, and a schism between Palmerston and Melbourne, who, looking upon themselves as Canningites, had hitherto gone hand in hand. Ministers are doing all in their power to contradict the belief that there is any disagreement among them ; but what I tell you is the exact truth, and, what is more, it is known to the world. Lord Grey told me in

---

[1] Madame de Lieven was probably unaware that her own *sobriquet* in English society was ' The White Bear,' but not on account of her appearance or her manners.

general terms that he was quite satisfied with Count Nesselrode's despatch of December 22, and I know that the
general opinion is that the misunderstandings with Russia
have been got over. He is satisfied, too, with the turn things
have taken in Spain—that is, with the fall of Zea,[1] and the
begining of a revolution there—for it is really that. He told me,
too, a heap of absurdities (about the Spaniards), for really the
people there are crazy. I merely remarked that it was lucky
that Louis Philippe was wise and prudent, because with such
a conflagration in a neighbouring country his position would
become difficult. 'Very lucky indeed,' he replied, 'but very
natural, for France is unanimous for peace, and the existence
of the King demands it. Louis Philippe would be the first
victim if peace were disturbed.' He went on to say a lot of
pretty things on this subject, and then suddenly seemed to
be afraid that he had said too much, and that I might gather
from them too great an assurance of tranquillity.

He then passed to the subject of Belgium to tell me that
he was wholly indifferent whether the business was brought
to an end or was left where it now rests, that Leopold was
able to get on quite well with the provisional arrangement, that
the country was very prosperous, and that as the convention of
May 21 guaranteed peace this provisional state might last
thirty years, and that he regarded the affair as settled until
bankruptcy should put an end to Holland.

He spoke of the Prussian treaty of commerce as being a
political rather than a commercial matter,[2] adding that there
were some who thought that it would be prejudicial to the
commercial interests of England, but this was all nonsense.

This is my budget of Lord Grey's babbling ; show it to
Count Nesselrode, adding that the Ministers affect to be
completely united, and say that they are perfectly sure of
their position in Parliament. You may also tell him that the
Tories are discouraged, because Peel is the most selfish and

---

[1] Señor Zea Bermudez, the Spanish Prime Minister, was dismissed by the
Queen, and Señor Martinez della Rosa, a Liberal, was appointed.

[2] Eighteen German States had by this time joined the Zollverein, started by
Prussia in 1818, and a Treaty of Commerce with Great Britain was concluded
through its action.

most cautious man in the world, yet they cannot do without him. Further, that the present Ministry inspires neither esteem nor confidence in any quarter ; next, that although England as a whole desires peace, a few noisy speech-makers might lead her into war ; and lastly, that in this country there is not left a single man of sense—where formerly there were so many.

After this catalogue of unpleasant truths—of which you may believe all or none—good-bye, dear Alexander. I embrace with all my heart, you and all the others.

CXLV

London : January 8 (N.S.), 1834.

Here we are back again from Brighton, dear Alexander, after a stay of ten days, during which we were constantly with the Court. The King treated us, if possible, with greater kindness and attention than ever, and all that I saw and heard there contrasts strongly with the bad relations in which we find ourselves with England. I cannot habituate myself to the ridiculousness of these relations, for in reality that is the feature in them which strikes me most forcibly. At the point at which we have arrived there are only two alternatives—to laugh or to fight. For my part, I think it is the former which will come about. They admit that they have been mistaken, and pass the sponge over a period of illusion and unreasonable suspicion. It seems that already there are symptoms of throwing off this nightmare, and that the Court Ball of December 6/18 was an effort in this direction. So far I know nothing beyond a few words let drop by Lord Grey to-day during his visit to me ; but he seemed flattered by the interview which the Emperor had accorded to Mr. Bligh, and told me that his Majesty's words were most satisfactory and pacific. I remarked that his thoughts and intentions had always been so, and that it was greatly to be regretted that they had been so long misinterpreted here, that the time had come to look at things in the face and in a clear light, which would be to everyone's advantage. He warmly asserted that that was his way of thinking also, and that the peace of the world did not depend on England. At this he broke off with a deep sigh, saying that it was not the East which was disturbing him, but Portugal, where everything was going badly ; and that Spain was in as bad a plight as Portugal ; that the Queen Regent was without authority, Zea surrounded by enemies, the Captains-General independent and ignorant, the insurrection thoroughly organised, and Portugal in hopeless confusion—in a word, it was a cataract of groans and sighs over everybody and everything. For my part I am delighted, for anything which disturbs and annoys the English Ministers commends itself to my liking. M. de Talleyrand finds himself in an awkward position here. On his return he promptly discovered that Ministers would not deal with him,[1] that all business matters were being carried on between M. de Broglie and the British Ambassador in Paris ; that, however pleasant Lord Palmerston might appear, he would tell him nothing ; that although they might write flattering letters to him from the Tuileries, yet his Cabinet left him in total ignorance of their intentions. For a man of his known ability and talent such a *rôle* was scarcely flattering, and he is quite dumfoundered. Madame de Dino[2] weeps—and he does not laugh. It is said that he has recently lost 800,000 francs in the Funds ; he gambles in accordance with the policy he directs, or else he settles his policy in accordance with his financial news, and now he cannot manipulate one or the other. Lord Grey is devoted to him, Lord Palmerston detests him, Lord Holland tells him all the Cabinet secrets—but in the long run Lord Palmerston laughs at his colleagues' game and at all the world. His hostility has completely paralysed Talleyrand, who wished to bring our two Cabinets more closely together. He rather

[1] ' It would seem rather that M. de Broglie in the debate on the Address in the French Chamber (January 7–8) had attenuated, almost to extinguishing, the strength of the protests made at M. de Talleyrand's instigation against the Treaty of Unkiar Skelessi.

[2] Princess Dino, daughter of the last Duchess of Courland, married in 1808, through the intervention of Alexander I., to Talleyrand's nephew, on whom the title of Prince Dino was conferred. His wife divorced him after a few years, and she lived with Talleyrand until his death, when she assumed the title of Duchesse de Sagan.

boasted in Paris that he was coming here with that object ; Palmerston was informed, and anticipated him by making conciliatory overtures to my husband. Talleyrand was quite taken aback when he found this out. I fancy that what he wished done by himself does not please him when done by others. We are apparently on the best of terms just now, but he is an unprincipled rascal.

January 10.

I am closing this without being able to add anything except that Lord John Russell assures me that Lord Grey regards the squabble with Russia at an end, and that not a single Minister dreams of war. One must not believe all —but still less nothing—of this assurance.[1] Experience has taught me that the truth lies mid-way. What is certain is that the present Ministry are a poor lot. Good-bye, dear Alexander ; I love and embrace you tenderly.

CXLVI

London : $\frac{\text{January 25}}{\text{February 6}}$, 1834.

I thank you ever so much, dear Alexander, for your two kind letters received by the Petersburg courier of January 4–16 —a thousand thanks, too, for the patterns of the national costume. I find it magnificent, and am just ordering one for myself. The national air ' Боже Царя храни !' is charming ; it is always running in my head, and I cannot tell you the pleasure you have given me by sending it.

Everything which Count Nesselrode receives to-day goes to prove that the people here are both cowards and fools. If they go on to the Day of Judgment they will never send direct declarations, but merely pitiful roundabout criticisms. Palmerston fancies himself still in a Rhetoric class, working at his theme. He will never be more than a schoolboy, and is not brilliant as that. We shall muddle on with such as long as they remain, but Europe will never be able to get on with them. The best plan is to think about them as little as

---

[1] 'The storm that impended over Europe has blown off, and there seems to be no danger of any interruption of the peace. Esterhazy and Madame de Lieven both told me last night (February 12) that they thought so now.' (*Greville's Memoirs*, ii. 56.)

possible. For us this is easy enough ; our position is excellent, and sometimes I am tempted to think that they have helped us to it, and that it is really ingratitude on our part not to like those who have so nicely allowed us to manage our own affairs as we wish. Either the Tories or the Radicals would have hampered us very much more ; these good creatures have forced us to place ourselves at the head of Conservative Europe, and have thereby doubled the moral strength of our gigantic empire. I believe that my view of the situation is correct.

I am delighted to hear that the Poles have been trying to get up a revolution in Savoy.[1] In time the world will learn what to think of that *canaille*. Already the statements and documents submitted by the Ministers to the French Chamber of Deputies have produced their effect. Sympathy for the Poles will soon die out—I don't hear of a single one who has come to live in England.

I have a wretched cold on my chest, which prevents my going on with my letter. I have written a long letter to the Empress in reply to a short but charming one she addressed to me. Tell me if our Grand Duchesses have grown. I shall have twenty questions to ask you. I like all these little details, especially those about the Imperial family. Good-bye, dear brother ; I am dead. I embrace you all.

CXLVII

London : 16/28 February 1834.

Here is a good opportunity, dear Alexander, for sending a letter ; but as ill-luck will have it I have nothing to say— but anything is better than that my courier should arrive empty-handed. He is Buckhausen, our Consul-General, who is going to Petersburg. I recommend him to you first as a

---

[1] A few Polish refugees had united themselves with the Italian republicans. In all about fifty started from Voreppe, on the confines of Savoy and Switzerland. They passed through a few villages, arousing the inhabitants with cries of 'Vive la république!' captured a post of Custom-house officers and some carbineers ; but their march on Chambéry was promptly stopped by Sardinian troops, and the band dispersed.

worthy man, and also as one who thoroughly understands his business, and, in a measure, England also. He is quite competent to answer any questions you may put to him about the state of this country. I don't know the cause of his journey, but in any case a few civilities on your part will not be out of place.

Ministers make a sorry show ; at variance among themselves, they stand badly with Parliament and in public opinion. They give no thought to the rest of Europe, occupied as they are each morning in speculating whether they may not be upset in the evening in the House of Commons. Reform has made the path of the Government very difficult ; the cleverest would find difficulty in extricating themselves, but these idiots are totally incapable of doing so. Wellington said to me a short time ago : ' Take my word, Reform must be reformed, or else government is impossible.' Another Englishman—a Whig—said to me yesterday : ' Parliament should be prorogued, and not summoned again ; we should be all the better for its absence.' In fact, it is quite possible that this is what it will come to. You may guess that this spectacle amuses me vastly, but from a distance it must look ridiculous The world will have to go through more disturbance before it becomes once again tranquil and happy, and we can afford to look with pity upon all these attempts to upset everything for the happiness of the people, for, thank God, we are not in search of happiness—we are already possessed of it.

Louis Philippe is getting very near the ' Ordonnances. which cost his predecessor his throne—and Louis Philippe is right, for one must be master when one has done so much to be King.[1]

Good-bye, dear Alexander ; kiss for me wife, children, and everybody. Remember me kindly to Count Orloff— I often think of him. My best love to you.

[1] There had been disturbances in Paris and Lyons, which Louis Philippe had firmly repressed, and the Ministry of the Duc de Broglie gave notice of a new Bill dealing with the right of public meeting.

CXLVIII

London : 13/25 April 1834.

We have had, dear Alexander, our little attempt at disturbance in London also ; [1] it was inevitable that their friends and brethren in France and Belgium should find imitators in England. It did not suceeed, however, and, as I have said before, this sort of thing cannot do so in England, because the masses (*canaille*) here are cowardly and the classes are courageous. Thirty thousand men marched through the streets in good order and strict discipline to the Home Office to ask for the reprieve of certain men, sentenced to transportation, who had been taken in the act of administering the oath of association to workmen. The Minister refused to receive a petition presented in such a threatening way ; the thirty thousand men took the refusal without a murmur, and went back to their own homes. The measures adopted by the Government were excellent ; not a single policeman was on the route of the procession, but police, troops, and cannon were ready and at hand. Grey on the previous day had said to me : ' At the first sign of disorder I begin with the cannon—and that will settle the business.' His decision was the right one, its execution was unnecessary ; absolute order was maintained throughout.

France and England have agreed upon a treaty to put a stop to the dissensions in the Peninsula.[2] For my part, this seems to be for us a matter of total indifference. The terms of the convention are so delightfully vague that its actual execution may give rise to a thousand causes of misunderstanding between the two Powers. At any rate, this affair will give them plenty of occupation for some time to come, and Europe will remain for an indefinite period the theatre of confusion, which cannot but give more striking prominence

[1] This was the first procession organised by the Trade Unions with a view of arousing public opinion in London, as well as of obtaining the release of the men convicted at the Dorchester Assizes.

[2] This was the Quadruple Alliance, France and England joining Spain in support of Queen Christina and Portugal in support of Doña Maria. It ultimately brought about the estrangement of England from France.

to the conservative principles of the three great monarchical Powers of the Continent. Politically it is impossible for France and England not to quarrel over the question of preponderance in the Peninsula. Already the partition of its influence in Portugal is a British blunder, which makes M. de Talleyrand die with laughter. He cannot get over his astonishment at the imbecility of the English Ministers.

Do you know that the King of England seems to me in a fair way to become as mad as his father.[1] This is the result of my own observation, for I have had some strange scenes with him since my return from Russia; but recently confidences made to me from various quarters have confirmed me in my idea. Yesterday, too, when talking with the Duke of Wellington we both of us arrived at the same conclusion. What I was not aware of, but recently learnt, is that in 1828 he was so violent for a fortnight that it was found necessary to put him in a strait waistcoat. Wellington, who was Prime Minister at the time, knew all about it. This is another source of trouble and confusion for England. I entreat you not to allow anything of this secret to get abroad.[2]

Ministers are now in a better position in Parliament, and there are no imminent dangers ahead. Lord Palmerston and M. de Talleyrand are still personally antagonistic. The King has just invited the Spanish and Portuguese Envoys to Windsor in honour of the recently concluded treaty; Palmerston prevented M. de Talleyrand being invited also.

Good-bye, dear Alexander; I embrace you heartily.

CXLIX

London : 6/18 April 1834.

Dear Alexander,— . . . You may imagine the effect produced here by the news from France. In the first place, the resignation of M. de Broglie is looked upon as a symptom of

---

[1] 'The King has been exhibiting some symptoms of a disordered mind, not, however, amounting to anything like actual derangement, only morbid irritability and activity—reviewing the Guards and blowing up people at Court.' (*Greville*, iii. 81.)

[2] 'As betting is a feature of public opinion in this country, I will inform you that now the general bet is that Clarence is in a strait waistcoat before the King (George IV.) dies.' (Letter from Sir Henry Cooke to Lord Fitzgerald, May 1830.)

the decline of English and the rise of Russian ascendency. Next the rioting at Lyons, and then in Paris—followed, as they necessarily must be, by rigorous measures.[1] All this is wholly at variance with the ideas of the English Government of the day.   Blame cannot be expressed because she is an ally ; praise cannot be given, because that would be anti-liberal. Hence a nice dilemma ; so the matter is scarcely mentioned. But in the midst of all this comes our despatch, polite, pacific, amiable—and beneath the surface *persiflage* from beginning to end.

The auspices under which it arrived were such that it had to be taken with the best face.   M. de Talleyrand did not a little to bring this about.   Lords Grey and Palmerston pretended to be satisfied, and both affected to resume their former attitude even of friendship—especially the younger man. Talleyrand laughs and repeats ' The great word of your despatch, the word so well chosen, is " Forget." I tell them all that is the word they should repeat over and over again—it must find an echo.'

It is easy to understand that France in revolution, or placed under a military despotism, cannot be an ally who can be led to the Dardanelles.   All the British calculations are upset, and any plan which Palmerston may devise is doomed to failure.   As for ourselves, it is impossible for us to stand higher than we do in the eyes of friends and enemies alike.   The Emperor has conducted this treaty business with a skill and firmness before which all bow their heads.[2]

Therefore tell Count Nesselrode that his famous note of October 24 last is still to-day the object of universal admiration.   The Tories, the Radicals, even the Ministerialists, refer to it as a masterpiece of good taste, of adroitness, and of political superiority.   It has made an epoch in our diplomacy.

[1] The Chamber of Deputies rejected the proposal of Ministers to vote an indemnity to the United States for claims arising out of the great war.   M. de Broglie and General Sebastiani at once resigned.   At Lyons the *Mutuellistes* (Trade Unionists) rose against the Government, and were imitated by the workmen of Paris ; the insurrection at Lyons was only suppressed after much bloodshed.

[2] It had just transpired that a further treaty had been concluded at St. Petersburg (January 29) by which a further strip of Turkish territory in Asia, including Kars, was ceded to Russia.

It is generally repeated in various quarters that the revolutionary party in France is intimately associated with the English Radicals ; but although a rising of the working classes of London is announced every week, I don't believe a word of it—the English populace are too great cowards. It seems that there have been horrible scenes in Paris and Lyons—French ferocity differs altogether from English.

M. de Talleyrand continues to laugh at Lord Palmerston, and does his utmost to upset him. He has completely destroyed Lord Grey's opinion of him ; still, there is always great difficulty in getting rid of a Minister unless defeated in Parliament, as witness the case of de Broglie.

I conclude, dear brother, in embracing you and all around you.

CL

London : $\frac{\text{April 29}}{\text{May 11}}$, 1834.

You can have foreseen, dear Alexander, the effect which the news brought by the Consul-General Buckhausen would have had upon me. A complete change of career, of moral and material habits and surroundings after twenty-four years, is a serious epoch in one's life. It is said that one regrets even one's prison after spending many years in it. In this respect I may well be permitted to regret a fine climate, a delightful social position, ways of comfort and luxury which I can find nowhere else, and many friends wholly independent of politics. This is my sigh—now for my hopes. To live near the Emperor and the Empress whom I love with as much warmth of heart as if they were not my masters,[1] with as much admiration and respect as their titles impose upon me ; to live among you all and to prepare a future for my two boys ; to live in that Russia which has ever been the object of my pride and of my love—for, dear Alexander, I love it well, and perhaps I have served it well also, in my long absence—at least I have striven to do so. So I am happy at the prospect before me ; and the only doubt which mingles

---

[1] Prince Lieven was appointed Governor of the Tzarevitch and the Princess was to take up her duties as a Lady of the Empress's household.

with my joy is whether that future will be long-lasting. I have reached the age in life at which our mother was taken from us—an age which needs care and precautions. Shall I be able to support our winters? or will it be that the beginning of my life with you will be its end? I put aside such thoughts, for I love life; but it comes back again and again, and chills my heart.

I was so much upset for the first few days after the arrival of the news that my mind was unfit to take note of what was going on around me, but many things have happened which deserve notice. The King has shown unequivocal symptoms of madness. His Chancellor, Lord Brougham, is not a little mad also. Ministers lose ground every day. In the country every by-election turns in favour of the Tory candidates. In the Lower House they can carry no measure without the support of Peel; in foreign policy they only provoke the smiles of their own supporters.

I am sending to Count Nesselrode a short summary of what Lord W. Russell, just returned from his mission to Lisbon, has told me. He is a furious Whig, but an honest gentleman, who sees things as they are and tells what he has seen. His opinion is that, despite the tardy protection of Lord Palmerston, Portugal, and indeed the whole Peninsula, will for a long time offer the spectacle of confusion if they persist in imposing a liberalism wholly distasteful to both nations. As a rule it is a plant which flourishes only in England, and even here one can see whither it threatens to lead. It will be a salutary example for other countries. M. de Talleyrand is never tired of saying to me: 'The old governments alone offer repose and happiness to individuals. Constitutions are follies; nations will have nothing to do with them, because they have the conservative instinct.'

You would scarcely believe what good and sound doctrines one finds in this disciple of all forms of government, in this political *roué*, in this personification of all the vices. He is a strange creature, but there is much to be learnt from his experience and to gather from his wit—and at eighty years his wit is still fresh.

Goodbye, dear Alexander, for I have much to write. I shall await your letter with impatience, for you wrote so laconically, and I want to hear all the details. Here is a life which is about to be entirely changed ; tell me, therefore, all that you know. I embrace you with all my heart.

CLI

London : 18/30 May 1834.

My dear Alexander,—A volume of writing for Count Nesselrode has exhausted all my strength and leaves me no materials for a letter to you. But I must repeat myself upon one point—the respect, the affection, the esteem, and the general regrets of which my husband is the object. There is no need for exaggeration on my part ; the Government, the Tories, and even the Radicals alike look upon his departure as a catastrophe. He is much touched by these proofs of regard, and it would be strange if it were not so.

Dear brother, I am half dead with fatigue—I must say good-bye. So far as we can see, we shall be leaving here in the first fortnight of July. Best love to all.

CLII

London : 4/16 July 1834.

Dear Alexander,—It is some time since I last wrote. You have been away at Yalta,[1] and moreover my letters to Count Nesselrode are in a way addressed to you also. I must refer you to them again to-day, but I must write you a few lines, probably the last, from here, as in a fortnight we hope to have got through all our wearisome packing and to embark. What a nuisance it is either to carry off or throw away the contents of a house like ours—and that is our present perplexity. We are bringing away all that is useful for the household, and getting rid of all that is merely super-fluous or valuable, because I imagine that we shall find our new home furnished. I am getting impatient to know where that home will be, and you leave me, dear Alexander, in

---

[1] In the Crimea, a favourite health resort of the Imperial family.

complete darkness on such points. I have asked Count Nesselrode for his protection and for letters of introduction. He has been very good—do not you be behindhand.

Yet another English crisis, and do not fancy that it will be the last ; there will be another, perhaps, before we leave. It is impossible that with rebuff after rebuff this Ministry can continue to exist. Grey has not held on six weeks after Stanley's defection. How, then, can the wretched remaining dregs get on without Grey ? Melbourne is a man of honour—a gentleman—but why is he so suddenly endowed with energy ? This crisis has been brought about by Brougham to get rid of Grey and to put himself in his place. He was successful in the first part of his scheme, but has failed in the second ; but he, the restless intriguer, will be the moving spirit of the Cabinet, and will upset them all, one after the other. For the moment Melbourne leads the majority in the Cabinet, but they know not what to do with Durham. It is not impossible that he may be named Viceroy of Ireland ; at this moment he is at open warfare with his father-in-law. The French Ambassador does not make any pretence ; he is frankly Tory and a bitter enemy to all Radicals, and still more so to Lord Palmerston, and determined to go back to France in a fortnight—not to return so long as the present administration is in office. He has said so openly, and will do what he says. The diplomats here are as contemptible as the Ministry. Miraflores, Envoy for Spain, Sarmiento for Portugal, and Tricoupi for Greece are three rogues (*canailles*) who adore Lord Palmerston. The most important personage after Talleyrand's departure will be M. de Bülow,[1] and alas ! I was about to place him with the other three.

The flight of Don Carlos is a brilliant feat of audacity, an immense event [2]—should the same boldness and the same

---

[1] Prussian Envoy, whom Wellington once described as 'a wise fool,' who was constantly discovering something remarkable in every trifling incident.

[2] Don Carlos had come to England in an English ship of war with a large retinue and taken up his residence at Gloucester Lodge, where Canning had lived for some time. He had refused to be bound by any conditions. After a month's stay he left London (July 1) accompanied by a single attendant, reached Paris

success attend him later on.   The English Ministers are thunderstruck—they could not have been more duped.   Good-bye, dear Alexander.

I will send you a few lines to say when the day of our departure is fixed.   The English Government is very polite, and has offered us a ship for either Hamburg or Petersburg.   I have not yet made up my mind whether to accept or not.   Happily the offer was made by the First Lord of the Admiralty,[1] one of our old friends, for if it had been made by Palmerston I should have declined it without hesitation. Good-bye again, I am overwhelmed and wearied by visits, packages, and sighs—my own as well as those of others. I shall get no rest until the day of our departure.   I embrace you tenderly, dear brother.

on the 4th, went to the theatre, travelled unrecognised to Bordeaux and Bayonne, crossed the Spanish frontier on July 9, and on the next day found himself at the head of his followers.

[1] Sir James Graham.

APPENDIX

THE DUKE OF YORK (p. 85)

FREDERICK, DUKE OF YORK, second son of George III., was born in 1763 and at the age of seven months was nominated by his father, the Elector of Hanover, to be Bishop of Osnaburg. He entered the army and served in Germany, where he attained the rank of General in 1782. In 1791 he married, in Berlin and afterwards in London, the Princess Frederica of Prussia, the King of Prussia paying the Duke's debts, amounting to about 20,000*l.*, and Parliament giving him an allowance of 37,000*l.* a year. The Royal couple first lived in Whitehall in what was subsequently known as Dover House (now the office of the Secretary for Scotland), which was subsequently exchanged for Lord Melbourne's house in Piccadilly, now the site of the Albany. In 1793 he was sent in command of the English army to co-operate in the Low Countries with the Austrian and Prussian forces, but failed to earn distinction. On his return, however, he was appointed Field Marshal, and in 1795 succeeded Lord Amherst as Commander-in-Chief, but in 1799 again took the field in command of the ill-fated Walcheren expedition. In 1809 his name was unfortunately mixed up with a scandalous traffic in commissions and promotions in the army carried on by a Mrs. Clarke, who had obtained great influence over the Duke. He temporarily resigned his post as Commander-in-Chief, but on being exonerated from any share in the transactions was restored to office by the Prince Regent, and during his tenure and by his advice many important reforms were introduced into the army. His warm attachment to his brother, the Prince Regent, led him into many financial difficulties and political intrigues, and was the cause of a duel with Colonel Lennox. Like other members of his family, he was a strong Protestant, and resisted the Catholic Emancipation Bill to the utmost. His last official acts were to approve the arrangements made for the despatch of troops to Portugal, and to obtain the King's sanction for a method of insuring promotion to old subalterns, which he had long desired to carry out. He died in London in January, 1827, after a long illness, having survived his wife over six years.

DUKE OF CUMBERLAND (p. 138)

Ernest Augustus, Duke of Cumberland, born in 1771, was perhaps the best endowed, but certainly the most unpopular, of George III.'s sons.   He was privately educated at Kew and afterwards sent to the University of Göttingen.   In 1790 he entered the army, and four years later commanded a brigade under Marshal Walmoden in the Low Countries.   In an engagement he lost an eye and was otherwise severely wounded, but after a short time was able to rejoin his brigade.   At a later date he fought with the Prussian army, and showed great bravery but little military knowledge. Soon after his return to England his name was brought into prominence by the attempt made on his life by his valet Sellis, a Corsican. The would-be murderer, to escape arrest, committed suicide, but so strong was public feeling against the Duke that rumours that the valet had been the victim of his master's ungovernable temper were readily accepted.   The evidence given at the inquest, however, satisfactorily disproved this calumny.   In 1814 he married the Princess Frederica Caroline Sophia, daughter of the Grand Duke of Mecklenburg-Strelitz, who had already been married to Prince Frederick of Prussia, and on his death to the Prince of Salm, by whom she had been divorced.   The marriage was received at first with approval by the aged Queen Charlotte, but on learning subsequently the circumstances under which Princess Frederica's second marriage had been dissolved she absolutely refused to receive her daughter-in-law at Court.   The Duke showed his resentment by remaining for some years abroad, but after the Queen's death he returned to England and interested himself in English politics.   His influence over his brother George IV. after the death of the Duke of York was very considerable, and during the discussion of the Catholic Relief Bill, to which he offered the strongest opposition, he openly quarrelled with and insulted his brothers the Dukes of Clarence and Sussex in the House of Lords.   At the same time he was making use of the King's name to defeat the Bill, which the King had sanctioned and Wellington was pressing.   To further his ends he bitterly attacked Wellington, denouncing him as a man never again to be trusted.

On the accession of William IV. the Duke's influence behind the throne ceased, and the relations of the two brothers were well expressed by a toast given by the King at one of his own dinners : 'The

land we live in, and let those who don't like it leave it.' The crisis,
however, was delayed for a while. At length the Duke of Cumberland
as Gold Stick gave orders that no carriages should be admitted (presumably on levee days) through the Horse Guards' gateway into
St. James's Park, and the Duke of Wellington and Peel, on their way
to Court, were turned back. Upon this the King determined to take
from the Duke of Cumberland the command of the Household
Cavalry, and to place this corps, like the rest of the army, under the
Commander-in-Chief. The Duke protested that Gold Stick was
a military not a Court office, and that by taking his orders from the
Commander-in-Chief (Lord Hill) he would, as Field Marshal next in
seniority to the Duke of Wellington, be taking orders from a junior.
The Duke of Wellington was disposed to treat the matter leniently,
and although an estrangement followed it was only temporary.
His conduct towards Lady Lyndhurst, wife of the Lord Chancellor,
was less easily condoned. After grossly insulting that lady in her
own house, he went about making the most calumnious statements,
which soon found their way into the newspapers. His subsequent
conduct after the death of William IV. was as little to his credit as
much of his earlier career had been. He was openly accused of
wishing to set aside the Queen's (Victoria) rights in favour of a prince.
On her accession he withdrew to Hanover, of which the sovereignty
under Salic law passed to him on the death of William IV., and, to the
surprise of all, his Government was marked by ability, common sense,
and even an amount of liberalism, which was not restricted after the
general outbreak of revolutionism in 1848. He died at Hanover in
1851, but not before he had vented his spleen upon the Great Exhibi-
tion which in that year had attracted so many people to London, and
promised to inaugurate an era of peace and good will.

DUKE OF GLOUCESTER (p. 138)

William Henry, Duke of Gloucester, was the younger son of
Frederick, Prince of Wales, and brother of George III., who in 1766
married secretly Lady Waldegrave, an illegitimate daughter of Sir E.
Walpole, brother of Horace Walpole, and mother of the 'three
Ladies Waldegrave.' grouped in Reynolds's famous picture. The
marriage was not made public until after the passing of the Royal
Marriages Act, 1772, but after some time the King consented to
recognise it. In 1787 a separation took place between the Duke
and Duchess owing to differences of opinion over the education of
their daughter, the Princess Sophia. He died at Weymouth in
1803. The son, William Frederick, who became Duke of Gloucester,

born in 1775, was not distinguished by his talent, and early in life earned the sobriquet of 'Silly Billy.' In later times he was known chiefly for his Ultra-Toryism, but he showed great regard for Warren Hastings, and was on intimate terms with that statesman, and afterwards stood by Sir Robert Wilson, who also had fallen into disgrace. In 1809 the Swedish Diet, having dethroned Gustavus IV., offered him the crown of Sweden, but the English Government declined the offer. He married his cousin, the Princess Mary, in 1816, and died at Bagshot House in 1834.

DUKE OF CAMBRIDGE (p. 145)

Adolphus Frederick, Duke of Cambridge, seventh and youngest son of George III., was born in 1771, and, like his brothers York and Kent, after a brief stay at Göttingen University entered the army, and fought in Flanders, being wounded on one occasion and temporarily taken prisoner on another. In 1818 he married the Princess Wilhelmina Louisa, daughter of the Landgrave of Hesse-Cassel, who on coming to England had been most cordially received by the Queen and public, but gave great offence to her mother-in-law by her behaviour towards the ostracised Duchess of Cumberland. The Queen's illness, writes Mr. Greville in June 1818, 'was occasioned by information which she received of the Duchesses of Cumberland and Cambridge having met and embraced. This meeting took place by accident, but really by appointment in the Kensington Gardens : and the Duke of Cambridge himself informed the Queen of it.' After having been created a Field-Marshal the Duke was appointed Governor of Hanover and resided much abroad until after the death of William IV., taking less part in English politics than his elder brothers. On coming to England he distinguished himself as a patron of music, being himself a respectable amateur, and of public charities, and was perhaps more popular than either of his brothers, although the least prominently brought into public notice.

CHARLES JOHN XIV. (p. 150)

Jean Baptiste Jules Bernadotte, the son of a French *avocat* at Pau, was born in 1763, and at the age of seventeen enlisted in the Marines. He began his career in Corsica, and for some years served in the ranks. Receiving his first commission in 1789, in 1793 he had risen to be colonel. He served under Kleber at the battle of Fleurus as General of brigade, and as General of division under Jourdain on the Rhine, and under Napoleon in Italy. In 1798 he was sent as

Ambassador to Vienna, and in the same year married Mdlle. Desirée Clary, sister-in-law to Joseph Bonaparte. For a short time he was Minister of War and a strong partisan of Napoleon, by whom he was appointed Commander-in-Chief in the West, and as such did much to pacify La Vendée. After the proclamation of the Empire Bernadotte was created a marshal and given the command of the army of Hanover, where by his considerate conduct he gained the good will of the population. He distinguished himself in the campaign, 1805-6, and was created Prince of Pontecorvo. He was severely wounded at the battle of Spandau, but was able to resume his position as Commander-in-Chief of the army of the Baltic and North Sea littoral, and was instructed to occupy Denmark in the event of Sweden not breaking off friendly relations with Great Britain. In this he was anticipated by the bombardment of Copenhagen and the capture of the Danish fleet. A revolution shortly afterwards broke out in Sweden, Gustavus IV. was deposed, and his uncle, the Duke of Sudermania, succeeded as Charles XIII., after the crown had been successively offered to the Duke of Gloucester, and declined in his name by the English Government, and to Napoleon, who was then pledged to friendly relations with Russia and Denmark. In 1809 Bernadotte was appointed to the command of the 9th Army Corps, with his headquarters at Hanover, but, notwithstanding the coalition of the European Powers against Napoleon, he not only suspended hostilities against Sweden, but opened the Baltic ports to Swedish vessels. After the battle of Wagram, at which he was present, he issued an address to his troops which greatly offended Napoleon, who ordered him to retire to Paris. His services in checking the British expedition to Walcheren did not restore him to favour. Napoleon refused to reinstate him in his command, and after a stormy interview at Vienna Bernadotte finally broke with his master. His kindness towards the Swedes, however, had not been forgotten, and the Swedish Diet on August 21, 1810, elected him Prince Royal of Sweden under the title of Charles John, and he was shortly afterwards received into the Lutheran Church. He devoted himself especially to cultivating good relations between Sweden and Great Britain, and to obtaining the assent of the latter to the union of Sweden and Norway. He attended the meeting of the Emperor of Russia and the King of Prussia after the retreat from Moscow, but was coldly received until the Emperor of Austria wrote saying that the co-operation of Sweden with the allies was absolutely necessary. He was then given the command-in-chief of the Army of the North, and fought with the allies throughout the campaign 1813-4. In recognition of his services the union of Sweden and Norway was agreed to at Vienna, but the Danish Prince Christian asserted his right to the Regency of Norway and war seemed imminent. Christian, however, was induced to give way, and Charles XIII., having been acknowledged by the Storthing and accepted the Norwegian Constitution, was elected King November 1814. He died February 15, 1818, and was succeeded by Bernadotte under the title of Charles John XIV.

The matter referred to by Madame de Lieven is thus summarised in a despatch from Lord Bloomfield (Minister at Stockholm) to the Earl of Aberdeen, Foreign Secretary, dated October 17, 1828 : ' His Majesty (Charles John XIV.) turned to the approaching marriage of Prince Gustavus (son of Gustavus IV.), upon which subject his Majesty seems to labour under the most extraordinary excitement. H.S.M. dwelt confidently on the good offices of my King and his Government should his Netherlands Majesty persevere in giving the title of Prince of Sweden to his future son-in-law. The King of Sweden then dilated largely on the great services he had rendered to the King of the Netherlands, and finally declared it to be his intention to avenge the wrongs offered to the Swedish nation, should they be persevered in, by force of arms.'

The King of Sweden also wrote protests to the Courts of Europe. Austria and Prussia suggested the reference of such a delicate question to a general European Council, but after much letter-writing and squabbling it was arranged that Prince Gustavus should no longer be styled Prince of Sweden, but of Wasa, in the Imperial Army List and on all state occasions in Austria. To this the King of Sweden assented, although he would have preferred the title of ' Prince of Holstein-Gottorp.' [1]

Prince Gustavus, however, insisted upon his rights, and the King of Holland being unwilling to offend the Powers, who had recognised Bernadotte as King of Sweden, the projected marriage of the dethroned Prince with the Dutch Princess was broken off.

GRAND DUKE CONSTANTINE (p. 37)

Constantine, born in 1779, although the eldest son of the Emperor Alexander, never bore the title of Tzarevitch until 1799, when it was conferred upon him after his Italian campaign under Suwarrow. In 1796 he married Princess Julienne of Saxe-Coburg (a sister of Leopold, subsequently King of the Belgians) when she was only fifteen years of age, but the marriage, which was an unhappy one, resulted in a separation in 1800, and the Princess returned to

[1] Lord Bloomfield's *Diary*, ii. 165, &c.

Germany. It was not, however, formally dissolved until 1820, when Constantine fell in love with Joan Grudzinska, the daughter of a Polish gentleman, and married her privately according to the rights of the Romish Church. Constantine was described as 'adding to the savageness of the *moujik* the courtesy of a man of the world.' He was certainly eccentric, impetuous, and at times even brutal. His ruling passion was for military affairs, in which he showed a pedantic adherence to the smallest details. In 1815 he was made Viceroy of Poland, and by his severity and narrow-mindedness became unintentionally the main agent in betraying his brother's Government into an unconstitutional course, which at length by its insufferable tyranny brought about a disastrous revolution. His second marriage, after some little difficulties had been surmounted by the tact and firmness of his wife, turned out happily, and she was held in high esteem by the Emperor, who invested her with the Duchy of Lowicz and bestowed on her the title of Princess.

The order of succession to the throne of Russia had been established when Michael Feodorovitch Romanoff, by free election of the three Estates, had received the crown on the condition that it should descend by right of primogeniture. Peter the Great first disturbed the order in 1722 by the ukase which gave to the Russian Sovereign the right of choosing his successor—even outside the Imperial family ; but in 1797 Paul I. re-established the succession by hereditary descent in the male line, and this arrangement was confirmed by Alexander I. in 1807 and again in 1820.

DUKE CHARLES OF BRUNSWICK (p. 107)

Charles, Duke of Brunswick, whose fantastic career closed in 1873, was the elder of the two sons of the Duke of Brunswick who fell at Quatre-Bras. His mother had died in 1808, and the two lads became wards of George IV. (then Prince Regent). From a very early age he was the source of constant trouble to his guardians, and ultimately accused both the King and Count Münster, the Governor of Hanover, of breaches of trust and sent a challenge to the latter. Moreover, on coming of age and succeeding to the Duchy he refused to recognise those of their political acts which bore the appearance of any concession to liberal opinions. His subjects appealed to the German Diet, and judgment was given against the Duke, who was ordered to fulfil the pledges to his subjects and to apologise to his guardian. He refused to do either, or to withdraw the libels he had published. Serious difficulties might have arisen from this contumacy, but in 1830 his subjects unanimously voted his deposition,

and transferred the crown to his brother, Duke Wilhelm. He spent
much time in England, where his wild freaks and extraordinary habits
aroused much indignant remonstrance, and later on made him the
victim of many outrageous calumnies, which frequently brought him
before the law courts. In 1831, after the accession of William IV.,
the King and the Duke Wilhelm joined in a declaration that Duke
Charles was insane. He subsequently associated with Prince Louis
Napoleon (afterwards Emperor) and furnished the means by which
the latter was able to effect his escape from Ham prison in 1845. A
joint 'treaty' was drawn up between the two, according to which
both parties solemnly swore that whichever first came to power
should support the other 'par tous les moyens possibles.' The
Duke, moreover, was, if possible, to make Germany a single united
nation, and to give it a Constitution adapted to its habits, its needs,
and the progress of the times. The Duke continued to live in
ostentatious style for some years at Brunswick House in the New
Road, Regent's Park, regarding himself as a sovereign prince and
above the ordinary law, with which he was constantly in conflict. In
1851 he left England for Paris, travelling by balloon, in which he
ascended from the Vauxhall Gardens. He established himself in
what had been Lola Montes's house in the Champs-Elysées, which
was gorgeously decorated and at the same time strongly protected
against possible burglars and assassins, of both of whom the Duke
lived in dread. Although 'the treaty' was never carried out, he
continued on friendly terms with the Emperor Napoleon, and made
a will bequeathing his immense wealth to the Prince Imperial. At
the outbreak of the Franco-Prussian war he removed to Geneva, and
on the downfall of the Napoleonic empire he revoked his will and
left everything to the city of Geneva, where he died on August 18,
1873, and where his costly tomb and the new opera house com-
memorate his vanity and his taste.

PRINCE METTERNICH (p. 59)

Clemens Wenceslas Nepomuk Lothario, Count and Prince Metternich, who played an important part in the history of Europe for so
many years, was born at Coblentz in 1764, where his father, the first
of the family of princely rank, held a post under the Austrian
Government. His son was successively educated at Coblentz and
Strasburg University, and passed through a course of law at Mainz.
In 1794 he married Maria Eleonora, granddaughter of Prince Kaunitz,
the Austrian statesman, and simultaneously obtained his first post at
Court. It was not, however, until three years later, when as Austrian
Plenipotentiary at the Congress at Rastadt, he became known as a

diplomatist. On the break-up of that meeting he was sent to Berlin in order to bring about a better understanding between Austria and Prussia, and to induce the latter to abandon its policy of neutrality. He, however, soon returned to Vienna, and remained there until 1806, when, as Count von Coblentz, he was sent as Ambassador to Paris in order to negotiate the marriage of Napoleon and the Arch-Duchess Maria Louisa.   On the rising of Central Europe against Napoleon after the Russian campaign, Metternich proposed a Germanic Confederation, consisting of Austria, Prussia, Bavaria, Hanover, and Würtemberg ; but he opposed the entry of the lesser German States, including the Grand Duchy of Baden.   In all thirty-four princes and free cities insisted on the right of being represented in the Confederacy, and, their claims having been astutely taken up and urged by Prussia, they were eventually admitted to the Bund. Meanwhile Metternich had summoned and presided over the famous Congress of Vienna, which was to re-settle the Continent and to re-establish autocracy in Europe.   His later policy was marked by the treaty known as the Holy Alliance, by the enforcement of absolutist rule, and in the stern repression of free political life. He lived to see the total collapse of his policy in 1848, having, by the irony of fate, been forced to take refuge in England, which from the time of Canning had most steadily opposed his policy.   His second marriage in 1827 is referred to in these letters, but there is no allusion to his third marriage, in 1831, to the Countess Melanie Zichy von Ferraris.

COUNT NESSELRODE (p. 22)

Charles Robert, Count Nesselrode, was born at Lisbon, 1780, of a Westphalian family, settled in Livonia for nearly a century.   He was educated at the Military College, St. Petersburg, and admitted by Catherine II. into the Imperial Guards, appointed aide-de-camp to Paul I., but soon after abandoned the military for a diplomatic career.   In 1802 was appointed *attaché* at Berlin, and from 1804-6 was *chargé d'affaires* at The Hague ; but after a short stay in Paris he was called by the Tsar Alexander I. to take a high post in the Russian Foreign Office, and was instrumental in bringing about the meeting of Napoleon and Alexander at Tilsit.   From 1812 onwards he was the principal director of Russian diplomacy, although it was not until 1816, and after he had represented his country at the Congress of Vienna, that he was formally made Secretary for Foreign Affairs in conjunction with Count Capo d'Istria, an arrangement which lasted until 1820, when after the Congress of Verona the latter quitted official life, and Count Nesselrode became sole Minister and gave a

general support to Metternich's policy. On the accession of Nicholas
Count Nesselrode retained his office and gradually increased his
influence by promoting the wishes of the Tsar with regard to the
incorporation of Poland, the partition of Persia, and the expulsion
of the Turks from Europe. In various ways he made the influence of
Russia dominant in Eastern and Central Europe, but on the breaking
out of the revolutionary movement in 1848 he withdrew his country as
far as possible from all relations with Western Europe. He was generally supposed to have been opposed to the Russian war 1854–6, but
after the signature of the Treaty of Paris he retired from public life,
retaining, however, the honorary title of Chancellor of the Empire.

PRINCE ESTERHAZY (p. 19)

Prince Paul Esterhazy de Galantha, a Hungarian magnate, son of
Prince Nicholas Esterhazy, born in 1786, was successively Austrian
Minister at Dresden and in Westphalia. In 1814 he was sent
as Ambassador to Rome, but was transferred in the following year to
London, where he remained until 1818. After an interval he
returned to London in 1830, where he continued Ambassador until
1838. On his retirement he went to live in Hungary, and in 1842
declared for the National party, and was Minister of Foreign Affairs
in Count Bathyanyi's Hungarian Cabinet in 1848, but after its fall
took no prominent part in politics. He was one of the largest landowners in Europe. His property, of which the chief centre was
Eisenstadt, comprised 29 fiefs, 21 castles, 60 towns, and 414 villages,
besides the countship of Edelstetten in Bavaria and large estates in
Lower Austria. In 1860, a year before his death, owing to his
enormous debts, his property was sequestrated and administered for
the benefit of his creditors. His son, Prince Nicholas, married in
1842 Lady Sarah Villiers, daughter of fifth Earl of Jersey.

COMTE DE FLAHAULT (p. 22)

Count Auguste Charles de Flahaut (or Flahault) de la Billarderie
was the son of Adelaide Marie Filleul. At the age of fifteen she was
married in 1779 to the Comte de Flahaut, aged fifty-seven, a Knight
of Malta, whose devotion to the Royal cause brought him to the
scaffold in 1793, but who, according to Gouverneur Morris, ' had
denied himself no excess of dissipation. His wife found herself
coldly neglected. The Abbé Périgord, who had performed the
marriage ceremony for her, became her friend, companion, and
instructor, for to him she owed the opening training of her intellect
and he became also the father of her only child, who was named

Charles, after the Abbé.'[1]   After the death of her husband Madame
de Flahaut wrote several novels, of which 'Adèle de Sénanges'
(1794) was the most popular.   She was forced to emigrate to Hamburg, where she met and subsequently married the Comte de Souza,
a Portuguese diplomatist, and returned to Paris on the restoration of
order.   A long account of Madame de Souza and her son Charles
will be found in the recently published 'Memoirs of the Countess
Potocka' (London, 1901).

MADAME DE FLAHAULT (p. 12)

Miss Margaret Mercer, to whom reference is frequently made in
these letters, and afterwards as Madame de Flahault, was the daughter
of Admiral Lord Keith by his first wife, Jane, eldest daughter and
coheir of Colonel William Mercer of Aldie and Meiklour, county
Perth; grandson of second Baron Nairne.   In addition to the
numerous aspirants to Miss Mercer's hand mentioned in these letters,
and to many others, it appears that Byron was at one time thought
likely to marry her.   She and Lady Jersey stood by Byron at the
time of the latter's separation from his wife.   On leaving England
Byron sent Madame de Flahault a message saying that he should
not be going into exile had he married a woman like her.[2]   The
truth of the statement that by her marriage with M. de Flahault she
relinquished a large portion of her fortune can neither be substantiated
nor refuted.   It is by no means unlikely that, belonging to a strictly
Presbyterian family, her marriage with a Roman Catholic may have
involved the renunciation of some of her income.   Her father, Lord
Keith, married as his second wife Hester, daughter of Henry Thrale
of Streatham Park, which was frequently let to the Lieven family.
Madame de Flahault succeeded to the Barony of Keith in 1823,
and to that of Nairne in 1837, although her claim to the latter was
not admitted until 1874.

COUNTESS LIEVEN (p. 37)

Charlotte Kaarlow, wife of Major-General Baron Lieven, of an
ancient Livonian and Courland family upon which the Kings of
Sweden had conferred the title of Baron, was born in 1743.   She was
selected by the Empress Catherine II. in 1783 to superintend the
early education of the Grand Dukes Nicholas and Michael and their
sisters.   In 1794 she was appointed a Lady of the Bedchamber, and
in 1799 advanced to the rank of Countess.   In 1825, on the occasion
of the coronation of the Emperor Nicholas, she was created Princess.

[1] *Diary*, i. 4.   [2] Murray's *Biographical Edition*, iii. 253.

It is asserted of her that during the forty-five years she spent at Court she did not make an enemy or lose a friend.

Her eldest son Charles, born in 1770, entered the army in 1797; he became Major-General in 1827, having in the interval (1817–25) been the Curator of the University of Dorpat, where he acquired the reputation of being more devoted to mysticism than to science. Nicholas, shortly after his accession, made him a member of the Council of the Empire, and for several years up to 1833 he was Minister of Public Instruction. Her second son, Christopher, the husband of the writer of these letters, was born in 1772, began life as a soldier, and in 1798 was aide-de-camp to the Emperor Paul. In 1809 he was sent as Envoy to Berlin, where he remained until 1812, when he was appointed Ambassador in London, and held that post until 1834. On his recall he was named Governor of the Tzarevitch Alexander, retaining that position until his death at Rome in 1839.

THE ORLOFFS (p. 19)

The Orloffs, of whom frequent mention is made, were a powerful family in Russian Court circles, and were either antagonistic to or jealous of the Lieven-Benckendorf influence with the Emperor. Among the chief members to whom reference occurs were :

(a) Count Gregory Vladimirovitch Orloff, the last legitimate male representative of this great princely family, was born in St. Petersburg, but on account of his delicate health resided chiefly abroad in Italy and France. He was a liberal patron of literature and art, as well as the author of several works in French. He was appointed a Senator, and came to reside in Russia on the accession of Nicholas, but died soon afterwards in 1826.

(b) General Alexis Orloff, born 1786, served in the Russian army in the wars with Napoleon 1812–15, became an officer of the Imperial Guards, and as such took a prominent part in the suppression of the military revolt at St. Petersburg in 1825 on the death of the Emperor Alexander. For his services on this occasion the Emperor Nicholas, whose life he saved, conferred on him the title of Count. He was by general repute 'an honest man justly esteemed.' He was given the command of a division in the Turkish war 1828–9, and, in conjunction with General Diebitch and Count Frederick (Fritz) von Pahlen, negotiated the Treaty of Adrianople 1829. He was next employed to put down the Polish insurrection 1831–2, and was later given command of the army sent to protect Turkey against Ibrahim Pasha, with whom he negotiated the famous Treaty of Unkiar Skelessi. In 1833 he was sent to The Hague and to London to bring about a solution of the Belgian question. He filled many diplomatic posts, and finally represented Russia in 1856 at the Congress of Paris after the Crimean War, and for his services received the title of Prince. On the death of Prince Lieven in 1839 he became travelling companion to the Tzarevitch.

(c) Michael Foedorovitch Orloff was an illegitimate son of Count Foedor Orloff, youngest brother of Gregory Orloff, the principal actor in the revolution which had placed Catherine II. on the throne. Michael Orloff was born about 1785, and entered the army, in which he gained rapid promotion, and in 1814 was one of the signatories of the capitulation of Paris. He was a man of great intelligence, high education, and noble sentiments. He repeatedly urged the Emperor Alexander to reform the Russian administrative system. In conjunction with Tourguenieff he was one of the founders of the 'Society of Russian Knights,' formed to promote the welfare of the people. He also attempted to introduce into the army and among the children of the soldiers a system of mutual education. Under a very thin disguise his work and character can be traced in more than one of Tourguenieff's studies of Russian life.

POZZO DI BORGO (p. 8)

Charles André Pozzo di Borgo, of an old Corsican family, was born near Ajaccio in the same year as Napoleon Bonaparte, his life-long enemy. From their earliest youth the two were antipathetic, Pozzo belonging to the Nationalist and Napoleon to the French party in the island. In 1789 he was secretary to the *noblesse* of Corsica, and was sent as Deputy of the island to the National Assembly, where he voted with the Girondists. On the fall of that party Pozzo became an object of suspicion, and his life was in danger. He returned to Corsica, which had temporarily passed into the hands of the English, and was appointed President of the Constitutional Assembly called together by Admiral Elliot. Two years later, Corsica was recovered by the French party, and Paoli and Pozzo found refuge in England. Pitt speedily discovered the value of Pozzo and sent him on various diplomatic missions. While at Vienna he received an invitation from Alexander to enter the service of Russia, and successively represented that country at Naples, Constantinople, and Vienna. After the Peace of Tilsit he withdrew from the councils of Alexander to Vienna, where he was able to advise Metternich, but, Austria having been crushed at Wagram, Napoleon, in the treaty that ensued, expressly stipulated that Pozzo should be expelled from both the Austrian and Russian services. He then came to London, where he was warmly welcomed by Lord Castlereagh.   On the breaking up of the Franco-Russian alliance in 1812, which he had fore-told, he was recalled by Alexander, and on his way to St. Petersburg stopped at Stockholm, where he helped to overcome Bernadotte's indecision and persuaded him to join the allies.   Throughout the war which followed the retreat from Moscow Pozzo was attached to the Emperor's personal Staff, and entered Paris with him.   After the restoration of peace he was appointed Russian Ambassador in Paris, where he remained many years.

COUNT CAPO D'ISTRIA (p. 41)

Giovanni Antonio, Count Capo d'Istria, was born at Corfu in 1776 of parents disaffected to the British Government. He was educated at Padua and Venice for the medical profession, but turned to political life on the expulsion of the French from the Ionian Islands by the Russians and Turks, and during the interval, 1802–7, occupied various administrative posts.   In 1807, on the restoration of the islands to France under the Treaty of Tilsit, Capo d'Istria entered the Russian Foreign Office, and as Russian Envoy to Switzerland played an important part in framing the Swiss Constitution, which lasted from 1813 to 1848.   In 1816 he was recalled to St. Petersburg and appointed Minister of Foreign Affairs, and as such his absolutist views were more in accordance with those of the Russian nobility than with those of the Emperor.   In 1822, however, he was forced to resign, but throughout his tenure of office he had steadily kept in view the liberation of Greece from Turkish control, and on his retirement identified himself more closely with the policy of the Greek national party.   In 1827 he was elected President of that party, and after a full but secret understanding with Russia, and after a short stay in England, disembarked at Nauplia, calling upon the Greeks to rise against their oppressors.   His popularity, how-ever, was short-lived.   The strict discipline he attempted to enforce was repugnant to the Greek insurgents.   His influence was neverthe-less sufficient to prevent the election of Prince Leopold of Saxe-Coburg to the throne of Greece, which he hoped to secure for Russia.   He was assassinated at Nauplia on October 9, 1831, as he was entering the Church of St. Spiridion, by a Mainote, one of a large tribe of which the chief family, the Mauromichalis, had re-volted against Capo d'Istria's arbitrary rule.

GENERAL MOREAU (p. 5)

General Moreau, a distinguished officer under the Republic, had commanded the French Army of the Rhine 1796–7, and again 1799–1800, when he displayed masterly ability.   After a brilliant career he quarrelled with Bonaparte, then First Consul, and intrigued with Pichegru.   He was arrested, sentenced to imprisonment, which was changed to banishment, and he retired to America in 1804.   On the news of the disasters of the Russian campaign he returned to Europe and took counsel with Bernadotte.   By the advice of the latter he presented himself to the Emperor of Austria at Prague, by whom he was warmly received and attached to the Allied Army as general adviser. He was present at the battle of Dresden, and on the second day (August 27), while seated on horseback beside the Emperor Alexander, he was mortally wounded by a cannon ball from a battery which had been specially brought into action under Napoleon's orders and supervision.   The fact that Moreau was with the Russian army was made known to the French after the battle, by the capture of a dog, found in the hut to which the wounded officer had been first carried.   On the dog's collar were the words : ' J'appartiens au Général Moreau.'

LORD DUDLEY (p. 25)

John William Ward, only son of third Viscount Dudley and Ward, was educated under conditions which were scarcely likely to give his studies uniformity of method or aim.   After passing through the hands of several private tutors, he went to Oxford, matriculating at Oriel and graduating at Corpus Christi College.   Thence he went to Edinburgh to study under Dugald Stewart for a short time before entering Parliament.   Returned as a Tory for Downton, Wilts, he gave his allegiance successively to Pitt, Canning, Grenville, and Fox, and similarly he shifted his seat from Downton to Worcestershire (1803), Petersfield (1806), Wareham (1807), Ilchester (1812), and Bossiney (1823).   He travelled much on the Continent after the restoration of peace, and in 1822 was offered, but declined, the Under-Secretaryship of Foreign Affairs under Canning.   In 1827 he became Foreign Minister in Canning's short-lived Ministry, and continued under the Duke of Wellington for a few months, resigning with the rest of the Canningites.   He was chiefly known by his vagaries and absent-mindedness, having on one occasion put into an envelope addressed to the Russian Ambassador a despatch intended for his French colleague.   He signed, in 1827, on behalf of Great Britain the treaty with France and Russia for the pacification of Greece, and at a later

date, when in opposition, was a violent objector to the Reform Bill.
He is credited with having said to Metternich in 1817, when the
latter was denying the genius of Napoleon, ' Il a rendu la gloire passée
douteuse et la renommée future impossible.'

THE EARL OF DURHAM (p. 276)

John George Lambton, born in 1792, the son of William Henry
Lambton, M.P. for Durham, began life in the army and served
for about two years in the 10th Hussars.   In 1811 he was elected to
Parliament for the city of Durham, and during his earlier years took
a prominent interest in foreign politics generally, attacking the policy
of Lord Liverpool and the appointment of Mr. Canning as Minister
to Lisbon in 1817.   In 1821 he seconded a resolution censuring
Ministers for taking proceedings against Queen Caroline, and in the
same year brought forward his motion for Parliamentary Reform, which
was defeated by only twelve votes, although his proposals embraced
electoral districts, household suffrage, and universal suffrage.   During
the next few years he took little part in politics, but on the break-up of
the Goderich administration he was created (1828) Baron Durham.
In 1816 he had married as his second wife Lady Louisa Grey,
daughter of Earl Grey, and on his father-in-law's accession to office
in 1830 he was made Lord Privy Seal, and, in conjunction with Lord
Duncannon and Lord John Russell, framed the first Reform Bill,
although it is asserted that his dislike to the Russells had induced
him to influence Lord Grey to exclude Lord John Russell from the
Cabinet in 1830.   When the struggle between the two Houses arose,
Lord Durham was in favour of an unlimited creation of peers, and
Lord Grey's objection to the proposal led to an unseemly outburst
of temper at Lord Althorp's dinner-table on the part of Lord
Durham.   He did not resign, and Lord Grey took no offence, but
in the summer of 1832 sent him on a special mission to St. Petersburg, Berlin, and Vienna, whence he returned without obtaining any
concessions either with regard to Turkey or Poland, and ' more odious
than ever ' to his colleagues and the Cabinet.   Few Ambassadors,
however, had ever been despatched under more disadvantageous
circumstances.   An exaggerated reputation for ultra-liberal principles was not calculated to inspire the autocrats of Eastern Europe
in his favour, but he nevertheless, by his manners and straightforwardness, conciliated their personal regard.   His irritable and
overbearing temper prevented him from assenting to the policy
of concession and compromise which Lord Grey's Government
had been obliged to adopt, and on Lord Palmerston's refusal to

cancel the appointment of Stratford Canning as Ambassador to St. Petersburg, which the Emperor of Russia had insisted upon to Lord Durham, he resigned (March 14, 1833), and was created Earl of Durham. Lord Palmerston, however, writing to his brother, attributes the resignation wholly to ill-health, believing that nothing would otherwise have induced Lord Durham to leave a Ministry in which he hoped to occupy a more prominent place. He did not withdraw from politics, but opposed the Irish Church Temporalities Bill, the Irish Coercion Bill, and other Government measures. He became one of the recognised leaders of the Radical party, and engaged in controversies with Brougham, Bishop Phillpotts, and others. Even his appointment in 1838 as Ambassador to Russia was the cause of a violent outburst of temper, because the Emperor's consent had been obtained before the post was offered to Lord Durham ; but his embassy was signalised by the honourable adjustment of a serious matter—that of the ship *Vixen*—which might have led to serious consequences. He returned to England on the accession of Queen Victoria, and in 1838 was appointed High Commissioner of Canada to adjust the troubles which had arisen in that colony. His high-handed proceedings gave rise to attacks on the Government as soon as they were known in this country, and they were disavowed by the Government. Lord Durham resigned in October 1838, and on his return sent in his famous report on the affairs of British North America, which had been drawn up by his secretary, Charles Buller. He attended Parliament in the ensuing Session and spoke on Canadian affairs, but his political career was closed, and he died in the summer of the following year.

LORD STRANGFORD (p. 152)

Percy Clinton Sydney Smythe, sixth Viscount Strangford, was born 1780, and after a brilliant career graduated at Trinity College, Dublin. Two years later he entered the diplomatic service as Secretary of Legation at Lisbon, and in 1803 published a volume of 'Poems from the Portuguese of Camoëns.' In 1806 he was left in charge of the Legation at Lisbon, and in November 1807, on the advance of the French, persuaded the Prince Regent of Portugal to embark for Brazil. Strangford returned to England shortly afterwards, and on his arrival in December drew up an account of the proceedings, dating his despatch November 29, 'on board H.M.S. *Hibernia* off the Tagus.' On the appearance of the first volume of Sir William Napier's ' Peninsular War ' in 1828 a controversy arose between the author and the diplomatist, as to whether to the latter or to Sir William Sydney Smith was due the credit of getting the Regent away from Lisbon. Meanwhile Lord Strangford had received many distinctions and had been sent in 1808 as Minister Plenipotentiary to the Portuguese Court which had estab-lished itself in Brazil. In 1817 he was employed as Ambassador to Stockholm and in 1820 at Constantinople, and as such was present at the deliberations of the Congress of Verona. On his return he was charged with the sole care of Russian interests in Turkey, and obtained several important political and commercial concessions for Russia. He finally quitted Constantinople in the autumn of 1824, and in the following year was sent to St. Petersburg, but only remained there for about a year, and with the special mission to Brazil his diplomatic career closed. He subsequently took an active part in conjunction with the extreme Tory party in parliamentary life, and vigorously opposed the Reform Bill. He also took a considerable interest in literary and historical questions, although he produced no work of importance. He died in 1855, his two sons in turn succeeding to his title, each leaving a considerable reputation but no children.

The action referred to by Madame de Lieven arose out of the following article which appeared in 'The Sun' newspaper, August 7, 1828 : 'We direct the admirers of Lord Strangford to an article in the "Times" of this morning. . . . For such a character we would not accept the embassy to the Brazils. To the friends of liberty and liberal principles it must be very consolatory that the reviler of Mr. Canning's memory would hardly be believed on his oath, cer-tainly not on his honour, at the Old Bailey. But his lordship is a poet as well as a politician, and accordingly draws upon his fancy for the few facts which give a colour of verisimilitude to his works. He is confessedly the best Irish translator of Portuguese that has lately appeared in diplomatic affairs, and renders the meaning of his author in a style that strongly reminds us of the celebrated echo of the Lake of Killarney, which on being asked "How do you do?" replied "Very well, thank you." It was this hint which enabled his lordship to write that very characteristic piece at the English Opera entitled, "He lies like truth." '

In consequence of this article Lord Strangford commenced pro-ceedings against Murdo Young, publisher and printer of 'The Sun,' and on November 29, in the Court of King's Bench, on the applica-tion to make the rule absolute, Brougham and Alexander appeared for the defendant and argued against the rule. Lord Tenterden (with Justices Park and Bayley) found against the rule, and ordered it to be discharged.

LORD HERBERT'S MARRIAGE (p. 13)

Lord Herbert (afterwards twelfth Earl of Pembroke), born in 1791 married August 17, 1814, Princess Octavia Spinelli, daughter of the Duke de Lorine, and widow of Prince Butera-Rubari. The story of Lord Herbert's marriage as given by Madame Lieven seems to reflect the current gossip of the day. It tallies with that given by the Margravine of Anspach,[1] not always a trustworthy authority, according to whom Lord Pembroke himself went to Sicily to prevent the marriage. Lord Herbert, having been informed of his father's arrival, urged the Princess to consent to a clandestine marriage by a Roman Catholic priest in the presence of two witnesses. This took place on August 17, and by a further religious ceremony he ratified his promise. The newly married pair, however, were promptly separated by the civil authorities; Lord Herbert was confined in the castle of Palermo, and the Princess sent to the neighbouring monastery of Stimmali. On November 13 Lord Herbert succeeded in escaping from confinement, leaving a letter addressed to his wife, which, according to the Margravine, was never delivered to her.

A somewhat different version of the story is given by Mr. Pryse L. Gordon,[2] according to whom Lord Herbert, at the time of Prince Butera's death, was twenty-three years of age and the Princess some fifteen years older. He had for some time previous to the Prince's death been *cavaliere servente* to the Princess, a position which provoked no scandal. But, according to the rules of Sicilian etiquette and morals, such relations could not be continued when the lady had no longer a husband. The choice, therefore, lay between marriage and separation, and from whichever side insistence may have come the ceremony was gone through. Immediately afterwards Lord Pembroke reached Palermo on an English frigate. He at once obtained an audience of the King, and four-and-twenty hours later Lord Herbert was carried off from the house he was occupying and lodged in prison, and the Princess conveyed to a convent, where, according to the Sicilian law, she would be imprisoned for five years. The former speedily made terms with his father and was liberated on promising to abandon his wife. On his return to England a suit was commenced in the English courts. The case for restitution of conjugal rights was tried in the Consistory Court, Easter Term, 1819, before Sir William Scott (Lord Stowell), who gave judgment in favour of the validity of the marriage. From the evidence it appeared that the kidnapping of both bride and bridegroom was by orders of the

[1] *Memoirs*, ii. 400 *et seq.*   [2] *Personal Memoirs*, ii. 200.

King at the solicitation of the Earl of Pembroke.[1]   The Princess obtained a separate maintenance of 800*l.* per annum, which was subsequently increased.   Afterwards she took up her residence in Naples, succeeding in 1827 as Countess of Pembroke, which title she preferred to that of Principessa Butera.

I am, however, indebted to the courtesy of the archivist of the Butera family for another version of the incidents of this affair. The Princess Octavia was scarcely more than fifteen years old when she was taken from Naples to Palermo in December 1798, where the Neapolitan Royal Family and Court had taken refuge. She was a girl of remarkable beauty, and soon after her arrival was married, as his second wife, to Prince Butera, already an old man. Lord Herbert at first sight fell in love with the Princess, and became wholly devoted to her. On the death of the Prince he urged her to marry him, and with difficulty obtained her consert to a ceremony which was a private one. As soon as the news reached Lord Herbert's family his father used his powerful influence with the Ministry to enlist the services of Lord William Bentinck, then British Envoy to the fugitive Neapolitan Court. Through his aid Lord Herbert was shipped off on board a British frigate, and Lord William Bentinck, acting on behalf of the Pembroke family, agreed to the payment of an annuity of 1,000*l.* so long as she remained apart from her husband, but recognising her claim to bear his name. She lived in Naples until 1857, where her home was the meeting-place of persons of all ages and nationalities, especially of the young, in whose society she took special pleasure.

THE ARAKTCHEIEFF TRAGEDY (p. 77)

General Count Alexis Araktcheieff, the son of a poor country gentleman, was born in 1769, and in 1787 having obtained a commission in the army, subsequently shared in the military education of the sons of the Grand Duke Paul, afterwards Tsar. He early distinguished himself by avoiding the use of any language but his own, but this did not prevent his early rise in his profession, for in 1797 he was Governor of St. Petersburg, a Major-General in the army, a baron, and the wearer of many orders ; and at the same time he gained the character of a man of great cruelty and harshness, especially towards the cadets. His career was marked by violent changes, alternately in favour and disgrace. He was supposed to have been concerned in Count Pahlen's conspiracy in 1799, which had for its object the dethronement and exile of the Emperor Paul.

[1] *Phillimore,* iii. 58.

He was reinstated by Alexander as Inspector-General of Artillery, and did much to reform this branch. In 1808 he was Minister of War, and after the peace it was by his advice that military colonies were established in various parts of the Empire. For many years the personification of Old Russia, he was the chief counsellor of both Alexander and Nicholas, and was more dreaded throughout the Empire than the Tsar. He had for his mistress the wife of a sailor. One day she ordered one of her maids to be whipped ; her brother, exasperated by the sight of the girl's sufferings, determined to assassinate the mistress. He found accomplices among his comrades, and twenty-one were arrested, tried on the spot by the Count himself, and sentenced, several of them to be broken on the wheel, and the others to the knout. Moreover, by Araktcheieff's action the amnesty consequent upon the accession of the new Tsar was withheld and the sentences were carried out. A revision of the trial was subsequently ordered, and Araktcheieff fell completely into disgrace. He passed the later years of his life in seclusion, but occupied with acts of useful benevolence, many of which bore some reference to his devotion to the Emperor Alexander ; and by his will he left the whole of his fortune to the reigning Emperor to dispose of as he should think fit. He died in 1834.

DOM MIGUEL (p. 212)

Dom Miguel, third son of John VI., King of Portugal, was born in 1802, and was taken by his parents to Brazil on the invasion of Portugal by the French in 1808. His education was so shamefully neglected that on his return to Portugal, when his father in 1821 quitted Brazil, he could neither read nor write. During the absence of John VI. a Constitution had been proclaimed in Lisbon and Oporto, which on his arrival he accepted. His wife, the Infanta Carlotta, sister of Ferdinand VII. of Spain, refused to take the oath to it, and, placing herself at the head of the clerical opposition, she put forward her son, Dom Miguel, as pretender to the crown. Two abortive attempts to bring about a revolution having convinced Dom Miguel of the weakness of his cause, he made his submission and was pardoned by his father. Soon afterwards he was appointed Commander-in-Chief of the Portuguese army, and the first act of his authority was to cause the assassination of the Marquis de Loulé, his father's intimate counsellor. This was followed by a third attempt at revolution in 1824, which caused the King to fly from Lisbon, but on the energetic intervention of the foreign Ambassadors John VI. returned and Dom Miguel was banished, taking up his residence first in Paris and afterwards in Vienna. On the death of King John VI. (March 10, 1826) his eldest son, Dom Pedro, elected to remain Emperor of Brazil, ceding to his daughter, Doña Maria da Gloria, his rights to throne of Portugal, and at the same time offering her hand to Dom Miguel with the rank of Regent. These conditions were accepted by the latter, who further swore to respect the Portuguese Constitution (which Dom Pedro had sent over by the hands of the British Minister, Sir Charles Stuart). After visiting Paris and London, Dom Miguel proceeded to Lisbon and took the oath on February 26, 1828. The English troops were shortly afterwards withdrawn, whereupon he dissolved the Chambers, annulled the Constitution, and summoned the old Constitual Cortes, by which he was proclaimed King. He also repudiated the hand of Doña Maria, refused to allow the ship which was bringing her to Portugal to enter any of his ports, and drove into exile Palmella, Saldanha, and other Constitutionalists. His accession to the throne was recognised by Spain and Great Britain, and his conduct apparently approved by Wellington, and, notwithstanding his violence and outrageous follies, he was able, until the death of his mother in 1830, to maintain himself on the throne. Meanwhile Doña Maria had returned to Brazil, and was betrothed to Prince Augustus of Leuchtenburg. In 1831 Dom Pedro resigned the throne of Brazil in favour of his infant son, and came to Europe to support his daughter's cause. He came to London, and with the countenance of Earl Grey and the Whig Ministry then in power raised a loan, and with a force of 7,500 embarked for Portugal, landed at Oporto, claiming the throne and promising a charter. The Miguelist fleet was first crippled by Admiral Sartorius (October 1832), but for some months the Miguelites made a determined resistance until they were at length overpowered by Sir Charles Napier at sea off Cape St. Vincent, and by Marshal Saldanha on land. Dom Miguel, supported by Spain, attempted to carry on the struggle, but was ultimately forced to sign the capitulation of Edora and to submit to perpetual banishment. He took up his residence in Rome, where in 1851 he married Princess Adelaide Lowenstein, and died in 1866.

INDEX

TO NAMES REFERRED TO IN THE LETTERS

SUPPLEMENTARY LETTERS

1829–1832

THE CATHOLIC RELIEF BILL—EARL GREY'S CABINET—LORD PALMER-
STON FOREIGN SECRETARY—BROUGHAM AND THE CHANCELLORSHIP
—DEFEAT OF THE FIRST REFORM BILL—SIEGE OF ANTWERP—
GENERAL ELECTION.

THE following letters were not discovered among Madame de
Lieven's correspondence until this volume was already in type. It
was consequently impossible to introduce them in their proper place.

The first letter refers to the negotiations which resulted in the passing of the Catholic Relief Bill. The second, written in ' sympathetic '
ink (*en citron*), although undated, can confidently be assigned to the
date given in view of the incidents referred to. It is of considerable
importance historically as well as politically, for it suggests that at one
moment at least Madame de Lieven exercised an important influence
over Earl Grey, and gives additional point to Lord Chelmsford's
remark quoted in the preface. The assertion that it was at her
solicitation that Lord Palmerston was made Foreign Minister and
Lord Lansdowne set aside will doubtless arouse some controversy. I
have stated, in connection with another reference to the same subject,
that there is no evidence to show that any definite offer was made to
Lord Lansdowne, and it may be inferred from the present letter that
the intention never went further than some vague rumour or suggestion, which may have reached Madame de Lieven through an
irresponsible channel. The version of Lord Grey's attitude on the
second reading of his first Reform Bill is in accordance with general
knowledge : but the difficulties which beset the English Government in
their determination to support King Leopold have been generally lost
sight of. The obstinacy of the King of Holland was strengthened by
the advice of friends who were unable or unwilling to assist him by
arms, whilst the co-operation of France with England was seriously
suspected of being far from disinterested, and it was felt that any
attempt of the former to recover her ' lost frontiers ' would be the
signal for a renewal of hostilities upon the Continent, and would raise
questions in the settlement of which Great Britain would claim a
right to be heard.

A

Day after day, dear Alexander, I feel more and more acutely the disappointment you have caused me by refusing to confide little Marie to my care.   The more I think of it, the less do I understand the reason.   It is clear that nothing in Constantine's will is said as to the bringing up of his children, for you yourself, on reaching Petersburg, mentioned to my son Paul your wish that I should have her, and even suggested that he might take charge of her on the journey to England.   How do you now explain your change of mind—on the ground that our dear Constantine did not wish her to leave Russia ?

It is only natural that I should ardently desire to have charge of Marie, and that I should have come to believe that it would be for her good also.   Having no daughter of my own, all my care and love would be centred upon the dear child.   I am growing old ; my experience of life qualifies me for being a good guide to a young girl, and my aim would be to make her resemble her dear mother.   You have many daughters, dear Alexander, and you have Coco, who takes the place of a son to you ; why, then, do you refuse me, who have no daughter, a happiness which can only be profitable to the child?   Our dear Constantine loved me dearly, and he would not have refused my appeal—indeed, had he foreseen his death he would have anticipated this wish of mine.   Think it over again, dear brother ; my rights are as strong as your own, and can only be set aside by some written proof of Constantine's wishes.

A week has passed since Parliament assembled.   Party warfare is becoming violent—that is to say, the Ultra-Tories are doing everything one might expect from men fanatical in their belief, who suddenly discover that they have been duped.   As for the others, they cordially support the Government, and are enjoying the success of their efforts of the last thirty years.   Political parties at this moment may be classed in this fashion : (1) The Conquerors (the Whigs) ; (2) the Converts (the Ministry) ; (3) the Imbeciles (the Tories told to obey orders, but not told why or wherefore) ; and (4) the Obstinates (the Ultra-Tories who resist to the last). These last, as you may see, are a small minority, at whose head stands the Duke of Wellington as Commander-in-Chief. The Bill will pass—there's no doubt on that score. In the Commons they reckon upon a majority of 100 votes, and in the Lords of 38 or 40.

The Catholics have spontaneously dissolved their formidable Association, and by the advice of the Whigs rely without reserve upon the Duke of Wellington's promises. This is the stage which after nine days the Bill has reached ; it may drag on some time longer, but in six weeks all its stages will have been got through. In the midst of all this Europe slumbers, and will be allowed to slumber in the English Parliament, except perhaps in the case of Portugal.

Good-bye, my dear brother. We are still charmed with Matuscevitz, and he is delighted with England, especially as his coming is at an interesting moment. We let him see everybody, and introduce to all parties, which in the present state of confusion is fair and legitimate. I embrace you heartily ; a thousand loves to your wife and children. A parcel for the former has arrived from a Mr. Forrester. I will send it by the next courier. My best remembrance to Count Nesselrode.

B

Richmond : November 1830.

Here is the composition of the new Ministry as finally settled last night. Lord Grey, First Lord of the Treasury ; Lord Lansdowne, President of the Council ; Lord Durham, Privy Seal ; Lord Palmerston. Foreign Affairs ; Lord Melbourne, Home Office ; Duke of Richmond, Master-General of the Ordnance ; Lord Althorpe, Chancellor of the Exchequer, and Leader of the Commons ; Sir James Graham, First Lord of the Admiralty ; Mr. Grant, Board of Control ; Lord Holland, Duchy of Lancaster. The Chancellorship, the Secretaryship of the Colonies, and the Presidency of the Board of Trade are not yet settled. In all likelihood, Lord Goderich will take the Colonies, the Marquess of Anglesey will be Viceroy of Ireland, and Mr. Stanley his Chief Secretary. The Duke of Devonshire has been offered the post of Lord Chamberlain, and Lord Hill will probably remain Commander-in-Chief.

As there is no rule without its exception, I thought that I was entitled to make one to the rule I have always observed of never meddling with the political matters of this capital. Lord Grey wished to give the Foreign Office to Lord Lansdowne. I suggested Palmerston, and Grey consented at once in the hope that the choice would be agreeable to our Court. Have no fears, not a soul here has the least idea of the influence by which this has been brought about. I assure you that I pass for being altogether ignorant of what is going on. My living at Richmond disarms suspicion.

Lord Grey has assured me that we shall have reason to be satisfied with him, and that his policy is to maintain peace. I added—and the observance of treaties? He smiled and asked me not to press him upon any special point at this moment. It went without saying that he would fulfil all engagements made in the name of England. He promised to take cognisance of the state of affairs, and repeated to me his assurance that we should be satisfied, and that what he most desired was the union of all, in order to assure the tranquillity of Europe.

He explained to me his extreme dislike of Talleyrand, who, he thinks, had given expression to unfavourable opinions about him. Similar suspicions exist in his mind with regard to ' Matou,'[1] and the other members of the diplomatic body with the exception of Bülow. I told him plainly that there was nothing to be surprised at, for his speech had naturally aroused mistrust on all sides. I defended Matou, and assured Lord Grey that, whilst objecting to his doctrines, Matou had the greatest admiration for his talent, and that like myself he was convinced that when the Earl became better acquainted with the actual state of affairs, he would see the need of adopting other opinions. Lord Grey returned once more to the subject of his promises, speaking even more

---

[1] Matuscevitz ?

explicitly, and he left me thoroughly convinced that he will frankly, but more firmly than the late Ministry, pursue the policy of the Duke of Wellington. He then gave me an account of his various audiences of the King. He is quite overcome by the complete confidence with which his master treated him. Lord Grey in his first interview laid down the principles of his policy : (1) Maintenance of Peace ; (2) Economy ; (3) Moderate Parliamentary Reform.

The chief cause of embarrassment now is Brougham. If he is not humoured, he is capable of raising the standard of Radical Reform, and then, in view of his great talents and the actual state of public opinion, he might be the source of real danger. The hope of high office has for the last few days kept him fairly in subordination to Lord Grey, who regards him at once as a foe and as a most dangerous friend. The bold remedy of making him Lord Chancellor suggests itself. As this is the highest prize of all, he might then be reckoned upon, and having become a peer of the realm, he would abjure democracy and attack it as vigorously as he had formerly defended it. This nomination will, if it be made, cause a great outcry, but after all the calculation will in all probability be found justified. The King, moreover, has some objection to the proposal, the only one he has taken to the names put forward by Lord Grey, but even in this matter he has in case of necessity allowed him *carte blanche.*

Lord Grey having exacted the promise from me that I would say a word to nobody about his ministerial arrangements, and that I would write to nobody but to you and only in cipher, I have been forced to have recourse to this secret method. In future whenever you find my signature at the end of any letter, as in this case, throw it into the fire. I implore Count Nesselrode to await the first words and the first acts of the new Ministry before judging it. I may almost venture to say that they will satisfy us. In this case we shall have gained by the change, for with the will there is also the power, which was wanting to the late Government. Lord Grey anticipates very little opposition in either House during the next few months. DOROTHEA.

C

The debate on the second reading of the Reform Bill in the Lords opened on 3rd inst. I saw Lord Grey an hour before he went down to the House. He was in a vile temper that day, irritable and violent, and under these conditions he made a speech distinguished by its bitterness and its imprudence. He declared that he would not remain Minister for a single day if the peers threw out the Bill, and held over the threat of a revolution in the country, and of a Bill far more democratic than that under discussion. The more moderate members of the Upper House—those who, without approving the Bill, were of opinion that instead of rejecting it they should amend it in Committee—took alarm at Lord Grey's speech. Recognising the hopelessness of obtaining any concessions, they sided with the Tories, and from the very first night formed so formidable an opposition that the Government was at once convinced that the Bill would be thrown out. It was in vain that the other members of the Government attempted to soften down Lord Grey's words ; the impression had been conveyed, and five nights' debate only served to strengthen it. On Friday morning (7th October) the King sent for Lord Melbourne, the Home Secretary, to assure him of his support, and to tell him to urge Lord Grey not to lose courage. This mark of royal favour, on which I think Lord Grey had scarcely reckoned latterly, gave him great hope, and the same night in closing the debate he paid a touching and eloquent tribute to the King, and ended by declaring that he would not abandon his master, whatever might happen.

The result of the division astounded him. An adverse majority of 41 was beyond what he had ever contemplated. A Cabinet Council was hastily summoned on Saturday morning. It was unanimously agreed that the idea of creating new peers must be given up ; that Parliament must be prorogued, and that the Ministry should remain in office. A letter from the King to Lord Grey was delivered whilst the Council was sitting. It was a pressing appeal from his master to retain the management of affairs, assuring him in the strongest terms of undiminished confidence and support.

The Tories had been unable to conceive any other alternative to resignation but a *coup d'état* (the creation of sixty peers), and were prepared to meet it by a Bill of impeachment for high treason. They had already been drawing up lists of the new Ministers, and even now they do not realise the truth.

Tuesday, 11/22 October.

The House of Commons, by a majority of 131 votes, passed a resolution that Ministers enjoyed the confidence of the country. This morning Lord Grey demanded and obtained the dismissal of the Queen's Chamberlain on account of his having voted against Reform. These satisfactions having been obtained, all is now settled—the Ministry remains, and Parliament will adjourn. Good-bye, dear Alexander ; this is a dry bulletin rather than a letter, but I have not a moment to spare even for you. I embrace you.

D

Brighton : 1/13 December, 1832.

Dear Alexander,—I have just seen in the *Journal de Pétersbourg* the announcement of the honour conferred upon you on the occasion of the baptism of the Grand Duke Michael. I hasten to tell you the pleasure which this has given me, and to congratulate you and your good wife most heartily. The Emperor is lavish of his favours, but they are well deserved.

I have been spending three weeks here, where I have been treated with the greatest kindness by the Court. This, combined with my gratitude for having escaped London fogs, has enabled me to bear more philosophically the turn which affairs have taken. At the same time, it must be allowed that this Anglo-French expedition sets to work in a funny way. On the one hand, the English fleet, after blockading a few cruisers which had caused it no damage, has returned to port ; the Orders in Council issued by the British Government against Dutch commerce have been withdrawn because it was found imprudent to adopt hostile measures against a country which refused to indulge in re- prisals. On the other hand there are 100,000 French soldiers engaged in bringing to terms 4,000 Dutchmen, so far without much success—a siege undertaken and to be finished in three days, which has already lasted fifteen—and a number of folk quite surprised to find that it rains or freezes in winter, that soldiers get their feet wetted and are laid up with colds. On his side, too, Leopold seems to have been making a pretty mess of it, by inviting guests who are eating him up and are on the point of burning one of his finest cities, and who seem quite ready to settle down permanently on his territory. For, after all, what is going to be the outcome of this Belgian business? It is enough to make one die of laughing.

The elections have been going on throughout England and in a few days will be over. There were no disturbances in London, and very few in the provinces. Here at Brighton under the eyes of the King, the Ministerial candidate has been defeated, and two violent Radicals have been returned to Parliament. This has greatly annoyed a number of persons but, on the other hand, by way of compensation in other divisions Ministerialists and Radicals have been forced to give place to Tories. The result would seem to be that there will be in the new Parliament a large number of Whigs, that the Tories and the Radicals will both be in force, and that those members whose actual principles are doubtful, but whose number is considerable, will attach themselves to one or other party as soon as Parliament meets—and this takes place on January 29.

The King is in the best health. I am writing by the ordinary post, dear Alexander, because I did not wish to wait for a courier to send you my congratulations as well as to your dear Countess. A thousand good wishes, my dear brother.

A Classified Catalogue
OF WORKS IN
GENERAL LITERATURE
PUBLISHED BY
LONGMANS, GREEN, & CO.
39 PATERNOSTER ROW, LONDON, E.C.
91 AND 93 FIFTH AVENUE, NEW YORK, AND 32 HORNBY ROAD, BOMBAY

CONTENTS.

INDEX OF AUTHORS AND EDITORS.

18714963R00238

Printed in Great Britain
by Amazon